Letters of H. L. Mencken

BOOKS BY

H. L. MENCKEN

THE AMERICAN LANGUAGE

THE AMERICAN LANGUAGE: Supplement One

THE AMERICAN LANGUAGE: Supplement Two

HAPPY DAYS
NEWSPAPER DAYS
HEATHEN DAYS
} which, taken together, constitute *The Days of H. L. Mencken*

A NEW DICTIONARY OF QUOTATIONS

TREATISE ON THE GODS

CHRISTMAS STORY

A MENCKEN CHRESTOMATHY (with selections from the *Prejudices* series, *A Book of Burlesques, In Defense of Women, Notes on Democracy, Making a President, A Book of Calumny, Treatise on Right and Wrong,* with pieces from the *American Mercury, Smart Set,* and *Baltimore Evening Sun* and some previously unpublished notes)

MINORITY REPORT: H. L. MENCKEN'S NOTEBOOKS

THE BATHTUB HOAX and Other Blasts and Bravos from the *Chicago Tribune*

LETTERS OF H. L. MENCKEN, Selected and Annotated by by Guy J. Forgue

H. L. MENCKEN ON MUSIC, Edited by Louis Cheslock

These are BORZOI BOOKS *published by* ALFRED A. KNOPF *in New York*

Letters of H. L. MENCKEN

SELECTED AND ANNOTATED BY

Guy J. Forgue

WITH A PERSONAL NOTE BY

Hamilton Owens

[1961]

Alfred·A·Knopf NEW YORK

L. C. catalog card number: 61–12312

THIS IS A BORZOI BOOK,

PUBLISHED BY ALFRED A. KNOPF, INC.

 Manufactured in the United States of America.
Published simultaneously in Canada by
McClelland & Stewart, Ltd.

FIRST EDITION

H. L. MENCKEN

A Personal Note

A YEAR or so ago, August Mencken called me to say that he had a young Frenchman with him who proposed to do a book about H. L. M. His guest, he said, knew of my long and intimate association with Henry and would like to question me about him as well as look over some of the letters in my files.

M. Forgue showed up the next morning. We had not talked long before I perceived that he was well-informed about his subject. To me this was surprising because, so far as I knew, the French paid little attention to present-day American literature and if any of Mencken's books had been translated into their language I had not heard about it. Nevertheless, my visitor had ranged through the whole of his production. His ultimate object, he said, was to do a searching work for the Sorbonne on all the available material. In the meantime, he thought that a book might be written for American publication that concerned itself mainly with correspondence with literary figures.

I am not certain that M. Forgue comprehended what a massive task even this limited undertaking would turn out to be. Mencken came to my office once or twice nearly every week for almost thirty years. In addition we saw each other at the meetings of the Saturday Night Club, at occasional beer evenings at Schellhase's and at each other's houses. Extended correspondence was thus unnecessary. Yet his letters in my strongbox number in the hundreds. The total of his production must be in the scores of thousands. Moreover, they are scattered about in a dozen libraries and private collections. Alfred Knopf had been hoping for years to find someone with the energy and patience to undertake a complete editing of them. The hope had so far been in vain. Still, with Mr. Knopf's encouragement, M. Forgue persisted.

Here, then, are the admirable results; and now that I have read them all, seriatim, I begin to realize that however well I knew their author, I comprehended only certain aspects of his personality and was certainly not aware of the enormous extent of his activities in other fields. And you are to remember that what we have here is a mere selection, however expertly and sympathetically made. Yet these letters somehow leave the impression that the man wrote them all as a kind of enjoyable side line, that most of his thought and most of his energy were concentrated on the production of his own almost unbroken flood of news articles, essays, and books. Henry Mencken wrote incessantly, inspired and directed a whole generation of authors (castigating those who uttered a false note), and in the intervals led a joyous and gregarious social life.

No one denies, nowadays, that Mencken, first in the *Smart Set* and then more emphatically in *The American Mercury,* set the tone of American letters during the decade and a half following World War I and greatly influenced political thinking even later. There is evidence that the present post-war generation is not entirely ignorant of him. Some would belittle him by saying that it was the times rather than the qualities of the man himself which gave him his pre-eminence. There is, naturally, a shred of truth in such an argument. It is undeniable that the thoughtful young people of the twenties were a disillusioned lot. Bearing in mind that they had been told to expect a millennium and were handed Harding, Coolidge, and prohibition with its attendant horrors, they had a right to feel cheated. It is thus understandable that the loud roars of contumely and contempt emitted by Mencken and Co. were just the sort of music they wanted to hear. To change the metaphor, his diagnoses gave a name, at least, to their spiritual malaises, put a finger on their boils. Many of them became social surgeons overnight—not all of them competent.

But to say that Mencken was a product of the times does not explain him or come anywhere near doing it. He would have been his own unprecedented self had there been no World War I, no Woodrow Wilson, no Harding, no Coolidge, no Volstead, no Bible Belt. His riotous vitality, his learning, his skill with words, his sense of the human comedy (closer to farce, for him), his scorn for frauds and hypocrites, his gift for hyperbole and, above all, his deep sympathy for any intelligent man struggling with the riddle of life—all these things would have brought him to the forefront regardless of the times.

As a matter of fact, his reputation as iconoclast was established years earlier. His book on George Bernard Shaw was published in 1905, that on Nietzsche in 1908. He became literary critic of the *Smart Set*, largely at Dreiser's suggestion, in the same year and was accepted forthwith as the spokesman for those even then in rebellion against the stuffed-shirtism then prevailing. His "Free Lance" column in the Baltimore *Evening Sun* made its first appearance in 1910 and soon became more than a local feature. Journalists all over the country read it and, more often than not, imitated it as far as their capacities and their publishers permitted. Isaac Goldberg's *The Man Mencken* covers this period of dcvclopment with understanding.

In the capitulation above, I purposely omitted from the list of his characteristics the one that may be the most remarkable of all. Most of us arrive at maturity with no notion of life's significance or lack of it, no understanding of its myriad complexities, no philosophic system to guide us save copybook and Biblical maxims. As we grow older, we adopt first this rule of thought and action and then that one, only to discard each in turn as experience proves it false or inadequate. It is only when our arteries begin to harden and we begin the slide toward the funeral parlor that we find it possible to adopt a satisfying or nearly satisfying view of things in general, a pattern or mode of life. Usually this pattern even then is an "as if" one. That is to say, although we have acquired no knowledge of ultimate truth and no longer expect to, we conclude that we can at least order our lives *as if* certain rules, certain precepts, had continuing value. We painfully agree, inside ourselves, to pretend that we have free will and so conclude that there is comfort and ease, if not virtue, in conforming outwardly to the mandates of the society in which we live.

Mencken, more than any man I have ever heard of, avoided this painful intellectual progress through life. Read some of his earlier writings and you will see what this means. When he wrote about Nietzsche in 1908, he displayed in his comments not only understanding of that tortured philosopher but also an ability to see his shortcomings. He was meticulously careful to underwrite only those attitudes that conformed to his own. The point of view thus expressed is precisely the same as that set forth in his posthumous *Minority Report*. Read again his debate with Robert Rives La Monte (1910) on the subject of socialism; again the same unswerving refusal to accept the notion that the majority is wise or ever can be. Here we find the same withering scorn of the uplift and the same contempt for reformers that were so gloriously trumpeted all through the twenties and thirties, to the horror of the powers. Pallas Athena, they say, sprang full-formed from the brow of Jove, with her wisdom all filed and indexed behind her beautiful brow. Jove did not survive to procreate our subject but the evidence all suggests that the young Mencken's concept of the world and of the men and women in it, whatever its source, was complete when he first contemplated the great outdoors from the windows of the red brick house on Hollins Street. He gathered facts to support his congenital prejudices and filled out the details as he went along. He learned how to express himself in ever more resounding phrases, but the point of view never altered.

I recall, in some detail, the first time I met him. It was at the performance of one of those well-contrived French plays popular around 1910. I was a cub reporter sent to write my first theatrical notice. Perhaps the regular critic was tight; such things happened in those days. In my naïve way, I thought the play pretty good, but during an intermission I checked with Mencken, then doing occasional dramatic notices for the *Evening Sun*, a new and bumptious offspring of the stately morning paper. In five minutes he pointed out the silliness of its theme and the falsity of its view of life. After that I could hardly fashion half a dozen stumbling sentences about it for my paper. But the following afternoon in the rival *Evening Sun,* he set forth his scorn in words so pungent that I can still quote some of them verbatim. Some day a scholar will dig out those fugitive reviews and republish them. Most drama critics could learn something from them. Perhaps the late George Jean Nathan did.

His impact on me at this first meeting was similar, one might conclude, to that he produced on the young men of the generation following World War I. They were floundering in their disillusionment, uncertain where to turn for guidance. Some fled to the Left Bank to fritter away their talents. Those who remained at home did better: they discovered Mencken. His was the point of view they wanted. His harsh realism, his complete scorn for the prevailing patriotic hypocrisies, his "destructiveness" and above all his uproarious gusto while swinging his ax on the idols gave them that sense of direction which they had lacked. They followed him in the thousands in enthusiasm if, alas!, in almost complete misunderstanding of the doctrine he preached. I know from direct observation how far from comprehension many of them were for, as editor of the *Evening Sun* of which he was so potent a part, I received scores of their manuscripts, probably *American Mercury* rejects. Too many of them labored under the illusion that by copying his vocabulary, or such of it as they could master, and exaggerating in what they thought was his fashion, they could achieve like eminence. Their subjection was pitiable when it was not ludicrous.

Their hero was not deluded by their acclaim. They were indeed a large part of his audience and as such helped to support him. He used to say, with some truth, that if another came along who could put on a better show, they would abandon his overnight. Therefore he put on the best show his talents could provide. There was material enough in those days, Heaven knows! What he could not utilize himself in the *Smart Set*, in the *Mercury* or in that flood of books, he would turn over to the *Evening Sun*. Our files were overflowing with his suggestions, not all of them practicable for a family newspaper but all of them stimulating. And, of course, there was always that two-column article from him for Monday afternoon. Many of these dealt with local issues in the manner of the old "Free Lance" column; others had to do with his pet aversions, such as prohibition (which we always called Volsteadism), censorship in general, the Methodist Board of Temperance and Public Morals under Bishop Cannon, the anti-evolutionists, the imbecilities of the Bible Belt, and so on.

Some of these articles were so extreme that I passed them with dread of the consequences, for libel suits can be a costly nuisance. On one occasion he sent in a piece which argued that, having given up wine for grape juice at the communion table, the next step for the evangelical sects was certain. He therefore formally predicted that before long Coca-Cola would be the tipple at such rituals. Accustomed to his exaggerations as I was, this seemed to be going too far, so I called him and told him so. His answer on such occasions was always the same: "You're the jail editor. Change it to suit yourself". The offending passage was blue-penciled and the article appeared without it. But not more than three or four days later he sent in an envelope enclosing an advertisement torn from a daily paper in Colorado. It was a big display, three or four columns wide, inserted by the manufacturer or distributor of some kind of soft drinks. It consisted of the reproduction of the letterhead of an obscure church on which the parson had written that on the previous Sunday he had substituted a cola drink (not Coca-Cola, however) for the customary grape juice at the communion table and that the members of his congregation had commented upon its excellent taste. Mencken's hyperbole always held some element of truth. His own rule was "Never underestimate the booberie of the booboisie".

There was something almost miraculous about the activities of the man in those days of the twenties and thirties. He was, of course, editing the *Mercury* for most of the period. That involved frequent trips to New York. He was writing long pieces, including several book reviews, for every issue. He was reading and editing manuscripts. He was reading a score or so of novels every month and other books besides. He was collecting material for his dictionary of quotations. He was similarly collecting material for the several revisions and supplements to *The American Language*. All these professional undertakings involved heavy correspondence and every letter was answered the day it was dropped in the mail slot in his front door. Yet at least once a week, sometimes twice, he spent the afternoon in the *Sun* office at what we called a conference but was usually an audience gathered to listen to a gusty Mencken monologue, more often than not in criticism of the paper's current news or editorial policies.

Nor was this all. Never was a man more gregarious, never one who strove more generously to keep his friendships green. There was the famous Saturday Night Club, a small orchestra made up of music-loving cronies. They sawed away for two hours, usually ending with a Strauss waltz, then adjourned to Schellhase's *bierstube* for seidel after seidel. Each seidel was engraved with the member's name. Visitors received seidels engraved "deadhead". If a member or any other friend fell ill, Henry was the first to arrive at the hospital with flowers or a basket of delicacies. Visitors from out of town were numerous. They were taken to dinner at Schellhase's if male and for lunch or tea at some smarter restaurant if female. Schellhase's, of course, was labeled a Seafood Restaurant. In Baltimore, in the days of prohibition, a seafood sign always meant that beer was on tap. If no visiting fireman demanded attention in the evening, he would call me or some other friend and spend the evening guzzling and talking. Usually, in my case, he talked; I listened.

Now and then, usually on Henry's initiative, the Maryland Free State Association, of which he was the acknowledged chief executive, would hold a really bang-up dinner at the old Rennert Hotel. The manager thereof was one Jeff Davis whom we insisted was *the* Jeff Davis. Usually these were stag affairs in honor of some visiting dignitary known for his opposition to Volsteadism, such as the late Jim Reed, U. S. senator from Missouri. But now and then, especially after Sara Haardt appeared on the scene, ladies were included. Such affairs were decorous, however freely the wine flowed. Dr. Raymond Pearl, the biostatistician, Dr. Curt Richter, psychologist from the Johns Hopkins Hospital and the inimitable Willie Woollcott, author and composer of the song celebrating ironically the virtues and beliefs of the "One Hundred Per Cent American", were active in the Free State Association. I was the recording secretary or official chronicler and my main job was to prepare elaborate certificates on vellum conferring honorary citizenship in the Free State upon worthy visitors. Fortunately, fitting candidates were few.

Sara Haardt, who became Mrs. Mencken in 1930, was a native of Alabama who had graduated from Goucher College in Baltimore. She had considerable imagination and skill as a writer and attracted Henry's attention for that reason, just as a dozen other women had done. She was one of the "Violets" in "The Sahara of the Bozarts". Under his stimulation she submitted several manuscripts to the *Evening Sun,* some of which were published. In addition to such occasional writing, she produced several major works, including *The Making of a Lady,* a novel that received much critical praise. Most of Mencken's friends discounted the likelihood of marriage, for they bore in mind his numerous dicta on the joys of bachelorhood. Still, there was always that famous sentence in one of the *Prejudices* to this effect: "The reason the average bachelor of thirty-five remains a bachelor is really very simple. It is that no ordinarily attractive and intelligent woman has ever made a serious and undivided attempt to marry him". Several women of our joint acquaintance insisted that Sara was making such an attempt, but I have never been able to accept that as the real explanation of his marriage, certainly not the main one. More likely there was something of a paternal or protective instinct involved. Sara, however clever and ambitious, was a semi-invalid during much of her mature life. She wrote under the handicap of continuous weakness and even pain. It was impossible for him not to feel concern for one so pretty, so amiable, so patient. Moreover, she obviously adored him.

She died in the early morning of May 31, 1935. Before noon that day Henry was in my office. He seemed to feel a need to unburden himself, if that is the way to describe it. He concluded his talk in words so poignant that I can quote them almost verbatim. "When I married Sara," he said, "the doctors said she could not live more than three years. Actually she lived five, so that I had two more years of happiness than I had any right to expect". To my mind, those do not sound like the words of a man ensnared against his will. Perhaps they also explain why, after a few confused months, he moved from the Victorian apartment overlooking Mt. Vernon Place, so redolent of Sara's dainty presence, back to the original Hollins Street homestead. There, thanks to brother August, he could work mightily in familiar surroundings and rest his eyes and his brain by gazing out on Union Square, that little green oasis in a decaying neighborhood.

The brief but successful venture into marriage, with its sorrowful ending, had in some degree interfered with his output. During those five years, as might have been expected, domestic duties and delights consumed both time and energy. But once back in the old familiar surroundings he began to boil again and at as high a temperature as before. But the emphasis had changed. With no *Mercury* to drain his vitality, no book reviews to write save as the mood seized him, he concerned himself more and more with the political scene on both the national and international level. Roosevelt Minor, as he called him, provided the most available target. The Sunpapers had supported F. D. R. in 1932 and with that decision Henry went along, with no more than the usual misgivings. Hoover, that "fat Coolidge", had disgusted him. Any change was for the better, particularly as prohibition disappeared in the shuffle.

Some of us on the *Sun* expected the devaluation of the dollar when we learned that the new president was enamored of the theories of J. M. Keynes. Mencken, whose contempt for economics was deliberate and articulate, refused to believe such a step possible. When it came, his anger was explosive. With all the vehemence of which he was capable he insisted it was downright robbery. He talked about taking court action in person. He had not got over his wrath at this revolutionary step when the proposal to pack the Supreme Court came along. That finished him. Thereafter there was no epithet strong enough to characterize the man who had become his personal villain.

His political judgments were sometimes faulty, perhaps because his prejudices fed his emotions. In the beginning Hitler was a joke to him. He could not believe the Germans would follow such an obvious clown. Indeed for a period he took the Austrian monster so lightly that on all hands he was frequently denounced as a Nazi and an anti-Semite. Letters poured into the *Sun* office using these words. By his direction most of them were published, with only the necessary editing. At first he laughed them off but I remember that one day he came into the office and quite seriously asked: "Hamilton, you don't believe that I am a Nazi or anti-Semitic, do you?" Reassured, he made one of the frankest confessions of faith I ever heard from him. "I believe", he said in effect, "in only one thing and that thing is human liberty. If ever a man is to achieve anything like dignity, it can happen only if superior men are given absolute freedom to think what they want to think and say what they want to say. I am against any man and any organization which seeks to limit or deny that freedom".

I made the obvious comment, that he seemed to limit freedom to superior men. His reply was simple, to the effect that the superior man can be sure of freedom only if it is given to all men. So far as my observation goes, that little exchange gets close to the core of the Mencken philosophy.

When the Sunpapers came out in favor of American entry into World War II, he withdrew from active participation in our policy discussions. He thought the course we pursued idiotic and said so publicly on more than one occasion. But he did not resign from the board of directors and there was no break in any of his personal friendships with members of the staff. His mood, however, seemed more often morose than happy. But, by contrast, the major work he produced in this period, the three "Day" volumes, were full of high spirits. When Henry reminisced, he was always at his most entertaining and these were reminiscences *in excelsis.* From the time the first of them appeared in *The New Yorker,* it was clear that he was once more in the ascendant. Now more than sixty, he was regaining not only the survivors of his original audience but a good part of the new generation as well.

The explanation was perhaps simple. His life had been a full one. Few men had more colorful personal experiences to draw upon. Still fewer had command of the fitting prose style in which to express themselves: from the earliest days, despite his love for music, he had insisted that writing good prose was the highest art of all and in these recollections he was reveling in his own superb skill. He still slaved, as in duty bound, over his *American Language;* he still added to the pile of aphorisms which, unearthed after his death, made up his *Minority Report.* But reminiscence was his joy, in the workroom and in the *bierstube.*

No need here to recall the series of events which preceded his final illness. William Manchester has detailed them with good understanding in his *Disturber of the Peace*. The second cerebral hemorrhage had somehow affected the connection between his thought and his command of words. He could read only with great difficulty and write not at all. In conversation he fumbled badly and, if August had not been almost always at hand, communication with visitors would have been almost impossible. His faithful physician of those days, Dr. Philip F. Wagley, struggled hard to help him bypass the barrier. On his instructions, I went frequently to the Hollins Street house, primed in advance with memories of doings we had shared. Henry would clearly appreciate and enjoy these efforts for a while but would soon relapse into a kind of tired hopelessness. Once Dr. Wagley suggested that his patient might be stimulated if I were to write some of these recollections down in as close to the Mencken style as I could manage, read them aloud to him and persuade him to edit them verbally, so that he might have some feeling, however indirect, that he was producing. He listened patiently to this desperate proposal and thought it over for a week. At our next meeting, with something of his old pride and firmness, he said that he had never put his name to anything other than his own work and that it was too late for him to change now. He was so clearly right that the project was abandoned forthwith.

There was little that friends could do but wait. His watchful and ever affectionate brother (Henry sometimes said he got his best ideas from August) did his utmost to make those weeks pass agreeably. Part of the time the patient would sit at the front window and gaze at the little green square across the street. He acquired an amused admiration for the single watchman who cared for it and policed it, keeping the children from its flower beds and making them rid it of their own litter. On good days he sat in the sunshine in the little backyard, doubtless admiring the mellowing brick wall he had put up himself many years before and, to visitors, calling attention to the inserted death mask of Beethoven with the theme of the Fifth Symphony, which he had reproduced in concrete. On such days he seemed almost happy.

* * *

Perhaps a word of caution should be offered to readers of the letters that follow. Mencken's delight in the hoax was known to all his friends and regular correspondents. Most of them had received in the mail their certified chips of the famous "madstone" that guaranteed cure for all diseases save impotence. Some had been invited to accept medals or honorary degrees from the "American Institute of Arts and Letters (Colored)" or to contribute to the "Loyal Legion of American Mothers" dedicated to preserving the purity of American womanhood and to the enforcement of the Constitution of the United States, especially the Eighteenth Amendment. There was no end to such things. Most of his letters to intimates were written in the same mood. They were full of minor hoaxes, grotesque hyperbole, and wholly fictitious accounts of exploits at the table or at love. Many of the letters herein follow that pattern. The discerning reader will soon learn how to differentiate between truth and hoax. Let others beware.

HAMILTON OWENS

A NOTE FROM THE EDITOR

THE NUMBER of letters written by H. L. Mencken will probably never be ascertained. Those deposited in public libraries or held in private collections amount to about fifteen thousand. There are presumably many more at large. The unmanageable quantity of letters, as well as the fact that not a few of them are nothing but social notes of little interest to the general public, make it inadvisable to attempt any complete edition of Mencken's correspondence. Among the more important ones there are letters of all kinds and, despite the similarity of their style, they deal with topics so varied that it is hard to imagine them grouped together under a common title. H. L. Mencken's interests were nothing short of encyclopedic; the letters devoted to linguistic matters alone must run into the thousands. Consequently the editor of this volume has chosen to restrict this selection to the best of Mencken's *literary* letters, along with a number of others that best express his *personality* and give the most vivid and lifelike picture of the man and his literary activities.

For nearly half a century Mencken was in constant correspondence with most of the major writers in the country and thus played an important role on the literary scene. The value of his letters was recognized very early in his career, and many abortive attempts have been made at publishing all or part of them. Critic Burton Rascoe wrote around 1925: "He early established a sort of personal relationship with every promising writer in the country. . . . I have yet to meet a man under thirty-five with articulate ideas who has not a sheaf of those lively, hearty notes whereby Mencken conveys a maximum of good cheer and boisterous comment within a minimum of space." [1] This is corroborated and amplified by Sherwood Anderson: "At that time Henry Mencken was our great hero. We all read the old *Smart Set* and later Mencken and Nathan's *Mercury*. Many of us had got letters from

[1] Ernest Boyd: *H. L. Mencken* (New York: Robert M. McBride; 1925).

Mencken. He was the great letter writer. At that time he must have been in correspondence with all of the young writers in the country. . . ."; and further: "We got the letters and the letters made us proud. 'Well I had a letter from Henry Mencken today.'

"You said it offhand, but in your heart you felt that it was like being knighted by a king.

"You knew damn well the others felt the same." [2]

Mencken's correspondence abounds in amusing and often penetrating remarks on contemporaries or on the passing American scene. Sometimes they provide us with a day by day commentary on what is going on in literary America. Nearly always they reflect the writer's personality, his critical acumen and his unfailing humor.

Not all of Mencken's acquaintances could be reached or persuaded to part with their letters, and so this collection does not presume to represent an absolute cross-section of Mencken's correspondence; although the editor believes that it is a selection of the best items available at present, other letters may turn up from time to time and prove to be of equal or even superior interest. It is hoped, however, that the present volume will contribute to correct some of the current misapprehensions about Mencken, and perhaps emulate others to search for and publish more of this fascinating correspondence.

The letters in this selection are arranged chronologically and alphabetically by addressee within each day. Each letter is preceded by the name of the addressee and a symbol indicating the origin and the nature of the document. The following symbols and abbreviations have been used:

AAK Letter in the possession of Alfred A. Knopf

CC Carbon copy of a letter

CU Microfilmed original from Cornell University Library

EPL Transcript from a letter; at the Enoch Pratt Free Library in Baltimore

EPT Transcript of an original letter, made in Italy for the editor by Ezra Pound in 1959

HU Microfilmed original from Harvard University Library

MS Manuscript letter. Typewritten letters have no special symbol

---

[2] Sherwood Anderson: *Memoirs* (New York: Harcourt, Brace & Co.; 1942).

OFP Microfilmed original from the Princeton University Library

PT Transcript of an original letter made at Princeton for Dr. Julian P. Boyd in 1942 or about. Now at the Princeton University Library

PU Original letter from the Princeton University Library

UP Microfilmed original from the University of Pennsylvania Library

UV Microfilmed original from the University of Virginia Library

YU Original letter from the Yale University Library

As is customary, headnotes have been used to explain the circumstances in which each letter was written or to summarize the contents of the letter which it answers. Footnotes serve to clarify references, identify addressees (at the first occurrence of their name), and to supply any other relevant information.

No attempt has been made to reproduce the exact arrangement of the lines or the appearance of the originals; marginalia and postscripts are not differentiated by a change in the typography. Punctuation and spelling remain as in the original documents. The date of each letter and the place where it was written have been printed in the upper right-hand corner. Square brackets enclose information supplied by the editor, such as conjectural dates and words that seem to be missing in the original. In some cases the exact date of the letter is uncertain. Where the day of the month is unknown I use the symbol [?]. Where the month is unknown but probable I use a simple question mark after the month.

The quotations from Theodore Dreiser's letters have been taken verbatim from *Letters of Theodore Dreiser* (Philadelphia: University of Pennsylvania Press; 1959).

Most of the letters in this selection have been printed in their entirety. Occasional deletions have been made to protect living persons or to suppress trivial or irrelevant material; three dots in brackets indicate that one or a very few words have been taken out, and a complete line of dots that one or more paragraphs have been suppressed.

The letters identified by an OPT symbol were copied from the transcripts made in Princeton from the originals borrowed by Julian P. Boyd in 1942; consequently it has not been possible to verify the accuracy of their contents. Lastly, though most of the references contained in the letters have been explained in the various notes, the others are bound to remain unclarified as long as the letters sent to H. L. Mencken are not made available to scholars in the New York Public Library—until 1971, according to the terms of his will.

GUY JEAN FORGUE

ACKNOWLEDGMENTS

THANKS ARE DUE first to August Mencken and the *Mercantile–Safe Deposit and Trust Company*, Baltimore, Maryland, for permission to use the H. L. Mencken letters to which they possess the literary rights. I am also grateful to the Princeton University Library for permission to copy the letters in the H. L. Mencken collection; to the Yale University Library, for permission to copy the letters from H. L. Mencken to Carl Van Vechten, Fania Marinoff, Bradford F. Swan, Walter White, Sinclair Lewis, Ben Abramson, William Lyon Phelps, Wilbur Cross, Wheeler Sammons, Arthur D. Ficke, A. L. S. Wood, Amélie Rives, Dudley Nichols, Isaac Goldberg, Lawrence Gilman, and Marvin C. Ross; to the University of Pennsylvania Library, for permission to copy the letters from H. L. Mencken to Theodore Dreiser, Helen Dreiser, and Burton Rascoe; to Cornell University Library, for permission to copy the letters from H. L. Mencken to George Jean Nathan, James Joyce, and F. C. Prescott; to the University of Virginia Library, for permission to copy the letters from H. L. Mencken to Guy Holt and Edward Stone; to the Harvard University Library, for permission to copy the letters from H. L. Mencken to the unknown editor of the *Youth's Companion* and to Mr. Duncan; to Mrs. Burton Rascoe, for permission to use the letters addressed to her husband; to Ernst, Cane and Berner, executors of the Sinclair Lewis Estate, for permission to copy the letters to Sinclair Lewis; to Harold Ober, Associates, executors of the Sherwood Anderson Estate, for permission to reprint the quotation from Sherwood Anderson's *Memoirs* in the introduction to this book, and to copy the letters from H. L. Mencken to F. Scott Fitzgerald; to James T. Farrell, for permission to use his letters from H. L. Mencken; finally, too, I wish to thank the Bollingen Foundation, whose grant has helped to offset the expenses incurred in the preparation of this volume.

For permission to quote from *Letters of Theodore Dreiser*, my thanks go to the University of Pennsylvania Press; for permission to quote from Ernest Boyd's *H. L. Mencken* (New York: Robert M. McBride; 1925), to the Robert McBride Company and Mrs. Burton Rascoe.

I should like to thank the following persons who to various extents have been helpful to me: Miss Betty Adler, Mrs. Stephen Vincent Benét, Mrs. Ernest Boyd, Huntington Cairns, Alexander P. Clark, Carrol Coates, H. L. Davis, John Dos Passos, Robert Elias, Donald Gallup, Gaston Hall, Mrs. Joseph Hergesheimer, Miss Sara D. Jones, Alfred A. Knopf, Mrs. John W. Lohrfinck, Mrs. Percy Marks, Mrs. Henry Miller, Arthur Mizener, Hamilton Owens, Ezra Pound, George S. Schuyler, Ellery Sedgwick, Upton Sinclair, Bradford F. Swan, Carl Van Vechten, Mrs. Neda Westlake, and Mrs. Walter White.

For biographical data, I am also greatly indebted to *The Irreverent Mr. Mencken,* by Edgar Kemler (Boston: Little, Brown and Co.; 1950); *Disturber of the Peace, the life of H. L. Mencken,* by William Manchester (New York: Harper & Brothers; 1951); and *Theodore Dreiser, Apostle of Nature,* by Robert H. Elias (New York: Alfred A. Knopf; 1949).

Thanks are also owed to my wife and to Honoré Guillefort, who have both contributed to the preparation of this volume more than I can ever hope to acknowledge.

In concluding, I wish to add that although he first conceived the idea of this volume and played a large part in collecting material for it, Dr. Julian P. Boyd had nothing to do with this work as it now stands, and that I claim entire responsibility for the editing of these letters.

G. J. F.

New York and Paris
August–December 1960

CONTENTS

LETTERS OF H. L. MENCKEN

[1915] CONTINUED

[1916]

[1917]

[1917] CONTINUED

[1918]

[1919]

[1 9 1 9] CONTINUED

[1 9 2 0]

[1 9 2 0] CONTINUED

[1 9 2 1]

[1 9 2 1] CONTINUED

[1 9 2 2]

[1 9 2 3]

[1 9 2 3] CONTINUED

[1 9 2 4]

[1927] CONTINUED

[1928]

[1929]

[1930]

[1 9 3 0] CONTINUED

[1 9 3 1]

[1 9 3 2]

[1934] CONTINUED

Letters of H. L. Mencken

1900

To THE CORRESPONDING EDITOR OF THE YOUTH'S COMPANION, *Boston, Mass.*
[HU]

[*In the Summer of 1899 H. L. Mencken began his journalistic career at the Baltimore* Morning Herald. *But he worked so hard to become its star reporter that the next year he fell ill and was sent to Jamaica for a few weeks' rest. This is where he got the inspiration for "The Defeat of Alphonso," one of the 20-odd stories he wrote as early as 1900 for various popular magazines, among them,* Short Stories, Youth's Companion, Everybody's, Hearst's, *and* Frank Leslie's Popular Monthly, *then edited by Ellery Sedgwick.*]

Baltimore, November 18 [*1900*]

DEAR SIR,

Enclosed you will find the MS. of a short story entitled "The Defeat of Alphonso", which I trust will prove available.

In your letter of September 26 you informed me that the Companion was in need of stories of adventure, "containing at least one effective incident and dealing with the formation or illustration of character." I hope that you will judge the enclosed to fill these requirements.

The story is based upon a score or more of yarns told to me by an American "tramp dentist" whom I met last summer in Jamaica.

The local color, I know, is accurate. Should you object to the fact that the hero of the tale is a gentleman of little virtue, I beg to point out the further fact that, as the curtain falls, he is kicked vigorously.[1]

I am sorry that I have been unable to work up any more of the boy's stories regarding which I wrote to you. As soon as I have time I will do so, and if your kind invitation still holds, will submit them to you.

Awaiting a reply, I am,

Yours truly,
Henry L. Mencken

[*Almost 30 years later, Mencken fondly recalled his early writings in this letter dated September 11, 1929:*]

Dear Duncan:

God will reward you throughout eternity. I am delighted to have the magazine with my story and am depositing it into my secret archives at once. The story itself, re-read after nearly thirty years, seems to me to be not at all bad. I was indeed a talented fellow in them times. In late years, woes and sorrows have corrupted my imagination.

My best to Mrs. Duncan.

Yours,
H. L. Mencken

[1] The American tramp dentist depicted in this story is a familiar character in Latin America. With Kingston, Jamaica, as a base he makes annual trips to the cities and towns of all of the republics, from Mexico to Argentina. While on his travels he moves in state and is often accorded the reception of an ambassador. Sometimes his earnings exceed $15,000 a year. In the West Indies the author met a champion "extractor" who had cleared $350 in a day. Often these wandering Americanos add to their incomes by taking a hand in mining, railroad and filibustering schemes. They are commonly of rather dubious antecedents and few of them ever return to the states without changing their names. (H. L. Mencken) [This footnote by Mencken was later appended to a letter he wrote to Duncan, to whom he had sent the November 18, 1900, letter for his collection. It is now at Harvard University Library. Ed.]

1909

◇◇◇◇◇◇◇◇◇◇◇◇◇◇◇◇◇◇

To THEODORE DREISER
[UP]

[*H. L. Mencken left the* Morning Herald *for the Baltimore* Sun *in 1906. In 1908 he agreed to ghost a series of articles for Leonard K. Hirshberg, a Baltimore physician; the doctor approached Theodore Dreiser, then editor of* Woman's Home Companion, *who eventually published them. In March, Mencken visited Dreiser in order to discuss the rest of the series. An account of their picturesque meeting can be found in Isaac Goldberg's* The Man Mencken (*New York: Simon and Schuster; 1925*). *The medical articles written by Mencken were brought out in 1910 by Butterick Publishing Co. as a book signed by Dr. Hirshberg:* What You Ought to Know about Your Baby. *"It is the only job of ghost-writing that I ever did," Mencken wrote to Bradford Swan* (*December 14, 1929*).]

H. L. Mencken
1524 Hollins St.
Baltimore
March 7th [1909]

MY DEAR DREISER:–

Thanks for your letter of the 4th. I take it that you want an article dealing especially with improvements in nursing. For instance, fever patients are now given all the water they want, whereas a few years back they were compelled to go dry. Again, it is now possible to allay the pain in many diseases which were formerly accompanied by agonies. If this is your idea, I shall ask Hirshberg to get material together at once.

I am afraid I must beg off on the Rural Life stuff. I went to Washington Tuesday, but could find no one in authority, on account of the Inauguration. It may seem foolish, but it is a fact that I won't have time to return next week. Happenings at the Sun office have kept me sweating, I have been in indifferent health, and La Monte is howling for copy for the Socialist book.[1] This evening Hirshberg is to employ his saw upon a small part of my anatomy, and I suppose that a certain soreness will ensue.

All in all, I find that I have too many irons in the fire. To get more time for the work I want to do, I must withdraw some of them. I am getting along toward thirty and it is time for me to be planning for the future. Specifically, I want to write a couple of books for you within the next few years. Specifically again, I want to write a play that now encumbers and tortures my system. You will understand what a stew I am in.

Incidentally, I have happened upon two foreign books that may interest Dodge & Co. The first is Nietzsche's autobiography, "Ecce Homo", which was recently issued by Friedrich Richter in Leipzig in a limited edition of 1250 copies. (I had to pay $6.70 for mine.) The book is a semi-insane rhapsody, but I rather think it would sell. I have had no communication with the publisher and so don't know if the English translation rights are still open. I rather think they are. I wouldn't care to make the translation myself, because my German is full of scars and knot-holes, but I could get a slave, I believe, to translate it word for word, and then tease it up. The book, of course, would need a good introduction, and some explanatory notes.[2]

II. The posthumous letters and papers of Ibsen are about to be

---

[1] Robert Rives La Monte (b. 1867) was a socialist writer who, having read Mencken's antisocialist blasts in the Baltimore *Sun*, suggested that they publish jointly a book of letters discussing Socialism; this resulted in *Men versus The Man* (New York: Henry Holt & Co.; 1910), the first volume of Mencken's correspondence ever published.

[2] H. L. Mencken's interest in Nietzsche had already produced *The Philosophy of Friedrich Nietzsche* (Boston and London: John W. Luce & Co.; 1908); Mencken was also to write *The Gist of Nietzsche* (Boston: John W. Luce & Co.; 1910), preface the Nietzsche-Wagner correspondence in 1921, and finally translate and edit *The Antichrist,* which formed the third volume of the Free Lance books, published by Alfred A. Knopf in 1920.

issued in three volumes by the Hegel firm of Copenhagen, and I have already applied for the American rights.[3] The three volumes, by judicious editing, could be brought down to one. I have a first class Danish translator on my staff and would be glad to undertake the work. So far, I have got no response from Hegel, and the whole thing, of course, is heavy with ifs and buts.[4]

If these things interest you, I'll go into them more carefully.

Sincerely yours,
H. L. Mencken

To WILLARD HUNTINGTON WRIGHT[5]
[OFP-MS]

[*Mencken had begun contributing monthly book reviews to the* Smart Set *as early as November 1908. Here we find him congratulating* W. H. *Wright's style, which was actually an imitation of his own.*]

H. L. Mencken
1524 Hollins St.
Baltimore
Oct. 28, 1909

MY DEAR WRIGHT:–

Believe me, your two essays knocked me over—not because their doctrine startled me, for I knew your position, in part, and suspected the rest, but because of their electric style. You have here got into English the thing that Nietzsche got into German—a loud heart beat, an assertive clang. There is the resounding wallop of heavy strokes, the clash of hammer on anvil. If anyone talks to you of style, bidding you read Addison and Walter Pater—my curses on him! May he be

[3] The Gyldendal firm.

[4] Mencken's interest in Ibsen probably stemmed as early as 1904 from his interest in G. B. Shaw. Mencken collected a great mass of Ibseniana which he gave to the University of Leipzig in 1928. In 1909 he was working with H. A. Koppel, the Danish Consul in Baltimore, at a translation of Ibsen's plays; as a result of this, he wrote an introduction and notes to *Little Eyolf* and *A Doll's House* (Boston: John W. Luce & Co.; 1909).

[5] Willard Huntington Wright (1888–1939), who took the pseudonym of S. S. Van Dine in 1926, was then literary editor of the Los Angeles *Times*. He became assistant editor of the *Smart Set* soon after and gained complete control of the magazine in 1913.

forever damned! Your style is already there: guard it, by all means, from feminization. I'll have more to say when your book comes out—a lot more. Let it be got under way at once. And you are already elected to the Review—elected and inaugurated. When the time comes, you *must* come in.

It was a great pleasure to see you and a great pleasure to make acquaintance with your essays. More!

Yours,
H. L. Mencken

◇◇◇◇◇◇◇◇◇◇◇◇◇◇

To THEODORE DREISER
[UP]

[*Regarding "The Decay of the Churches," one of Mencken's articles for the* Bohemian, *Dreiser had questioned the theory that men are wholly independent from the gods. Dreiser said that he believed in fixed rules, that scientific knowledge was a kind of prayer and that all men were religious, although in different ways; he asked Mencken to add a paragraph to that effect (Dreiser to Mencken, November 2, 1909).*]

H. L. Mencken
1524 Hollins St.
Baltimore
November 3rd [1909]

MY DEAR DREISER:–

I have no copy of the editorial on the decay of the churches, and so can't fix it up until I get back the copy I sent in. If you will do it, I'd much prefer to have you add the qualification you mention. You know exactly what you mean to convey. I am in your hands.[6]

In all honesty, I can't follow you. The scientific impulse seems to me to be the very opposite of the religious impulse. When a man seeks knowledge he is trying to gain means of fighting his own way in the world, but when he prays he confesses that he is unable to do so. The essential thing about prayer is that it assumes that the moods of

[6] In the summer of 1909 Dreiser had become editor of the *Bohemian;* during four months, Mencken contributed a number of articles on various subjects grouped under the title "At the Sign of the Lead Pencil".

the gods are *not* fixed and invariable. If they were, it would be silly to ask the gods to change them. This idea, I think, explains the decay of religion.

The feeling of abasement, of incapacity, is inseparable from the religious impulse, but against that feeling all exact knowledge makes war. The efficient man does not cry out "Save me, O God". On the contrary, he makes diligent efforts to save himself. But suppose he fails? Doesn't he throw himself, in the end, on the mercy of the gods? Not at all. He accepts his fate with philosophy, buoyed up by the consciousness that he has done his best. Irreligion, in a word, teaches men how to die with dignity, just as it teaches them how to live with dignity.

But all this is only my personal view of life, and I freely confess that I may be wrong. Therefore, I shall be glad to see you put something of your view into the editorial.

A few other things, before I forget. If the Sun is on the Bohemian's exchange list, will you please cut it off. Sending the magazine can do no good, and if any of my stuff is recognized there may be a kick. No. 2: Has any conclusion been reached regarding the Ibsens? No. 3: I'd like to have "Abaft the Funnel" to review in the S. S. jointly with "Actions and Reactions". No. 4: How are you? No. 5: Suite A is being made ready for you.

Sincerely,
H. L. Mencken

1911

To THEODORE DREISER
[UP]

[*On February 24, 1911, Dreiser announced that he had finished* Jennie Gerhardt *and was halfway through* The "Genius".]

H. L. Mencken
1524 Hollins St.
Baltimore
March 3rd [*1911*]

DEAR DREISER:–

Bully news! You know I am one of those who hold "Sister Carrie" in actual reverence, as one of the best novels this fair land has ever produced. What is more, I have often said so in print, in a clarion voice. What is still more, I have really meant it. So I look forward eagerly to "Jennie Gerhardt" and to her successors. Give the game a fair trial: you have got the goods, and soon or late the fact will penetrate the skulls of those who have anything within. Whether you know it or not, "Sister Carrie" has begun to soak in. Such fellows as Wright in Los Angeles are enthusiastic about it, and you will see the result when your next one comes along. The money be damned. You will not grow as rich as McCutcheon and Garvice, but there's a good living in it.

Unluckily, I can't attend the lobster party, but I'll have a mass said for you. Here's hoping that Mrs. Dreiser has recovered her health and that you are well. My folks send their best regards.

Yours,
H. L. M.

To THEODORE DREISER
[UP]

[*In his letter of March 10th, Dreiser had asked Mencken what he thought of David Graham Phillips's books.*]

H. L. Mencken
1524 Hollins St.
Baltimore
March 14th [*1911*]

DEAR DREISER:–

As for Phillips, I am a great admirer of his later work—particularly "The Hungry Heart" and "The Husband's Story". Such stuff as "The Fashionable Adventures of Joshua Craig" seems to have been done to get the money. In the S. S. for Jan. I had an article entitled "The Leading American Novelist", in which I pointed out a few of P.'s merits. Unluckily, there was no space for a long and serious discussion of him. I have no doubt that you find him immensely interesting, for your own method, as shown in "Sister Carrie", suggests his. I suspect that "Sister Carrie" taught him something. Incidentally, I seize every opportunity to ram in the idea that your book must be read. In the S. S. for Dec. (p. 165) there was a note about it. Here we behold, not a yearning to please a friend, but honest admiration for an arresting work of art. I look forward eagerly to "Jennie". Meanwhile, the bock beer delights and the season of boiled hard crabs dawns.

Yours,
M.

Don't answer this: stick to your work!

(1911)

To Theodore Dreiser
[UP]

H. L. Mencken
1524 Hollins St.
Baltimore
April 23rd [*1911*]

Dear Dreiser:–

When "Jennie Gerhardt" is printed it is probable that more than one reviewer will object to its length, its microscopic detail, its enormous painstaking—but rest assured that Heinrich Ludwig von Mencken will not be in that gang. I have just finished reading the ms. —every word of it, from first to last—and I put it down with a clear notion that it should remain as it stands. The story comes upon me with great force; it touches my own experience of life in a hundred places; it preaches (or perhaps I had better say exhibits) a philosophy of life that seems to me to be sound; altogether I get a powerful effect of reality, stark and unashamed. It is drab and gloomy, but so is the struggle for existence. It is without humor, but so are the jests of that great comedian who shoots at our heels and makes us do our grotesque dancing.

I needn't say that it seems to me an advance above "Sister Carrie". Its obvious superiority lies in its better form. You strained (or perhaps even broke) the back of "Sister Carrie" when you let Hurstwood lead you away from Carrie. In "Jennie Gerhardt" there is no such running amuck. The two currents of interest, of spiritual unfolding, are very deftly managed. Even when they do not actually coalesce, they are parallel and close together. Jennie is never out of Kane's life, and after their first meeting, she is never out of his. The reaction of will upon will, of character upon character, is splendidly worked out and indicated. In brief, the story hangs together; it is a complete whole; consciously or unconsciously, you have avoided the chief defect of "Sister Carrie".

It is difficult, just rising from the book, to describe the impression I bring away. That impression is of a living whole, not of a fabric that may be unravelled and examined in detail. In brief, you have painted so smoothly and yet so vigorously that I have no memory of brush strokes. But for one thing, the great naturalness of the dialogue sticks in mind. In particular, you have been extremely successful with Gerhardt. His speeches are perfect: nothing could be nearer to truth. I am well aware that certain persons are impatient of this photographic accuracy. Well, let them choose their poison. As for me, I prefer the fact to the fancy. You have tried to depict a German of a given type—a type with which I, by chance, happen to be very familiar. You have made him as thoroughly alive as Huck Finn.

These are random, disordered notes. When the time comes, I'll reduce my thoughts to order and write a formal, intelligible review. At the moment I am too near the book. I rather distrust my own enthusiasm for it. Perhaps I read my own prejudices and ideas into it. My interest is always in the subjective event, seldom or never in the objective event. That is why I like "Lord Jim". Here you have got very close to the very well-springs of action. The march of episodes is nothing: the slow unfolding of character is everything.

If anyone urges you to cut down the book bid that one be damned. And if anyone argues that it is over-gloomy call the police. Let it stand as it is. Its bald, forthright style; its scientific, unemotional piling up of detail; the incisive truthfulness of its dialogue; the stark straightforwardness of it all—these are merits that need no praise. It is at once an accurate picture of life and a searching criticism of life. And that is my definition of a good novel.

Here and there I noted minor weaknesses. For one thing, it is doubtful that Jennie would have been able to conceal from so sophisticated a man as Kane the fact that she had had a child. Child-bearing leaves physical marks, and those marks commonly persist for five or six years. But there are, of course, exceptions to this rule. Not many readers, I suppose, will raise the point. Again, if I remember correctly, you speak of L. S. & M. S. "shares" as being worth $1,000 par. Don't you mean bonds? If bonds, the income would be fixed and could not fluctuate. Again you give Kane $5,000 income from $75,000 at 6 percent. A small thing—but everywhere else you are so utterly careful that small errors stick out.

A final word: the least satisfactory personage in the book is Jennie herself. Not that you do not account for her, from head to heels—but I would have preferred, had I the choice, a more typical kept woman. She is, in brief, uncompromisingly exceptional, almost unique, in several important details. Her connection with her mother and father and with the facts of her life grows, at times, very fragile. But I can well understand how her essential plausibility must have reacted upon you—how your own creation must have dragged you on. There is always Letty Pace to show Jennie's limitations. In her class she is a miracle, and yet she never quite steps out of that class.

But I go back to the effect of the book as a whole. That effect, believe me, is very powerful. I must go to Hardy and Conrad to find its like. David Phillips, I believe, might have done such a story had he lived, but the best that he actually wrote, to wit, "The Hungry Heart", goes to pieces beside "Jennie". I mean this in all seriousness. You have written a novel that no other American of the time could have written, and even in England there are not six men who, with your material, could have reached so high a level of reality. My earnest congratulations. By all means let me see that third book. "Jennie" shows immense progress in craftsmanship. As a work of art it is decidedly superior to "Sister Carrie".

I'll return the ms. by express tomorrow morning. Maybe chance will throw us together soon and we'll have a session over "Jennie". At the moment I am rather too full of the story as a human document to sit down in cold blood and discourse upon its merits and defects as a work of art. I know that it is immensely good, but I have still to get my reasons reduced to fluent words.

God keep you. As for me, I lately enjoyed the first of the season's rashers of crab à la creole. With genuine Muenchener to flush the esophagus afterward.

Yours,
H. L. M.

Reading this over it seems damned cold. [What] I really want to say is just—"Hurrah!" You have put over a truly *big* thing.

[*In his letter of April 28th, Dreiser thanked Mencken for his appreciation of* Jennie Gerhardt *and compared his critical acumen to Huneker's. In answer, Mencken wrote on September 20th:*]

Dear Dreiser:-

[. . . . .]

My second reading of "Jennie Gerhardt" has increased my enthusiasm for it. Let no one convince you to the contrary: you have written the best American novel ever done, with the one exception of "Huckleberry Finn". It hangs together vastly better than "McTeague". It is decidedly on a higher plane. The very faults of it are virtues—as I argue in my S. S. article. But of all that anon.

If the Harpers want my review in advance they can get a proof of it by telephoning to Norman Boyer at the S. S. It is in type by now. God bless all honest men. . . .

[*The* Smart Set *review was printed in the November 1911 issue.*]

To THEODORE DREISER
[UP-MS]

H. L. Mencken
1524 Hollins St.
Baltimore
May 8th [*1911*]

DEAR DREISER:–

"The Mighty Burke" pleased me a lot: I am in favor of any effort [to] knock out that curse of fiction, the formal plot. The short story of tomorrow will be of the pattern of Galsworthy's sketches in "A Commentary". Damn the O. Henry stuff. "Jennie Gerhardt" sticks in my mind—a fine piece of work. That it will be a best-seller I doubt, but I suspect that it will make you. I hope Heinemann does it in London.

That scheme for bottling beer is interesting—but only academically. Down here, we don't bottle it, but drink it. As well preserve roses in cans!

[Yours,]
H. L. M.

To THEODORE DREISER
[UP-MS]

H. L. Mencken
1524 Hollins St.
Baltimore
Aug. 15th [*1911*]

DEAR DREISER:–

No word, as yet, from the Harpers—but there is still time to stir them up. If the worst comes to the worst I'll ask you for a few names—and write from memory.

My compliments to Huneker whenever you see him. He and William Archer, two very different men, have given me more ideas than any other living critics. Tell him he simply *must* do a volume on the new dramatists—Synge, Galsworthy, Barker, Brieux, Gorki, Wedekind, Schnitzler, Barker, Bennett, etc. The material is at hand, or at least part of it, in his *Sun* articles. Meanwhile, the blessings of S. S. Anhaüser & Busch be upon you!

[Yours,]
H. L. M.

◇◇◇◇◇◇◇◇◇◇◇◇◇

To HARRY LEON WILSON[1]
[PT]

Baltimore, September 4th [*1911*]

MY DEAR MR. WILSON:–

A curse on Luther! [2] He hadn't ought to have shown your letter to me, and he hadn't ought to have shown my letter to you. (I use American, that lovely tongue.) But if, perchance, his diabolical indiscretion leads, some day, to a joint ingestion of stimulants—the Orange Blossom in Carmel or real Loewenbrau (a secret and limited stock) here in old Baltimore—then, say I, let him escape the Hell he deserves. That epistle of mine was composed, I needn't say, in some biliousness of spirits. The provocation reached me in hot, moist weather. I sat in my drawers and undershift, under a Welsbach, reviewing poetry by fair survivors of ovariotomy. In came Luther's letter—and then the discharge of bile! It was not that we diverged, but that we agreed. Sehen Sie? Next day, of course, I was sitting up and feeling better—and then came the consoling thought that, after all, you had probably never actually read the S. S., any more than I had myself. From J.A.T. come pleas, demands, orders that I read it monthly.[3] My price is $100, and he won't pay it: so there you are. Oct. 1 the price rises to $125. A man must guard his health, and magazine reading is very hard on my system. Novels are not so bad: the canned reviews help. . . . By the way, do you know Bennett's "The Truth About an Author"? Certainly you must. Well, there is a sound theory of book-reviewing—not of criticism, but of book-reviewing. Criticism is as hard to sell as postmeridian virtue. I have tried it.

---

[1] Harry Leon Wilson (1867–1939): writer and former editor of *Puck.*
[2] Mark L. Luther was editor of the *Smart Set.*
[3] J.A.T.: John Adams Thayer (1861–1936), publisher and owner of the *Smart Set* from 1911 until 1914. See his autobiography: *Out of the Rut* (New York: G. W. Dillingham; 1912).

As for Howells and Bennett, I am with you, heart and soul. Howells is a somewhat kittenish old maid—in brief, a giggler. Not since "The Rise of Silas Lapham" (which I read in my nonage) has he done a stroke of honest work. And by the same token, Bennett is stupendous —a man of tomorrow rather than of today. His two plays, "Cupid and Commonsense" and "What the Public Wants" knocked me in a heap. Wells, I believe, is very near him, especially in "The New Machiavelli". And Moore, in "Memoirs of My Dead Life" (the English edition, of course, *not* the denaturized Putnam edition) is even ahead of him. I compare here, not ideas, but workmanship. In ideas, Moore is nearer Henry James.

Good old Hank! I defend thee, sweet Hal, and get into rages about thee, and yet thou knowest that "What Maisie Knew" is the one book of thine that I can read. "The Golden Bowl"—ye Gods! Still, the artist is there, and on the whole I believe that his influence has been for the good. He led the escape from the old novel of external incident —the true Victorian novel—the Hop Smith, William Allen White, G. B. McC, H. Mcg. novel—the dephlogisticated piffle of the department stores. If, on the one hand, he has set a pack of Lizzies to writing involved balderdash, don't forget that, on the other hand, he has given us George Moore, and above all, Joseph Conrad. If you don't know Conrad, I pray you, in nomine Domini, to get him at once—"Youth", "Typhoon", "Lord Jim", anything he has done. If "Youth" is not the best short story in English, and "Heart of Darkness" the next best, and "Falk" the next best, then on with the bastinado and tear my hide to shreds! Conrad is the greatest of them all—and Robert McClure once told me that a Conrad book sold 1,000 copies in the United States! The English government lately gave the poor fellow a Civil List pension of $500 a year. Why be decent?

Of course, I know "McTeague"—know it and wallow in it, or at least in the first half of it. I doubt that he would have done a better book had he lived. The occult rubbish was getting into him. Witness "The Octopus". It has made a tedious bore of Augustus Thomas. As for Dreiser (the "Sister Carrie" man), keep your eye on him. He has lately finished a new novel, "Jennie Gerhardt", in which he tells the story of "Sister Carrie" again, but with vastly better workmanship. Dreiser and I are old friends and so he sent me the ms. Believe me, the story is an astonishing piece of work, recalling Bennett on every page, though Dreiser has no humor. It will score a knockout in England, but over here it is not apt to sell more than 6,000 or 7,000. The lady critics will denounce it—as "The Bookman" denounced "Jude the Obscure". God, what a country!

The Town Talk interview is good stuff. Give 'em hell. The greatest sport in the world is a stand-up bawling match. I am constantly in them—and enjoy it to the limit. Cale Young Rice is the latest to have at me. I refuse to apologize for saying that his so-called poetry is rotten, and defend myself on the ground that the pain caused by my saying so will tend to make it less rotten in future. Progress is by opposition: the cell doesn't act, it *re*acts. A case in point: My Oct. S. S. article, written in the midst of two or three nasty rows, is the best I had ever done. An honest damn is worth 200 God bless you, my boys. If "A Doll's House" had been praised, there would have been no "Ghosts".

Some day, God willing, you will come East and we'll victual together. I'd give four square inches of velvety cuticle to see California and the ocean from your front yard—but the railroads demand cash. The best I can do is another bier-semester in Munich—maybe next Spring. Daily newspaper work is killing me: I haven't had a holiday for 3 years.

A seidel of that Orange Blossom—Prosit!—Skaal!

Achtungsvoll,
H. L. Mencken

P.S.—Good old Luther!

To HARRY LEON WILSON
[PT]

Baltimore, October 25th [*1911*]

MY DEAR WILSON:–

When Arnold Bennett landed in New York the other day and Howells and the Harpers camorra began filling his bowels with tea, he slipped out by the hind door and called up Dreiser. He didn't know Dreiser, but he did know "Sister Carrie", and he yearned for a palaver. On Sunday, in the Times, he gave Dreiser a fine boost. Naturally enough, Theodore was vastly pleased. I saw him in N. Y. last week. He is hopeful that "Jennie Gerhardt" will stir up the plain people, despite the fact that the Harpers cut about 25,000 words out of the ms. I read the ms. and it floored me. What the book will do, God knows. Such ruthless slashing is alarming. The chief virtue of Dreiser is his skill at piling up detail. The story he tells, reduced to a mere story, is nothing. Of course you will read the book. Give me a line or two telling me how it strikes you as it stands. He has another and even better thing, "The Financier", in his trunk—an elephant of 300,000 words.

Conrad is one of my superstitions, and so I can't argue about him intelligently. The trouble with him, I fear, is a deficiency in the sense of form. He often staggers into his stories in a crazy manner. Observe, for example, his story in the current Harper's. The thing is clumsy, inept, maddening. Its long prologue has no sense. You will find the same fault in "Lord Jim"—and yet that same "Lord Jim" is colossal. I read it once—and damned it. Then I went back—and began to fathom it. Now I put it at the head of all Conrad's longer stuff—"Nostromo", "Almayer's Folly" and all the rest. But his very best work is in shorter forms—for instance, "Youth". I once gave "Youth" to Paul Armstrong, a man who seldom reads books.[4] It knocked him flat. Then I gave it to a college professor—a learned pundit. And he went down, too. A third type: Channing Pollock.[5] I met him the other day—and we were yowling over "Youth" in a minute. It turned out that the thing which struck him hardest was something that I had overlooked. My own pet scene is the last. When I was 20 I was condemned by medical survey and sailed for the West Indies in a smelly banana boat. The seventh day out, at 3:30 in the morning, we arrived in Port Antonio harbor. Stillness. The sweet tropical smells . . . Up came the dawn—and there, all around the boat, were the palms . . . skiffs full of niggers . . . high mountains . . . the blinding, pea-green water. Later on, when I read "Youth"—but you can imagine how it got under my hide!

As for Moore, I hand [it?] to the "Memoirs". Do you know the English edition? What of "The Lovers of Orelay"? The idea here, as I understand it, is that such a joust, far from being vile, may be actually poetic, elevating, civilizing—and to both parties. The Glyn tried to preach the same doctrine in "Three Weeks", and (despite Percival Pollard's eloquent dissent) made a mess of it. But what a bully piece of writing Moore has made of it! His English constantly tickles my ear. It has all of the music of Walter Pater's—and lacks the simpering striving. Pater is Chopin; Moore is Mozart. And now the old buck issues a proclamation that he will write English no more. The neo-Celtic movement has wrapped its tentacles about him, and he swears he'll write nothing but Gaelic hereafter. In the next breath he confesses that

[4] Paul Armstrong (1869–1915): a playwright.

[5] Channing Pollock (1880–1946): author, dramatist and dramatic critic of the *Smart Set.*

he knows no more Gaelic than an Irish comedian. A queer old rooster.

Patterson the Socialist is a fellow who shows signs of doing decent work later on. His "Rebellion" is full of rotten writing, but somehow his characters stand out clearly. I hear that the play was cheap drivel. The novel is certainly not. If he could only get a few of his banal theories out of his system, he would come to something. But Socialism seems to be an incurable disease. Not poppy, nor mandragora, nor even salversan can stop it. Another promising gent is Henry Milner Rideout, who lives somewhere in your vicinage.[6] His "Dragon's Blood" was a fine imitation of Conrad.

What are you doing in the lit'ry way? Why don't you and Tarkington publish your plays? Don't say no publisher will fall for it. I have good reason to believe that Bobbs-Merrill will. Play-reading is increasing in this fair land, and the old objections to publishing, on the score of piracy, have been waved away by the new copyright law. "The Man From Home" should go between covers, at least. I have been trying for years to induce Frank McKee to print the Hoyt plays. He owns them and has made a fortune out of them. Stock companies still do them. But the old fellow always puts it off. Hoyt, of course, never got far from the seltzer siphon, and yet he was close to our national notion of humor, and so he is worth standing on the shelf.

Anon! Anon! The clock in the steeple strikes one!

Sincerely,
H. L. Mencken

To WILLARD HUNTINGTON WRIGHT
[OFP]

H. L. Mencken
1524 Hollins St.
Baltimore
December 20th [*1911*]

DEAR WRIGHT:–

My sincere congratulations on the Christmas Book Section.[7] You have got guts into it: the stuff is sound and has an air. In particular, I like the notice of "The Indian Lily".[8] For why? Because I sent the S. S.

[6] H. M. Rideout (1877–1927), an author.
[7] Of the Los Angeles *Times*.
[8] *The Indian Lily*, by Hermann Sudermann (New York: B. W. Huebsch; 1912), was reviewed by Mencken in the *Smart Set* for February 1912.

last week a notice that follows yours almost idea for idea! You'll see it in the February number—a plain psychic steal from you. The book disposes of the notion that Sudermann is a dead one. Who else could have done "The Purpose", or "The Song of Death", or "Autumn", or that Christmas story? Once more I bang my seidel on the table and bawl "Die Wacht Am Rhein". We Dutch may be vulgar eaters, but we have a few good men left.

Poor Pollard passed in painlessly, but very pathetically.[9] A month or so ago headaches seized him and pretty soon he began to show signs of mental disturbance. On December 5, the bonehead horse-doctors at Milford having diagnosed grip, his wife brought him to Baltimore for treatment. Unfortunately she landed him, before I knew anything about it, in an E flat homeopathic hospital. There nothing seems to have been done for him. The homeopaths said he was getting on "nicely"—and Mrs. Pollard went back to Milford to lock up the house and get some clothes. While she was away Pollard was suddenly paralyzed and became unconscious.

That was last Sunday a week. I was out at dinner and couldn't be found, but an old fellow named Burrows, who knew Pollard, happened to drop into the hospital and found out what was going on. He set up a loud and righteous bellow and demanded a consultation with Harvey Cushing, of the Johns Hopkins, the greatest brain surgeon in America. Cushing diagnosed a brain abscess and decided to operate at once. But Mrs. Pollard was somewhere on the road and couldn't be reached. Poor Burrows, until he found me, after midnight, was in a hell of a sweat, being afraid that Pollard would die on the table and that he (Burrows) would be blamed. But I joined with him in authorizing the operation (there was nothing else to do, for Pollard was dying) and Cushing operated at 1:30 in the morning. He found one whole lobe of the brain involved. The thing was utterly hopeless. So Pollard was put to bed and there was nothing to do but wait for the end. Fortunately enough, when Mrs. Pollard returned next morning, she approved the whole proceeding.

Pollard lasted until the past Sunday. He never regained consciousness a moment. Yesterday, according to his wish, we cremated him at the local crematory. Present: Mrs. Pollard, Mrs. Burrows and another woman; Ambrose Bierce, Neale the publisher and myself. A pathetically small party for so clever a fellow, so decent a friend. I had an

[9] Percival Pollard (1869–1911) was a Baltimore critic and the former literary reviewer of *Town Topics*.

Episcopal preacher I know (he also knew Pollard slightly) read a few words at the undertaker's. Then we went to the crematory, the women returning at once, but Bierce, Neale and I waiting to the end. The business there was over in five minutes. I am holding the ashes here. Later on they will probably be sent to Iowa, where Pollard's parents are buried. Mrs. Pollard went back to Milford this afternoon. She has an invalid mother and a sister, but no child. I think Pollard left property enough to keep her.

Pollard's last book, "Vagabond Journeys", came out on the day of his funeral. Neale came down from New York with the first three copies. He landed at the undertaker's with them. They actually went to the poor fellow's funeral.

I'm glad you get a chuckle, now and then, out of the Free Lance stuff.[1] Most of it, of course, is purely local. Privately, I am thinking of reducing my newspaper work a good deal to make time for other business. Thayer of the Smart Set pursues me with propositions and I am inclined to take some of them. This under your hat. I want to stay in Baltimore, on account of my family and the property that will have to keep me when I am old. This, I believe, can be managed. Thayer, by the way, is willing to start that knock-em-down quarterly I mentioned to you, though it may be a year or two before he gets the Smart Set going and can come to it. You are elected and inaugurated in advance. He will pay cash for stuff. Of all this, of course, say nothing.

If you can possibly manage it, you must make that Munich trip with old MacDannald and me.[2] Mac is a noble beer-drinker: a Virginian with a figure like Taft's and German brains. We sail April 16 and return by June 3 or 4. Total cost: not over $450.

Yours,
Mencken

---

[1] The Free Lance was a column that Mencken wrote for the Baltimore *Evening Sun* from May 8, 1911, until October 23, 1915, and in which he commented freely and somewhat tartly on local or general matters. It was discontinued because Mencken's position had become untenable after the war broke out in Europe.

[2] A. H. McDannald was a Baltimore *Sun* reporter, who later became editor of the *Encyclopedia Americana.*

1912

◇◇◇◇◇◇◇◇◇◇◇◇◇◇◇◇◇◇◇◇

To THEODORE DREISER
[UP]

H. L. Mencken
1524 Hollins St.
Baltimore
October 6th [*1912*]

DEAR DREISER:–

I have just finished "The Financier". Frankly, there are spots in it that I don't like a bit. It is not that you have laid on too much detail—I am in favor of the utmost detail—but that you have laid on irrelevant detail. Why give the speeches of the lawyers in full? Why describe so minutely the other prisoners sentenced with Cowperwood? Why describe particularly the architecture of the jail in which Cowperwood spends his five days? All of these things are well described, but they have nothing to do with the story. On the other hand, there are essential things left undescribed. For instance, Cowperwood and Aileen in their flat—their conversation, the girl's initiation, the dull days (they always come!), her probable alarms, the constant menace of the remote chance of pregnancy, perhaps a bad scare or two.

But all these things, after all, are but minor blemishes on a magnificent piece of work. You have described and accounted for and interpreted Cowperwood almost perfectly. You have made him as real as any man could be. And you have given utter reality to his environment, human and otherwise. No better picture of a political-financial camorra has ever been done. It is wholly accurate and wholly American.

Again, you have given great plausibility and interest to the affair between Frank and Aileen, from beginning to end, despite the reserve I have mentioned. It is credible that such a girl should succumb in such a way; it is credible that such a man, after marrying Lillian, should respond. Yet again, old Butler is excellently done, particularily as he appears in conflict with Aileen. These, to me, the most difficult of all the scenes, are done best of all. The reality in them is absolute. All sense of fiction is lost.

That is the feeling, indeed, that I get from the book as a whole. The very particularity of it helps. The irrelevant, in the long run, becomes, in a dim and vasty way, revelant. As you laboriously set the stage, the proscenium arch disappears, the painted trees become real trees, the actors turn into authentic men and women. And at the end, you stop upon just the right note. The big drama is ahead. We have seen only the first act.

I can't praise too much the evident painstaking of the whole thing. The story of Cowperwood's financial transactions is superbly thought out: it hangs together beautifully. And the same care shows in minor ways. The Cowperwood houses may be a bit too exhaustively described, but at any rate they are accurately described. There are no smudges here. Every line is distinct. So with the people: down to the least of them they stand out in the round.

Is the book too long? I doubt it. "Clayhanger" can't be much shorter. You are trying to lay in a large landscape and to draw its people to the last dot. That requires space. The reader who once ventures into the story will not be apt to complain of its length. He may rebel at some of the chapters and even skip them, but you have kept the feeling of impending events, of drama just around the corner, strong throughout. In brief, the story is well managed. Its machinery works.

So much for first impressions. I want to go through certain parts again. By the way, how long may I keep the proofs? My December article has gone in, but my January article, out December 15, is yet to be written. Will the book come out in time for me to review it in that article? I hope so. Meanwhile, I must get together material for the review, and so I'd like to have the proofs for a few days more. But if the book itself is due very shortly I can wait for it.

More anon.

Yours,
M.

[*Far from taking exception to this letter, Dreiser thanked Mencken for his suggestions, asked for more, and once more praised Mencken's critical faculty* (*October 6 and 8, 1912*).]

To THEODORE DREISER
[UP]

H. L. Mencken
1524 Hollins St.
Baltimore
October 8th [*1912*]

DEAR DREISER:–

Don't take too seriously my objections. I think you have done well to make the cuts, because the redundant matter breaks the back of the story, but that story, as a whole, is a splendid piece of work. Nothing could be finer than some parts of it, and what is more important, it hangs together. That is to say, it does not blow one way in one place and another way in another. Cowperwood is a genuine man from first to last. The fair Butler is as real as any hussy I ever met on the field of honor. And old Butler is a fit companion for old Gerhardt, for all his differences.

I'll keep the cuts in mind in writing my review, which goes into the Jan. S. S., out December 15. How far have you got with the next volume? There you will be in the midst of Cowperwood's greatest adventures. I am eager to see it.

Caution for clergymen: Be ascetic, and if you can't be ascetic, then at least be aseptic.

Yours,
M.

To THEODORE DREISER
[UP]

[The Financier *had a cool critical reception, and the sales dropped sharply*.]

(1912)

H. L. Mencken
1524 Hollins St.
Baltimore
November 4th [*1912*]

DEAR DREISER:–

Don't let those notices worry you. There is a certain justice in their complaints, true enough, but none the less the general effect of the book is excellent, and I have the utmost confidence that the second volume will be a knockout. You have paved the way and you have got a thorough grip on Cowperwood. What these fools will have to understand, soon or late, is that you are not trying to produce a thriller, but a work of art. Let them read Conrad's "Lord Jim" or George Moore's "Sister Theresa", and it may occur to them at last that allegro furioso is not the only tempo known to man. But, as I have said, there is a certain truth in their charge of wordiness. Well, you will avoid that next time.

I had a telegram from the N. Y. Times Saturday asking me to do their notice. I have sent it in, but it is decidedly un-Timesy in style, and so I await the issue. If they make any complaint I'll take it back and give it to Wright. My S. S. review went in today. The main thing in it, and in the Times notice, is the idea that the present book is merely an overture to the next one.

Lebe wohl.

Yours,
M.

To THEODORE DREISER
[UP]

H. L. Mencken
1524 Hollins St.
Baltimore
Dec. 10th [*1912*]

DEAR DREISER:–

It is amusing to see the virtuosi of virtue on the job. Some day I am going to write an essay on the moral mind: its inability to see anything save as a moral spectacle. Naturally enough, Cowperwood's cleanly paganism was bound to disgust such snouters into man-made muck. Down here I am in constant conflict with such vermin. At the moment they propose a law making copulation a felony, with a penitentiary penalty for the first offense and castration for the second! Imagine it! Remember, I mean simple copulation, fornication—not adultery. I meet a woman of full age, propose a harmless recreation, she consents, and we co-operate. Result: both of us to the pen for a year's hard! I venture an epigram: A moralist is one who holds that every human act must be either right or wrong, and that 99 percent of them are wrong.

The reply of Dell is excellent.

Yours,
M.

Did I ever send you a copy of "The Artist"? You are its grandpa & must have it.

[*Dreiser answered that he considered* The Artist *one of the best things he had ever published in the field of satirical humor (December 17, 1912).*]

To HARRY LEON WILSON
[PT]

Baltimore, December 10th [*1912*]

MY DEAR WILSON:–

You hit the nail so squarely on the head in your remarks about "The Financier" that I wish to God Dreiser had had your note in time. Privately, the book was even worse in its first form, and fully 10,000 words must have been cut out of the court scene. In brief, D. got drunk upon his own story and ran amuck. He piled into it a vast mass of irrelevant stuff, and at the same time he left out a lot of important things. For instance, it seems to me that the seduction scene is hopelessly underwritten. I am much more interested in the way Cowperwood initiated Aileen than I am in the decorations of his house. Again, I have made the very objection that you make: that the progress of the love affair is too smooth. A man may conceivably get on with his wife without rows, but I doubt if any man ever did it with his girl, particularly when she ran such risks and was in such constant terror. However, all this hath been duly set before Dreiser and he sees the force of it. Allowing for it, I still believe, with you, that "The Financier" is full of first-rate stuff. And I am certain that the second volume will be magnificent. D. has his faults plainly before him—and he knows Chicago. In this first volume, I think, the business of accumulating material overwhelmed him. He got together so much stuff that he couldn't make tracks through it, and when the work of composition began he was like a drunken man, ever falling over his own feet. A man who knows the stock market tells me that the technical details are perfect, that the book hasn't a single error in it from end to end. But who cares a hoot?

The book, for all its faults, has got some excellent reviews. The Chicago Evening Post gave it half a page and has since defended it against silly attacks made by virtuosi of virtue. The N. Y. Evening Sun, after some qualifications, called it great, and the Boston Transcript praised it loudly. Elsewhere, there have been savage attacks, mainly on the ground of Cowperwood's unmorality. (What a curse this brummagem moralizing is to our fair land!) I myself wrote the N. Y. Times notice, not to mention those of the Los Angeles Times, the Baltimore Evening Sun and the Smart Set. Dreiser is a sensitive fellow and easily dashed. He needs a little help over this rough place, but that help must take the form, at least in part, of frank truth-telling. If you know him, I wish you would send him a few lines. You stiffen up so well the criticisms made by the rest of us.

I observe your gay peregrination through the [S.E.P.], but put temptation behind me and wait for the book. Of all the maddening enterprises ever invented by man, the reading of serials is the maddest. If I got interested in a novel it would kill me with impatience to spread it over 15 weeks. What becomes of proportion? How the devil can a serial reader get any intelligible notion as to what the thing is about? I suppose you publish at once and that the book will reach me soon. That will land my notice in the March S. S.[1]

I am having a hot row down here with Vice Crusaders and have aroused the good old dears to a state of incandescence. I wish you were nearby to see the fun.[2]

A tale is current in the local kaifs to match your niggero yarn. A Moor stands on the scaffold, the rope around his neck. The Moor (to

---

[1] H. L. Wilson's book: *Bunker Bean* (New York: Doubleday, Page & Company; 1913).

[2] The row mentioned by Mencken took place in Baltimore with the clergy and the Christian Scientists, whom he assailed in his Free Lance column; Mencken coined the names "Baltimoralist" and "Baltimoron" to designate them.

the assembled witnesses): "Gen'lemen, dishyer cert'ny will be a lesson to me."

When are you coming East? I may get to the Coast next summer —possibly, possibly!

With best regards,

Sincerely,
H. L. Mencken

1913

To Harry Leon Wilson
[PT]

Baltimore, May 27th [1913]

Oh, Excellent Wilson!

If I didn't tell you, per private post, what a high old time I had over "Bunker Bean", then I do it now. The way you announced it, if you recall it, wasn't assuring. You gave me the idea that it was a hack job, done for the mazuma, and with little of you in it. But what I found was something I enjoy above everything—a first-rate comic novel—save "Zuleika Dobson", the only good one in years! So I bawled through it during a happy evening, and next day began giving it to my friends. Imagine a book reviewer, steeped in graft, *buying* and giving away books! And yet I done it—and altogether, I suppose, a dozen times. What is more, I steered others to the shambles, and made them leak. Such eloquence of the act transcends all the puny rhetoric of book reviews. I offer it in testimony of genuine joy.

I wish I knew Ade—not formally, officially, but well enough to put him to bed without impertinence.[1] I must know twenty of his friends, but he himself I have never even seen. Someday, it will occur to William Lyon Phelps or some other such fellow, that "In Babel" is one

[1] Ade: George Ade (1866–1944), author of *Fables in Slang* (Chicago and New York: H. S. Stone & Co.; 1900).

of the best things in our literature, and then Ade will be ranked almost as high as Henry Van Dyke, perhaps even with Hamilton Wright Mabie. As it is, the Brownells and Paul Elmer Mores are all busy with Thoreau and William Cullen Bryant. Phelps, who is a professor at Yale, is better than most. In his essay on Mark Twain he shows how the donkeys of the 80's underestimated Mark, and is properly indignant. But then he ends up with the plain insinuation that "Huckleberry Finn" is much inferior to "The Scarlet Letter". It may be so, but damme if I believe it.

What are you up to? A new novel, I hope. As for me, I am sweating over a book to be called "The American", a sort of ironical character sketch of [the?] animal.[2] The Smart Set is using six chapters in much abbreviated form. The book will be full of studied insult, and may help me along. I do only a part of Hatteras—about half.[3] The rest is done by George Nathan and Willard Wright, with incidental aid from Joe Miller. The London article was a hack job, done to please J.A.T. I met him in London by accident. He gave me a box of cigars and ordered three articles—Munich, London and a third to be written.[4] Then he proposed dinner at the Cheshire Cheese. Then I escaped.

Life down here is one darn crusade after another. Two-thirds of the cat houses have been closed, and about 175 saloons. In some neighborhoods a man now has to walk three blocks for a kettle of beer. Result: the streets are alive with street-walkers and the suburbs are full of open-air blind-tigers and al fresco bridal chambers. Some of the fornicati adopt the trick of going to a real estate agent, getting the key of a furnished house "to inspect it", and then using it that night. Sometimes the agent gives out two keys, and they have to shoot dice for the best room. Such is virtue!

I see hard work ahead all summer and no trip to the coast—yet. But aren't you coming East? Here is Pilsener! Here are soft crabs!

Yours,
H. L. Mencken

---

[2] *The American,* six chapters of which appeared consecutively in the *Smart Set* in 1913, was never published as a book.

[3] Hatteras: Major Owen Hatteras was one of the pseudonyms under which Mencken, Nathan, and Wright wrote satirical articles in the *Smart Set* entitled "Pertinent and Impertinent", and mainly directed at current American beliefs.

[4] The two articles mentioned here were parts of *Europe after 8:15,* later published as a book by Mencken, Nathan, and Wright (New York: John Lane Co.; 1914).

To Theodore Dreiser
[UP-MS]

H. L. Mencken
1524 Hollins St.
Baltimore
August 1 [*1913*]

Dear Dreiser:–

This review (by Wright) bears out what I said the other day: that you are gaining a definite place, by general acceptance, as the leading American novelist. I see you mentioned constantly, & always with the same respect. New serious novels are no longer compared to "Silas Lapham" or to "McTeague", but to "Sister Carrie" & "Jennie Gerhardt". I think you will note this plainly in the reviews of the new book.[5]

Temperature here: 105.

[Yours,]
H. L. M.

To Willard Huntington Wright
[OFP]

The Sun
Baltimore, Md.
August 17th [*1913*]

Dear Wright:–

Here's hoping that your tonsils are on the track again. Why are we constantly tortured with such ills? What low, bar-room comedian is boss of this world? There is need of a Czolgosz in Hell.[6]

The story is excellent—full of sap and paprika.[7] But I have several small changes to suggest. In the first place, in the title "Night Life in Vienna" somehow recalls the Police Gazette: it has the air of a lure held out to the Puritanical and dirty-minded. There is something cheaply pornographic about it. I would much prefer "Wiener Blut", " 'S gibt nur a Kaiserstadt!" or something of that sort. Give each of the

[5] The new book: *A Traveler at Forty* (New York: The Century Co.; 1913).
[6] Czolgosz: the assassin of President McKinley, executed in 1901.
[7] Wright's article: "The Night Romance of Europe: Vienna", published in the *Smart Set* for October 1913.

four articles a different name, and keep off of the secret revelation suggestion. We are appealing to the sophisticated, not to the yokel, and to the sophisticated there is something disgusting about a guide-book to sin. The guides in Paris make one sick: one yearns to kick them in the ass. I strongly advise against the present caption.

In the first line, change "tourist" to "Sunday-school superintendent". You are trying to picture the adventures of the true yap, the shouting American, the fellow who is pure at home, but yearns to throw his leg over a hoor on the continent. He is the archetype of the American tourist: the god-fearing deacon on the loose, the vestryman returning from Jerusalem. Kid him more in the introduction. Be a little more satirical in dealing with his hunt for joy. Picture him as one who has doubts and qualms, who is almost afraid to find what he is looking for. In line six make it "for surgical and psychic shock" instead of "for wooing". And in the third line from the bottom (page 1) make it "deviltries" instead of "lecheries".

Again, is the proper spelling "Weaner?" (Page 1 again). I know very little about the Viennese dialect: in German it would be Wiener. As I have heard the couplet, the initial "Es" is cut down to " 'S". Thus:

'S gibt nur a Kaiserstadt,
'S gibt nur a Wien.

You will find it correctly given in one of the early chapter's of Lady Randolph Churchill's reminiscences. I haven't the book by me. Get it at the library and make sure. And be careful of all the other quotations: it is important to get them exactly right.

But the whole tone and swing of the story is excellent: it has real atmosphere in it. The one suggestion I make is that the searcher after hidden sweets be kidded more in the first four or five pages—that he be depicted more grotesquely—and that you keep a firm restraint on phrase. These things are small. A few words here and there will do the trick.

You and George are to come down two weeks hence, by all means.[8] It is dinner day at the club. Incidentally, we will show you some Wiener waltz playing that will satisfy you. I stir up the mountaineer: He does nothing in this hot weather but fry in his own unguents.

Yours,
M.

---

[8] George: George Jean Nathan.

(1913)

◇◇◇◇◇◇◇◇◇◇◇◇◇

To WILLARD HUNTINGTON WRIGHT
[OFP]

[*W. H. Wright was then planning to bring out a violently anti-Puritan review entitled* The Blue Review; *he had a dummy issue of it printed at the expense of Thayer who, not having been consulted, declined to pay the bill.*]

H. L. Mencken
1524 Hollins St.
Baltimore
November 12th [*1913*]

DEAR WRIGHT:–

Eureka! I begin to feel like a new man. Once that weekly is launched, it will become a pleasure to manufacture prose. As soon as you get your Christmas supplement into shape, let me know how Thayer received the dummy. No need to beat the bush for men until the New Year. I have great faith that, once you get close to Thayer's ear, you will be able to pump sense into his head. He must realize by this time that the Zenda stuff is murdering the S. S.[9]

Boyer notifies me that he is coming down to Baltimore Friday and so I am in for a long session.[1] I am going to tell him the truth, however much he may mistake it for soreness over recent events. The S. S. is too valuable a property (to all of us) to be turned into a sugar-teat.

I enclose a few lines about Dreiser's book. The N. Y. Evening Sun has just come to the bat with a smashing fine review, and the Boston Transcript gives it an eloquent boost among the highbrows. I think D. will get away with it. He is a real fellow and deserves all the help he can get. Some day, I believe, we will be glad to think that we gave him a hand. He is bound to win out.

When are you coming East? It tickles me to death to think that we'll now have many chances for palavers. Philadelphia on Sunday is

---

9 The Zenda stuff: refers to the melodramatic romance, *The Prisoner of Zenda* by Anthony Hope (New York: H. Holt and Company; 1894).

1 Norman Boyer: a former Baltimore reporter, then managing editor of the *Smart Set;* there was some tension at the magazine because of Wright's policy of printing objectionable articles.

an easy meeting place, and beside, I hope to get to N. Y. more often than in the past.

I think I'll turn down that rum job.[2] The money is enough to make me dizzy, but I fear it would mean contact with brewers and such-like swine and a lot of uninteresting work. I tackle "The American" tomorrow, God willing.

Congratulations and good luck.

Yours,
M.

◇◇◇◇◇◇◇◇◇◇◇◇◇

To THEODORE DREISER
[UP]

The Sun
Baltimore, Md.
Sunday [*November 16?, 1913*]

DEAR DREISER:–

No need to say that I have read the travel book[3] with interest: some parts of it show the best writing you have done since "Jennie Gerhardt". But I wish that you had held it down to 350 or 400 pages. The whole Italian section is dragging in tempo: you have got in a lot of stuff that is unimportant, and you have put little of yourself into the rest. After all, it is nothing new to praise Rome and the hill towns: the thing has been done before. Nor is there any novelty in the story of the Borgias. The defect here, I believe, lies in the fact that there is more description than narration. You are at your best in those parts wherein narration is to the fore—for example, in the English chapters.

These English chapters I have enjoyed immensely, and particularly those telling of the incidents of your visit to Richards. The Smart Set chapter on street-walkers is also excellent, and so are the Paris chapters. But in the latter I note an effect of reticence. You start up affairs which come to nothing. The Riviera section is a fine piece of work—beauty seen through a personality—a soul's adventures among masterpieces. That week must have been a superb experience. I must see the Coast the next time I go to Europe.

But don't assume from the foregoing that the book has disappointed me. Far from it. You have got into it, not only a definite

[2] The Brewers' Association had asked Mencken to write its advertising matter.
[3] See footnote, page 32.

revelation of your personality, but also a clear statement of your philosophy. Do you know that this last is substantially identical with Joseph Conrad's? You will find his confession of faith in "A Personal Record". He stands in wonder before the meaninglessness of life. He is an agnostic in exactly the same sense that you are—that is to say, he gives it up. You put down your own ideas very clearly: they lift the whole book above the level of travel books, and make it significant and different. Without the slightest doubt it will be read eagerly by all who admire your novels. I am glad you have done it, and I hope you will follow it with that volume of essays. What you want to enforce is the idea that you are not a mere storyteller, but an interpreter of the human comedy. That is precisely the difference between a bad novelist and a good one—say Chambers and Wells.

What is the present state of the second volume of "The Financier?" [4] My advice is that you bring it out as soon as possible after the travel book, to take advantage of the discussion of the latter. And let that story of the artist (when am I going to see it?) follow quickly. I believe you are injured by long intervals between books. You ought to have seven or eight volumes on the shelves, instead of only three. Once you get them there, you will be discussed more, and also read more.

I note that the sheets of the travel book need not be returned. If you don't want them yourself, let me have them. I have a lot of postcards from you, covering the whole route, and I want to bind them with the sheets, thus enriching my library with a novel work of art.[5]

Take the Doran offer, by all means. I hear only good of Doran, despite his publication of bad books by Irvin Cobb, Will Levington Comfort et al. He is more secure financially than the Harpers, and he has an incomparable finer taste in books. I think you will find him a comfortable publisher.

Two ships laden with Pilsner arrived from Bremen yesterday. After all, the world is not so bad.

Yours,
H. L. M.

---

[4] The second volume of *The Financier: The Titan* (New York: John Lane Company; 1914). Dreiser gave the book to Harper's, who printed it in March 1914, but suddenly decided to stop publication. The book was later rescued by the John Lane Co.

[5] Mencken's project of binding the sheets of *A Traveler at Forty* with postcards from Dreiser was carried out, and the volume is now in the Mencken collection of the Enoch Pratt Free Library in Baltimore.

(1913)

To Willard Huntington Wright
[OFP]

The Sun
Baltimore, Md.
December 8th [*1913*]

Dear Wright:–

My best thanks for the Forum. The article is a fine piece of exposition, and I, for one, have got a lot of information out of it.[6] When your brother gets in I am coming over to palaver with him. One thing has always stuck in my untutored mind: that too much stress is laid upon subject in painting. That is to say, it is a fallacy to assume that every painting must represent something. As for me, I get pleasure very often out of a wholly meaningless arrangement of lights and colors. There are fabrics which tickle me vastly. I have, for example, an Irish poplin necktie of purple shot with vague greens that pleases me more than most pictures. In music I am suspicious of program stuff: the pleasure I get out of Richard Strauss has nothing to do with his banal "plots", but with the sheer exuberance of his orchestral colors. I remember a climax in "Feuersnot" which once lifted me out of my seat, but I haven't the slightest notion what it was about. If I had a lot of money my house would be filled with beautiful woods, metals and pottery, but there would be darn few pictures.

I have a long letter from Thayer on the subject of tonsils, the uplift and the Smart Set—a ghastly farrago of nonsense. It must be hell to listen to such stuff day by day. Here I am in the midst of forward-lookers. Yesterday I spent an hour listening to Grasty's creed.[7] I think he stated it honestly. I know that it almost made me sick. It is staggering to think that an intelligent man whould believe in such puerile bosh. And yet, as right-thinkers go, he belongs to the aristocracy. He lets me cavort as I please, of course within reasonable limits, and he shows little of the Puritan blood-lust. But a country fed on such ideas!

I have the $3 check for epigrams, but so far the cohorts of com-

---

[6] Wright's article in the *Forum:* "Impressionism to Synchronism" (December 1913).

[7] Charles H. Grasty: the former owner of the Baltimore *Evening News* (to which Mencken had contributed for a few weeks in 1906), then editor of the Baltimore *Sun;* Mencken was having some difficulties with him owing to public reaction to his Free Lance articles.

merce have not rewarded me for the December Hatteras. Stir them up. Within an epigram.

The Christmas dinner is changed to Sunday, December 21. I take it that this will suit you just as well. Come down on Saturday afternoon. My tonsils are nearly healed, and it tickles me to think that I didn't miss a day's work at the office. Why is the consciousness of physical toughness so agreeable?

Yours,
M.

Let me have news of the Europe book and your Nietzsche.[8]

[8] The Europe book: *Europe after 8:15*. Your Nietzsche: *What Nietzsche Taught*, by W. H. Wright (New York: B. W. Huebsch; 1917).

1914

To THEODORE DREISER
[UP-MS]

[*On January 8th, Dreiser thanked Mencken for his generous review of* A Traveler at Forty, *but expressed his fear that he would never be able to make a living out of his books.*]

H. L. Mencken
1524 Hollins St.
Baltimore
January 11th [*1914*]

DEAR DREISER:–

Certainly you'll reach the place where your novels will keep you. I think it is just ahead. "The Titan", with its melodrama, ought to make both a popular and an artistic success. And once you escape from Harpers all of the books will pick up. What are the results of your meetings with Doran? Let me hear about them.

I am in rotten shape physically and mentally, but look for improvement.

A hell of a world.

[Yours,]
M.

(1914)

◇◇◇◇◇◇◇◇◇◇◇◇◇

To HARRY LEON WILSON
[PT]

Baltimore, February 8th [*1914*]

DEAR WILSON:–

The Hatteras pedigree is perfectly correct, and I hasten to add details. The ravishment of Mlle. Verlaine did not take place in Paris, but during a storm at sea, and while it was going on Nietzsche, who was present, played the Valkyre motive on a viol da gamba. And the geburtshilfer at the accouchement was Dr. Crippen. I pass it on to George Nathan for further embellishment.

What Thayer is going to do with the Smart Set God only knows. I saw him in N. Y. two or three weeks ago, and found him scared half to death and without an idea in his head. Hatteras has been killed, not by his act, but by the refusal of Wright, Nathan and I to go on. My book-article contract runs until next October. Aside from these articles I am to do nothing for the magazine, and neither is Nathan. A good many other men, such as Untermeyer, have also pulled out, though there is copy from some of them in the safe. Mark Luther is leaving in a month or so. This will leave Thayer and Boyer to get out the magazine. I hear that Charles Hanson Towne has been offered the editorship, but don't know.[1] Thayer blames me for foisting Wright on him, and is fortunately not burdening me with his confidences.

It was simply impossible for Wright to go on. Thayer's friends in N. Y. are all forward-lookers of the sort who read the N. Y. Times, and every time an issue of the magazine came out they scared him with their horror. For nearly a year Nathan and I bucked him up. I made at least five trips to N. Y. for the sole purpose of quieting his fears of Comstock.[2] In October he was so far reassured that he offered Wright a three-years' contract at a very good salary. But just then came a sharp decline in circulation and he got into a pitiful panic. This decline was felt by all of the magazines, but he saw it as ruin, and thereafter he began making so many complaints and proposing so many absurdities

---

[1] Charles Hanson Towne: editor, author, poet; he formerly edited the *Smart Set*.
[2] Anthony Comstock (1844–1915) was at the head of a Y.M.C.A. campaign against obscene literature; he was special agent for the P. O. Department, founder of the Society for the Suppression of Vice and leader of the Boston Watch and Ward Society. He promoted the "Comstock Law" (1873) to bar vicious matter from the mails. He allegedly caused the arrest of more than 3,000 persons, destroyed 50 tons of books and nearly four million pictures.

—among other things, a series of articles exposing the looting of the New Haven! Fact! I heard it with these ears!—that Wright began looking for a job. At Christmas there came an open row, and Thayer rushed down to Baltimore to pour his woes into me. On his heels came Wright. I advised both of them to part at once. Fortunately enough, Frank Adams left the N. Y. Mail for the Tribune January 1st, and his job was offered to Wright. He accepted, he and Thayer tore up their contract, Thayer paid him a good bonus in cash, let him keep the money he borrowed from the magazine when his father died, and shook hands.

The essential fact is, of course, that Thayer is wholly unfitted to run such a magazine: his proper measure is the Ladies' World. I never met a man with less appreciation of good writing: the stories he admires are precisely the worst that are printed. What is worse, he is very tight with money. George Nathan and I had a devil of a time getting $100 an article out of him. Over Hatteras there were constant rows. He wanted to pay 5 cents a word for epigrams! That worked out to about $1 an epigram. Beside, he shed buckets of cold sweat every time we put a loud one over. Last Spring we went on strike, and he raised the price to $2.50. Yet again, he wanted to cut in on the book rights, and on the dramatic rights of the one-act burlesques. The net result was that I used to average $25 a month for a week's work—paying my own expenses to Philadelphia or New York, when Nathan and Wright and I met to put the stuff together.

Thayer told me about his telegram to you, and it made me laugh. He would probably offer you $400 for such a thing as "Bunker Bean". He paid $225 for George Howard's novelette a month or two ago—and yelled at the price. And yet, up to a few months ago, at least, he was averaging $3,000 a month net profit on the magazine. He told me so himself, and Wright, who has seen the books, confirms it. Meanwhile, he pays no attention whatever to the advertising department. So far as I know, indeed, he hasn't called on a single advertiser since he took over the magazine. My one hope is that he sells out to someone better fitted to run it. This, I believe, he is likely to do. He says he paid $265,000 for the magazine, whether in cash or not I don't know. In addition, he took over $100,000 in 5% bonds. When he was in the midst of his panic he told me he would sell out at a loss of $100,000. I tried to dig up a sucker here in Baltimore, but failed.

All this, of course, for your private ear. What are you doing in the way of labor? Mowing down the pages of a new book, I hope. As for me, I am in hell's hole. Since last June I have been entertaining a mysterious discomfort in the mouth. The learned chirurgeons of the Johns Hopkins—I happen to be friendly with the best of them—change their view of its nature every month, but it continues to worry me, and all work save the merest routine is impossible. I have a book on the stocks, with 30,000 words written, but can't go on. All the doctors seem to agree on is that there is no tumor, and that I am free [from ?] that general infection which the suffragettes so love to gloat over. Their last theory is that the thing is a sort of neuritis. I have had my tonsils cut out and three pieces cut out of my tongue for observation, all to no effect.

Virtue descends upon these parts like a pall. The Kenyon red-light law went into effect in Washington yesterday, and is soon to be passed in Maryland. The penalty for adultery is to be raised from $10 fine—the present humane maximum—to $500 fine and a year in jail. There is a bill before the Legislature providing $100 fine and 30 days in jail for any man who enters "any house or room" (I quote exactly) occupied by ladies of accommodating virtue. Such is the uplift! How is life under the suffrage?

Sincerely,
H. L. Mencken

◇◇◇◇◇◇◇◇◇◇◇◇◇◇

To Theodore Dreiser
[UP]

[*After printing a few thousand copies of* The Titan, *Harper's had been frightened into stopping publication.*]

H. L. Mencken
1524 Hollins St.
Baltimore
March 18th [*1914*]

Dear Dreiser:–

A copy of "The Titan", unbound, has just come from Miss Tatum.[3] I'll read it tonight. You'll never see it again.

An eternal pox upon the Harpers. And Doran be damned for his

[3] Miss Anna P. Tatum: a New York friend of Dreiser's.

flight. God knows, this country needs that weekly I once planned.[4] The forward-lookers are eating us up. Even the Smart Set is now as righteous as a decrepit and converted madame. The Owen Hatteras stuff that I used to do is now being done by some member of the Men and Religion Forward Movement.

When the carbuncles? I certainly hope they have all vanished. A painful, and often dangerous pestilence. My tongue could be worse. I sail April 11th.

Yours,
M.

To THEODORE DREISER
[UP-CC]

[The Titan *had been accepted by the John Lane Co., a British firm recently established in the United States under the management of J. J. Jones.*]

H. L. Mencken
1524 Hollins St.
Baltimore
March 23rd [*1914*]

DEAR DREISER:–

I have just finished "The Titan". Believe me, it is the best thing you have ever done, with the possible exception of "Jennie Gerhardt", and the superiority there is only in the greater emotional appeal. "Jennie" is more poignant—but "The Titan" is better written. In fact, some of the writing in it is far ahead of any of your past work—for example, the episode of the honest Mayor snared by the wench. I am delighted that you are striving hard in this department. You are more succinct, more dramatic, more graceful. In brief, you are superimposing a charm of style upon the thrill of narrative.

Let Lane have it, by all means. There is not a word in the book that will give Comstock his chance. He must go into court with some specific phrase—something that will seem smutty to an average jury of numskulls. The fundamental and essential immorality of the book is

[4] That weekly: W. H. Wright's projected "Blue Review."

beyond his reach. Believe me, the whole thing has made me kick up my heels. It is the best picture of an immoralist in all modern literature—at least, since Thackeray's "Barry Lyndon". You are not standing still: you are moving ahead. I wish you would print that book of serious philosophy. And the essays you once told me about.

Curious note: "A Traveler at Forty" made such a hit with Chas. H. Grasty, publisher of The Balto. Sun, that he has applied to the Century Co. for permission to reproduce extracts from it.

More anon.

Yours,
Mencken

[On March 25th, Dreiser thanked Mencken warmly for his appreciation of his book: ". . . your view . . . cheers me because I have such implicit faith in your honesty—intellectual and every other way . . ."]

◇◇◇◇◇◇◇◇◇◇◇◇◇◇

To THEODORE DREISER
[UP]

H. L. Mencken
1524 Hollins St.
Baltimore
March 27th [*1914*]

DEAR DREISER:–

Within the Lane telegram. The Chapman letter hasn't come in yet. Lane is in the proper attitude of mind: I'm glad you came to terms with him. It is high time that you stopped listening to the vapid criticisms of publishing donkeys. Such vermin overestimate their own sagacity, and what is more, their own importance. Imagine Kennerley objecting to a book of yours! The impertinence of the fellow makes me laugh. He was scared stiff by the "Hagar Revelly" affair.

The more I think of "The Titan", the more I am convinced that some of your best work is in it. In one thing, of course, it seems to fall below "Sister Carrie" and "Jennie", and that is in its lack of poignancy. In other words, Cowperwood does not appeal to the sympathies; he does not grip the more responsive emotions, as Carrie and Jennie do. But I think the book is better planned and better written than either of the others. You are making progress in workmanship, or, to use critical cant, in technic. You get your effects with greater ease, and they are subtler effects. I have tried out the book on a typical intelligent novel reader, and he is enthusiastic. I see no hook for Comstock to hang upon: he must go before a jury with some definite phrase. The profound unmorality of the book is beyond him. It is a great Nietzschean document.

Willard Wright (who has just gone to Europe) lately made a book out of various travel articles that he, Geo. Nathan and I wrote for the Smart Set, and Lane, I hear, is to do it. I have not seen the final ms. and know little about it. My own share in it is slight. The Smart Set is now as pure as the Christian Herald. I am doing nothing but my monthly book article: my contract runs to next Oct.

An eternal curse upon the Harpers. Give them a chapter in your reminiscences, following the Doubleday chapter. . . .

I sail on the Laconia April 11th.

Yours,
Mencken

To Louis Untermeyer[5]
[OFP-MS]

H. L. Mencken
1524 Hollins St.
Baltimore
Aug. 3rd [*1914*]

Dear Untermeyer:

If the Smart Set survives until May, 1915, which is improbable, and I am still doing its books, which is even more improbable, I'll return to "Challenge", and lay on a thin film of cocoabutter.[6] "God's Youth" tickled me much.[7] The moment I get time I'm going to write a thin (but valuable) work on the low, pothouse wit of the Lord God, with examples. Nine-tens of *us* are inexplicable—save as cheap witticisms.

[5] Louis Untermeyer (born in 1885): the poet and anthologist; until 1923 he was manager of his family's jewelry factory, hence some of Mencken's jokes.
[6] *Challenge:* a book by L. Untermeyer (New York: The Century Co.; 1914).
[7] "God's Youth": a poem by L. Untermeyer, later published in *Poems for Youth* (New York: E. P. Dutton and Co.; 1925. Edited by William R. Benét).

Wie geht's Geschäft?—I mean with "Challenge". Bad German, but you know me, Al! . . .

[Yours,]
M.

◇◇◇◇◇◇◇◇◇◇◇◇◇

To THEODORE DREISER
[UP]

[*On August 10th, Dreiser had announced his intention of writing a book of plays in which he would include three that he had already completed; he asked Mencken to put in a good word in order to get* In the Dark *produced at the Princess.*]

H. L. Mencken
1524 Hollins St.
Baltimore
August 11th [*1914*]

DEAR DREISER:–

In plain truth, you overcome me with the offer of one of your mss. There is nothing I'd be more delighted to have: it would be the arch of my collection of Dreisereana. But can it be that you really mean it? Trying my damndest to think evil of the man, I am filled with suspicions that you have taken to heroin, Pilsner, formaldehyde. Purge your system of the accursed stuff—and then offer me "Sister Carrie". And see me jump! [8]

By all means, do the plays as a book. And meanwhile, do me this favor: give me an option on them for two weeks. The reason must be kept confidential: I am at work on a plan which may give me editorial control of the Smart Set, and I want to blaze out with some Dreiser stuff. The chances, at the moment, are rather against success, but I am hanging on, and may know the result in a day or two. George Nathan is with me. He, in fact, is doing all the final negotiating. If the thing goes through there will be a future in it for both of us. The S. S. is losing very little money, and the cutting off of certain excessive overhead expenses—high rent, extravagant salary to Thayer, etc.—will quickly make it self-sustaining. And we are associated with a truly

[8] In answer to this letter, Dreiser sent Mencken the manuscript of *Sister Carrie,* now at the New York Public Library.

excellent man of business—one who is no mere talker, but has actually made a success elsewhere.[9] Thayer is a sorry quitter. He got into a panic at the first fire.

All this for your private eye. If our scheme fails, I want to be in a position to make decent terms with the new boss, whoever he is. Hold up the plays for two weeks. I think we can easily come to terms.*

I offer no formal thanks for the ms. offer. I would esteem it more than the gift of a young virgin. (Thus we old fellows talk! Diablerie senilis!)

Yours,
M.

* That is, cash on the block.

To THEODORE DREISER
[UP]

The Sun
Baltimore, Md.
August 17th [*1914*]

DEAR DREISER:–

With my usual stupidity I went to N. Y. without the memorandum that I had made of your address and telephone number, and so I couldn't get to you Sunday. My news is brief: if all goes well, Nathan and I will be in full editorial control of the Smart Set this week. Nathan, in fact, is already in the office, and I have gone through a lot of ms. The Thayer regime is at an end. We are putting up no money and taking no financial risk except the loss of our time. Warner, who has made a success of Field and Stream, starting on a shoe-string, is in charge of the business office and gives signs of making it a go. He has backing. I am to stay in Baltimore. My chief job will be to get and read ms. and negotiate with authors. Nathan will look after the office work, which is very slight.

Both of us want at least two of your plays. In fact, we simply *must* have something from you. It goes without saying that we are not rich, but if you will give us a couple of weeks to turn around, it will be possible to get you your money out of the first cash available. I therefore exercise the option you gave me, and hold the plays that long.

[9] Man of business: Warner, who had previously run *Field and Stream* successfully under Crowe.

What will you take for "The Blue Sphere"? Make it as cheap as possible, if you have a heart. This looks like an excellent fighting chance. The magazine, with our retrenchments, has income enough to keep it going. Give us a lift now, if you can, and I think there will be good times ahead. All our plans, of course, include the theory that we will get copy from you pretty regularly. We want to make this magazine thoroughly first class.[1]

This is a great rush. I'll probably be in N. Y. again next week, and I'll make sure that I don't forget the memorandum. . . .

Yours,
H. L. M.

◇◇◇◇◇◇◇◇◇◇◇◇◇◇

To ELLERY SEDGWICK[2]
[OFP]

H. L. Mencken
1524 Hollins St.
Baltimore
August 25th [*1914*]

DEAR SEDGWICK:–

I certainly hope you are purged of all typhoid by now, and eating a large succulent beefsteak daily. The one fear is that you will grow buxom anon, attaining in the end to my own matronly diameter. However, the curse is more imaginary than real. I positively enjoy being fat.

Incidentally, John Adams Thayer has vanished from the Smart Set to a low comedy tune, new owners are in charge, and I am general editorial adviser, with George Nathan as the editor on the job. We shall have to go slowly for two or three numbers, but our marks will be on November and December, and by January we should get out a good one. That is, if we survive so long—which now seems probable. My work will not take much time after the first few weeks: it will consist in the main of gunning for mss. If the plan succeeds, there will be something in it for me; if it fails, I'll not lose much. All of this in

[1] The *Smart Set* under Mencken and Nathan published three of Dreiser's plays: "The Blue Sphere", "Laughing Gas", and "In the Dark", respectively, in December 1914, January 1915, and February 1915.

[2] Ellery Sedgwick (born in 1872) was then editor of the *Atlantic Monthly,* to which Mencken contributed "Newspaper Morals" in March 1914. In 1900, as he edited *Frank Leslie's Popular Monthly,* Sedgwick had made his acquaintance when he had bought a few short stories from him.

petto; no announcement is proposed for the present. The story of Thayer's last six months would make a capital opera bouffe.

Our policy, I needn't say, is to be lively without being nasty. On the one hand, no smut, and on the other, nothing uplifting. A magazine for civilized adults in their lighter moods. A sort of frivolous sister to the Atlantic. Ideal authors: George Moore, Max Beerbohm, Otto Julius Bierbaum, Maurice Baring and Lord Dunsany, with Dreiser and Joseph Conrad now and then. If you see anything that we might use and you can't I'll be very grateful for a tip. And maybe I can repay in kind.

I begin to feel scribblerish: beware of manuscripts anon!

Sincerely yours,
H. L. M.

To ELLERY SEDGWICK
[OFP]

[*Sedgwick had suggested that Mencken write an article on the causes of the war, and particularly the acceptance by the German bureaucracy and the universities of the Nietzschean doctrine. This was to be "The Mailed Fist and its Prophet", printed in the* Atlantic Monthly *for November 1914.*]

H. L. Mencken
1524 Hollins St.
Baltimore
September 1st [*1914*]

DEAR SEDGWICK:

You have an excellent idea—if you want to stir up the animals! There can be no doubt that Nietzscheism has been superimposed upon the old, unintelligent Prussian absolutism, and that it is largely responsible for the astounding efficiency now visible in peace and war.

When Nietzsche began writing he was the bitterest of all enemies of German culture. He hated the whole theory of *junkertum*, and he hated, too, that German sentimentality which found its expression in the so-called *biergemüthlichkeit*. But that was back in the early 70's. Since then the old aristocracy of birth and vested rights has given place to a new aristocracy of genuine skill, and Germany has become a true democracy in the Greek sense. That is to say, the old nobility has taken a back seat and the empire is now governed by an oligarchy of its best men. And with this new cult of efficiency there has come a truly Nietzschean disdain for all merely theoretical "rights".

This my general notion of an article. If you fall in with it, I'll begin writing at once. The chances are that it will not be long. And if you don't like it no harm will be done, for I can use it in the Baltimore Sun in my regular column, and so recover the time devoted to it.

But if you don't like my thesis, there is Dr. Thomas S. Baker, of the Tome Institute, Havre de Grace, Md., to fall back on. Baker is a Hopkins PH.D., a sound German scholar, and one of the first Americans to write about Nietzsche.

Meanwhile, my best thanks for your thought of me. I am laboring with both hands, but your plans are full of attractions.

Sincerely,
Mencken

By the way, the Smart Set work, after the first reorganization, will not be a great burden. I'll have nothing to do with the make-up, nor with the finances. The business office is in competent hands, and Nathan is to do the editorial office work. My only regular business will be to keep on the lookout for good stuff, and in this I am helped by the fact that my book articles for six years past have put me on good terms with the very authors—e.g., Dreiser—that we want to cultivate. Also, I have good connections in England. For the rest, I'll look through a ms. or two of an evening.

M.

To ELLERY SEDGWICK
[OFP]

[*Mencken's article had been eagerly accepted by Sedgwick on September 10th.*]

H. L. Mencken
1524 Hollins St.
Baltimore
September 12th [*1914*]

DEAR SEDGWICK:–

I am delighted that the article meets your ideas. The story of the writing of it is a tragi-comedy that you must hear some day. The day of miracles is not past.

Please let me see the proofs. There are two or three verbal corrections. I think you will find I made it plain that Nietzsche poisoned the universities first: I speak of the enthusiasm of the young intellectuals, the rulers of tomorrow. And I also tried to show that public opinion, in Germany, runs from the top downward.

Isn't "Germany at the Feet of Nietzsche" a bit unfriendly? I don't want to appear to be pooh-poohing either Nietzsche or Germany. Why not "The Prophet of the Mailed Fist"?

With thanks again,

Sincerely yours,
H. L. Mencken

To ELLERY SEDGWICK
[OFP]

The Sun
Baltimore, Md.
October 10th [*1914*]

DEAR SEDGWICK:–

Lichtenberger and Dr. Oscar Levy are both trying to show that Nietzsche has had no influence in Germany, but without success.[3] I am in constant communication with Levy. As a German residing in England he has been forced into this position. Lichtenberger is in the same boat in France. The evidence on the other side is overwhelming. This morning, for example, came an article (in German) by Nietzsche's sister beginning:

"If there ever was a friend of war, who loved warriors and fighters *and upon them set his highest hopes,* it was Friedrich Nietzsche."

I planned the paper on American newspapers as my swan song, but I am still tied to the machine. However, I may get to it before long—once the work of reorganizing the Smart Set is over. Things there, by the way, seem to be going very well. Our total debt is now less than $15,000, and we are showing a profit on the month's business. If we can stagger along until January 1st all the chances will be in our favor. The authors we want to print are responding nobly, and though

[3] Oscar Levy: the translator and editor of Nietzsche's works, and the owner of the British rights in them.

we haven't much money we are paying cash on acceptance for everything.

If you would care for an indictment of England I could do it easily, for all the materials are at hand. But it would be red-hot. The war discussion down here has been extraordinarily furious, and I have been bombarded daily, but public sentiment seems to be rapidly turning in favor of England. Even such Germanophobic papers as the New York World now denounce the English for their astounding efforts to suppress and sophisticate the news. I enclose a couple of samples of German deviltry.[4]

With thanks and regards,

Sincerely yours,
H. L. Mencken

To THEODORE DREISER
[UP]

H. L. Mencken
1524 Hollins St.
Baltimore
October 13th [*1914*]

DEAR DREISER:–

Nathan is so full of the notion that this "Lost Phoebe" lies far off of the Dreiser that we want to play up that I begin to agree with him. Ah, that we could get a chunk of "The Genius" to follow the plays! Those plays are fine stuff, but they involve, as it were, winning a new Dreiser audience. What we ought to have, to follow them, is a return to C major—that is, to the Sister Carrie–Jennie Gerhardt–The Titan style. Is any such stuff in sight? I wish Lane would hurry up "The Genius". I believe I could saw out an isolated episode or two that wouldn't spoil the serial rights in the slightest. What else is in sight? *Is there any left-over matter from "The Titan"?*

Nathan tells me that the plays are mentioned in all advertising sent to other magazines. There was to have been a page announcement in the Nov. number, but it was killed at the last minute by an unexpected adv.

Yours,
M.

---

[4] E. Sedgwick declined Mencken's suggestion, but instead requested "a hot article on another subject" (Sedgwick to Mencken, October 13, 1914).

To THEODORE DREISER
[UP]

[*Irritated by Mencken's letter of October 13th, Dreiser had answered it the same day, canceling the arrangement and demanding that the three plays be returned to him. He also reminded Mencken that he had recalled* The Lost Phoebe *from* Red Book *at a loss in order to do the editors of the* Smart Set *a favor.*]

H. L. Mencken
1524 Hollins St.
Baltimore
October 14th [*1914*]

DEAR DREISER:–

I take all the blame and offer my apologies. But you are quite wrong as to any doubts about the merit of the plays, or, for that matter, of the story. I think the plays are excellent in plan and execution, and Nathan quite agrees with me. They are sure to make a strong appeal to the very sort of people we want to have in our audience. But at the moment we are still confronted by the Thayer audience, and until we get rid of it and build up our own, we will obviously have to handle the situation with some discretion. That is the sole basis for my eagerness to print something in your more *familiar* manner. We want to get as much wind from "Sister Carrie" and "The Titan" as we can. Once we get going we'll have them ready for anything *you* want to do, and even now we are willing to take every chance, but when the choice offers we naturally turn to the stuff which comes closest to the public notion of you, and so takes full-steam advantage of your following. Hence my eagerness to get an episode or two out of "The Genius", or even something cut out of "The Titan". I knew you probably had some such stuff on hand, and I also knew that it was otherwise unsaleable, and so I made my suggestion.

But the thought now sticks in my mind that we made a definite arrangement about "The Lost Phoebe". If that is your recollection also, we'll run it directly after the plays, and take our chances on the other stuff later. My confusion must be blamed on the damnable load of negotiations and counter-negotiations I have been carrying on—and writing a load of copy to boot, as the Nov. S. S. will show you.

As for the plays, I sincerely hope you don't push your demand for their return. Believe me, I appreciate your goodness in letting us have them, and if there was the money in the drawer I'd cheerfully pay a lot more for them. "The Blue Sphere" is already in type for December, and it was only an unexpected emergency that kept out a large announcement of it. I think you know how such things can happen, particularly when an office is upside down. We got out the Nov. number by the skin of our teeth. But the Dec. number will have hard and earnest work in it, and I think that you will like it. I needn't tell you that a Smart Set without your stuff in it would lose a good deal of its interest for me.

If I go to Nathan with such a demand as you make, it will kick up the very row that we must now avoid. Let me have "The Lost Phoebe" and forget it. And don't get the notion that I am sniffing at everything you write. If I could get a novel of yours, and had the money to buy it, I wouldn't hesitate to devote a whole number to it, and Nathan would go along.

Yours,
M.

◇◇◇◇◇◇◇◇◇◇◇◇◇◇

To Ellery Sedgwick
[ofp]

H. L. Mencken
1524 Hollins St.
Baltimore
November 2nd [*1914*]

Hochwohlgeboren Herrn Redakteur:–

Viewing the Nietzsche article in the Atlantic, the forward-lookers down here are again assailed by a damp, greenish, uncomfortable suspicion that, after all, I must be respectable. It is such doubts that shake them to their Methodist Episcopal foundations and palsy their arms. Allah il Allah!

I have seen two brief notices, in the New York Tribune and the New York Evening Sun. The former is very favorable; the latter 'arf and 'arf. If any hot ones show up, I wish you would let me see them.

Did I ever suggest to you a brief article on Theodore Dreiser? He has made a good deal of progress in England—Frank Harris, W. J. Locke and Arnold Bennett have all called him the greatest living

American novelist—but so far as I know, no one in this country has ever attempted a serious discussion of him. I know him very well and understand his aims thoroughly. If you have never read his "Sister Carrie" you have missed something that even Frank Norris never exceeded. (Norris, by the way, discovered Dreiser: a good story in itself.) The poor fellow is now in the dumps, and talks of giving up. I rather think that a careful article on him would attract some attention.[5]

If I could do it gracefully, I'd offer you congratulations on the November Atlantic. It is a good magazine, believe me.

Sincerely yours,
Mencken

To ELLERY SEDGWICK
[OFP]

H. L. Mencken
1524 Hollins St.
Baltimore
November 6th [*1914*]

DEAR SEDGWICK:

No doubt you are right about Dreiser: in any case, it would be well to wait until after his next book, "The Genius". The plan was suggested by Bliss Perry's complaint in the current Yale Review. Perry is not far from right. Dreiser sent me all of the notices of "The Titan", perhaps 100. Not one of them gave any coherent account of what he had tried to do, nor did any of them offer any criticism that would help him. After he had read them he was frankly muddled. It seems to me that so honest and talented an artist has a right to expect something better of his country. But I agree with you fully about the difficulties of printing anything about him now. Later on.

If you get a letter from one Albert Mordell, of Philadelphia, please pay no attention to it. This Mordell is a tedious fellow who writes childish criticism for newspapers, and pesters a lot of men (me among them) with long letters and requests for opinions about his work. He has cadged encomiums from two or three and uses them for purposes of advertisement. I mention him because a letter came in

[5] Sedgwick answered that Mencken should not attempt to sum up Dreiser in mid-career; he also expressed his dislike for long books in general, and *The Titan* in particular (Sedgwick to Mencken, November 4, 1914).

from him today, saying that he was about to favor you with his views on Nietzsche. I never answer his letters.

The Johns Hopkins still withholds my hard-earned D.D., but the Germans of Baltimore talk of making me a Geheimrat.

Sincerely,
H. L. M.

To JOSEPH HERGESHEIMER
[OFP]

H. L. Mencken
1524 Hollins St.
Baltimore
November 25th [*1914*]

DEAR MR. HERGESHEIMER:–

Surely we must meet for a long palaver. I am in Philadelphia at rather longish intervals and shall be delighted to look you up, particularly since I am now gunning for good stuff for The Smart Set! What have you? A novelette? I hope so.

You are, of course, quite wrong about "The Lay Anthony". You got an idea into it, whether you wanted to do so or not, and what is more, it was a good one. You cannot depict humanity without having some idea about it—that is, without viewing it in some specific manner, seeing some specific drama in its actions, setting it in some sort of opposition to an ideal. The baldest description of anything so complex as a man must needs be nine-tenths expression of opinion. But of all this when we meet. I hope it may be soon.[6]

Sincerely yours,
H. L. Mencken

To THEODORE DREISER
[UP]

[*On December 8th, Dreiser had sent Mencken the remainder of* The "Genius" *and asked his opinion on the 100,000-word serial that had been taken from the book and run in two magazines.*]

[6] In the *Smart Set* for December 1914, Mencken had severely criticized Joseph Hergesheimer's first novel, *The Lay Anthony* (New York: Kennerly; 1914); the two men, however, were soon to become close friends.

(1914)

H. L. Mencken
1524 Hollins St.
Baltimore
Wednesday [December 9, 1914]

Dear Dreiser:–

The remainder of the ms. will come just in time for me. I have been taking the first part slowly, reading five or six chapters each evening. Surely I'll be glad to go through the proposed serial. The crude cuts, of course, leave the thing as it stands rather disjointed, but I think I grasp its general drift. Two criticisms by the way:

1. I think Witla's artistic progress is under-described in the first part, that is, down to his New York days. The successive steps are not very clear. Suggestion: Start him in Chicago, cutting out the Alexandria part, and then go back to it briefly later on, à la Joseph Conrad.

2. There is no such word as "alright". I notice that you correct it to "all right" in one place, but elsewhere it stands.

More anon.

Yours,
M.

1915

To THEODORE DREISER
[UP]

Smart Set
456 Fourth Avenue,
New York
Wednesday [*January ? 1915*]

DEAR DREISER:–

I'll look into the matter of literary clubs in Baltimore and let you know by Monday. There is an organization called The Saturday Night Class which used to invite me to eloquence, and I think there are several women's clubs which run to beautiful letters. If the worst comes to worst I'll get an invitation for Powys from the Brew-Workers' Union, No. 22.[1]

The Rogers case is a mere beginning.[2] The uplifters have sworn to put down the villainous practise of copulation in this fair republic, and I begin to suspect that they will do it, just as they will put through prohibition and prevent any increase of the army. Their ideal is a nation devoted to masturbation and the praise of God. The American of the future will do his love-making in the bath-room, and he will be found in the same place when his country is invaded. If I ever get out of my present morass I shall begin the serious study of German, to the end that I may spend my declining years in a civilized country.

A letter from Harry Leon Wilson yesterday lavishing high praise on your plays. Not the first, by any means. They have made an un-

[1] John Cowper Powys (born in 1872): British author and lecturer.
[2] The Rogers case: an adultery and murder case.

mistakable hit, and it is worth noticing that the persons best pleased by them have been writers. I think the banzais that should please a man most are those of his own profession. . . .

Yours,
M.

To HARRY LEON WILSON
[PT]

Baltimore, January 26th [1915]

DEAR WILSON:–

My family roars over your new one weekly, and I have a devil of a time keeping out of hearing of whole columns of it.[3] Reading a serial drives me crazy. I always wait for the book and then take it at one sitting. I'll get this new one the moment it is out. Judging by the domestic chuckles it is worthy son of the unforgettable "Bunker Bean". Believe me, you done noble there. It sticks in my mind beside Max Beerbohm's "Zuleika Dobson", both genuine satires, both wholly free of the Wallingford-Earlderrbiggers species of whimsicality.

It tickles me beyond expression that you are finding the resurrected Smart Set readable. We are doing just what you supposed: that is, going out for the 150,000 civilized Americans. We start with about 50,000 and face hard times at their damndest, but things are beginning to loosen a bit, and we are full of hope. Yesterday we signed a contract for 12 full pages of whiskey ads; the circulation situation looks promising; in another month we'll pay off the last dollar of Thayer's debts. The tale of the past five months is one that screams for telling. Nathan and I and Warner (our business office partner) started on a shoe-string. The property was in a truly amazing condition of disorganization, with useless people cluttering the office and creditors whooping for their money and the safe full of bad stuff and a couple of fine law-suits threatening and the magazine a sort of one-horse imitation of Snappy Stories.

We lay about us with axes, cutting expenses about $2,000 a month and getting rid of the whole stock company. We are still on very short rations, and so labor under the distressing necessity of robbing poor

[3] Your new one: *Ruggles of Red Gap* (New York: Grosset and Dunlap; 1915), which was being serialized in a magazine.

authors, but we are paying spot cash for what we can buy at all, and the money situation grows better every day. Unless all the present signs fail we'll be back on the track by May 1, debt-free and with money in the bank. Nathan and I are absolutely at one as to what we ought to do. We have an agreement whereby each has the right to veto, but it is seldom exercised. And Warner is a hustler and a very ingenious money-saver. He disposed of more than $10,000 worth of debts by various compromises, chicaneries and appeals to the higher sentiments. Finally, the advertising situation brightens.

I wish to God I could accept your invitation to come to the Coast. It fills me with the wanderlust. But both Nathan and I will have to stick to the grindstone all summer. It is now or never. We have to write stuff and rewrite stuff. The sort of copy we want—brisk, sophisticated, showing some style—is enormously hard to get. We want to avoid the whorishness that Wright fell into (a natural reaction against Thayer's puritanism) and the namby-pamby inanity that Boyer pursued. Novelettes fitting into our program are almost unobtainable; we have to make a compromise monthly. "The Funeral King" I dug up here in Baltimore; the author had never written a line before. It was a sort of fluke; his second story was impossible. Dreiser, by great good luck, had his plays ready, and they were almost unsalable elsewhere. Pretty fair short stories bob up, but I have had to write nearly all the fillers and epigrams myself, under such aliases as Francis Clegg Thompson, R. B. McLoughlin, W. L. D. Bell, Raoul della Torre, Owen Hatteras, Sherrard Mullikin, William Fink, George Weems Peregoy, Marie de Verdi, Harriet Morgan, Pierre d'Aubigny, Irving S. Watson, Robert W. Woodruff, J. D. Gilray, William Drayham, James P. Ratcliffe, etc. Ye gods, what a list!

Which brings me to a commercial matter. Have you an idea for a novelette of 30,000 words, dealing with well-to-do people and lively in tone? If so, and the spirit moves you to write it hereafter, at what price in current money will you be able to sell it? I here play a future. We haven't got the money now, but by the providence of God we may have it in the autumn—and something of yours, particularly if a bit daring, would lift us over the stile. I doubt that we'll ever get within 80 degrees of latitude of Saturday Evening Post prices, but we hope eventually to concentrate on one big thing a month, and you may be sure that there will be no objection to a reasonable use of alcohol by the dramatis personae. In truth, we'll go so far as to let you keep them soused, one and all, from curtain to curtain. (An idea!) I open this subject diffidently, as one who still merely dreams of money, but I feel it in my bones that the S. S., soon or late, will genuinely attract you, and that our estimable treasurer will be able to insult you in the right manner. Keep it in the back of your mind. Maybe something will hatch.

Meanwhile, my best thanks for your quick comprehension of what we are trying to do, and your hearty encouragement. Believe me, the day you get into the magazine, and say that the rest of it is good, we'll be where we want to go.

Yours,
H. L. Mencken

Thayer is living at Westport, Conn. We are on good terms. Wright is in London. Boyer, I hear, is to be editor of Snappy Stories. Wright's book on Nietzsche will be published in a few days by B. W. Huebsch. We are thinking of making Thayer an offer for his appendix to "Astir", now under way. It deals with his Smart Set adventures.

My tongue is still a damned nuisance, but there is no tumor, malignant or otherwise, and I hope for relief before long. It has crippled me a lot.

M.

To THEODORE DREISER
[UP]

[*Dreiser had requested a comprehensive list of "fugitive realistic works of import", aside from those by Howells, James, Norris, Phillips, Wharton, Garland, Herrick, and London, and* excluding *Whitlock, H. B. Fuller, and Stephen Crane (Dreiser to Mencken, March 22, 1915).*]

Smart Set
456 Fourth Avenue,
New York
March 25th [*1915*]

DEAR DREISER:–

Counting out the authors you mention, and yourself, there have been very few realists in this fair land. Kennerley is just bringing out a very remarkable book, "One Man", by Robert Steele (pseudonym), but it is too full of autobiography to qualify as a novel, though it is called "a novel" on the title-page. Don't miss it. Others:

"Love's Pilgrimage" and "The Jungle", by Upton Sinclair.

"A Song of Sixpence", by Frederic Arnold Kummer.

"The Inside of the Cup", by Winston Churchill.

"The Golden Age", by Mark Twain and Chas. Dudley Warner.

What else? Damned if I know. Realism doesn't seem to appeal to most American writers.

What are you doing? Are you making any progress with that story of the condemned man? It sticks in my mind.

Yours,
M.

To THEODORE DREISER
[UP]

[*Dreiser wanted to know if H. L. Wilson's* The Spenders *had any realistic value; he had inquired about W. L. Comfort, Alice Brown, Mary E. Wilkins and Margaret Deland, and enclosed in his letter a few British reviews of* The Titan (*Dreiser to Mencken, March 29, 1915*).]

Smart Set
456 Fourth Avenue,
New York
April 1st [1915]

DEAR DREISER:–

If I left out Harry Leon Wilson's "The Spenders" it was an oversight. Comfort's stuff is gorgeously romantic, and even fantastic. He deals with Mystic Motherhood, the Fourth Lustrous Dimension and other such bosh, and is a crazy gynophile. Alice Brown, Mary Wilkins and Margaret Deland I don't know.

The London reviews, on the whole, are very decent. Locke's is excellent. It is amusing, by the way, to see how the English fear and hatred of Germany bob up, even in book reviews. The English Review is full of it every month. The English are beginning to realize what it means to fight Germans. They are finding that this is no Boer war, and the discovery is paralyzing them. I have a tip from the highest sources that a Zeppelin raid on a grand scale will be undertaken shortly, and that it will be a lulu.

"Working as usual". But on what? What of that story of the condemned man?

The Smart Set, by the way, seems to be making progress. The returns are declining steadily and the advertising department is bringing in new contracts for 6, 9, and 12 months. I begin to believe that we'll put it over. But what a sweat!

Yours,
M.

◇◇◇◇◇◇◇◇◇◇◇◇◇◇

To THEODORE DREISER
[UP]

Smart Set
456 Fourth Avenue,
New York
April 6th [*1915*]

DEAR DREISER:-

If you have ever given the resurrected Smart Set a glance, and can do it without injury to your conscience, and have no scruples otherwise, I wish you would dash off a few lines saying that it has shown progress during the past six months and is now a magazine that the civilized reader may peruse without damage to his stomach. This for chaste publication in refined announcements, along with the statement that you are a high-class novelist, a faithful Elk and a swell dresser on and off the stage. We are turning the corner and a help will actually help. But if the lie is too vast for you, say Nix in a loud tone, and no one will ever hear it save myself. Meanwhile I continue to pray for your conversion to orthodox Swedenborgianism and Lake Mohonkery.

Yours,
M.

By the way, the New Republic approached me lately with a proposition to do an article on you. The sheet is so damnably slimy and pecksniffian that I bucked, thinking it would injure both of us, but I may go back to it during the summer. There is no more oleaginous and forward-looking gazette in These States.

◇◇◇◇◇◇◇◇◇◇◇◇◇◇

To JAMES JOYCE
[CU]

Smart Set
456 Fourth Avenue,
New York
April 20th [*1915*]

DEAR MR. JOYCE:–

Two of your stories, "The Boarding-House" and "A Little Cloud" are in the May Smart Set; I am having two copies of the number sent to you by this post. We were unable to take more because the American publisher of "Dubliners", Mr. B. W. Huebsch, of 225 Fifth Avenue, New York, planned to bring out the book at about this time.[4] Apparently it has been delayed a bit, but I assume that Mr. Huebsch still proposes to do it during the Spring. The publishing business in the United States has been hard hit by the war, and there are constant changes of plans among the publishers. I think you are fortunate to get into the hands of Mr. Huebsch in this country. He is one of the few intelligent publishers in New York.

Mr. Pound sent me cuttings of the first 15 or 20 instalments of "A Portrait of the Artist as a Young Man", and I read them with much interest, but the story, unfortunately, is too long and diffuse for The Smart Set.[5] We do not publish serials, but do a whole novel, or rather novelette, in each number. Sometimes it is possible to carve a novelette out of a novel of the usual length, but, as I wrote to Mr. Pound, I felt that it would do unpardonable violence to your story to attempt anything of the sort. If you ever have a plan for a novelette, say of 30,000 words, I surely hope that you let us hear of it. As you may know, we also publish an English edition, and so we desire both the English and the American rights whenever it is possible to get them. In the case of your two short stories we had to send other stories to England, thus, of course, doubling our expense.

---

[4] The two stories mentioned here are included in *Dubliners* (New York: B. W. Huebsch; 1917).

[5] Pound: Ezra Pound.

Please don't hesitate to ask if I can do anything for you here in America. And keep The Smart Set in mind! Mr. Nathan and I took charge of it just as the war began, and we have had an uphill battle, but it is now, I am glad to say, in good financial condition, paying cash for everything and with both circulation and advertising increasing. We have to go slowly, but it is our aim ultimately to make it the best magazine in America. In particular, we want to print all the good novelties that the other editors baulk at. Curiously enough, our most successful novelty so far has been an omission: we have not printed a line about the war, not even a war poem!

Sincerely yours,
H. L. Mencken

To THEODORE DREISER
[UP]

[*Answering Mencken's letter of April 6th, Dreiser had written:*

I wish that I could say whole-heartedly that I liked the Smart Set, or that it has shown the kind of progress that I like in the last six months. Under Mann in its profitable social days it had a glittering insincerity and blasé pretence which I rather liked, shallow as it was.

Under Wright, when the society act had become a chestnut, it reflected a kind of shameless blood-lust, too fulgurous and unrelieved to suit me entirely, but still forceful and convincing.

Under you and Nathan the thing seems to have tamed down to a light, non-disturbing period of persiflage and badinage, which now and then is amusing but which not even the preachers of Keokuk will resent seriously. It is as innocent as the Ladies' Home Journal. Really the thing is too debonair, too Broadwayesque, too full of "josh" and "kid", like a Broadway and Forty-second Street curb actor. Everything, apparently, is to be done with a light, aloof touch, which to me is good but like a diet of soufflé. I like to feel the stern, cool winds of an Odyssey now and then.

Why publish so many things in one number? Wouldn't it be better to have one or two occasional very fine things than so many trivial ones? Why couldn't you have published Crainquebille by Anatole France, or Flax's study of Octave Mirbeau? (See Greenwich Village.) Or De Casseres' "From the Cusp of the Moon" or Masters'

"To a Greek Altar"! I called your attention to Masters months ago and you pass him over completely for third raters like Witter Bynner and Untermeyer. When you started six or seven months ago I was hoping that along with the touch that you now have—just a touch, however,—you would take a tip from Reedy and the Masses and the International, and do the serious critical thing in an enlightening way. There are splendid indictments to be drawn of a score of things before the world right now—things which could be sandwiched in between the things you do use and real literary achievements, such as a play by Chekhov or a satire by Andreyev. Once I was on the point of writing you. I felt that you were helplessly in tow of the Broadway-bebraided George Jean, for whom I have some respect as a lighter touch. But I decided not. Now, since you ask it I offer this as a purely personal opinion and one which, if followed, might cause your circulation to drop. Personally I think you are sound as a critic of books and that the magazine as you are doing it has some interest, but not enough to call forth from me the praise you want. The things haven't enough real interest for me.

Take the April number. Your leading story is entitled "When Fancy Leaves the Narrow Path". To me it is thin stuff, poorly done—traditional to the point of weariness and mediocre in style. The next thing that arrested my attention was "The Windy Shot". It was only fair—lacking in poetic poignancy—but fair. Then I went back and read "The Uplifters". It seemed trivial and along a line which is now becoming a little thin. Then, for interlude, I read the three things by Lord Dunsany who is good as a philosopher-humorist, but not fascinating enough to warrant three contributions in one volume. Also I read "Cameron's Conclusion", (fairly clever), "Jealousy"—William Anderson, (not worth doing), "Grandmother"—Woljeska (fair). "Flirt", Thomas Ransford—(trivial but good for the society game and as a filler). Then I stopped and turned to the poetry. "Annunciation"—Witter Bynner, (truck—uninspired), "Evening"—Martin Greif (a useless filler), "Transpostion"—Thompson Rich (rather good—traditional), "The Victory"—Whitford (a dull mechanical idea—made to sell), "April Song" (charming but the eightieth millionth of its kind), "Love's Pilgrimage"—Middleton (mediocre), *"The Last Poet"—Johns (not bad at all—rather good), "The Ancient One" (truck), "In Donegal" (truck—lost space), "Certainly, It Can Be Done," (Should have been done in prose and then torn up), "Lines for Music" (only fair—sweet old style), "Disembodied"—H. K. (not worth space), "Love's*

Need"—Scollard (a dull rhyme), "The Reason"—A. W. Peach (suitable for Godey's Lady's Book).

To finish I read "A Careful Surgeon"—clever but in the same joshing vein as eight or nine others in the book and not to be included with so many of its kind. "The Moral Defeat"—Harvey—(clever but in the same vein—good another month), "The Flight"—(without serious charm), and finally "With the Minstrels of the Moment" (I don't think George Jean is mentally in a position to pass on Granville-Barker) and "The Grand Stand Flirts with the Bleachers" by Henry L. Mencken—whose diatribes I always enjoy and whose strictures in the main I accept as sound.

Does this sound severe? I don't mean it to. Frankly I think you are infinitely better than the paper you produce. Why is this?

Dreiser

(Dreiser to Mencken, April 20, 1915)]

Smart Set
456 Fourth Avenue,
New York
April 22nd [*1915*]

Dear Dreiser:–

These notices are marvellous revelations of English pecksniffery. They are obsessed by moral phantasms—and the other fellow, of course is always wrong. The Germans are putting holes through that philosophy, and they will put a lot more before this war ends.

I am sorry that The Smart Set doesn't please you. As it stands, of course, it represents a compromise between what we'd like to do and what the difficulties that we face allow us to do. We had to buck a falling circulation and a bad reputation. The former has swung back; the latter we are trying to live down. We haven't money enough to take long chances. We have to give them, to some extent at least, what they seem to like, and more particularly, what we are able to get. I agree with you that "When Fancy Leaves the Narrow Path" was an execrable novelette. But, believe me, it was the very best that we could get. We got promises of stuff on all sides, but not a line of actual copy. The May novelette is very much better, and so is that we have scheduled for June. Where July's is to come from I haven't the slightest idea. Nothing whatever is in sight. Read the novelettes in the other magazines: you will find that they are even worse than ours. I know it because I have read most of them in ms. and declined them.

But the light touch you protest against is what we want. The Smart Set—consider its title!—is no place to print the revolutionary fustian of De Casseria and company. One of the first things I did last August was to invite De Casseria, Dell, Herts and all the rest of the red-ink boys to send in stuff.[6] I read it diligently and hopefully, but found it inexpressibly empty. These fellows are all sophomores; they have nothing to say, and they say that nothing very badly. My study of their stuff cured me of all belief in neglected geniuses. The whole red-ink bunch, and particularly the International bunch, is hollow-headed and childish. I couldn't find a single intelligible idea in 50 mss. Harry Kemp is the only tabble doty genius who has given us anything fit to print.

As for Masters, I bought a long ballad from him three months ago, and only recurring make-up difficulties have kept it out so long. It is scheduled for the July number. Harris Herton Lyon has sent us two good stories. We printed one, "The Pact", in December; the other dealt with an abortion, and, though well done, was quite impossible. A novelette that he submitted was full of faults; he is still tinkering with it. Nothing else from the Reedy crowd. You missed the best two stories in April, "Little Girl" and "Felix and Carlotta". It was, however, a bad number.

But let it go! We are not trying to shock 'em, but to entertain 'em! The June number will be better.

Yours,
M.

To THEODORE DREISER
[UP]

[*On April 26, 1915, Dreiser replied in these terms to Mencken's letter of April 22nd:*

You make a mistake in regard to my supposed interest in "the red ink fraternity", as you call them. I hold no brief for the parlor radi-

[6] De Casseria: Benjamin De Casseres (1873–1945), then book-reviewer and proofreader for several New York newspapers and magazines. He wrote a book on Mencken: *Mencken and Shaw* (New York: Silas Newton; 1930). Herts: Benjamin Russell Herts, Socialist writer and newspaperman.

cal. Viereck, Rethy, Herts and a score of others whose names have come and gone are of a thin cloth, but when you mix in Dell and De Casseres with them, and then pause to praise Lyon and George Bronson Howard you are sound asleep, also having taken over into your camp the empty Kemp. Produce me a poetic philosophic dissertation (recent) the equal of "From the Cusp of the Moon", by De Casseres, or better poems than some of Dell's, and I will eat these words without salt.

The trouble with you is that in the fury of your riding you plunge over all merit on foot. The International, the Masses, Rogue, Greenwich Village, the Mirror, and the like are, let us say thin things. Admitted. Yet if they can pick things like Crainquebille, "From the Cusp of the Moon", The Spoon River Anthology and things of that sort, and you can't or don't, where do you get off? A man like Max Eastman, radical though he is, lays his finger on notable pecksnifferies, sore and shames. You don't. Yet they are everywhere at hand. It may be important for circulation to print gay trifles—I know it is in part—but why attempt to ride down the other fellow until you are sure that he is not doing some of the things you ought to be doing. I am genial—not angry.

I sometimes think that because I have moved into 10th Street and am living a life not suitable to the home streets of Baltimore that you think I have gone over to the red ink family and "the brothers of the hollow skull". Give yourself one more guess. I have never had a better line on myself than at present, and the advice I am giving you is straight from the shoulder. You may increase your circulation and make some money by the unrelieved "light touch" you mention—(the "unrelieved" part being the only thing I complain of)—and the desire not to shock is commendable where the cash drawer is concerned, but it is not necessarily at war with the desire to entertain. Personally I would say that if you would mingle a severe jolt now and then, or a loud shrill scream, you really would entertain and keep up your good character in the bargain. But for a man with your critical point of view the stuff you are publishing is not literature and there are those who are getting it under your nose. But— But here's to all storm and sudden death! I see that the Catholics are quoting you.

Dreiser

If I can think of anything to suggest I will do so with pleasure. It is helpful criticism you want, not grape juice.]

Smart Set
456 Fourth Avenue,
New York
Thursday [*April 29, 1915*]

DEAR DREISER:–

Pish! What slush is this about "living a life not suitable to the home streets of Baltimore"? Do you take me for a Methodist deacon—or a male virgin? For far less insults I have had gentlemen killed by my private murderer, a blackamoor but a deft hand at the garrote.

Moreover, your allegations are chiefly damphoolishness. I tackled Masters the moment I heard of him (through you), and bought a long ballad from him out of the first and only batch he offered. He tells me he has been sick all winter. His Spoon River stuff was all printed when I got to him. I read all the stuff that De Casseres sent in, and bought the only good thing in the lot. I read all of Dell's stuff and found nothing. I have bought three or four things from Kemp, not one of them "a gay trifle". I did not mention George Bronson Howard in my last letter, and have bought nothing from him. I have read The International for three years, and have seen nothing in it worth a dam save a philippic against Maeterlinck by André Tridon. I have read Rogue, and found nothing in it save the sort of "wit" that school-boys chalk on pissoir walls. I have read all the books published by the Nortons, etc., and told the truth about them in the Smart Set.

I grant you that there has been a decided lightness in the magazine—but we had a condition, not theory, before us. The experiment with whores and horrors had failed; the experiment with cheap melodrama had failed; we had to try a new tack or go down. On August 15 The Smart Set owed $24,000 and was losing more than $2,000 a month. The circulation was cut to pieces; there was no advertising at all; we actually had to borrow money to pay interest on the debt. We guessed that satire would save it, and we guessed right. But we have steadily endeavored to lift the thing as much as possible. April was our worst number, and you picked out the worst things in it. For example, you missed the two stories by James Joyce (his first published in America), the excellent "Little Girl", by Lee Pape; "The Man Who Waited", by Lina Bernstein; "Felix and Carlotta", by Edna Marion Hill (sentimental stuff); and "The Desert is Not Fifth Avenue".

But away with debates! We'll prove it to you yet, old top! If you see anything likely, for Goddes sake sound the alarrum! I have no prejudices, save against the Methodists.

In nomine Domini.
M.

◇◇◇◇◇◇◇◇◇◇◇◇◇◇

To THEODORE DREISER
[UP]

Smart Set
456 Fourth Avenue
New York
Sunday [*May 1? 1915*]

DEAR DREISER:–

A thought: you are constantly coming into contact with aspiring authors. Why not spread the following whisper: that I'll be glad to see the manuscripts of any ambitious new one, buck or wench, and to give them my prompt and personal attention? This may develop something and so help both the magazine and the authors. In particular, I'll be glad to read any novelette or play. Even on the red ink question I am still willing to be convinced. All I say is that the stuff actually sent in by the tabble doty revolutionists was uniformly feeble and empty.

Incidentally, what has become of your own novelette—the one about the man condemned to the chair?

[. . .] In nomine Domini!
M.

◇◇◇◇◇◇◇◇◇◇◇◇◇◇

To ELLERY SEDGWICK
[OFP]

The Sun
Baltimore, Md.
May 22nd [1915]

DEAR SEDGWICK:–

My apologies for this delay in answering your letter of May 18. I have been in New York since Tuesday.

As I wrote last week, I agree with you that it would be unwise to print the article at this time.[7] It seems to me very improbable, in truth, that it will be possible to print it later on, for if Dr. Wilson does not

[7] The article: an article against democracy, representing the United States after their conquest by the Germans and "the subsequent increase in civilization"; also perhaps that referred to in Mencken's letter to H. L. Wilson (July 2, 1915).

goad the Germans into war this time he will undoubtedly do so next time. Despite his pacific protestations, I hear on the best of authority that he is full of a Puritan bellicosity, and that he will enter the war at the first opportunity.

If you care so, I shall be glad, of course, to have you keep the manuscript, but with the clear understanding that you thereby incur no obligation whatever. It may be that the skies will clear, and that, in some form or other, it may become printable. But please let me see a proof before you actually print it. I don't want to appear as a spokesman of Germany, for I am an American by birth and the son of native-born Americans. Nor do I want to appear as yielding an inch to the super-patriotic fustian which now goes 'round. Such fustian seems to me typical of the United States. I am getting an enormous mass of capital material for my book, "The American".

Here's hoping that you are in the best of health.

Yours,
Mencken

◇◇◇◇◇◇◇◇◇◇◇◇◇

To HARRY LEON WILSON
[PT]

Smart Set, New York, July 2nd [*1915*]

DEAR WILSON:–

My best thanks for the clipping and your letter. I have concocted a flaming advertisement based on the clipping, and added the fortissimo asseveration that you meant the Smart Set, and the copy has gone to Warner. If my prayers are answered, a large wood-cut of your countenance will accompany and adorn it. Incidentally, the statement will appear that you are—but let it go!

I am delighted that you liked the June number. Nathan and I thought that it was the best to date. The July number shows a falling off, but August will be much better, and September will be the king of them all. For it we have a corking novelette by Avery Hopwood, author of "Nobody's Widow", etc. More, we have an even better novelette for October. Yet more, by dint of copious sweating, we have dug up some genuinely decent short stories. Altogether, things begin to look very good, despite the fact that the war talk in May knocked circulation galley-west. The seasonable drop in that month, of course, was also partly to blame. July, August and September are the best selling months, judging by the records of past years.

But meanwhile, despite set-backs, we have at last clawed the old hulk out of debt, and if the war ever ends we'll have a fine property. Rosy dreams! But with the Pilsner supply cut off it is hard to be happy. I had a session with Huneker in New York the other day, and he was almost tragic. Certain New York kaffy-keepers, it appears, lately began to mix Pilsner with a debased native brew, and he had drunk eight or ten barrels of it before discovering the cause of the unearthly, graveyard flavor. Result: he fell out of an automobile and broke his nose. Second result: he is talking of taking the veil. I still see him at Luchow's, weeping into his lentil soup. His only consolation lies in the continued deviltries of F. M. von Mackensen.[8]

I agree with you about Wister's Atlantic article. I wrote a column notice of it for the Baltimore Evening Sun, the one which went to you yesterday. Incidentally, the war gabble in May cost me an Atlantic article of my own—one arguing that it would be well to examine into the causes of the German success, and so borrow a few useful ideas, instead of harping forever on the moral string. Sedgwick had ordered it, but he now hesitates to print it, and I agree with him. Later on, perhaps, I'll work it over. What with two jobs on my hands, I wrote it under difficulties, and so hate to lose it.

What are you at? Another "Ruggles", I surely hope. Along about February, God willing, you will be approached with a proposal to do a novelette for a certain grey magazine, with all the rules thrown overboard and the Saturday Evening Post spit in the eye. Meanwhile, the blessings of St. Aesophagus. And again thanks.

Sincerely yours,
H. L. Mencken

To James Joyce
[cu]

Smart Set
331 Fourth Avenue,
New York
July 24th [*1915*]

Dear Mr. Joyce:–

Mr. B. W. Huebsch tells me that on account of the financial situation in the book-trade he has been forced to give up his plan to repub-

[8] Mackensen: a German general.

lish "Dubliners" in America.[9] Things are quite at a standstill, and they threaten to grow even worse. Our cheque for the American serial rights, by the way, was sent to Mr. Richards at the time the two stories were accepted.

We cannot consider a novel because our space-limit for a single story is about 30,000 words. Nor can we print a three-act play. But if you write any more short stories I'll be very glad to see them. Whenever possible we want both the English and American serial rights. If we are given the American rights only we are forced to buy something else for our English edition, which is both costly and troublesome.

If you happen upon Arthur Abbott in Zurich, please give him my best regards. At last accounts he was British Vice-consul there. I visited him in Munich 15 months ago, and have a great liking for him.

Sincerely yours,
H. L. Mencken

◇◇◇◇◇◇◇◇◇◇◇◇◇

To THEODORE DREISER
[UP]

[*On October 9th, Dreiser had offered Mencken "The Light in the Window" and "A Spring Recital" for the* Smart Set.]

Smart Set
452 Fifth Avenue,
New York
Friday [*after October 9th, 1915*]

DEAR DREISER:–

Frankly, I am against using this, and for a simple reason. It would strike a note of anti-climax after the other three and spoil their effect both for you and for us. The difference between it and them is plain enough. In each of the three there was a definite dramatic transaction, and a resultant dramatic suspense. In "The Blue Sphere" there was curiosity as to what would become of the imbecile child; the atmosphere grew steadily more sinister. In "In the Dark" there was the conflict between murderer and police, with the issue in doubt until the end. And in "Laughing Gas", of course, there was that poignant sus-

[9] *Dubliners,* which had appeared in England in 1914, was not published by Huebsch until 1917.

pense which always hangs around a surgical operation. But in "The Spring Recital" there is no suspense at all. It is atmospheric, not dramatic. And so I think, as I say, that it would be very injudicious to print it after the other three. The effect would inevitably be disappointment.

I am not arguing, mind you, that the play is bad. Not at all. On the contrary, I think there is a good deal of color in it. In the book, sandwiched between two of the other plays, it will go down. But standing alone in a magazine I am convinced that it will seem weak, and I believe you will agree with me when you think it over.

By the way, you have forgotten to put in the name of the composition the organist "drifts" into at the bottom of page 4.

What of the novelette you mentioned—the electrocution story? Is it coming on? I begin to hope that we will have a few bucks in bank by the time it is ready.

Thine,
H. L. M.

To THEODORE DREISER
[UP]

H. L. Mencken
1524 Hollins St.
Baltimore
December 25th [*1915*]

DEAR DREISER:–

This is the impression the group of poems makes on me: the first three are hopelessly commonplace, and two of them open with intolerable banalities, but the last four are truly excellent. "Wood Note" is genuinely superb; I am enthusiastic over it. "For a Moment the Wind Died" is almost as good. "Ye Ages, Ye Tribes" is a fine statement of your philosophy. Even "They Shall Fall as Stripped Garments", despite the obviousness of the thought, is a sound poem. But why hook up these with such obvious and hollow stuff as "Life is so beautiful" and "How pleasant is the waterside"? I am wholly unable to understand the idea beneath the grouping. My recommendation is that the first three be dropped entirely and the last four be made into a group. The former will hurt you; the latter will be sure to do you good. I am so strongly of this opinion that I urge it with the utmost vigor, and if you dissent from it call for arbitration by some disinterested party, say Masters or Wright. Believe me, "Wood Note" is first-rate stuff. If you have more things of its kind you should print a volume of them, by all means. Nobody in this country is doing better. But please don't tie up your best with things so empty as "Life".[1]

I hold the copy for your decision, which I hope will be favorable to my contention. If not, I'll come to New York week after next and tackle you head-on.

Yours in Xt.,
M.

◇◇◇◇◇◇◇◇◇◇◇◇◇

To Ellery Sedgwick
[OFP]

H. L. Mencken
1524 Hollins St.
Baltimore
December 29th [*1915*]

Dear Sedgwick:–

I seem to be forever making excuses, but surely it is not because I have not labored! The truth is that I have put in a lot of very hard work on the proposed Down-with-democracy article, but at every turn I run into the war. I thought I could steer clear of it, and of Wilson, but the thing is quite impossible. The only way I seem to be able to do it is a way that would not please you at all. It is, in fact, out of the question for a man of my training and sympathies to avoid the war, for it is forced into his notice at every turn. How can I preach upon the dangerous hysterias of democracy without citing the super-obvious spy scare, with its typical putting of public credulity to political and personal uses, *e.g.*, by Snowden Marshall, who prosecuted old Buenze? After writing a lot of stuff, and tearing up a lot, I have come to the conclusion that I had better put the project aside, at least for the present. I thought it would be easy, but it has turned out quite the reverse. My chance will come when the inevitable reaction comes, and the American people begin to see how they have been deceived and played upon by dishonest newspapers and self-seeking patriots.

[1] These Dreiser poems were later included in *Moods, Cadenced and Declaimed* (New York: Boni and Liveright; 1926).

When will you be in New York? I am very eager for a talk with you. I get there myself every two weeks, and shall be there Monday and Tuesday of next week.

Sincerely yours,
H. L. M.

[*Sedgwick answered Mencken that the spy scare was not as dangerous as the bad policy and ill-defined aims of the United States.*]

1916

◇◇◇◇◇◇◇◇◇◇◇◇◇◇◇◇◇◇◇◇

To THEODORE DREISER
[UP]

[*Dreiser had offered Mencken a few poems free of charge* (*Dreiser to Mencken, after February 5, 1916*).]

Smart Set
331 Fourth Avenue,
New York
February 18, 1916

DEAR DREISER:

I am here in New York and have gone over the financial situation with Nathan. I seize and embrace your offer to give us your poems free of charge, cost or expense and accept it with respect to three of them. With respect to the fourth entitled "Wood Note", we find ourselves unable to see our way clear to take advantage of your kind hospitality. We therefore insist upon paying $25 cash for this poem, which works out to $3.62–½ a line. With the cheque, which will reach you next week, go the blessings and prayers of the firm.

Your book of plays has reached me this very minute from Jones, and I shall bury my snout in it on my way home tomorrow.[1]

Let us pay strict attention to our religious duties during the next

1 Your book of plays: *Plays of the Natural and the Supernatural* (New York: John Lane Company; 1916).

month or two. I believe that both of us will be killed by patriots within six months.

Yours,
H. M.

P.S. I notice that opposite to the title page of the book Jones gives a list of your works included in the "Trilogy" and that the third volume of "Trilogy" is represented by a row of stars. The thought seizes me that it would be a capital idea to use this row of stars as the title of the third volume. The novelty would be sure to interest and inflame the boobs. Jones, by the way, has made a very beautiful book.

I saw Wright last night and he, too, is preparing for death.

M.

To LOUIS UNTERMEYER
[OFP]

Smart Set
331 Fourth Avenue,
New York
April 19, 1916

DEAR LOUIS:

Your letter, as always, is a noble contribution to serious literary criticism. My own taste is toward poetry of a far more solemn and horrible type than that which we print but I have convinced myself that The Smart Set is not the place for it. The fat women, who read our grand family magazine, like sweet stuff, and sweet stuff we shall give them.

I am delighted that you find Lilith Benda interesting.[2] She seems to me to be the most cunning new-comer that has bobbed up in a year past. Unluckily, she is full of delusions that her stuff is very bad and it is a hard job to make her write at all.

Dr. Billy Sunday is, at present, spreading the word of God in Baltimore and I regret that you are not here to hear him.

Within you will find a few documents that may help you to a better life.

Yours in Xt.,
H. Mencken

---

[2] Lilith Benda: Lucia Bronder, an author of short stories.

[*Mencken used to send various grotesque material, such as advertisements, religious pamphlets or the like, for the pleasure and edification of his correspondents. At other times, he would write parodies such as the following undated letter addressed to Louis Untermeyer:*]

◇◇◇◇◇◇◇◇◇◇◇◇◇

1524 Hollins Street
Baltimore, Md., U.S.A.

DEAR SIR:–

Our buyer, Miss Katzenstein, says your Mr. Rifkin has the wrong idea about them trimmings. Such things positively ain't worn this season. We would say further our Miss Katzenstein knows the business from A to Zet; also, furthermore she was once on the stage, and is very tasty. We therefore adjust your bill accordingly, hoping it will be satisfactory. Our cashier, Mr. Kone, will mail you a check come Sabbath. We don't say nothing about that North American Store concern, but if they would take such goods then we have our opinion too.

Trusting for a renewal of your favors,

Yours truly
THE SMART SET SHOP
per B. Rashkind
Mgr.

[. . . . .]

◇◇◇◇◇◇◇◇◇◇◇◇◇

To THEODORE DREISER
[UP]

H. L. Mencken
1524 Hollins St.
Baltimore
April 22, 1916

DEAR DREISER:

From some unknown hand I receive notice that you have taken to the stump and will read one of your plays before an intellectual gathering next Sunday. In vicarious expiation of this crime, I am going into a monastery to serve ten days. Moreover, I shall have my ruffians at the meeting and in the midst of your eloquent burbling, a dead cat will approach you at terrific speed. This is too, too much; henceforth I consign you to hell along with Alfred Noyes and Henry Van Dyke.

Yours in Xt.,
M.

To THEODORE DREISER
[UP]

H. L. Mencken
1524 Hollins St.
Baltimore
May 12, 1916

DEAR DREISER:

I have been working on a chapter about you for a book that I have under weigh and find myself stumped for one or two facts.[3] In the first place, I have been unable to make out to what extent, if any, you were influenced in your early days by Frank Norris. "McTeague" was published in 1899 and "Sister Carrie" in 1900, but it sticks in my mind that you once told me that you had not read "McTeague" when you wrote "Sister Carrie". Is this true? The two books, in many ways, show a similar attitude of mind though the differences between them are numerous and important. What is your remembrance of the influences you stood under at the time you began to write? You have told me that you had not read Zola or any of the Russians. Did Hardy influence you? I know that this is difficult ground, for a man can scarcely determine such things himself, but it occurs to me that you may remember some enthusiasm of that period and that it may account, to some extent, for your utter divergence from what was then the main stream of American fiction. Saving H. B. Fuller, I can think of no American novelist of the 80's or 90's who steered in anything even remotely approaching your own direction.

Incidentally, what was the name of that novel by Arthur Henry which you spoke of in your house the other night?[4] I don't know that

[3] The book was *A Book of Prefaces* (New York: Alfred A. Knopf; 1917).

[4] Arthur Henry: a close friend of Dreiser's; he played an important part in encouraging Dreiser to write fiction; at the same time as Dreiser was laboriously composing *Sister Carrie,* Henry was writing another novel to keep him company, and as a sort of challenge to him: *A Princess of Arcady* (New York: Doubleday, Page & Co.; 1900).

I will mention it at all but if I should happen to do so, I will want to get its title accurately.

Another thing: how long after the suppression of "Sister Carrie", by Doubleday, Page and Company, did William Heinemann bring out his London edition?

Yours in Xt.,
M.

Again, let me have that long Sheridan review in the *Nation,* and that Chicago wench's review—the one in which parents are warned to defend their children against German kultur.

M.

To THEODORE DREISER
[UP]

H. L. Mencken
1524 Hollins St.
Baltimore
May 15th [*1916*]

DEAR DREISER:–

My best thanks for your letter.[5] It clears up a lot of dark places and heads me in the right direction. Curiously enough, though I never heard you mention Hardy, I had written a long paragraph arguing that he probably influenced you. The exact facts are excellent. Let me keep the clippings for a while; I won't get back to the essay for a couple of weeks. This afternoon I am going to New York, but whether I'll see you God knows; the office is in a mess. But I'll surely go over the whole thing with you before I send my book to Lane. Four of the eight chapters are blocked out and four-fifths written—those on you, Conrad and Huneker, and one on American best-sellers.

"The 'Genius'" is still my blind spot; more and more I put "The Titan" first, not for its contents, but as a work of art. Your best writing, and by long odds, is in it. Nor do I think that "Laughing Gas" is your best play. "The Blue Sphere" and "In the Dark" seem to me to be much better. If there is time, I want to get the Old Home Week book and "The Bulwark" in.[6]

[5] In reply to Mencken's letter requesting details about the writing and publication of *Sister Carrie,* Dreiser had written at length on May 13th.

[6] The Old Home Week book: *A Hoosier Holiday* (New York: John Lane Company; 1916).

The San Quentin letter is immense. All the best Americans will be in prison in a few years.

Yours in Xt.,
M.

To THEODORE DREISER
[UP]

[*Dreiser had just put the first volume of* A History of Myself *in the John Lane vault; in the event of his death, the manuscript was to be given to Mencken so as to be protected against any interference on the part of Dreiser's family.*]

H. L. Mencken
1524 Hollins St.
Baltimore
June 26, 1916

DEAR DREISER:

1. I have had three copies made of the insert and am inclosing two of them herewith.

2. I shall insert the name of Kitchener in the proper place. I notice several errors and omissions. For one thing, you speak of Gustavus Myers' book on the great American fortunes as in four volumes. My copy is in three volumes. Was a fourth ever published? Curiously enough, I have had it in mind for some time to write an article on this work, which has been so much neglected that it is practically unknown. Despite a lot of Socialist fustian, it is one of the best books ever done in America. Naturally enough, it was not done by an American.

3. I note what you say about your autobiography and shall leave a memorandum among my papers providing for its disposition in case of my death. It is conceivable that we may enjoy the felicity of dying together—for example, in battle for the Republic. Let us discuss the question of a substitute editor when we meet.

4. I will be delighted to do the catalog notes for "A Hoosier Holiday" and "The Bulwark", but it had better be put off until I see you. I suggest that we meet at the Lafayette at 6:30 on Friday evening and

put in the rest of the evening discussing the problems of theology and statecraft. If I don't hear from you, I shall assume that you will be there. Meet me in the entrance hall.

5. No; I didn't write "The Vivisectionist of Women". The thing was actually done by Vere Tyler. But I wrote the whole of the first chapter and re-wrote parts of all the rest. The idea, however, was Mrs. Tyler's and so was the plan of the story in every detail. I didn't insert a single incident. Even in the first chapter, I followed her general idea faithfully. The difficulty with the novelette as it reached us was that it was badly written. But the scheme of it was well devised and the characters well thought out.

6. I have read about 75,000 words of "A Hoosier Holiday" and I am proceeding forward steadily at twenty-five miles an hour. The book is full of excellent stuff—some of the very best you have ever done. I am constantly outraged, however, by banalities, and it seems to me that they should come out. My hands itch to get at the job. I hope that I will be able to convert you to it when we meet. The pastoral scenes are beautifully written. How long is it? I feel it must run to 200,000 words or even more. This is too much for such a book.

Yours in Xt.,
H. L. M.

◇◇◇◇◇◇◇◇◇◇◇◇◇◇

To THEODORE DREISER
[UP]

Smart Set
331 Fourth Avenue,
New York
July 5th [*1916*]

DEAR DREISER:–

Unexpectedly, I have been able to put in two days on the ms., and so I have got through it, and am returning the last half by express today. The changes I propose are relatively few, and making them will leave no appreciable mark on the book. Most of them involve the excision of repetitions: your discussion of the nature and meaning of life, for example, is repeated a dozen times, and often in very similar words. Again, there are many smaller repetitions. Yet again, certain words are overworked—for example, secure—and I have substituted synonyms. Yet again, I have performed some discreet surgery upon the Day Allen

Willy episode, and upon others of its sort. In the main, I have let the discussion of the Catholic church stand. They are against you anyhow. Why not strike back? You do it very effectively. So with the Puritans.

The book, on a second reading, seems very good to me. It contains, in fact, the best writing you have ever done. A genuine feeling for style is in it.

I'll be in New York in about a week.

Gott mit uns!
M.

To HARRY LEON WILSON
[PT]

[*Baltimore,*] *July 10, 1916*

DEAR WILSON:

Your scheme for a series of burlesque short stories is capital and you could do it to perfection, but I would consider it a deliberately unfriendly act to urge you to do it with the other markets so good. The more the other magazines get into difficulties, the more the Saturday Evening Post seems to prosper. You would be a maniac not to go out for all that money while the going is good.

I doubt that newspaper experience would have helped you to quicker writing. Undoubtedly it would have taught you how to slash out a lot of stuff in a few hours, but that stuff would be by no means the sort of thing you are doing now. In my own somewhat narrow experience, the value of writing seems to be in inverse proportion to the ease of writing. Whatever flows freely and bubblingly turns out to be sorry stuff a week later. Whatever goes like pulling teeth tickles the eye.

At last I am able to accept your invitation—not for this year but for next year. If it so be God's will, I shall start on a long tour of the West some time next summer, and it goes without saying that I shall stop off to pay my respects. I may be accompanied by a literary gent known to you, but on this point I can report nothing at present. He is a healthy and free-drinking man and so worthy of all respect.

If you run through the August Smart Set, I hope you take a look at a story called "The End of Ilsa Mentieth" by Lilith Benda. This Benda is a Polish woman whom I discovered six or eight months ago and all of her published work has appeared in the Smart Set. She is still somewhat crude but it seems to me that a few years of experience would make a very respectable authoress of her. One of her short stories, "The Pernicious Influence" is in the July number. Unluckily the poor girl is suffering from tuberculosis and like most Poles, she is pessimistic and faint of heart. Last week she solemnly informed me that her day was done and that she would never write another line. I have hopes, however, of getting her back to work.

I am writing this from Baltimore, where the Elks' convention has just begun. Fortunately, a heavy rain is falling. The demonstrations are truly astounding and in one public square there has been erected a so-called Court of Honor that deserves to be re-produced in marble as a perpetual memorial to the American Kultur of 1916. I have seen Père Lachaise cemetery in Paris and the worst of the German halls of heroes, but this is incomparably more hideous. I begin to long for the roar of artillery and the measured tramp of the Japs. A couple of Zeppelins in the sky would charm me.

I hope you are in good health. Barring the natural infirmities of age, I am in fair condition.

Sincerely yours,
Mencken

To THEODORE DREISER
[UP]
[*On July 27th, 1916, Dreiser had informed Mencken that the censors had "descended" on* The "Genius" *and that they had denounced its alleged blasphemy and immorality; Jones, the publisher, had been ordered to withdraw the book from the market.*]

H. L. Mencken
1524 Hollins St.
Baltimore
July 28 [1916]

DEAR DREISER:

Can you get a bill of complaint from the moralists—that is, an exact statement of the passages they object to? In the absence of such details it is impossible to make any plans of defense. As you know, I have been in combat with these gentlemen on various occasions and know something of their methods of work. I needn't tell you that it is an extremely difficult thing to combat them in court for all judges are eager to appear as moral gladiators, and though they hate the Comstocks, nevertheless, they want to cut a pious figure in the newspapers. The charge of blasphemy need not bother you. No such crime is known to American law. But the charge of immorality is more serious. It seems to me that Jones is approaching the matter in a wise way. The thing to do with the moralists in the case of such valuable a property as "The Genius" is to offer some sort of compromise and so force them into the position of negotiating with you. In the end, if the thing is properly managed, it will be unnecessary to take out more than a few sentences. My feeling is that it is always better to do this than to risk the complete suppression of the book. After all, we are living in a country governed by Puritans and it is useless to attempt to beat them by a frontal attack —at least, at present. The war against them is so badly organized and the average American is such a poltroon that it is next to impossible to get help. I'll tell you when we meet the story of the Parisienne case, and in particular, that part of it dealing with the desertion of the gentlemen we had trusted. The country is in a state of moral mania and the only thing for a prudent man to do is to stall off the moralists however he can and trust to the future for his release. If this attitude may seem to be pessimistic, please don't forget that it is born of extraordinarily wide experience. My whole life, once I get free from my present engagements, will be devoted to combatting Puritanism. But in the meantime, I see very clearly that the Puritans have nearly all of the cards. They drew up the laws now on the statute books and they cunningly contrived them to serve their own purposes. The only attack that will ever get anywhere will be directed—not at the Puritan heroes but at the laws they hide behind. In this attack I am full of hope that schrapnel will play a part.

I shall be in New York on Monday and shall try to get into communication with you. Not a word has come from Jones. Please keep the whole matter quiet.

Sincerely yours,
M.

◇◇◇◇◇◇◇◇◇◇◇◇◇◇

To THEODORE DREISER

[UP]

[*Seeing that nobody wanted a compromise, Dreiser decided to fight it out* (*July 31st*).]

(1916)

H. L. Mencken
1524 Hollins St.
Baltimore
August 4, 1916

Dear Dreiser:

Going through the pages marked by the moralists, I find they have fallen into their characteristic extravagances. Page after page marked as indecent is utterly harmless, and I can't see more than half a dozen pages that they could reasonably take before a jury. This examination of their own evidence very considerably augments the chances that they may be beaten. If, as you say, Jones has got over his alarm and is ready to fight, I begin to believe that your plan may be the best one after all. The chief danger, aside from those I mentioned in my last letter, lies in the faintheartedness of your associate in the defense: that is to say, if Jones is convinced that the moralists have a good case, you yourself can scarcely hope to beat them, but if Jones is convinced that he can win, then I believe that the chances of actually doing so are very greatly improved. As for the charges of profanity, they are childish and need not concern you. The Postal Act says nothing whatever about profanity. Its exact words are: "any obscene, lewd, lascivious, filthy, or disgusting book". It would be straining a point to call such phrases as "God damn it" disgusting. The New York Act of March 4th, 1909, uses the words "obscene, lewd, lascivious, filthy and indecent". Here again you will find no mention of blasphemy. As a matter of fact, I believe that blasphemy is a crime unknown to American law. Surely, the occasional use of "Jesus Christ" in "The Genius" is not a violation of any existing act. If they base any process on it at all, it will have to be under the common law and I doubt that the common law still runs in such matters.

Let me know the result of Jones' conference with his directors. Wright told me on Wednesday that Jones had left town for three weeks and so I made no effort to see him, though I had business with him regarding my own books. After trying in vain to get hold of you, I was told by M that you were out all day investigating records at the World office. I return to New York on August 14th, ten days hence. Let us have a meeting. My experience in the Parisienne case may offer some suggestions. The thing I am most afraid of, as I wrote to you, is the introduction into the case of the German spy fear. A man accused of being a German has no chance whatever in a New York court at this time. He would be better off, if anything, before an English court.

My best thanks for your corrections in my Sun article. I'll make all of them. More installments will reach you from time to time.

Please don't get the notion that I am disinclined to tackle the moralists. The one thing I am against is tackling them with both hands tied.

Yours,
M.

To Ernest Boyd
[OFP]

[*Ernest Boyd, who had met H. L. Mencken in Baltimore where he was British Consul, was then back in Europe. Later he was to abandon the diplomatic career and settle in America as journalist and critic.*]

1524 Hollins Street,
Baltimore, Md.
September 6, 1916

Dear Boyd:

Just a few lines to report the state of moral progress on this side of the ocean. The Post Office Department still hangs reluctant upon the brink of the Dreiser affair and so far as I can make out, no actual decision to prosecute has been reached. But meanwhile, preparation of the defense goes on. Greatly to my surprise, the executive committee of the Authors' League passed a resolution last week definitely pledging the support of the League to Dreiser, and since then the executive committee has adopted a minute which is to be presented to the Post Office by the Secretary in person. This minute states that all authors must stand behind Dreiser and that the principle behind his proposed prosecution is one that they feel themselves obliged to combat to the last extremity. In addition, the Authors' League has taken over the business of getting signatures for the public protest of authors, and the prospect seems to be that this protest will be a formidable document. Moreover, the executive committee has notified Jones that even if he jumps from under the case, it will continue the fight. I was present when Jones was notified and his apparent alarm showed plainly enough that he was contemplating a discreet surrender. As things now stand, he will either fight or be exposed as a faint heart. The Authors' League case is in the hands of an Irishman named O'Higgins, and he seems to be a very pugnacious and determined fellow. I am eager to see the issue joined. It will be a lot of fun.

Meanwhile, Dreiser himself plays the fool. It seems impossible for him to shake himself free from the Washington Square mountebanks. Yesterday I got a letter from him in which he said that arrangements were under weigh for an indignation meeting at the Liberal Club and that I was to be invited to speak. I have notified him that in case my name is mentioned publicly in connection with the Liberal Club, I will sue whoever so misuses it for libel. It will be difficult, however, to keep Dreiser himself out of the place. The plain truth is that he is a fearful ass and that it is a very difficult thing to do anything for him.

I assume that you have already landed by this time and that you are safe and happy. I am writing this note to avoid rehearsing the Dreiser case later on.

Sincerely yours,
M.

To THEODORE DREISER
[UP]

Smart Set
452 Fifth Avenue,
New York
Friday [*October 6, 1916*]

DEAR DREISER:–

This afternoon a Baltimore second-hand book-seller handed me a copy of the Authors' League protest, just received from Lane. I note that, despite our talk of last week, you have inserted the names of four or five tenth-rate Greenwich geniuses, including two wholly unknown women, and left out such men as Churchill and Ade. Let me say once more that I think this a damnably silly, perverse and dangerous policy. You are making it very hard for Hersey, who has already imperilled his job in your behalf, and spitting into the eyes of the rest of us. Just what satisfaction you get out of this course I'll be damned if I can see. Why start a fight in the trench while a bombardment is going on? All of these jitney geniuses are playing you for a sucker. They can't advance your reputation an inch, but you make a very fine (and willing) stalking horse for them.

Yours,
M.

◇◇◇◇◇◇◇◇◇◇◇◇◇◇

To Ernest Boyd
[OFP]

Oct. 9, 1916

Dear Boyd:

Although I have received no letter from you, I hear indirectly that you have proceeded to Spain. Last week I sent you a copy of the epigram book and in a week or so the other book will follow.[7] I shall see Jones in three or four days and find out exactly when he proposes to publish the Irish book.[8] I am also sending you some magazines. No doubt your letter to me is delayed by the censor. Of late, it has been taking from four to six weeks to get news from England.

In the matter of the Comstock prosecution, Dreiser, as usual, is playing the fool. The Authors League circulated a protest of American authors and hundreds had signed it, including such orthodox gladiators as Winston Churchill, Margaret Deland and Doty, editor of the Century magazine. But Dreiser, in sending out extracts from this protest, insisted upon adding the names of a lot of Washington Square jitney geniuses. The result is that the Authors League men in charge of the matter are violently enraged. I myself wrote him a hot letter two or three days ago. The old ass is ruining his case by his folly. These frauds flatter him and so make use of him. I am almost in despair of getting him on the track. Meanwhile, the Post Office Department still delays its decision and the circulation of the book is temporarily prohibited. Dreiser's association of his case with the names of mountebanks advocating birth control, free verse, free love and other such juvenile propaganda is hurting him very severely with the pundits at Washington.

Within is a photograph of the party at Phil Green's place. Unfortunately, the group of Jesi was spoiled in the developing. The inclosed, however, is a noble work of art.

Black has become a father. The child is a boy. Otherwise, there is no news.

Sincerely yours,
Jackson

---

[7] The epigram book: *A Little Book in C Major* (New York: John Lane Company; 1916). The other book: *A Book of Burlesques* (New York: John Lane Company; 1916).

[8] The Irish book: *Appreciations and Depreciations*, by E. Boyd (Dublin; 1917). Later published in the United States as *Appreciations and Depreciations: Irish Literary Studies* (New York: John Lane Company; 1918).

To THEODORE DREISER
[UP]

[In his letter of October 9th, Dreiser had accused Mencken of adopting a "harsh, dictatorial tone" and had forbidden him to meddle in his private affairs—that is, to criticize his friends the liberals.]

Smart Set
452 Fifth Avenue,
New York
Tuesday [*October 10, 1916*]

DEAR DREISER:–

Whatever the origin of that list, I still think it was wretchedly bad policy to circulate one bearing the names of such professional revolutionists as Abbott and Eastman and such nobodies as the two women.[9] On the one hand it hooks up your cause with causes that are definitely unpopular, and on the other hand it greatly embarrasses Hersey, to whom the support of the Authors' League is chiefly due, and who has been imperilled already by the suspicions and opposition of the respectables. I was wholly unaware that this list was made up before our talk. The presence of Rupert Hughes' name on it made me think, and quite naturally, that it postdated our talk.[1] What was my surprise then to encounter what appeared to be a gratuitous crack in the nose for the only men who have devoted any honest effort to the case, and done it any appreciable service!

I haven't the slightest right or desire to question your private doings. They are, I am informed, of a generally immoral nature, and hence abhorrent to a right-thinking man. But I would be a false friend if I stood idly by and let you do things certain to injure you, and some of your most faithful partisans with you. I have opposed the publication of the list, at least at this stage, for plain and simple reasons. If it were printed in full the names of the birth controllers, jitney Socialists and other such vermin would give the moralists the very chance they are looking for. And if a selected list were printed, then you would bring down upon yourself the bitter enmity of all the signers omitted, and

[9] Leonard D. Abbott (born in 1878): associate editor of *Current Literature* (1905–25). Max Eastman (born in 1883): editor of *The Masses* (1913–17).
[1] Rupert Hughes (1872–1956): formerly of *Criterion,* then with the army on the Mexican border.

some of them are in a position to do you serious injury. This is sound politics, and I stick to it. Once the case is decided I withdraw all objections. In fact, I am already planning to print a pamphlet about it myself, giving a full list of the signers [. . .] and exposing the pecksniffery of those who have refused to sign. To this end Hersey and I are carefully preserving all material.

I am coming to New York this afternoon, and shall call you up tomorrow or next day. Thanks very much for the Booth pictures. They are excellent.

Yours,
M.

There is, in fact, no secret grievance. You surely know me well enough to know that I never have secret grievances.

To Barrett H. Clark[2]
[OFP]

The Smart Set
34th Street and 8th Ave.
New York
Nov. 2, 1916

Dear Mr. Clark:

This play is an amusing piece of writing, but I am frankly in grave doubt that the average American reader would see anything in it. The trouble with it is that it rests immovably upon a strictly French conception of marital rights and duties. The old woman would not only not amuse Americans; she would probably horrify them. This is one of the plays which bear translation badly. There are many more, such as you know very well, in German. A capital example was Beyerlein's Zapfenstreich, which failed both in England and America, despite the fact that it was an excellent play. Our requirements in the Smart Set are not unlike those of the theatre itself; that is to say, we must make a good many concessions to popular taste. We cannot swing as far away from it as one may do in a book. By all means, let me see the other plays you speak of. Our supply of good one-acters is always distressingly short.

Sincerely yours,
H. L. Mencken

[2] Barrett H. Clark (1890–1953) was a critic, translator, and playwright.

To Louis Untermeyer
[ofp]

Smart Set
452 Fifth Avenue,
New York
November 3rd [*1916*?]

Dear Louis:–

Here, indeed, is good stuff—James Gordon Cooglar himself never done no better—but I am confronted by a double agreement with Nathan: on the one hand to avoid all discussion of the war, however innocent, and on the other hand to admit no poets into the house until we make some sort of hole in the Thayer stock. Nathan takes a look at that stack of rondels and triolets every morning, and the rest of his day is poisoned by acute dithyramobophobia. Last Sunday he burst into tears, hung around my neck and swore that poetry was suffocating him. Nevertheless I made him put through two things: one your obscene sonnet on the Chopin-chopper, and the other a few lines on Wash Day (fact!) by Lizette Reese. So you see what I am up ag'in. The man's fear of strophes is actually pathological; I think a sudden wallop with a dactyl, from the rear, would send him into puerperal convulsions.

The Chopin is being embalmed and will probably see the light in the Feb. no. By the way, did you ever know that the fair young boys taken on hunting trips by the Eskimos (their gnädige Gemahlinnen being left tu hum) are called *shopans*? A curious fact of sex hygiene, worthy of being put into a ballad. Somehow, Chopin's music always suggests to me unhealthy and abnormal things—for example, tenors. But here, of course, I wander into the realm of the lewd.

I wish you would have 10,000 copies of this counterblast struck off for my private use. I get at least 50 war poems a day from the hog-meat and hominy belts. Worse, in every one of them the Kaiser is called a [.... .....]! Well, maybe he is, but I am for him all the same. Once he has Europe by the neck, insurance on the hides of you Socialists will go up to 90 guineas per cent. But what a day it will be for us arrogant, sniffish, malty Dutch Junkers! As for me, I am going to revive my "von", and have a couple of scars cut across my right cheek—or is it left?

What a crack the forward-lookers got yesterday—what? Penrose, Uncle Joe Cannon, u.s.w.! Down with the uplift!

Yours,
von Mencken

I wish Oppenheim would send me his book for my annual poetry article.

M.

To Ernest Boyd
[OFP]

November 13, 1916

Dear Boyd:

I inclose a copy of my review and shall send you some more tomorrow. I shall also send a few to Jones. He is reprinting the article, somewhat reduced in length, as a pamphlet, and will distribute it widely. It was held up in the Sun office on account of the election, which naturally had the right of way on the editorial page.

The estimable Doctor suffered a bad scare.[3] It appeared on election night that he was badly beaten and it took three or four days of counting to establish the fact that he had really won. It seems to be generally agreed that he will now proceed to get revenge on those who presumed to oppose him. We shall see what we shall see.

The Dreiser case has taken a very favorable turn. John B. Stanchfield, a very clever New York lawyer, has volunteered his services and will manage the case hereafter. His plan is to force a decision and then sue Sumner for libel and apply for a permanent injunction against him. The chances are one thousand to one that the decision will be in favor of Dreiser. The United States District Attorney in New York has given a decision in writing that "The 'Genius' " does not violate the law and the Post Office Department has come to practically the same verdict. Sumner is already offering compromises, but Stanchfield refuses them. Stanchfield is the man who drove Sulzer out of New York. He is a trial lawyer of the most brilliant and effective sort and he has vowed to put a crimp into the moralists if it takes him all the rest of his life. Natural enough, Dreiser could not afford to employ such an attorney at the regular scale of fees. Stanchfield, in fact, will work for nothing. He will be sided by two Jewish lawyers of the utmost cleverness and by

[3] The Doctor: Woodrow Wilson, who had beaten Hughes by a narrow margin.

the Free Speech League of America, which has been collecting evidence against the moralists for many years and has accumulated an enormous mass of proofs of their imbecilities.

I have just returned from New York where I spent two or three days negotiating for newspaper commissions on the enterprise of which you know.[4] At this writing, it seems likely that I'll depart on January 1st and remain two or three months. I am now completely free of the two Louse magazines and have nothing to do save edit the Smart Set. I shall write three or four book articles in advance.

My best regards to Mrs. Boyd. Please tell her that I received the Goodfellow manuscript from Dublin but that I could not convince Nathan that it was the thing for us. It was, in fact, a good deal too elusive for the Smart Set fat women. But I have written to Goodfellow suggesting that he do other work for us and I am confident that we will come to terms. He has cleverness in him.

You will be astounded to find in the next Smart Set—that is, the January number, a page of epigrams by Harry Black. Nevertheless, they are authentic. He offered them to me very diffidently and I was astounded to find some excellent ones among them. What is more, he has since suggested an idea for a one-act play that is so good that Nathan is in ecstasies over it. The principal character will be a President of the United States.

Yours,
M.

To Max Broedel[5]
[OFP]

H. L. Mencken
1524 Hollins St.
Baltimore
Nov. 24, 1916

Dear Max:

Your letter emboldens me to touch you for something I have long wanted to have—that is, one of your drawings. I mean one of the

[4] The enterprise: Mencken had been commissioned by the Baltimore *Sun* to go to the German front as a war correspondent; he was scheduled to sail on December 28, 1916.

[5] Max Broedel (1870–1941) was a German-born illustrator of anatomy and physiology, who came to the United States in 1894 to work at the Johns Hopkins University as assistant professor. He was a lifelong friend of Mencken's.

anatomical drawings. If you have one knocking about that is of no present or future use to you, I'd be delighted to have it, properly autographed. The more I look at them the more they excite my amazement and admiration. Give me, my dear Mon chair, a portrait of a kidney. I'd really appreciate it very highly.

I daresay Jack London's finish was due to his chronic alcoholism in youth. He was a fearful drinker for years and ran to hard liquor. I have often argued that he was one of the few American authors who really knew how to write. The difficulty with him was that he was an ignorant and credulous man. His lack of culture caused him to embrace all sorts of socialistic bosh, and whenever he put it into his stories, he ruined them. In brief, he made a mess as an author of tendenzliteratur. But when he set out to tell a simple tale, he always told it superbly.

Sincerely yours,
M.

To Henry Sydnor Harrison[6]
[PT]

[*The suppression of* The "Genius" *originated when a minister of the 9th Baptist Church in Cincinnati called the Western Society for the Prevention of Vice, which, in its turn, barred* The "Genius" *from the bookstores and warned Sumner in New York. This letter is an example of the many Mencken wrote to various writers in order to persuade them to sign the protest.*]

Baltimore, November 25, 1916

Dear Mr. Harrison:

Thanks very much for your very agreeable letter, which followed me to my home in Baltimore. (Answer: because no self-respecting man can live in New York: think of the way they cook soft crabs!) It rather startles me to hear that you have found anything worth reading in my *Smart Set* stuff, for on the whole it has had to be light and inconse-

[6] Henry Sydnor Harrison (1880–1930): a novelist. Mencken had little esteem for his works, which he severely criticized in the *Smart Set.* About this letter, Mencken wrote: "My flattery of Harrison, of course, was largely hooey. He had a certain amount of talent, but he was by no means a first-rate writer. His books were inordinately sentimental." (Mencken to Julian Boyd, March 2, 1943)

quential; but nevertheless I have tried to get a coherent theory of the novel into it, and I am delighted to know that it has interested you. The thing that separates us, I daresay, is not so much a difference over the novel as a difference over things more fundamental. It seems to me, indeed, that men in general subscribe to two diametrically opposite theories of life, and that all the disputes of the world revolve around this fact. My own view of things is almost unbrokenly literal; I am a materialist of the materialists, and so my attitude toward idealism is invariably skeptical. I not only question it in prose fiction; I question it in politics, national and international, and in its supreme form of religion. I can no more change this view of things than I can change the color of my eyes. More, I am so constituted that I can't avoid combatting the contrary view—too often, I fear, with more noise than is necessary. But I at least try to keep before me the equal sincerity in the other fellow, and to accept his objections with the best grace possible. These objections, believe me, seldom come so pleasantly as from you. The idealist, both in politics and in art, almost invariably assumes that his antagonist is not only wrong, but immoral; and out of that theory comes much fustian. One example of it is to be found in the article of that college professor (in the *Nation*) who lately denounced Dreiser for subscribing to a purely animal theory of behaviour—quite forgetting the poor fellow's sentimentalization of Carrie Meeber and Jennie Gerhardt.[7] Another example was provided by Dr. Wilson's Manhattan Club speech, in which he posted all opponents of his scheme of preparedness as traitors—and then abandoned it himself two months later.

As for Dreiser, I shall not try to dissuade you from your decision, though I am frank to say that it would delight me to see you recant and sign. For this there are two reasons, the first being that the Protest has already accomplished substantially all it was designed to accomplish—(the case, in fact, is won), and the second being that you will inevitably change your mind in the long run, and be properly sorry. But purely for the sake of the record, I set down a few answers to your objections:

1. That you object to the wording of the Protest, and do not believe that "anybody is making efforts to destroy the work of Dreiser". The Comstocks, in point of fact, announce openly that, if they can bar

[7] The professor mentioned here was Stuart P. Sherman (1881–1926) whose attack on Dreiser in the *Nation* for December 2, 1915, was indignantly resented by Mencken.

"The Genius" from the mails, they will proceed against all his other books; their champions denounce him as one who must be put down; it is against this that Wells, Bennett and Locke have protested by cable. As for the text of the Protest, it is a collaboration, and hence bound to be unsatisfactory in detail. But it specifically says that "some of us may differ from Mr. D. in our aims and methods, and some of us may be out of sympathy with his point of view". Surely no Protest could have been drawn up that would have been perfectly satisfactory to *all* prospective signers.

2. Two horns to this objection. First, you haven't read "The Genius" and are "at the moment unable or unwilling to do so". Secondly, you believe, with Sumner, that "authors as a class are no better judges of what constitutes indecency than any other classes in the community". As for No. 1 I leave it to your blushful remorse. What you say is that you are unwilling to read a book by a man who is widely regarded in England, and by competent judges (*e.g.*, Bennett), as the foremost living American novelist, and is undoubtedly a conspicuous figure in your own craft. Imagine Brahms refusing to hear "Die Walküre"! . . . As for your second objection, it pains me even more. Who is better fitted to judge novels, in art and in morals—men of letters, or a small clique of filthy-minded Puritans? Have you ever read Comstock's pamphlets, "Not Art—But Morals"—the Bible of the smut-hounds? Read it, and weep!

3. That there is no occasion or necessity for this protest. That Dreiser delights in shocking the Philistines. That his position is fortified by such attacks . . . What you forget is that the Comstocks are trying to pillory him before the world as a merchant of mere pornography, a low and lewd fellow, a dirty swine; and that they are trying to send him to a Federal prison for five years. Is this a prospect that a man of self-respect can face unmoved? Is this a fate that other authors can see inflicted on one of their number, known to be an honest man, without making a protest? Is this the sort of thing that should go on unchallenged in a free republic?

I leave the rest to your conscience and the Great Jehovah. Personally, I don't care for "The Genius". I reviewed it very unfavorably, in fact, in the *Smart Set,* and dealt with it so severely in private that Dreiser and I quarreled. I believe that it is stupid, hollow, trifling and vulgar. But I know that, whatever its deficiencies, Dreiser himself is a sincere artist and an honest man, and that he wrote it in absolutely good faith. If we admit the right of arbitrary and disingenuous moralists to attack the work and liberty of such a man, if we put his failure to meet our personal notions of what literature should be above the principle that every bona fide artist should be free, then we plainly hand over letters to a crowd of snooping and abominable Methodists, and say goodbye to all we have struggled for.

The present persecution, I am convinced, is without merit. It did not originate in any bona fide complaint. It was started by a professional moralist in Cincinnati—a petty preacher. It is carried on in New York by men whose sole apparent object is to prosper their own obnoxious business, and who have refused an offer to submit the book to impartial judges, and to eliminate whatever is agreed to be objectionable. What is more, this view of their motives and character appears to be held also by the proper officers of the law, for they have refused to take any motion. The one aim of the Protest is to enter a caveat against all such vexatious and intolerable proceedings, and to give public notice that the authors of the United States, putting aside their personal likes and dislikes, are united against the common enemy, as the authors of France were in the Zola case.

My apologies for this infernally long letter. Your politeness makes me eager to present the facts to you in the best manner possible. But whether you sign or not in the end, I offer my thanks for your frankness, and I am sure that Dreiser will respect your position when you tell him of it. I need not add, in closing, that your own work has my sincere and hearty admiration. You don't write the sort of novels I like best, but you do your own kind superbly. After all, craft is the thing; it lies far above *tendenz* and content. You are the best craftsman among the American novelists of today.

Sincerely yours,
[*Unsigned*]

1917

To Ellery Sedgwick
[OFP]

1524 Hollins Street
Baltimore, Md., U.S.A.
[*1917?*]

Dear Sedgwick:–

Some day, when idleness afflicts you, cast your eye over the enclosed. Maybe you will see something that interests you.

Sincerely yours,
Mencken

I.

HIC JACET C_2H_5OH—A *Festschrift* to ethyl alcohol on its deathbed. Prose strophes in honor of its passing. A last, sad caveat to prohibition. What alcohol has done for man. Its enormous uses, now forgotten. Why men really drink it and need it—the true facts, not the current pseudo-facts. The psychological origin of the opposition to it. The moral frenzy of today. The messianic delusion. What its passing takes away from civilization. A serious, melancholy article, not protesting against national prohibition (which is certain to come shortly), but shedding a few philosophical tears over it.

II.

The Lack of Originality Among Millionaires—All of them spend their money in one or two of a small number of set ways. They show no imagination in getting rid of it. What a truly civilized man could do with $50,000,000. For example, in the courts. Yet again, in the propagation of ideas, particularly unpopular ideas. How much would it cost to convince the American people of the truth of any given absurdity, taken at random? The fun a millionaire could get out of sending 5,000 Mohammedan missionaries into the South, to stir up the niggeroes. The opportunities for an American Borgia.

III.

The Prussian—A character sketch. An attempt to see into the Prussian mind. Its obvious defects. Its concealed sources of strength. What other man could face the odds the Prussian faces? How he bears himself in the face of danger. His view of himself. A somewhat careful study, leading to the conclusion that, after all, the Prussian *is* really a superior animal. Some Nietzschean flavoring, to make it scandalous.

IV.

On Punishments—The disadvantages of their lack of variety in modern states. The tendency to reduce them to three: death, fine and imprisonment, and even to two. The superiority of the older system: ducking, branding, etc. The delusion that punishment can be purged of the vindictive purpose. Some better punishments for common crimes. How the courts constantly show the limitations of the present system—e.g., by condemning bad boys to join the navy. False squeamishness; the morality of the mob. Infernal cruelty concealed under bogus humanitarianism.

V.

Reflections of an Amateur Theologian—Some fallacies inherent in all modern religious systems. Points at which religion inevitably wars with intelligence and common observation. Religious ideas and practises that would not offend, and have not been tried. Defects in the argument by design, in the doctrine of free will, in the custom of worship. The true psychology of prayer. I think this could be done without giving offense to the godly, and yet show some novelty. It would probably take the form of Nietzschean paragraphs of say 200 or 300 words, not continuous, but organically related.

VI.

The Spy Mania—An analytical study. I have had a clipping bureau collect spy stories, and have a great many. A critical examination. The psychology of the frenzy.

(1917)

VII.

After the War—A consideration of some neglected possibilities. The moral frenzy of the moment versus the cold facts. Effects of the conflict on the Germans. How they view the future. Some shifts of interest that are likely. The Japanese factor. The control of the sea. The possibility of a sweeping German naval victory. Not pro-German or controversial, but a calm review of things that are overlooked.

To Ernest Boyd
[OFP]

The Smart Set
34th Street and 8th Ave.
New York
[April? 1917]

Dear Boyd:

The war has naturally affected all publishing ventures, but I don't think there will be any very formidable paralysis. The people will stop reading magazines for a while, but soon or late they will tire of the newspapers and go back to the magazines. Nathan and I are so firmly convinced of this that we are sticking to our resolution to print nothing about the war. When the reaction against alarms and headlines comes we'll pick up the circulation we now lose.

I have by no means lost sight of the new magazine scheme. In fact, I plug away at it constantly, and have even interested some capital. Black is one of these capitalists. More, he insists that you are the man to edit it, and Nathan and I agree. Therefore, direct your rev. chaplain to pray for the end of the war. Coming out before then, I take it, will be impossible. At the moment, of course, nothing resembling an intelligent magazine would have a chance. The country is reading nothing but buncombe. But, as the late Polonius aptly observed, wars can't last forever.

The literary situation here reflects the political situation. Dreiser is being hammered in most of the literary weeklies on the ground that he is a secret agent of the Kaiser, greatly to his astonishment. Huneker is ill and in retirement. Wright is being slaughtered for his book on the Encyclopedia, despite its highly patriotic tone.[1] Nathan is to do two

[1] Wright's book on the Encyclopedia: *Misinforming a Nation,* a sharp criticism of the *Encyclopaedia Britannica* (New York: B. W. Huebsch; 1917).

books in the autumn, one through Knopf and the other through a new publisher named Goodman.[2] I see no one else. I hear from no Irishmen save Joyce and Dunsany. Dunsany is now all the rage in New York and Joyce's "Dubliners" and "Portrait of the Artist" are very well received. We introduced both of them in this fair republic. I had a letter from Joyce lately; he is in Switzerland. I haven't heard from Dunsany for six weeks. We are doing three poems by him in June. Who Bierstadt is I don't know—probably some Harvard boy. He had better change his name to Cocacolaville.

The spy hunt over here takes on astounding forms. The other day the German Hospital in New York was raided by armed police on the ground that some one was signalling Zeppelins from the roof. It turned out that a couple of Low Dutch orderlies were cleaning brass spittoons. This is a mild sample. But I doubt that it goes much further, at least for the present. The position of actual Germans, of course, is very unpleasant. Some are already jailed; others are watched. Krieg ist Krieg!

My book can't be printed now, but it can wait. I am rewriting my prefaces from end to end; on getting home and re-reading the stuff I found it all tosh. Dreiser has sold a serial to the Saturday Evening Post, two stories to Hearst's and a play to a good manager. He has more money than he ever saw before, and is wearing silk shirts.

Conscription here stops at 27. It seems a century since I was eligible.

My best regards and my household's to Mrs. Boyd.

Yours in Xt.,
H. L. Mencken

To ELLERY SEDGWICK
[OFP]

1524 Hollins Street
Baltimore, Md., U.S.A.
[*Before April 5, 1917*]

DEAR SEDGWICK:–

Thanks very much for your letter. I'll be delighted to do a piece for you, but somehow a plan for it eludes me. What is your own notion? My newspaper stuff, running to nearly 30,000 words, pretty well exhausted the Gerard-Zimmermann seltzer-siphon and bladder-on-a-

[2] Philip Goodman (1885–1940), a theatrical producer, author of *Franklin Street* (New York: Alfred A. Knopf; 1942).

string combat. I did not tell the whole story, but I at least spoiled it. More of it will go into my book, "The Diary of a Retreat", but even there I'll have to use the soft pedal. What do you say to an article leaving out M. Gerard, but presenting some German views of the future course of things, along with a general picture of war-time Berlin? I could deliver it by the end of next week. Unluckily, I doubt that I could keep two convictions from creeping into it: (a) that the Germans will never starve, and (b) that it will cost 5,000,000 lives to beat them. But I could avoid controversy.

Alternatively, there is a possible article on Ludendorff, the real boss of the country—perhaps the best man that Germany has produced since Bismarck. I have some material about him that is quite new here. Also, I have some curious stuff about Hindenburg and Mackensen. I dessay I'll be jailed presently as a secret agent of the Kaiser, but I hope to get out promptly, and to put in most of 1917 doing long-delayed work. Your commands will get my prayerful attention. It is a staggering thing for an American to come out of Germany—and read the American papers. Our fair republic wanders in a maze of pink delusion. The truth is far worse than anyone seems to suspect.

The trip was a noble adventure. I had a week of actual war from a front bench, and then the Gerard-Zimmermann buffoonery, and then a fine journey through Spain, ending with a week in Cuba. How are you?

Sincerely yours,
Mencken

[*E. Sedgwick admired Mencken's* Diary of a Retreat, *and requested an article on Ludendorff.*]

To Ellery Sedgwick
[OFP]

1524 Hollins Street
Baltimore, Md., U.S.A.
[Before May 23, 1917]

Dear Sedgwick:–

Take your time, by all means. At the moment I am immersed in a book. Enclosed are some suggestions to add to the others.

Sincerely yours,
Mencken

Hindenburg A typical Junker. A lot of stuff about his family hitherto unpublished in English. The peculiarities of the man, as described by his old associates. His position before the war. His relations to the Kaiser. A pen-picture of the old walrus, and a discussion of some of his achievements.

Mackensen The German beau ideal. An amazing blend of dress-parade flummery and the highest military genius. His career before the war. The Nelson A. Miles of Germany. His family, his two marriages, his sayings, his books. No article on him, even remotely accurate, has been done in English.

The Psychology of the War An examination and discussion of certain American reactions. The growth of legends. The man-under-the-bed complex. The current conception of the German. A comparison between German and American attitudes toward the war and toward each other. The throttling of free discussion.

Wilson and the War: the First Stage An examination of Presidential pronunciamentoes. The effort to get through the espionage bill. Wilson's conception of American duty and destiny. Calvinism in international politics.

Dreiser The English view of him. His affronts to American prudery. The background of the man. The facts of his life. (I think I am the only person who can do this accurately. I know a great deal about him.) His point of view. Der Bauer im Frack. His heathenry. Why such men as Bennett, Wells, Watts-Dunton, and Frank Harris regard him as America's greatest novelist. His limitations.

James Huneker The only American critic of music who has ever gained any standing abroad. What he has done, and how. His aesthetic theory. A comparison of his work to that of Krehtiel, Henderson, Finck, Mason, et al. His inner history; how his style was formed.

Women The godless, immoral sex. Where they are heading. Current delusions and sentimentalities about them. Their new attitude toward marriage. Their opposition to masculine romanticism. Their general superiority to men. The need of a new valuation of them, purged of ancient fallacies. Changes in the sex war.

[*These suggestions were not accepted by the* Atlantic, *but the last three were worked into various books, and especially* In Defense of Women *and* A Book of Prefaces.]

◇◇◇◇◇◇◇◇◇◇◇◇◇◇

To VINCENT STARRETT [3]
[OFP]

The Smart Set
34th Street and 8th Ave.
New York
June 12, 1917

DEAR MR. STARRETT:

Since I last wrote to you Nathan has gone through "The Truth About Delbridge" very carefully. He agrees with me that it is a very fine piece of work but he raises an objection that I confess begins to make an impression on me—that is, the objection that a story dealing with such an abnormality would probably prove very offensive to a great many readers and perhaps bring down upon us the strong arm of certain moral gentlemen who constantly stand by awaiting their opportunity. I am not entirely in accord with this idea but his arguments shake me up to some extent. And so I hesitate definitely to take the story. If you see any way to change the ending so that the man need not dress himself up in woman's clothes, I would be inclined to grab the manuscript at once. It has been suggested in the office that it might be possible to get around the matter by making the man hang himself with a doll in his arm but without his present paraphernalia of silk stockings. I incline to believe that this would solve the problem. Please give it your thought and let me hear from you.[4]

Nathan joins me in assuring you that it would delight us very much to have you in the magazine regularly. You know how to write in the way that we like to see writing done. I surely hope that something else will reach us very shortly and that you will be able to overcome our qualms in the present case.

I trust that the two books of piety that I sent to you the other day are giving you the spiritual consolation that all of us need in these hard times.

Sincerely yours,
H. L. Mencken

---

[3] Vincent Starrett (born in 1886): a Chicago newspaperman and author, who was associated with the Chicago Renaissance movement.

[4] The article was later published in the *Smart Set* and is part of Vincent Starrett's *Coffins for Two* (Chicago: Covici-McGee Co.; 1924).

◊◊◊◊◊◊◊◊◊◊◊◊◊◊

To THEODORE DREISER
[UP]

To Rev. Theodore Dreiser
℅ H. B. Smith
R.F.D. No. 10,
Westminster, Md.

July 10, 1917

DEAR SIR:

Mr. Mencken requests me to inform you that he is quite ignorant of the matters to which you refer. He further instructs me to ask you to kindly refrain from pestering him with a long and vain correspondence. He is engaged at the moment upon patriotic work which takes his whole time and he has no leisure to fool with the bughousery of the literati.

Having no more to say, I will now close.

Very sincerely yours
Ferdinand Balderdash
Captain, 16th U. S. Secret Service

◊◊◊◊◊◊◊◊◊◊◊◊◊◊

To LOUIS UNTERMEYER
[OFP]

[*The August number of* The Masses *has been barred from the mails in early July because several satirical cartoons and an article by Max Eastman ("A Question") had been found subversive. The judge had enjoined the Postmaster to refrain from withholding the paper from the mails, but the censors had managed to render the injunction ineffective.*]

1524 Hollins Street
Baltimore, Md., U.S.A.
[*Late July 1917*]

DEAR LOUIS:–

The ferocity of the Masses business is almost beyond belief. But, after all, it is nothing new. In time of war, democracy always falls into such extravagances. Read Fisher's "The True Story of the American

Revolution". Its difficulty is this: that the very free speech it is based upon makes war impossible unless the desire for it is practically unanimous. When such unanimity is absent, as is usual, it has to abolish free speech by orgy. The spectacle is staggering, but not without its logic. To argue anything in such a time seems to me to be as impossible as to stop a stampede by playing on an E clarinet. It simply can't be done.

All appeals to any intrinsic love of free speech are futile. There is no such passion in the people. It is only an aristocracy that is ever tolerant. The masses are invariably cocksure, suspicious, furious and tyrannical. This, in fact, is the central objection to democracy: that it hinders progress by penalizing innovation and nonconformity. But here I am lured into dirty talk against socialism.

What we need is an accurate and objective record of the present process. I have a lot of material, but I have four or five other books to do, once the war is over, and may never come to working it up. Why don't you do it yourself. I don't mean a passionate protest, but a calm and analytical record, as cold-blooded as possible. No such writing has ever been done in America. In the midst of endless clinical material, we haven't a single study of democratic psychology. I can see forty sound books in what is now going on. Give this your prayerful thought.

All men with names like yours and mine will be jailed before Sept., 1918.

Yours in Xt.,
M.

To ERNEST BOYD
[OFP]

[*W. H. Wright had lost his job at the New York* Evening Mail *after being investigated for anti-American activities.*]

[*Late September 1917?*]

DEAR BOYD:–

The Wright affair turns out to be a masterpiece of imbecility. He hired a stenographer from an agency, and soon found out that the spy scare had unbalanced her. When, in the midst of an article, he dictated a German book title, she objected to writing it down. Later he found her making off with copies of his correspondence—harmless stuff about getting a passport for a naturalized Frenchman. Despite all this, well knowing that she regarded him as a suspicious character, he gave her a test letter deliberately designed to inflame her—and introduced the names of real men! She promptly made off with this letter and called the police. The letter, of course, was obviously nonsensical, but among the men mentioned in it is Leeds, who has been very seriously hurt, both at home and professionally, by the publicity.[5] I regard the whole affair as intolerably idiotic, and am so angry that I have not answered Wright's letters. To put such burdens upon innocent friends in such crazy days as these is an unforgivable offense. The net result is that Wright has badly injured Leeds, got himself into the spy-hunting newspapers, lost his job on the Mail, and well-nigh ruined himself. It is impossible, in the circumstances, to have anything to do with him. A man so silly is a public menace.

These are the exact facts. He maintains that he dictated no actual names, but told the stenographer to leave blanks. But this is a weak defense. The text of the letters made it obvious to the girl, who knew his correspondents, that he was addressing Leeds. She promptly inserted all the names, and the Secret Service, of course, tried to make it appear that Wright had inserted them himself.

There is no personal rancour in the matter; I myself was not mentioned; but what he did to Leeds in his childish folly he might have done to any of his friends.

Yours in Xt.,
H. L. Mencken

To ERNEST BOYD
[OFP]

1524 Hollins Street
Baltimore, Md., U.S.A.
[*Fall 1917*]

DEAR BOYD:–

Your book and the O'Sullivan book came in today.[6] My best thanks for both. You have done an excellent job, particularly with

[5] Leeds: a mutual friend of Mencken's and Wright's; he was Washington correspondent of the New York *Evening Mail.*

[6] Your book: *Appreciations and Depreciations.* The O'Sullivan book: *The Good Girl* (New York: E. P. Dutton; 1912).

Shaw: it is, by long odds, the most penetrating criticism that great flamingo has suffered. In these days nothing is heard of him on our side of the ocean. I'll review both books anon.

Dreiser, it appears, is subtly outraged by certain passages in my prefaces, and shows it by an idiotic petulance. With Wright excommunicated, this cuts me off from two of the three men I used to see in New York.

I send you an occasional copy of Pistols. This for the illuminati. The book has made a sensation.

Nathan and I are planning to organize an American Academy. We shall elect the members, appoint the officers, and publish the list in an anonymous pamphlet, along with the constitution and by-laws. An appendix will contain a waiting list, and a roster of the persons rejected.

I have been engaged in surgery on my dog. Two teats removed—and she still lives. Such is Wissenschaft.

My best regards to Mrs. Boyd. My family begs to be remembered. We still live, but it becomes steadily more difficult to eat. The S. S. is laboring heavily.

Yours in Xt.,
H. L. Mencken

To CARL VAN VECHTEN
[YU]

1524 Hollins Street
Baltimore, Md., U.S.A.
[*Postmark: October 12, 1917*]

DEAR MR. VAN VECHTEN:

I am delighted that the prefaces book interested you. The unspeakable Gael, Knopf, has not yet sent me a copy. My lawsuit against him, for disfiguring the title-page with the portrait of a dog, will be tried next month. In this great cause I expect the support of all authors.

Sincerely yours,
H. L. Mencken

To Ernest Boyd
[OFP]

[*Winter 1917–18*]

Dear Boyd:–

I have written to H. B. Sell, of the Chicago Daily News, suggesting that he make some arrangement with you (paid) for an occasional letter on literary affairs in Britain. His space is infernally crowded, but he may embrace the idea. No such letter (that is, of any sense) is now printed in America. The New York Times used to have one, but no more.

[. . . . .]

The book you mention will be published after the war. It embraces a detailed account of events that these eyes witnessed, and will be, I hope, a contribution to history. At the moment it would have no chance. I am still sweating over my tome on the American language—a superb piece of punditry, shaming the college professors. But you can imagine what a job it is to coordinate the material. I have just rewritten the first half. My further plans are as follows:

First, A Book of Prejudices—a general slaughter of the literary gods in America, already half done.

Next, A Book for Men Only—a critical consideration of la femme. Aphoristic, scandalous.

Then, a short history of the American effort to maintain neutrality in the war, with an analysis of the documents.

And then, for the dim future, a series of small aphoristic [books]: Democracy, War, Puritanism, Sex.[7]

Work enough for five or six years. Meanwhile, the S. S. yields me next to nothing, and I have had to do some newspaper work (for the N. Y. Mail, Chicago Tribune, etc.) to keep the lupus from the portal. We are paying expenses, but no more. The office owes me nearly $2,000 back salary. However, there is still hope.

Wright I have not seen since his collapse, and it is unlikely that I ever shall. He not only did a grave injury to Tridon and Leeds, entirely without excuse; he also failed to show any decent regret. Moreover, I suspect him of thimble-rigging me at a time when he was in

[7] About Mencken's projects, as expressed in this letter: A Book for Men Only became *In Defense of Women* (New York: Philip Goodman Co.; 1918); the other plans do not seem to have been carried out.

great difficulty, and I kept his roof over his head. Altogether, a swine. He is leaving New York, I believe. Don't fool with him. As for Dreiser, he is full of some obscure complaint against me, which I can't understand, and so I don't see him. In brief, I suddenly find myself very lonely in New York. Nathan has neuralgia and is pretty ill.

[. . . . .]

Poor old Tinker was 70 yesterday, and is very ill.[8] He has a cancer in the throat and it looks hopeless. Radium is being used on it. It is inoperable. The old boy still keeps up his spirits, but he has a terrible time ahead of him. Broedel has got the best Johns Hopkins men at work on him, but they can do little.

Do you remember Blankenagel, the flutist? He is just under 31, and has been drafted. He is a professor in Goucher College, but they have put him to work playing piccolo in a regimental band. Meanwhile the army is full of interpreters (with commissions) who still struggle with their habe gehabts.

Yours in Xt.,
H. L. Mencken

[8] Matthew Tinker was a nonplayer member of the old Saturday Night Club.

1918

To Philip Goodman
[EPL]

Baltimore, [*January 1918*]

Dear Goodman:

I announce with profound sorrow the death of Martin Meyerdirck. He left $5,000 to the orphan asylum, and many thousands to other worthy objects.

But I blush for you. What is to be thought of a man who turns the name of Major General Franz Sigel into Segal? Why not go the whole hog and make it Seagull? I was too young, of course, to be present at the banquet in Raine's Hall, when the general was entertained by Humbolt Lodge, but I will remember the evening he was the guest of honor at a Wine Kommers given by the Metzger Liedertafel, with Prof. Dr. Gustav Raabe in the chair. I have it from Fritz Buchsbaum, who had the catering contract, that the assembled bibuli drank 700 bottles of Erbacher—say 3.6 bottles to a man. The general made a speech lasting from 10.05 to nearly 2 A.M. and recounted in detail the whole story of his invasion of the Valley of Virginia, forgetting nothing. At one point he drew out a parchment and read the complete roster of his brigade. Here, however, he hunched a bit. That is, when he came to the Schmidt's, for example, he simply said 39 Schmidts, and didn't read their front names. Two of his staff officers, Oberstleutnant Himmelheber and Oberstabsarzt Gusdorff, were also present. Both grew mellow and shed tears.

But more of this anon. I am sweating on a mss. for a publisher of your name. Maybe you know him: a fellow of matronly habit, an ale drinker. One night lately he drank George Nathan under the table. But does it take any talent to drink George Nathan under the table? I doubt it. I'd like to match him against a real professor, for example, Hermann Schlens.

[*Unsigned*]

◇◇◇◇◇◇◇◇◇◇◇◇◇

To ERNEST BOYD
[OFP]

The Smart Set
34th Street and 8th Ave.
New York
February 14th [*1918*]

DEAR BOYD:–

Let the poems of La Lyster come on. I am under no illusion: you wrote them yourself. Unluckily, it seems to be unlawful to print anything in Gothic without filing a sworn translation with the Postmaster. This bars out her strophes in that harsh tongue. As for French stuff, we buy it in bulk from the Society of French Authors, paying, as I remember it, $25 a year.

The Little Review of this month contains three separate notices of my prefaces: one by Pound, one by la Anderson, and a very short one by someone unknown.[1] Needless to say, I shall watch for your own composition with vast interest. If you mention the typographical errors by Knopf, then be forever damned. Pistols, it appears, thoroughly enraged the righteous. According to Pound, even Orage regards it as immoral.[2] Well, let him wait.

I have finished my book of short essays—some of them no more than 100 words. Goodman, the publisher, wants to give it a bawdy title. It will be followed by a small volume to be called "The Infernal Feminine", or something of the sort. I think Goodman is the man for you.[3] Why not let me approach him? Just what have you?

Yours in Xt.,
H. L. Mencken

---

[1] A review by someone unknown: it was written by Jane Heap. Pound: Ezra Pound.

[2] Alfred R. Orage (1873–1934): an English writer; he contributed to the *New Age* and the *Little Review*.

[3] Mencken had temporarily abandoned Knopf as a publisher, and taken Philip Goodman, who promised larger sales and a more liberal approach. But displeased with Goodman's incompetence, Mencken was to go back to Knopf in July 1918.

Did you get Pearson's with Frank Harris' article on the Comstocks? I read Shaw on the doctors with much joy. Also, the long Harrison article.

What is your correct address, 2 Kildare Place or 25 Kildare St.?

◇◇◇◇◇◇◇◇◇◇◇◇◇◇

To Ernest Boyd
[ofp]

March 9th [1918]

Dear Boyd:–

I can't make out from your letter whether you have Huneker's "Unicorns" or not: you mention only the English edition. If not, let me know of it, and I'll send you a copy. Also, let me know what other books you want. All those on your previous list have been sent save "Visions and Beliefs", by Lady Gregory, and "Nowadays", by Dunsany. The publication of both has been delayed. I'll send them when they come out. Very few new books worth reading are being printed. The current fiction is horrible stuff. For the rest, there are only war books, and not one of them in twenty has any merit or interest. Not a single volume describing the military operations of 1917, simply and accurately, has been published.

My congratulations on your revolt against Moore. You probably feel as much relieved as I do, with Dreiser off my chest. The Greenwich Village radicals are now proposing a public dinner to him on the conclusion of "The 'Genius' " case, if it ever ends. You may be sure that I shall not be present at this convention of frauds. The newspapers will poke fun at it, and do D. a lot of damage. But the man is such a hopeless ass that he falls for any flatterer. Let some preposterous wench come in in a long blue smock, and call him "Master", and he is immediately undone.

I have sent you various papers and magazines, including the first issue of the Liberator, the copy of Pearson's with Frank Harris' article on the Comstocks, and several issues of the Gaelic-American. All these are admitted to the American mails, but whether or not they pass the English censor I don't know. In these days it is hard to make out what the rules are. Here in America, under a law forbidding the sending of magazines containing liquor advertisements into dry states, the Postmaster General has just issued a warning that it is unlawful to "advertise" any intoxicant in the reading matter. Thus a casual reference, in a piece of fiction, to Pilsner, Bass' ale or Chianti, may get us barred from the mails, and cost us $4,000 or $5,000. Such are the delights of life under a Methodist despotism. God knows what the end will be. This month Roosevelt's magazine, the Metropolitan, of which an Englishman is editor, is actually forbidden the mails. It is impossible to understand the rules, and there is no redress. Even a magazine which avoids politics absolutely and never mentions the war is constantly exposed to ignorant and unintelligible assault.

Money is anything but plentiful in my vicinage, despite our avoidance of bankruptcy. I have made a six months contract with the Mail for three articles a week—an eloquent proof of its paucity.[4] It brings in enough to keep me alive, even if all magazine income stops again. Books yield nothing. Knopf reports that he owes me $111. on the preface book. This is about all I'll ever get. The book of little essays will be published by Goodman in a week or so, and I am just finishing the woman book. These, together, will bring in about $175.

I shall see Jones the next time I get to New York, and find out just what he thinks about the French book. If he has any doubts, I can find another and better publisher for it. Also, it should be easy to get an American publisher for the Moore book. The trouble with Jones is that his mind wobbles. He is forever changing it. My relations with him, however, remain friendly.

The Ibsen collection is not actually in the market. Janvier printed that offer in an effort to establish a high price for it.[5] I have subscribed for Ed. Howe's Monthly for you. There is always a laugh in it. This month he has a long article describing his meeting with Nathan and me in New York. I send you all literary magazines and other such curiosities that come this way. Many of them are trivial, but with half of them lost en route, I run to quantity in the hope that a few good ones will get through.

I wish to God you could get out here. The times are difficult, but there are still plenty of openings on the newspapers and magazines, provided one avoids politics. I am working on various tomes to be printed after the war, when publishing conditions are better.

Yours in Xt.,
H. L. Mencken

---

[4] The Mail: The New York *Evening Mail.*
[5] Meredith Janvier (1872–1936): a Baltimore bookseller and local historian.

To Ernest Boyd
[OFP]

[*March 16, 1918*]

Dear Boyd:–

There is a plan on foot here to print a small book in honor of E. W. Howe, the Kansas Aristotle—a festschrift to mark his 50th birthday (he is actually 65).[6] The thing is being arranged in secret, and various illuminati will take a hand. Howe is one of the few genuine originals in the country; you know his stuff. What occurs to me is this: that it would be pleasant to have a few lines from you—the Old World's tribute to the only American philosopher. If you agree, write me a page or so in the form of a letter, saying that you heard of the proposed book in London. The whole thing will be kidding. Any extravagance at Howe's expense will go down. The idea is to accuse him of various crimes, and start off with a bogus biography of him, detailing his amours. But underneath, of course, there will be some soothing flattery for the old boy.

I finished my book on women tonight—33,000 words. There is some good stuff in it, along with much blather. It should be out by May 1st.

In Xt.,
H. L. Mencken

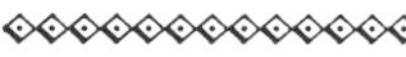

To Burton Rascoe[7]
[UP]

1524 Hollins Street
Baltimore, Md.
March 27th [*1918*]

Dear Rascoe:–

I wish you could see a story that Cabell sent in to the Smart Set a week or so ago—a superb piece of writing.[8] I only hope we can come to terms with him: he deserves five times as much as our cash-drawer can afford. The thing is really almost perfect. He has done nothing better, and very little so good.

---

[6] Edgar Watson Howe (1854–1937): a Kansas editor and writer.
[7] A. Burton Rascoe (1892–1957) was the literary editor of the Chicago *Tribune.*
[8] J. B. Cabell's article: "Some Ladies and Jurgen" (in the *Smart Set* for July 1918).

In the midst of your encomiums I begin to detect a central fact, to wit, that Cabell mirrors the disdain of a defeated aristocracy for the rising mob. He is the only articulate Southerner who is a gentleman by Southern standards: all the rest are cads. Thus one may account for his "decadence" in the midst of a crude and Methodist society. I shall pursue the point in a book I am doing for the autumn.[9] In this book I shall argue that most of the best blood in the South is now in the niggers. But more of this anon.

I'm sorry you made such a short visit and that I had Altberger on my hands. He is a noble old buck, but he has no interest in books, and not much in music. At the moment I am entertaining a mild dose of la grippe, acquired in New York. It fills me with depression.

You should get my damn book shortly.[1] The woman book is also finished.

Yours in Xt.,
M.

To ERNEST BOYD
[OFP]

April 20th [*1918*]

DEAR BOYD:–

Your letters of March 13, March 25 and April 8 have arrived within three days. To your inquiries first:

1. I sent you "I, Mary MacLane", the new book by the Buttess,[2] about the time I forwarded Macy's book on American literature.[3] If it doesn't reach you, let me know. Since then I have sent you my "Damn" book and various volumes by the more gaudy poets, and Nathan has sent you his little book of sketches.[4] Also, various papers, pamphlets, etc. I send six in the hope that two or three will survive the Hun.

2. Evans' "My Own People" has not yet arrived. I'll be delighted to have it. The small Stephens book is here, and also the two Corkery

---

[9] The proposed book: *Prejudices: First Series* (New York: Alfred A. Knopf; 1919).
[1] My damn book: *Damn! A Book of Calumny* (New York: Philip Goodman Co.; 1918).
[2] The Buttess: Mary MacLane, the author of the book, was from Butte; see *Prejudices: First Series.*
[3] Macy's book: *The Spirit of American Literature* (New York: Boni and Liveright; 1918).
[4] G. J. Nathan's book: *A Book Without a Title* (New York: Philip Goodman Co.; 1918).

books.[5] My best thanks. Please don't think of an eye for an eye in such times. I dispatch a lot of stuff simply because it reaches me for review. The English Review comes in regularly.

3. The Outposts book would probably be hopeless for the present. An amendment to the Espionage Act makes all discussion of American culture impossible. I have even had to rewrite parts of my book on women, surely a harmless piece of fooling. And yet a few chance phrases in it, questioning universal manhood suffrage, would have exposed both me and the publisher to 20 years imprisonment. The law is astoundingly drastic; nothing like it exists in England.

4. I don't know about Joyce's "Exiles". I must inquire of Huebsch.

5. Dreiser's "The Hand of the Potter" is not published. It has been . . . refused, and I am glad of it; the thing is really a stupid piece of pornography, and would hurt D. a lot. My fear is that Boni & Liveright or some other such firm will do it for the sake of the scandal, and so drink the old ass's blood. He is doing little writing, but devotes himself largely to the stud. I haven't seen him for six months, but hear from him indirectly. His case in the matter of "The 'Genius' " is still held sub judice.

6. What other books do you crave? I send you literary announcements from time to time. If you see anything that invites, let me know.

7. Unluckily, I haven't got [Repshin's?] "What Never Happened". I'll try to graft a copy.

Life over here is anything but a bed of roses. The cost of everything is gigantic; even railroad tickets are taxed. A decent meal in New York costs $2. Meanwhile, the magazine business gets more and more precarious. What the end will be God knoweth. A new bill in Congress proposes to draft men up to 45. I may yet appear as a cannoneer. My young brother has been rejected again—the third time—but is still liable to a new call. The draft has played hell with the bozart. All the young authors are drilling, and so there is a great scarcity of decent stuff. Of late we have had to buy English stuff through Pinker—among other things, a couple of Stephens sketches and a capital comic piece by Brighouse, otherwise a fifth-rater. John McClure is called up, and has stopped writing.[6]

The "Damn" book is getting furious notices; even some of my

---

[5] The Stephens book: *Reincarnations,* by James Stephens (London: Macmillan and Co., Ltd.; 1918). The two Corkery books: *A Munster Twilight* and *The Threshold of Quiet* (Dublin: The Talbot Press, Ltd.; 1917?).

[6] John McClure was an obscure *Smart Set* poet.

steady constituents are shocked by it. Imagine such hollow platitudes shocking anyone! Meanwhile, the first edition (1,000 copies, divided bogusly into Second Printing and Third Printing) is exhausted, and it is to go back to press. I shall change the name to "A Book of Calumny". "Damn" is too smart-alecky. Nathan and Goodman were hot for it, and I weakly let them have their way. But no more. You have the first edition—without any Second Printing gabble on the title page.

The Saturday Night Club still murders Mozart, but I begin to fear that its days are numbered.[7] One member, Hemberger, is an enemy alien, and as a result there is a great deal of watching, spying, solemn reporting, etc. The fact that another member is an Englishman, and that two more, Colston and Blankenagel, are in uniform, counts for nothing. The whole country is infested by volunteer secret agents, most of them asses. Some of their performances are amazing. The Floreston club is dead beyond recall.[8]

Not much news from Ireland is printed here. At the moment it is difficult to make out what has been done in the conscription matter. Nor is there any information as to the food situation. I surely hope there is food, if not drink. Over here there is still plenty to eat, but next Autumn will probably see some scarcity. I drink all I can hold while the going is good. The breweries will be shut down before the end of the year. I have laid in enough wine to last me 18 months. The California variety is still cheap.

My mother and sister offer their best regards to Mrs. Boyd. The bowl she presented to the house is in constant use. My chaplain, Dr. Pishposh, is on his knees daily in your interest. I often wonder how long he will survive prohibition.

Yours in Xt.,
H. L. Mencken

To Burton Rascoe
[UP]

1524 Hollins Street
Baltimore, Md.
May 15th [*1918*]

Dear Rascoe:–

The laryngitis has departed, and I am so far recovered that I

[7] The Saturday Night Club: a Baltimore club of amateur musicians, of which Mencken was a member. It is now extinct.
[8] The Floreston Club: a club for musicians and music-lovers.

have resumed work on "The American Language", a fat, formidable tome, certain to get me an S.T.D. from the North Carolina Baptist University. The Tapp book I have read: a stupendous piece of reasoning.[9] Old Ed. Howe used to carry a paid advertisement of it in his Monthly. It has had a large circulation in the hydrocele and nocturnal emissions belt. The other I have never heard of. This reminds me that I have a Bible for you if you want it. I stole it from the Astor Hotel. During the past ten years I have stolen 75 Bibles, perhaps the national record.

Cabell once sent me his witches article. It is excellent stuff. When is his book of essays to be printed?[1] I think it will give me a good chance to perform a piece on him. Lately I have been re-reading "The Rivet in Grandfather's Neck". What a slick, intriguing piece of writing! Nobody is doing any better.

I announce my arrival in Chicago, to lecture at Hull House on Maeterlinck, Sept. 1, 1918.

Yours in Xt.,
Mencken

To LOUIS UNTERMEYER
[OFP]

1524 Hollins Street
Baltimore, Md.
May 20th [*1918*]

DEAR LOUIS:–

Your spring line is so tasty that I can't choose, and so I am holding four samples for discussion with our Mr. Nathan. I dessay we will order at least two. If we do, we'll send them to John McClure to be trimmed.

Your piece on Pound is capital:[2] I have a feeling that you are right about him, and about Lindsay too. As for Aiken, I can't go his late stuff. Masters I have already buried. The doctrine that he is a Great Thinker has finished him, as it is finishing Dreiser and Gov. Whitman.

Maryland has just passed a law forbidding the transportation of

---

[9] The Tapp book: Sidney C. Tapp's *Sex, the Key to the Bible* (Kansas City, Mo.: The author; 1918).

[1] Cabell's book: *Beyond Life* (New York: R. M. McBride & Co.; 1919).

[2] Pound: Ezra Pound.

working girls per auto for natural purposes. A good second-hand Studebaker is for sale.

Yours in Xt.,
M.

"Betrayal" is now not lewd enough.

◇◇◇◇◇◇◇◇◇◇◇◇◇◇

To THEODORE DREISER
[UP]

1524 Hollins Street
Baltimore, Md.
July 16th [*1918*]

DEAR DREISER:–

You and I snort over it, and wallow generally in such florid fancies, but a fat woman with diabetes—the normal magazine reader—would stop her subscription. Hence my regrets.[3] If I had the gift of prayer I'd have you put to a novel with a Methodist as the central character: suave, sneaking stuff, turning him inside out. What has become of "The Bulwark"? Done as you can do it, it would be worth 100 burlesques. The attack must be made by indirection.

At least eight kind friends supplied me with prompt reports of the juridic evasion. After all, it didn't surprise me. The courts are simply afraid to be decent; the time has long passed for that sort of thing. What is the next move? If I understand the law of contract, "The 'Genius' " now reverts to you. Who is to do "The Bulwark"?

These are lovely days for a man with a taste for the ironical. The bondholders of the Mail, taking the paper back but NOT returning the money they got for it, now ban me on the ground that my stuff is immoral. My contract, running to Sept. 11th, is probably not worth a cent. They already hold up my money, honestly earned. I stand to lose about $500. It would cost twice as much to resist.[4] My pastor counsels prayer.

In Xt.,
M.

---

[3] The rejected Dreiser piece was "The Court of Progress".

[4] Mencken had signed a six-month contract with the New York *Evening Mail* for a series of three weekly articles, but in July 1918 the publisher, Edward A. Rumely, was arrested and jailed by federal agents on the charge of having received financial aid from the Wilhelmstrasse. Although he was innocent, Mencken was more or less involved in the scandal, and the new publisher broke his contract. Mencken threatened to sue, then compromised for a $250 settlement on a $450 debt. The next year, the newspaper went down.

[*In early 1917 Dreiser had sued Lane's to force them to release* The "Genius"; *the next year, the case was considered by the Appellate Division, but the court declared itself incompetent to render advisory opinions as to the impropriety of the book. Liveright reissued the book in 1923.*]

◇◇◇◇◇◇◇◇◇◇◇◇◇◇

To Ernest Boyd
[OFP]

1524 Hollins Street
Baltimore, Md.
July 23rd [1918]

Dear Boyd:–

If you have a copy of the photograph of Solomons' painting, let me have it for my gallery of sages. In the reproduction your beard seems to be made of concrete.

I daresay you have heard of the Evening Mail débâcle. Rumely, who ran the paper, is jailed on a charge of taking money from the Wilhelmstrasse. Whether or not he did it I don't know. My notion is that, if he did at all, it was only after his own money had become exhausted. He started out with a good deal, all inherited.

My own connection with the paper was slight, and fortunately of such a character that I had nothing to do with Rumely and his financing. The articles I did were not started until after the U. S. had got into the war, and had no relation to the war whatsoever. I was induced to do them, not by Rumely, but by Cullen, an old acquaintance here in Baltimore. Cullen is still on the job under the new management. This management nows tries to wriggle out of the contract with me to save the expense, but I am in hopes of getting my money. Altogether, a sweet-smelling episode. I was in New York when R. was taken, and had reporters and sleuths on my trail for four days. But this sort of thing is now usual. There must be at least 100,000 detectives at work in the United States. I was actually investigated on account of my "Damn" book. Scarcely a month goes by that some one doesn't complain about one of my book reviews.

I hear that conscription will be extended to us old bucks in a month or two. Before we depart this life I may have the felicity of assisting in the policing of Ireland. If duty ever calls upon me to arrest you I promise to do it politely.

Max B. is quite well again.[5] The tumor in his jaw turned out to be benign, but the surgeons chopped out a great cutlet and took three teeth. He is still sore, but can eat and drink once more. He lost about 20 pounds.

Yours in Xt.,
H. L. Mencken

To PHILIP GOODMAN
[EPL]

Baltimore, Md.
[*August, 1918*]

DEAR GOODMAN:

I have put Schultheiss' house in the hands of Adolf Klauenberg, secretary of the Hesse-Darmstradt Bauverein. Adolf is a capital man for such jobs. He visits 25 or 30 saloons every day, and hears all the new gossip instantly. The minute an engagement is rumored, he goes to see the bridegroom-elect, rents him a house, sells him the furniture on instalments, puts him up for membership in the Knights of Pythias ($500 in case of death; $15 a week in illness, up to 80 weeks), and gives him the name of Mrs. Hempel, the best midwife in town. Adolf deals in real estate, mortgages, insurance in all its forms, horses and wagons, Fords, fishing shores, pianos (including the automatic), baby carriages, home-made sauerkraut, and diamonds. His wife Berta, geb. Schneider, keeps his books, and is always throwing out hints about the amount he makes. It may be true or it may be false, but this I know: that he has $8,000 drawing 6 percent. in the Hesse-Darmstadt, and owns 7 houses in a row back of Patterson Park. And from what beginnings! Ten years ago Adolf was driving a wagon for Knefely, the cheese man. How he studied double entry bookkeeping under Old Man Kurtz, cashier of the Burghardt Brewery, and became a master of Bauverein finance—this is a story that would dim your eyes. He never takes a drink except on business, and gave up smoking a year ago. His father-in-law, Anton Stisser, opposed his marriage to Berta, but is now very proud of him.

I know of no man more useful to know. Say your roof leaks, and the tinner, collecting $17, only makes it worse. Well, you call up Adolf, and in an hour he is on the scene with an expert roofer from Elberfeld,

[5] Max B.: Max Broedel.

a man trained at the Hochschule there. Result: you pay $9, Adolf takes half—and your roof is tight. Or suppose you are giving a party, and want a reliable woman to make the Kartoffelklöse, wash the dishes, and otherwise help in the kitchen. Just send for Adolf, and he finds her, instructs her and guarantees her. Again, suppose you want to give your wife a diamond ring, and baulk at Castleberg's prices. Well, Adolf can get the precise ring from Hugo Wattenscheidt, the wholesaler, at 35% discount. Or suppose you buy a house, and then find that the title is shady, due to the carelessness of that shyster, Rechtanswalt Fischer. Well, Adolf quietly unloads it for you on a greenhorn who never heard of land records. Or suppose you have $1,000 loose and want to get it to work. Send for Adolf: he has mortgages on everything from a fish-stand in Belair Market to the new Gemeindehaus of the St. Mattias congregation. Altogether, a man of merit. Tell Schultheiss to be at ease. He will get his $6800—and Adolf will get a damned sight more than $20.

I remember Charlie very well. Ask him if he recalls the way we boys used to slip bullfrogs into his milkcans while he was taking something for his dyspepsia in Freund's family liquor store.

M.

To BURTON RASCOE
[UP]

1524 Hollins Street
Baltimore, Md.
August 9th [*1918*]

DEAR RASCOE:–

I surely hope you send me your stuff hereafter. The specimens are very well done.

Don't snort and brag about 102. It has been 105.4 here—the highest official temperature since the Fall of Babylon. My hide is red and blistery all over, and my work has gone to pot. The women book will be printed shortly, if ever the printers get the proofs corrected. The American Language will probably go over until after the war. As a bachelor, I am eligible under the new draft, and may soon be toting a gun. There will be few worse soldiers.

I don't envy you your novelists' job. But perhaps their cavortings are for the best. Remember this: that a hot slating always attracts more attention than praise.

Yours in Xt.,
H. L. M.

To Louis Untermeyer
[OFP]

1524 Hollins Street
Baltimore, Md.
August 21st [*1918*]

Dear Louis:–

Your suspicion of the worst is correct. The editorials in the New York Tribune have at last convinced me, and I am out for Methodism, vice control and the little nations. After all, this is no time for a patriotic man to be pulling against the revelation of God. Let Kremburg howl: I know that my Redeemer liveth.

If you die for democracy then I shall tear up the Old Testament. Your duty is plain: get into the Q.M. department, and then draft me as your clerk. You can imagine what chance I have down here, with all the patrioteers on my trail. I already practise the goose-step in secret.

Meanwhile, my best thanks for the kind word. I fear you are right about Pound.[6] He has gone the Dreiser route. Puritan pressure has converted him into a mere bellower. There is a lesson in this for all of us.

Yours in Sso. Corde Jesu,*
M.

* Ben Huebsch knows what this means.

To Fielding Hudson Garrison[7]
[PT]

Baltimore, August 30th, 1918

Dear Col. Garrison:

Your note followed me to New York and back again, and now

[6] Pound: Ezra Pound.

[7] Fielding Hudson Garrison (1870–1935) was a surgeon and a lieutenant-colonel in the army; he then became assistant librarian at the Surgeon General's Office, in Washington, D. C.; he edited the *Index Medicus.* Mencken, who was not well, and hence did not want to be drafted, had asked him for a job on the Medical History Board, and it seems that Garrison had refused to help him.

greets me in the midst of hay fever, with asthma by night and an astoundingly severe malaise by day. Always there is a new cure. This year it is Aestivin (Schieffelin), apparently an attempt to make a chemical antidote to the pollen-proteid toxin. One drops it in the eye, or has it dropped by one's wife. Result: nothing. It was sent to me with a humane letter by a man I don't know at all: J. G. Phelps Stokes, the millionaire Socialist, husband of Rose Pastor Stokes, lately jailed. Such an attention from a Socialist touched me. But I still have pollinosis.

One phrase in your letter is a straw thrust in my eye, to wit, "one of divided allegiance". Here you make an everyday mistake. That is, you assume that every man who stood against the United States favoring England did so out of "loyalty" to Germany. Nothing could be more erroneous. If I was "loyal" to Germany, why didn't I stay there in February, 1917, instead of coming back to the United States to face inevitable difficulties? My reason was plain. I had presented my views and they had been rejected. My sole remaining course, consistent with self-respect, was to submit to the decision and to accept its burdens. To this day I have never sought to change it, nor have I uttered a single word of protest, in public or in private, against its consequences.

The fact is that my "loyalty" to Germany, as a state or a nation, is absolutely nil. I haven't a single living relative there; I haven't even a friend there. It would do me no good whatsoever if the Germans conquered all Europe; it would do me a lot of damage if they beat the United States. But I believe I was right when I argued that unfairness to them was discreditable and dangerous to this country, and I am glad I did it. True enough, it doesn't pay to be honest in that way, but it at least caresses a man's vanity.

I surely hope we meet soon for a talk. For one thing, there are things to tell you about the Harden matter. As for the Medical History business, let it go behind the clock! There can be no doubt whatever that my notion to do something I could do creditably was corrupted by a notion of doing something pleasant. Now I am quite indifferent as to what I am put to, if anything. The press-agent jobs are not for me. I know too many of the bounders who now flourish in them.

Sincerely yours,
H. L. Mencken

(1918)

To GAMALIEL BRADFORD
[OFP]

The Smart Set
25 West 45th Street
New York
[After October 17, 1918]

DEAR MR. BRADFORD:

The high assurance of the *Smart Set* is largely artificial. I am myself the most complete skeptic since Pontius Pilate, and Nathan is a cynic who believes only in the incredible. But the American people crave positive affirmations, and so we give them to 'em. If conscience rebels then we salve it by answering that we at least do not speak for what everybody already believes. It is good fun, and it does no harm.

How you can believe in the Vice Societies I can't imagine. I am certainly in no rage against them, but they seem to me to be vulgar and even dirty, as, say, a Methodist revival is vulgar and dirty. If such virtue is approved by the Lord God Almighty, then the Lord God Almighty is a bounder, which, as Euclid says, leads to absurdity. The proof of a philosophy lies in the philosopher. What is the effect of making men good in the American sense? Answer: Kansas. Who would not prefer the society of a few amiable kidnappers, yeggmen and Follies girls?

What I had in mind was that you might be tempted to do some fiction now and then. In that department we have few prejudices. Our concern is chiefly with manner. A good piece of writing—and we swallow the doctrine. In poetry we are against all the rebels, chiefly because rebellion is now fashionable.

Your letter was forwarded to me from Baltimore. I'll be delighted to have the book, which is probably there now. I return tomorrow.

Your "Union Portraits" is a book I admire very greatly, and often read. It is anti-sentimental. It tries to tell the truth.

[Sincerely yours,]
H. L. Mencken

◇◇◇◇◇◇◇◇◇◇◇◇◇

To ELLERY SEDGWICK
[OFP]

H. L. Mencken
1524 Hollins St.
Baltimore
October 18th [*1918*]

DEAR SEDGWICK:–

You are too late with your Baltimore poem. The prize was won by an old friend of mine, and some of us celebrated the victory the other night. Casualties: 75 bottles of Pilsner, smuggled via Holland.

I am beginning today my last week of regular journalism. After Saturday I'll still be a member of The Baltimore Sun staff, but under no obligation to produce any definite amount of copy. This arrangement will give me, I hope, my long-delayed chance to enrich and embellish the beautiful letters of this grand and glorious république. I'd have quit a year ago if it had not been for the war. But the war is now in its last stages, and it is no longer good fun to lambast and make game of the poor English. I doubt that there will be any first-rate fighting after Christmas, by Easter the peace commissioners will be sitting in Lucerne.

Once it is over, I'll be glad to write for you, if you dare me, a frank statement of the experiences and sensations of an American of German blood, facing for a year or more the ecstatic Germanophobia of the rest of the population. It has been a curious time and I think it has changed me a lot.

Do you ever get to New York? Under my new schedule I'll be there one week in every month.

Here's hoping your visit to the woods made a new man of you.

Yours,
M.

◇◇◇◇◇◇◇◇◇◇◇◇◇

To CARL VAN VECHTEN
[YU-MS]

The Smart Set
25 West 45th Street
New York
[*Postmark: November 11, 1918*]

DEAR VAN VECHTEN:

If it were not for a depressing overstock of stories, poems, essays, dithyrambs, etc., about death, I'd take this at once. Something less mortuary, in God's name! Our safes, bins, vats, etc., are like morgues, etc.

Yours in Xt.,
H. L. Mencken

P.S.—I am reviewing "The Merry-Go-Round" with a bladder. The "Interrupted Conversation" is capital.[8]

To CARL VAN VECHTEN
[YU]

The Smart Set
25 West 45th Street
New York
November 15, 1918

DEAR VAN VECHTEN:

Several ideas for likely articles are in my mind and it occurs to me that they may possibly interest you. One is a serio-comic treatise on the grotesque amours of musicians and especially of singers—unprecedented polygamies, amazing marriages between eminent divas and obscure barbers, awe-inspiring carnalities, etc. There must be an enormous mass of material in the literature which you seem to know so well. If this appeals to you, you will have both an article for The Smart Set and a chapter for your next book.

Another piece that occurs to me is one dealing with ludicrous accidents of the operatic stage. I once saw a tenor in "Il Trovatore" fall out of the tower, bringing the whole structure down with him. He struck the soprano a glancing blow, inflicting a comminuted fracture of the right radial esophagus. The poor woman lost thirty-eight days of work. I also once witnessed a performance of "Das Rheingold" in which every member of the cast was tight. Many other such episodes must be stored in your mind. Let me know if either of these things inflames you. Our ideal length is about 4,000 words. Perhaps you have other ideas of the same sort—that is, in the line of your discourses of music and food, and the infinite lingering of archaic singers.

Sincerely yours,
H. L. Mencken

---

[8] About this letter, Carl Van Vechten writes: "It refers to a one-act play, never played or published, now at the New York Public Library."

(1918)

◇◇◇◇◇◇◇◇◇◇◇◇◇

To GEORGE STERLING[9]
[PT]

1524 Hollins St.
Baltimore
November 20th [*1918*]

DEAR MR. STERLING:–

London's widow I don't know, though I have talked to her by telephone. Her book on their Hawaiian affairs was a silly thing—written like a high-school girl's essay on the subconscious. He and she appear to have carried on love-making in moving-picture terms. I surely hope you manage to kill the love-letters. At the age of 24 I wrote one that brought an indignant husband on to my hands and damn nigh saddled me with his singularly idiotic wife. This lesson soaked in.

What is to be done about Phelps God knows. He is an amiable old boy and I hate to tackle him with all arms. I have written a few paragraphs of kidding. I doubt he does much damage. Even such fellows as Hackett and Bourne gag at him. After all, there must be some ass to write books for women school-teachers, and so mellow their sad lives.

Why don't you do some prose? The war has filled the country with mushy, hypocritical snuffling. Moralizing becomes a universal curse. I think that there will be a reaction, and that a few books will be enough to bring it on.

Yours in Xt.,
[*Unsigned*]

◇◇◇◇◇◇◇◇◇◇◇◇◇

To ERNEST BOYD
[OFP]

H. L. Mencken
1524 Hollins St.
Baltimore
December 20th [*1918*]

DEAR BOYD:–

[. . . . .]

---

[9] George Sterling (1869–1926): the San Francisco poet, disciple of Ambrose Bierce. He committed suicide in 1926 in a fit of alcoholic depression.

What happened to the Sinclair book God knows.[1] It left me whole. By this mail I am sending you a copy of a pamphlet by Stuart Sherman, proving that Methodism is official in America, and that anyone who dissents is hired by Hohenzollern. It is still forbidden to discuss this stimulating doctrine frankly, but I shall take at least a preliminary hack at it next month.

[. . . . .]

No reliable news from Ireland ever reaches us. The public, in fact, shows very little interest in the peace gossip. The war passes from the first pages. The troops getting home are hardly noticed. It is a curious phenomenon.

Moral is still held up, but I expect a production before February.[2] The American Language will be a formidable tome at $3.50, printed from type and probably numbered. The indexes still fatigue me. I'd tackle the philosophical treatise on democratic ideals at once, but most of my notes are out of my hands and I can't get hold of them until later on.[3]

Knopf is heated up to a very high view of your virtues.

Yours in Xt.,
H. L. Mencken

---

[1] The Sinclair book: possibly *The Profits of Religion* (Pasadena, Cal.: The author; 1918), by Upton Sinclair.

[2] *Moral:* the play by Ludwig Thoma, that Mencken and Nathan had translated and prepared for production in the U. S. A. A translation had already been published in America (New York: Alfred A. Knopf; 1916).

[3] The philosophical treatise: *Notes on Democracy,* long planned by Mencken, but not published before 1926 (New York: Alfred A. Knopf).

1919

To Gamaliel Bradford[1]
[ofp]

H. L. Mencken
1524 Hollins St.
Baltimore
January 17th [1919]

Dear Mr. Bradford:–

Thanks very much for your letter. It finds me ill, but gives me a lift toward recovery. The truth is that the business of writing the book turned out, in the end, to be fit for Hercules. I spent three weeks on the List of Words and Phrases, and came near murdering two stenographers, both virtuous and Christian girls, but utter damned fools. What with that labor and a lot of routine editorial work I closed the year in a state of collapse, and have been on a strict diet (not to mention the water-wagon) ever since. No more philology! My next book will be on politics, which requires no investigation.

It seems to me that you are better off, as a writer and as an American, in a small town than you'd be in New York. I thoroughly detest New York, though I have to go there very often. My home is, and always will be in Baltimore, where there is at least a civilized minority and the friends of today remain the friends of tomorrow. Have you ever noticed that no American writer of any consequence lives in Manhattan. Dreiser tried it (after years in the Bronx), but finally fled to California. Some time ago I visited Hergesheimer for a day in West Chester, Pa. A charming small town, much like the old county towns of

[1] Gamaliel Bradford (1863–1932), author and biographer.

Maryland. The people seemed friendly and decent. In New York they appear to be bounders. Some time before that, with Hergesheimer, I had been in Richmond to see Cabell. Another sensible man: he visits New York but once a year. Even Chicago is far better, as Boston used to be.

When is your book to be issued? [2] Canby was here a few weeks ago and said he expected to send it to me in ten days, but it has not appeared. In my review, I want to point out how you invented the Lytton Strachey scheme long before Strachey had ever heard of it.

Unable to do any work, I have been nosing around Washington, renewing old newspaper and political acquaintanceships. The net impression I get is that Balfour and company have swindled poor Hughes abominably, and that the treaties will have a hard time of it in the Senate. If they are ratified, then we had better form a Dominion at once, and apply for the same terms given to the Irish.

Thanks again. I am delighted that you liked the book. It is standing in type. I am awaiting the philological attack before letting Knopf cast the plates.

Sincerely yours,
H. L. Mencken

To ERNEST BOYD
[OFP]

H. L. Mencken
1524 Hollins St.
Baltimore
January 18th [1919]

DEAR BOYD:–

The Talbot Press scheme is a good one. Once things get back to normal over here there will be an outpouring of books, and some of them will be worth doing in England. I'll tackle Knopf on the subject when I see him again. He is doing well with Hergesheimer's novel, "Java Head". My American Language is corrected and indexed at last, and a copy should reach you soon after March 1st. Never again! Such professorial jobs are not for me.

My next tome now begins to get itself organized. It will be called

[2] Your book: *Portraits of American Women* (Boston and New York: Houghton Mifflin Co.; 1919).

"The National Letters", but it will cover a pretty wide ground.[3] On the heels of it will come "On Democracy"—a somewhat elaborate statement of democratic ideals and practises, defending them against the cynicism now prevailing.

The bibuli are crushed by the sudden triumph of prohibition.[4] All is lost, including honor. But I have enough good whiskey, fair wine and prime beer secreted to last me two solid years—and by then I hope to be far from these Wesleyan scenes. I sold my motor-car and invested the proceeds in alcohol.

Another great crusade is already under way. It is against copulation. A government bureau has been established to spread the news that the practise is not necessary to health—a heresy hitherto prevalent. Some of the literature is superb—I'll send you specimens. In the Middle West there is also a growing movement against tobacco. In a few years you will see a republic that is chemically pure. Pray for the day.

The literary news all belongs to buffoonery. Dreiser is trying to organize a society to save the national letters from the Baptists. George Nathan went to the first meeting, and came back almost a Baptist. The works of Joyce Kilmer, in prose and verse, have been printed in two stately volumes, with a preface hailing him as a genius.

I have sent you "Java Head" and Willa Cather's new novel. Also various pamphlets.

My family begs to be remembered. My brother is due here tomorrow to have his tonsils cut out. I'll have to hold his hand while the chirurgeons lay on. Influenza is again raging.

Yours in Xt.,
H. L. Mencken

To THEODORE DREISER
[UP]

H. L. Mencken
1524 Hollins St.
Baltimore
February 1st [*1919*]

DEAR DREISER:–

1. I have an impression that the Nouvelle Revue Française is a

---

[3] The National Letters: *Prejudices: First Series.*

[4] The 36th State, Nebraska, had just ratified the 18th Amendment and Prohibition thus became effective on January 16, 1920.

respectable magazine, somewhat on the order of the New English Review. But I am uncertain, and am asking Nathan to let you know. On general principles, I think you should embrace every opportunity to get into French. In this case, you don't risk much. "The Financier", as a piece of property, is worth far less than any other of your novels. If I were in your place, I'd let Gallimard have it, and then use its appearance as a means of planting "Sister Carrie", "Jennie Gerhardt" and "The Titan". To be translated at all is a great benefit.

2. "The Orf'cer Boy" is being set as a one-act opera by the Anglo-American composer, Emil Hugendubel. Beware of the Copyright Act!

3. To prove my absolute disinterestedness, I offer you one of those sanitary indoor closets entirely free of charge, if only you will agree to use it. It pains me to think of you going out into the yard in cold weather.

4. A man named Keating—George T.—has been writing to me. I had to be polite to him because our backer, Crowe, is under obligation to him. He hints that he had some sort of transaction or contact with you, apparently in the matter of "The 'Genius'". He seems to be wealthy. His aim seems to be to get your autograph. I have advised him that you and I are not on speaking terms, and that I can't help him.

5. Why in hell don't you move out of New York, settled down in some small town, and finish "The Bulwark"? In brief, get away from visible America. My own scheme is to move to Munich as soon as I can shake off my obligations. I have five or six books to write, wholly unlike anything I have yet done. Trying to write them while in active contact with American life would be like trying to read in a nail-factory.

In nomine Domini
M.

◇◇◇◇◇◇◇◇◇◇◇◇◇◇

To Ernest Boyd
[OFP]

H. L. Mencken
1524 Hollins St.
Baltimore
February 3rd [1919]

Dear Boyd:–

Your letter of December 16th got in this morning. A record passage, even for war-time: 49 days. The three Irish books reached me a month ago, and I wrote to you about them at the time. My best thanks for them. For some unintelligible reason, Follett's sophomoric platitudes seem to be on the black-list. This is twice that he has been held up. Perhaps the censor mistakes him for some Sinn Feiner named Follett. If so, it is a good joke. I have sent the Smart Set to you personally every month. Why it has not arrived, God knows. I am having the office send you all the back numbers. The sacred egoism pamphlet is impossible on this side at the moment. A publisher who did it would be exposed to such infernal annoyance, even supposing him to escape jail, that he'd be a maniac to attempt it. You may think it impossible, but it is a literal fact that the suppression of opinion on this side goes much further than in England, or even than in Ireland. The full story would stagger you. What is more, the existing laws, under one pretext or another, will probably remain in force. Free speech is absolutely abolished in America. It is worth a man's liberty to go counter to official opinion in the slightest detail. He is not only exposed to the direct accusation that he has a fee from the Hohenzollern in his pocket; much more importantly he stands a chance of having his publication barred from the mails (and thus ruined) on some obscure pretext, the exact nature of which he never learns. It has been decided time and again that the Postoffice need not tell a publisher *why* he is thus mauled. He gets no hearing, is not formally notified, and never even finds out just what he is accused of. In the case of The Nation no open accusation was ever made: the paper was simply barred from the mails. It was only by dint of great effort, and as a special act of grace, that Villard was finally informed that he had offended by sneering at Gompers, the late associate of the McNamara brothers.[5] Gompers, as a government press-agent, was sacred. I often think that the impatience with Irish aspirations now visible over here has some ground in these facts. When an American reads that Irishmen in opposition to the government are allowed to hold meetings, to organize a parliament and to issue statements of their case he wonders what in hell they are complaining of. In the United States all these things would be put down instantly. Moreover, the American reads that actual conspirators against the government in Ireland are given no more than a few years in prison, and then usually released long before their terms expire. In America the standard sentence for the most academic opposition runs from 10 to 20 years, and not a single prisoner

[5] Oswald Garrison Villard (1872–1949), editor and owner of the *Nation*.

has ever been released. Public opinion is strongly in favor of these heavy sentences. The only objection that I have heard of comes from small groups of Bolsheviki of the college professor type. To take a specific example: the great majority of Socialists approve the jailing of Debs, though even to such biliously anti-Socialist eyes as mine it appears absurd to call his platitudes treasonable. He appears to be merely a silly fellow, a professional martyr—the messiah complex. His case is now before the Supreme Court, but no sane man believes that he will be set free.

I have already sent you two copies of the Sherman pamphlet, and am sending another by this mail. Why it should be held up I can't imagine. It is a government publication, printed at the Government Printing Office, and bearing the specific imprimatur of Creel and the Secretaries of State, War and the Navy. It seems useless to send the Follett book again. The New Age has not yet reached me. I think it has been barred from the United States for some time: at all events, no dealer has ever been able to get a copy. I have received several clippings from it from Pound.

Black told me of his fellow lieutenant and showed me a photograph of him. A challenging face, by the gods! Black printed an article on Dunsany, with some mention of you, a week ago. He told me in advance that he would send you several copies. Marion has been transferred to Brest—a probable indication of an early return. It appears by her letters that I am a loose liver.

My present plan is to sail for Europe about August 15th, if I can get a passport and the price of passage is not too high. This will enable me to escape hay-fever. I am never able to work during September and October, and so I hope, in future, to cross the ocean every year, covering that time. Let us set aside a full week for a conference. All I ask is 10 gallons of beer a day. Are you still forbidden to go to London without special permission? If that rule remains in force, I'll come to Ireland. My book languishes. It is difficult to determine just how to write it. The supply of Michelob is about exhausted, but the Piel's dunkles still holds out. It is excellent. I have laid in 150 bottles against the coming drought.

The Saturday night club continues to flourish; we had 16 at table last Saturday. So with the dinner club: we never miss a dinner. At all meetings of both clubs you are commemorated in a ritualistic singing of "The Shite Hawk", followed by a libation to your spirit. The Saturday club will be paralyzed by prohibition, but the dinner club has laid in enough alcohol to last two years. However, even the former has hope of an illicit supply.

My apologies for this dreiserian bull. But you seemed to be under a misapprehension regarding publishing conditions here.

My family begs to be remembered to Mrs. Boyd.

Yours in Xt.,
H. L. Mencken

To THEODORE DREISER
[UP]

[*On the 3rd of February, Dreiser had reassured Mencken, who thought that he was not working; "it is your Dreiser complex", he wrote.*]

H. L. Mencken
1524 Hollins St.
Baltimore
February 4th [1919]

DEAR DREISER:–

1. I get the notion that I gave you the notion that I have the notion that you have been loafing. Nothing could be more inaccurate. I know very well that you have been sweating blood. But it so happens that "The Bulwark" sticks in my mind, and so I am eager to see it on paper. The "Twelve Men" book, if I understand the plan of it, is an excellent idea. What is more, it lies exactly under your hand—you can do it very effectively. All the other schemes are interesting too, save the publication of "The Hand of the Potter". As you know, I believe it will do you damage and make your position very difficult. Following a clean victory over the Comstocks in "The 'Genius'" matter, it would have been safe enough. But after failing to stop them, it will only give them (and all their friends on the newspapers) the precise chance they look for. In brief, publication of it will be a docile baring of the neck—highly delightful to the moral mind. They will not stop at mere accusations of polluting the innocent. They will seize on the perversion, roll it on the tongue, and quickly get you into training as the American Oscar Wilde. And against that there is no defense. I am opposed to hopeless fights. They not only injure a man; they make him ridiculous.

2. Don't get the notion that I give my imprimatur to Baldwin. He simply came to me as many other people come, and I listened to him for a couple of hours. So far he has done absolutely nothing worth reading. His proposal to write about you without having read your novels is so lovely that I shall discourse on it later on. Tell him to go buy your books. And hold all his letters. If any unpleasantness follows I may be able to use them effectively.

3. The Jones business is not surprising. Jones is simply a merchant trying to drive a good bargain. His fundamental motive, of course, is to recover advance royalties. Your remedy is to sue him for damages for his failure to carry out his contract. He doesn't own the book; he merely has your license to print it. If he fails to do so, the rights revert to you. Liveright ought to be willing to finance such a suit. In case you win, he will get the book without paying Jones anything. As for the advance royalties, Jones' only remedy is to sue you for their recovery. But the thing could be better arranged by friendly mediation. My impression is that Jones would come to terms if properly approached. More difficult is the question of the future of the book. If it is raided again, you will have the whole song and dance over again. Why be so eager to reprint it? My notion is that it does you far more good suppressed than it ever could have done you printed. The possible royalties in it are small. It gives an author a romantic glamour to have a suppressed book on his list. Remember this primary principle of the literary art: A man is always admired most, not by those who have read him, but by those who have merely heard about him.

4. I have started a book to be called "The National Letters". It will be the most violent philippic since the speech of the late Dr. J. C. Josephson on the scribes and pharisees.

Yours in Xt.,
M.

◇◇◇◇◇◇◇◇◇◇◇◇◇◇

To Theodore Dreiser
[UP]

H. L. Mencken
1524 Hollins St.
Baltimore
February 11th [1919]

Dear Dreiser:–

I shall read "The Hand of the Potter" with the highest attention. Maybe it will strike me quite differently than it did in ms. My objection then, of course, was not so much to the play intrinsically as to the folly of giving the Comstocks so noble an opportunity with the Genius case under weigh. That objection now fades. Far worse attacks on free speech than any Comstock ever dreamed of are now commonplace, and the end is not yet.

If you crave intellectual entertainment, send $1.50 to the Superintendent of Documents, Government Printing Office, for a month's subscription to the Congressional Record. Borah, France of Maryland and a few others are carrying on a fight for free speech that gets no notice in the newspapers. They will be beaten. See especially the Record for February 8th. The single copy may be had for 10 cents.

I have at last got the first four pages of my next book on paper—it took months to get so far. The volume will be a slaughter-house. Absolutely no guilty man will escape. Let me have a private list of your special enemies. I shall even denounce myself.

Yours in Xt.,
M.

◇◇◇◇◇◇◇◇◇◇◇◇◇◇

To Ernest Boyd
[OFP]

H. L. Mencken
1524 Hollins St.
Baltimore
March 13th [*1919*]

Dear Boyd:–

My chances of a trip abroad seem to be diminishing. On the one hand the passport regulations are made so stiff that it is practically impossible to make the voyage without great influence, and on the other hand I am thinking of venturing into a new cheap magazine scheme, and if I do it will tie me to New York all summer.[6] The opportunity is good and I need the money. If I could roll up as much, or a bit more, as I got out of the Parasite, it would make me foot-loose, and so I could depart these shores more or less permanently on the restoration of free seas. The paper situation is less acute than it was, and the existing magazines have lost their grip on the populace. A great

[6] A new cheap magazine scheme: *The Black Mask,* which Mencken and Nathan edited for some time, then sold to Crowe. The other two had been *The Parisienne* and *Saucy Stories,* in 1916.

opening for new ideas. The thing may fizzle out at once. On the other hand, it may grow big. If the gods send the latter result I may be in a position to seduce you from the despotism of the Romish satraps, and lure you westward. In any case, I have a superstition that we'll meet before the year is out.

Marion has got home, and is in a hospital in Atlantic City.[7] The horrors and privations of Brest nearly finished her. I doubt that she is seriously ill, but she is certainly much peaked. She talks of re-enlisting, but not for France.

I am sending you by this mail a copy of Eastman's magazine, but I doubt that it gets through.[8] It was barred from the domestic mails, but has since been restored—that is, this present number.

I am full of physical discomforts, and curse God daily. More anon.

Yours in Sso. Corde Jesu,
H. L. Mencken

To THEODORE DREISER
[UP]

[*On March 28th Dreiser had announced his intention of founding a magazine with Jones, and he asked Mencken to contribute articles.*]

H. L. Mencken
1524 Hollins St.
Baltimore
March 29th [*1919*]

DEAR DREISER:

The German mind is standardized. I thought of that book magazine idea two years ago. You pumped it out of me via Spafford or the Ouija board. I think it is excellent, provided decent stuff can be found. My one doubt springs out of the fearful difficulties I have encountered with the Smart Set. The obvious title is *The American Quarterly.* I offer you the Declaration of Independence translated into the American language, with an introduction showing that the average American

[7] Marion Bloom: a Washington literary agent, and a friend of Mencken's.
[8] Eastman's magazine: *The Liberator.*

cannot understand the original.[9] My share of the royalty to be payable to the German Red Cross.

I sent you "The American Language" today. It is a gaudy piece of buncombe, rather neatly done.

Yours in Xt.,
M.

To LAWRENCE GILMAN[1]
[YU]

H. L. Mencken
1524 Hollins St.
Baltimore
April 17th [1919]

DEAR MR. GILMAN:–

My very best thanks for your note and for your penetrating and generous review.[2] It accomplishes two things: (a) it tickles me enormously, and (b) it suggests ways to improve the next edition of the book. How I overlooked such euphemisms as "under the influence of liquor" I can't imagine. Probably it was because, in the midst of such huge Andes and Himalayas of material, I got myself lost. My notes would have made five such books. But I shall surely deal with euphemisms at greater length when I come to the revision. There is a lovely one that I used to encounter in Baltimore, perhaps a mere localism. When it was desired to indicate that a lady's husband had departed for parts unknown, the refined of the lower orders would say "He follows the water". Another I must mention is that the passion for euphemism even extended to the public stews, now extinct. The gals had sweet phrases to indicate all the processes of their sinister art. I collected many such phrases, and gave them to Henry N. Cary, formerly of the Times, who is compiling a dictionary of improper words. But I think I'll at least refer to them in my own book.

The conflict between American terseness and the American liking

[9] The Declaration of Independence "translated" into modern American was appended to the first edition of *The American Language,* then suppressed by Mencken as dangerous to his reputation as a scholar and a patriot.

[1] Lawrence Gilman: author, editor, composer, music critic, and radio commentator. He was associated with *Harper's Weekly* and *Harper's Magazine* and was music critic for the New York *Herald Tribune.*

[2] Lawrence Gilman had written a review of *The American Language* for the May 1919 issue of the *North American Review.*

for gaudy circumlocutions presents a psychological problem that I must work out far better than I have done. I had a feeling that I was shirking it while I was at work on the book, but, as I have said, the enormous mass of material rather befogged me, and at the first trial I had to evade more than one difficulty by disingenuous dodging. My plan is to wait a year or two, study the discussion of the book, and then re-write it from end to end, adding much new material and trying to readjust the emphasis. For one thing, I want to do the grammar of the vulgate more carefully. If any suggestions occur to you, I'll call on you as a fellow-member of the Knights of Pythias to let me have them.

Meanwhile, my best thanks again. You done a good job.

Sincerely yours,
H. L. Mencken

◇◇◇◇◇◇◇◇◇◇◇◇◇

To THEODORE DREISER
[UP]

The Smart Set
25 West 45th Street
New York
May 7, 1919

DEAR DREISER:

As I expected, I am forced to go home at noon today. I will probably be back next week.

It would be impossible at the moment, of course, to print my translation of the Declaration. The Espionage Act specifically forbids making fun of any of the basic ideas of the Republic. But once the Act expires by limitation I'll be delighted to do the thing. My present plan is to add a translation of the Constitution, including the amendments, and one of Lincoln's Gettysburg speech, and to preface them with a note arguing that all of these things are now incomprehensible to the average American. I shall support this argument by citing passages plainly beyond his understanding.

The "C. B." of the Baltimore Evening Sun is apparently Constance Black. Mrs. Black is an English woman and the wife of one of the owners of the paper. I know her very well. She is a great admirer of yours and constantly asks me to invite her to the party the next time you are in Baltimore. She is especially enthusiastic over "Twelve Men".

Yours in Xt.,
M.

(1919)

To Louis Untermeyer
[OFP]

H. L. Mencken
1524 Hollins St.
Baltimore
May 7th [1919]

Dear Louis:–

Why lie? I wrote the so-called Rascoe piece myself. It is my bilious answer to the constant charge that I imitate George Nathan. Incidentally, this idiotic imitation charge business deserves a satirical article. Half of the reviews I see contain it in some form or other. Coupled with it, in my own case, is the allegation that I am Vorhautlos. The Philadelphia Ledger is the last. Even Reedy hints at it. God knows, I begin to believe it. Sometimes I get so shaken that I haul out my lady novelist inspirer to make sure that the Vorhang is still there. Am I, or ain't I? Is there such a thing as a sect of unclipped Askenazim? I'll have to consult Knopf.

One Broening (observe the name) was elected republican mayor of democratic Baltimore yesterday, beating a professional patriot by a large majority. I left town over election day to evade suspicion.

Yours in [Xt.,]
M.

To Burton Rascoe
[UP]

H. L. Mencken
1524 Hollins St.
Baltimore
May 9th [1919]

Dear Rascoe:–

Here we begin to compare prejudices. Aiken is one of mine. Far from caressing my ear, his poetry seems to me to be full of cacophony. Moreover, his vagueness seems to me to go beyond what is fitting, and to become mere dull obscurantism. Worse, I respond to the old Jewish chanting of Oppenheim. But in this department agreement is always impossible; only idiots think absolutely alike. A man can't even agree with himself. I remember the time when Brahms irritated me. Today

I regard him as the greatest of symphonic writers, barring only old Ludwig. And maybe Mozart. As for La Lowell, it is obviously her social position, such as it is, that makes her talked of. Most of the new poets are cads—East Side Jews, small town wenches, etc. The notice of a Lowell enchants them. I am taking a hack at her in my next Smart Set article, and shall probably tackle her again in my book. Incidently, I am exposing Untermeyer's errors. He is an extremely clever fellow, though of course no poet. If he ever lifted anything from me, it was only a phrase or two. He builds his sentences on an entirely different plan.

The Dreiser notice will tickle the old boy very much. It is capitally done. I am sending it to him by this mail.

The Comstock verdict makes it quite safe to do "Mlle. de Maupin" —if you think it's worth while.[3] Also, a precedent is now set which will protect all the other books. Juries are sheep. You will see a big crop of damage suits against Sumner. He is, I believe, and I hope I do not exaggerate, a most foul and disgusting son-of-a-bitch. I have met the fellow. The perfect Y.M.C.A. face. The self-abuse complex to perfection.

Yours in Xt.,
M.

To CARL VAN VECHTEN
[YU]

The Smart Set
25 West 45th Street
New York
May 19, 1919

DEAR VAN VECHTEN:

Thanks very much for your suggestions. They are all excellent and I shall make good use of them in the next edition of the book. Knopf printed only 1500 copies of the first edition and he seems to have sold nearly all of them. The thing will have to be rewritten from start to finish. I am getting contributions from both sides of the Atlantic, and also many tart letters from Anglomaniacs who believe that it is felonious for us to have our own language. I am glad the book amused you.

[3] *Mademoiselle de Maupin* was published by Alfred A. Knopf as a Borzoi Classic; the Series was edited by Rascoe.

Both of your essays are rather long for us. But we like "The Variations on the Theme by Ellis" and if you agree we'll be glad to take about three thousand words of it. The most practicable arrangement would be for you to let me saw out this amount. The Ellis book is one of my old favourites. There are the raw materials of at least a dozen volumes in it. In general, you know what we want. We like to have a music article now and then, but it must deal, not with the intellectual doings of tone artists, but rather with their carnalities and imbecilities. Have you anything else in hand? The article on the rewriting of operas is rather over the heads of our subscribers. I am accordingly returning it herewith. Please let me know about the other essay as soon as you can, so that we may put it through and get you your cheque.

With regards,
Sincerely yours,
H. L. Mencken

To HARRY RICKEL
[OFP]

H. L. Mencken
1524 Hollins St.
Baltimore
May 23rd [1919]

DEAR RICKEL:–

The one memorable phrase in "[Le] Père Goriot" is near the beginning of the book, and has to do, if I remember rightly, with the smell of a boarding-house. But I may be wrong. It is a long while since I read the book. I left it sympathizing with the daughters, just as I always sympathize with Pilate when Pastor Oberndorfer, my spiritual adviser, begins ranting against him in Holy Week.

What are the innovations of you and the Braumeister? I plan to begin brewing on a colossal scale July 1st.

The Woodrow ukase is pure bull-shit.[4] He is trying to cultivate the wets without actually giving them anything. The fellow is an incurable mountebank.

Yours in Sso. Corde Jesu,
M.

[4] The Woodrow ukase: on May 21, 1919, Woodrow Wilson urged Congress to repeal wartime prohibition, so as to allow the sale of light wines and beer.

◇◇◇◇◇◇◇◇◇◇◇◇◇

To BURTON RASCOE
[UP]

H. L. Mencken
1524 Hollins St.
Baltimore
June 16th [*1919*]

DEAR RASCOE:–

All the same, I remain at least 51% right. True enough, Poe and Whitman set off the frogs, but the essential ideas of imagism, which are at the heart of the movement, originated in France, not in America. Poe was a wholly conventional poet. Whitman groped toward the imagist theory, but never quite reached it. Moreover, he had no *direct* influence at home. It was Frenchmen who were actually before the vers librists when they began their cackling, not Whitman. The whole movement is exotic and imitative. There may be 2% of Whitman in it, but there is obviously at least 75% of French heliogabalisme.

The Cox theory of the war is beautifully idiotic.[5] The gentlemen of England had nothing to do with it. The salient Englishman was Lloyd-George, who is no more a gentleman than Jack Johnson. The peace terms reveal what I have always preached: that the whole pretension to "chivalry, gentleness and character" in England, and in America, was and is a piece of buncombe.

I have finished Prejudices.
M.

◇◇◇◇◇◇◇◇◇◇◇◇◇

To JOSEPH HERGESHEIMER
[OFP]

H. L. Mencken
1524 Hollins St.
Baltimore
July 19th [*1919*]

DEAR HERGESHEIMER:

I am glad you got through that tome.[6] Fresh material is pouring

[5] The Cox theory of the war: probably refers to Marian Cox's book *Dry Rot of Society and other essays* (New York: Brentano's; 1919), and its theory that women enjoy wars.

[6] That tome: *The American Language*, about which Hergesheimer had wondered how a volume on the "construction of language" could possibly have given him pleasure (Hergesheimer to Mencken, July 18, 1919).

in from pundits all over the world, and when the mails are open I daresay the Germans will flood me. The job of rewriting the book is anything but appetizing.

If you have not read Anderson's "Winesburg", take a look. It contains some good stuff, and the general effect is excellent. When is Linda to come out in a book? [7] I can't read a serial. Knopf announces two new books of yours, but doesn't give dates. He is doing my Prejudices in September—a piece of tripe.

The weather here is so infernal—damp and hot—that, with a lot of work on hand, I pause every hour to damn the Blessed Trinity.

Yours,
[*H. L. Mencken*]

◇◇◇◇◇◇◇◇◇◇◇◇◇

To Louis Untermeyer
[OFP]

The Smart Set
25 West 45th Street
New York
July 23rd [*1919*]

Dear Louis:–

Thanks very much for the book.[8] It seems to me to be a very fine piece of work—not only the preface, but also the various notes on poets. In some cases, of course, my natural anaesthesia to dithyrambs incommodes my appreciation of the stuff printed. For example, there is Aiken. For the life of me, I can see nothing in his verse. Robinson is another fellow who seems to me to be overestimated. The enclosed, I think, meets him on his own ground, and lands brilliantly on his kishgish. But you make out a case, old top: you make out a case! A copy of the book ought to go to Frau Dr. Schönemann.

I have just finished revising the fair copy of The American Language. It runs to more than 250,000 words. Dreiser will be jealous. I have written a book larger than "The 'Genius' ".

Yours in Xt.,
H. Mencken

---

[7] *Linda* (*Condon*): a novel by Joseph Hergesheimer (New York: Alfred A. Knopf; 1930).

[8] The book: *Modern American Poetry,* by Louis Untermeyer (New York: Harcourt, Brace and Howe; 1919).

[*Equally about poets, Mencken had written to F. H. Garrison on June 2, 1919:*

(. . .) I rather think that the best recent American poetry is in Carl Sandburg's "Chicago Poems" (Henry Holt); James Oppenheim's "The Book of Self" (Knopf); John McClure's "Airs and Ballads" (Knopf) (. . .)]

To JAMES WELDON JOHNSON[9]
[PT]

Baltimore, July 29, 1919

DEAR MR. JOHNSON:

Have you anywhere in your files an estimate of the total wealth of the Negroes of the United States—that is, on the same basis that national wealth is reckoned? I have seen something of the sort, but I don't know where. They probably own at least a billion of property. Here in Maryland they have got very rich.

Your prophecies of serious race conflicts begin to come true. I hope you let me see what you write about the Washington affair.[1] I hear that the same sort of thing was very narrowly averted in Richmond. My guess is that Baltimore will be the last city to see anything of the sort. Despite a segregation ordinance, there is less race feeling here than anywhere else I know of. We have had but one race riot in years, and that was between Poles and Jews.

Sincerely yours,
[*H. L. Mencken*]

To ERNEST BOYD
[OFP]

H. L. Mencken
1524 Hollins St.
Baltimore
August 9th [*1919*]

DEAR BOYD:–

The advertisements of uplift literature have just come in. A noble

[9] James Weldon Johnson (1871–1938): author, secretary of the N.A.A.C.P., and poet.

[1] The Washington affair: a few days before, there had been race riots in Washington, D. C., in which white soldiers and sailors fought with Negroes. The casualties had run high, and a rumor had spread that martial law would be decreed.

collection. I see the influence of Dr. Sylvanus Stall, Dr. Frank Crane, Mme. Margaret Sanger and other great American thinkers. If you see any pamphlets that seem worth while, I'll be delighted to receive them. The mails seem to be quicker than formerly, and less harassed by censors. There are now regular mails between the United States and Germany, including parcels post. The day they opened the hyphenates here dumped in about 1,000 tons of Speck, oiled sardines, u.s.w. I have not yet heard from Sohler, but I expect a letter from him within a week. Levy I hear from regularly. He has been to Berlin, and reports a violent anti-Semitic movement on its legs. I do not share in his horror. We'll have one here before long. To Palestine or to the stake! The race riots in Washington and Chicago have shown a new feature. The coons have fought back—and pretty well beaten the whites. They are armed everywhere and apparently eager for the band to play. The war has made them rich. Tell Mrs. Boyd that our domestic cannibal now owns an automobile, whereas I have had to sell mine.

There is no literary news. Dreiser, I hear, is in a hell of a fix financially. His "Twelve Men" has not sold enough to keep him, and he has no other means. Worse, it will be hard for him to get a job. But this is not new. He was a great fool to give up his old job and try to live on books. It can't be done in America. Wright, I hear, is going downhill steadily; heroin has him by the neck. He is in San Francisco. C. talks of getting a divorce from the boob she married, but I doubt that she does it.[2] W. apparently lives on what she sends him. George Bronson-Howard is also full of heroin. He went to the war, was gassed and lost all his teeth. He says he was cured of drugs at the time, but that an army surgeon gave him morphine and so started him again. I saw him in New York two weeks ago, and he was very wobbly. Blankenagel has returned from France, and is going to Arizona to try ranch life. He says he will never profess in a college again. He was at Toulouse for four months, and reports the fornication very good.

Prejudices is on the press and should be out by Oct. 1st. Ditto the first two Free Lance Books.[3] In January Nathan and I will print The American Credo—a buffoonish piece. He has done the credo and I am

[2] C.: probably W. H. Wright's wife, Katherine. W. H. Wright was then music critic and art director for the San Francisco *Bulletin.*

[3] The Free Lance books were a series of philosophical works, so named after Mencken's famous column in the Baltimore *Evening Sun,* and prefaced by him. They were published by Knopf. The first two mentioned here were E. W. Howe's *Ventures in Common Sense* (New York: Alfred A. Knopf; 1919), and Pio Baroja's *Youth and Egolatry* (New York: Alfred A. Knopf; 1920).

doing a long preface on American character. We also think of printing our play, Heliogabalus. It is too lewd for an American production as it stands, but it may land on the Continent. If it is printed, it will be in a limited edition at a high price. We shall see that every Herr Intendant gets a copy. Are there any theatres in Denmark? If so, can you get me a list of their directors?

Hay-fever is due in ten days. I am taking no cure whatsoever. Maybe the Blessed Saints will come to the bat. I had planned to go to Mt. Clemens for a boiling out, but I hear that it would probably do no good.

Last week I came dam nigh getting into the New Republic by accident—a hair-raising affair. Hackett has taken a contract to edit an American edition of the London Nation, and asked me to do an article for him. I sent it to him while he was away from the office, and Croly, opening it, thought it was for the New Republic and slapped it into type. I killed it in time. Croly now proposes that I do something else for him. I am, however, very coy.[4]

Hearst has offered Nathan an enormous salary to edit the Cosmopolitan. The sum would make you set me down a liar. Nathan has refused. It would be killing work. But it was tempting, for the revenue from the S. S. never goes above a very modest level, and it still owes us 10 months salary. The Parasite saved our lives. We still live on the proceeds.

All well.

Yours in Xt.,
Mencken

To Edgar Watson Howe
[pt]

Baltimore, August 22nd [*1919*]

Dear Mr. Howe:

I had a letter the other day from E. A. Boyd, the Irish critic, who has been in Copenhagen. He tells me that he had a long talk with Georg Brandes, the famous Danish critic, who discovered both Ibsen and Nietzsche. He says that he found that Brandes was a regular reader of your Monthly and enjoyed it very much. He says that Brandes asked after only four Americans: Dreiser, Huneker, you and

[4] Herbert Croly (1869–1930): the editor of the *New Republic.*

me. I think Boyd added me to be polite. Brandes is now a man of 80 odd. He is probably the only genuine neutral the war has produced. He denounces both the Germans and the English as scoundrels, and believes that American participation in the war was due to press-agenting, both by Wilson and by the big financiers.

I'd like to do all the books you propose—but life is short! I have plans for at least half a dozen books, and year by year it grows harder to write them. My next, in the Spring, will probably be an attack on democracy—the most violent every made. I have a belly full of it, and long for the Japs.

So far no hay fever, but it will probably strike me within a few days. I ascribe the delay to the direct intervention of God.

Yours,
Mencken

As I anticipated, Knopf is meeting with delays in printing and binding. The printers here in the East are running amok. If you see your book by October 15th you will be doing well. My "Prejudices" book is already cast, but Knopf doesn't expect to be able to publish it until October 1st. Henry Holt once said that he started the Unpopular Review because he wanted to waste some money and was too old to keep a woman. It will soon be cheaper to keep a whole herd of women than to pay the printers' bills of a magazine.

To Ernest Boyd
[OFP]

H. L. Mencken
1524 Hollins St.
Baltimore
October 9th [*1919*]

Dear Boyd:–

I send you every few days some current specimens of American periodical literature, chiefly of the wilder sort. Does this stuff reach you? In particular, do you get such papers as the Liberator, Pearson's, the Appeal to Reason, the Gaelic-American, the New Republic and the Nation? Let me know which of these get through; perhaps some of them are forbidden by the censorship.

Some books that may interest you are now coming out. Which of the following do you want: Louis Wilkinson's new novel, Cabell's book, Lafcadio Hearn's "Fantastics"? They are all yours if you want them.[5]

The magazine situation is once more parlous. The strike of the pressmen makes it probable that we'll all miss our December issues. Meanwhile, overhead expenses will go on. The transportation strikes in England also affect us. Warner lately shipped 50,000 copies of The Parisienne and Saucy to England, and now they are rotting on the dock at Liverpool. But we hope to get through, and will probably set up several more cheap magazines. Nathan and I, of course, are out of the Parisienne, but we'll take a hack at the new ones. All costs of production are very high, but the public seems willing to pay. So far we have actually sold more Smart Sets at 35 cents than we were selling at 25. Meanwhile, the cost of living is gradually subsiding. Nearly all food stuffs are a bit cheaper than they were six months ago, especially meats.

Prejudices is doing fairly well. [Knopf] has sold about 1,000 copies, though so far no reviews have been printed. He is much handicapped by printing difficulties. He is asking $1.75, $2 and even $2.50 for small books—and getting it. The $1.35 novel is extinct. As you will see by the New Republic, sent to you today, most of the weeklies are printing on newspaper presses. The strike doesn't affect newspaper pressmen. The great advertising boom is causing all the newspapers to print from 24 to 48 pages a day. The result is that the consumption of paper is far ahead of the production, and that newsprint will probably go to 8 or even 10 cents. Two years ago it was at 2.80. The national advertisers are plunging for this reason: This year's war tax is much higher than next year's will be. Rather than give up the money to the government they are investing it in advertising, hoping to cash in next year. This also explains the steel strike. The steel men have an enormous surplus. If they divided it as dividends the government would take 75%. But if they invest it in trying to smash the unions they will cash in next year, when the war tax will be lower. Every dollar they spend on fighting the unions includes 75 cents from the public treasury. An altruistic, patriotic lot.

Yours,
M.

---

[5] Louis Wilkinson's new novel: *Brute Gods* (New York: Alfred A. Knopf; 1919). J. B. Cabell's book: *Jurgen* (New York: R. M. McBride & Co.; 1919).

To Burton Rascoe
[UP]

H. L. Mencken
1524 Hollins St.
Baltimore
October 13th [1919]

Dear Rascoe:–

Of course I'll be glad to contribute to a Vizetelly fund, but it would rather embarrass me to appear as hat-holder or anything of that sort.[6] The reason is that Vizetelly's brother, Frank, is now in this country and in good circumstances and I have had various friendly dealings with him. (My "American Language" set him off and he tried hard to induce me to join the Authors' Club, along with the other professors. I had to stall him off in the end by telling him that I was resigning from all American clubs and proposed to move to Europe and renounce my citizenship.) The point is that passing the hat for Ernest would be a devastating criticism of Frank, who should take care of him. No doubt Ernest is suffering from the same sort of stricture that killed his father, and has gone to the workhouse infirmary in order to be regularly catheterized. The old man was jailed by the English. Lying in a cell for 36 hours without being able to urinate, he suffered a rupture of the bladder and so died. Why Frank doesn't support Ernest decently I don't know: maybe some family feud.

I rather think you get at the truth about the Dreiser play.[7] Re-reading it, I am much less against it than I was. But I think I did Dreiser a valuable service when I induced him to withhold it while the Comstock case against him was still before the courts. The idiot wanted to print it at once, to show how brave he was. He wrote it with the same aim. Its publication would have caused the Appellate Division to decide against him. As it was, he at least got a hung court. Boni & Liveright set up the book nearly two years ago, but held it up until very lately. Dreiser is now on his way to California. He has got some money out of a movie company.

I shall not see Dunsany if I can help it. My news from Ireland is that he is vastly swelled up by his notoriety. The other day, in New

[6] Frank H. Vizetelly (1864–1938): British lexicographer and author, editor of Funk and Wagnalls *Standard Encyclopedia of the World's Knowledge.*
[7] The Dreiser play: *The Hand of the Potter.*

York, I met Hugh Walpole. A gigantic, red-faced Englishman, but apparently a decent fellow. When W. L. George is to arrive I don't know. Walpole is lecturing to the boobs and laughing at them behind the door.

The magazine situation is very disquieting. Unless the strike is settled this week we'll miss an issue. My own inclination was to pay the strikers what they asked—after all, not a great deal—and then pass it on to the yokelry. But the larger publishers insisted on fighting. I think we'll be licked. The publishers' side of the combat is managed by idiots—judging by their gabble, by former Liberty Loan orators.

Yours in Xt.,
M.

The review of "Prejudices" swells me up. You overestimate my philanthropy. I toy with the neophytes in order to dig up stuff for the Smart Set, and because it is good fun. But let it go. I only hope the book is readable. That is the hardest thing to accomplish. Any one can be accurate and even profound, but it is damned hard work to make criticism charming. I think "Solomon Eagle" fails. He avoids heaviness, but he often falls into the hollowest sort of Agnes Repplierish waggery —the *Atlantic Monthly* complex.

I think that next year's "Prejudices" will avoid books. I want to work off some bile against Xtianity, etc. Knopf has already sold 1,000 copies of No. 1, so the series seems safe.

My very best thanks.
M.

To FIELDING HUDSON GARRISON
[PT]

Baltimore, October 16, 1919

DEAR COL. GARRISON:

Did I ever say that? I remember the Chicago ham part, but not the child part. I dessay that my mellowness was caused by something out of a bottle. Alcohol always makes men better. I hope you don't print the notion that went with it—that the invention of the bichloride tablet was of greater influence upon human progress than the Constitution of the United States. Let me see the whole essay, by all means. I was astonished when you told me that pediatrics was a new fancy. I always thought that the ancients paid a great deal of attention to children—even more than we do today. The only child I know is my niece, aged four, and I see her but once or twice a year. It is amazing to observe her vanity. She already knows the whole art of dress, and watches her complexion carefully. I assume that the two pages are part of your ms. and so return them.

My American Language correspondence becomes enormous. Today I received from a man in Philadelphia the longest letter ever written—actually 10,000 words, and every page full of interesting observation. I am thinking of employing some professor to help me rewrite the book. It will run to 30 or 40 volumes folio.

Sincerely yours,
H. L. Mencken

To Burton Rascoe
[UP]

H. L. Mencken
1524 Hollins St.
Baltimore
October 22nd [*1919*]

Dear Rascoe:–

I am asking Harpers for Madeleine.[8] Who knows? Maybe I wrote it myself.

Obviously, you can't last on the Tribune forever. You ought to be striking out for wider and more comfortable waters. A couple of books behind you would help a lot. Why don't you do the Modern French book? I outgrew the Baltimore Sun long before I left it, and my last years were extraordinarily turbulent. The war took me much further than any newspaper could go.

You are absolutely deluded by marks.[9] I have no objection to his hero intrinsically; what I object to is his flatulent, quackish manner —his air of saying something profound. There is not a single good idea in his book. And his style is simply abominable—the worst sort of medical-journal English. I fear Louis Untermeyer put one over on you.

---

[8] *Madeleine,* the autobiography of a girl of pleasure; it had been raided by the censors.

[9] Marks: Henry K. Marks, author of *Peter Middleton* (Boston: R. G. Badger; 1919).

Prejudices is full of pishposh, but you probably pick the wrong places. The Arnold Bennett chapter is the most idiotic.

Yours in Xt.,
M.

To Gamaliel Bradford
[OFP]

The Smart Set
25 West 45th Street
New York
[Fall 1919?]

Dear Mr. Bradford:

You are doomed to read me, at least in part. Some of my worst prejudices come from you—were borrowed from you. I wish I could send you "The American Language" forthwith, but it is quite out of print, and I am quite unable to find a copy. Knopf printed but 1,500, from type; now he wishes he had been more optimistic.

You claim to be old! I beat you by years and years. I am at least 98!

[Sincerely yours,]
H. L. Mencken

To Fielding Hudson Garrison
[PT]

Baltimore, November 7, 1919

Dear Garrison:

My apologies for holding your ms. for so long. It goes back to you by this mail. It is amazing how much ground you have covered in your space, and how well you trace out the steps of the historical process. Why don't you make a separate book of it? It ought to have illustrations. The thing is articulated already; all it needs is a great accumulation of detail and example. I think such a book would sell very well. You have done an excellent job.

It turns out that Huneker's book is "Steeplejack", his autobiography. The name is absurd. He has also just finished a novel of 75,000 words and is sending me the ms. If it is at all printable I'll probably buy it for The Smart Set and print it in three numbers. But I suspect that it will be full of mystical fol-de-rol. The old boy is running to Rosicrucian ideas—if that is the way to spell it. Wagner's "Parsifal" is primarily responsible for setting him off. I have a long letter from him, appointing me his successor as poisoner of the right-thinking—gabble about passing on the torch, etc. He is obviously suffering severely from Biernot. When Pilsner disappeared he began to pick at his bed-clothes. But a charming fellow! There was never another such companion at the Biertisch. And never another such swashbuckler in the bozarts. He little realizes what a man he has been.

Thanks very much for the Brahms, for the incomparable Zietz play and for the two Sudermanns. I shall return the latter in a week or so. The Brahms is the very thing I need. My ignorance of his chamber music has gone on long enough. The trouble with our club is that we devote too much time to orchestral music, defectively arranged. The thing drapes itself around a piano four-handed; it ought to drape itself around a string quartet. But let us thank God for what we have.

The case of Dr. Welch puzzles me. Unluckily, I don't know him; he and Dr. Halstead are about the only Johns Hopkins men I have never met. I can easily imagine him being against the Germans in the war, if only as a matter of race loyalty, but what I can't understand is (a) his open alliance with the most extravagant and ignorant sort of German-baiters and spy-hungers, and (b) his almost childish assent to the Wilson buncombe. It seems to me that (b) is now obviously a proof of intellectual napping, and that (a) comes unpleasantly close to compromising his common decency. One does not ask an intellectual, in time of war, to stand against his country; one expects him to stand with his country—*but like a gentleman.* For example, like Lansdowne, like Arnold Bennett and like Anatole France and Richard Strauss, not like D'Annunzio, Kipling and Irvin Cobb. The course of Dr. Welch frankly gave me the shock of my life. Consider the sharp contrast offered by the course of other men, notably Halstead and Barker. Neither owed one-tenth as much to Germany as Welch owed, and yet both carefully avoided the slightest hysteria, and not a word came out of them from first to last that any reasonable opponent could object to today.

But all this I shall go into in a book to be done later on. Today I am entertained by my four-year-old niece. Ten minutes ago she caved in a doll's head in my office and set up a fearful caterwauling. Now she has gone to sleep.

Yours,
Mencken

To FIELDING HUDSON GARRISON
[PT]

Baltimore, November 17, 1919

DEAR GARRISON:

The war be damned. I am sorry I gave you the impression that I was filled with indignation. Indignation is a function of impotence, and I am no longer impotent. Think of the noble mark that American *Kultur* offers! My hands itch. The whole bilge of patriotism sickens me. During the war the Germans insisted on mistaking me for a German patriot, and the Americans tried their damndest to make me an American patriot. Between the two I was helpless. As for Welch & Co., I suppose they did the best they could, considering the times. I am against such fellows, but that is certainly no sound argument against them.

The war actually treated me magnificently. Its first shock gave me a business chance which brought me leisure, enabled me to escape from daily journalism, got me enough money to make me secure, and so helped me to write five books. Moreover, the ensuing festivities filled me with new ideas, greatly changed my aims, and flooded me with such an amount of material that I'll never be able to use a tenth of it. Still more, I had a lot of capital entertainment—some rough, gaudy debates, some curious adventures with spy-hunters, and even a taste of life in the field. So I'd be an ass to complain.

The other day Huneker came into my office with the ms. of his novel, and I read it on the train.[1] The thing turned out to be superb—the best thing he has ever done. But absolutely unprintable. It is not merely ordinarily improper; it is a riot of obscene wit. The old boy has put into it every illicit epigram that he has thought of in 40 years, and some of them are almost perfect. I yelled over it. There is one long chapter, in which the hero soliloquizes on women, that set me to such

[1] Huneker's novel: *Painted Veils* (New York: Boni and Liveright; 1920).

larfing that the Jews in the smoke room probably thought me insane. Huneker is either a great practical joker or he has no sense of humor (as opposed to wit) whatever. He actually submitted the thing for serial publication in the Smart Set. If we printed it, we'd get at least 40 years. But a fine piece of writing!

I had no notion of printing your name with that Senatorial burlesque. The book itself is hanging fire. A good deal of the stuff remains to be written—it is thought out, but not on paper. I surely don't blame you for canning the Hungarian pornographer. It is precisely such fellows who make Comstockery prosperous. Every man has a touch of Puritanism in him. In my case it takes the form of a dislike for smutty pictures. Collecting them is a curious form of self-abuse. How much better to view the gals themselves, comfortably in camera! Few women are beautiful, but now and then one strikes one whose hide at least shows a fine texture. Moreover, there is their artless prattle—about Ibsen, birth control, the question whether the hotel detective is suspicious, the novels of Hugh Walpole, and (if respectably married) the fiendish imbecility of their husbands.

Walpole, by the way, has been giving out an interview nominating Cabell, Hergesheimer, Willa Cather and me as the white hopes. He is, for an Anglo-Saxon, singularly obtuse. Hergesheimer is a Pennsylvania Dutch Jew,[2] Cather is half German, I am pro-Japanese, and Cabell, in "Jurgen", prints the most bitter attack on current American Kultur that I have ever read. I see Walpole going to Pentonville when he returns. "Jurgen", in part, is very fine stuff. It is too long, but the first half shows Cabell at his very best. A great deal of very deft deviltry is in it. I agree with you about "Beyond Life". It is very tedious reading.

The fair niece is notified that the candy awaits. I convey her best thanks. She will probably return soon. Her mother turns out to have a chronic appendicitis (diagnosed in Pittsburgh as hypoacidity and treated by dieting), and I am arranging with Bloodgood to operate. The other day I met Harry Kemp, the poet, in New York. His wife has just died of tuberculosis. She was under treatment for heart disease for three years. It was not until she was half dead that a correct diagnosis was made. Such things seem unimaginable, and yet they happen.

Yours,
Mencken

---

[2] This was meant by H. L. Mencken as a joke.

(1919)

To George Sterling
[PT]

1524 Hollins Street
Baltimore, Md.
November 29th [1919]

Dear Sterling:–

Alas, a bit over the wavering, impalpable line separating art from Blackwell's Island. The notion that perfectly good girls lean back with a sigh and murmur "Well, then, hurry up and let's get it over"—this doctrine makes progress. But it is still unlawful to argue (a) that the aged are constipated, (b) that aunts are ever Sapphist, and (c) that Tom cats are bawdy. Could you modify these lewdnesses? Change the name of the pamphlet to "Brotherhood of Men and Nations", by John D. Rockefeller, Jr. (It actually exists.) Make the Sapphic aunt merely diabetic. Halt the second paragraph at the word "night". Change William Lyon Phelps to Paul Elmer More. So castrated I'll be hot for it, and no doubt Nathan will join me.

I was horribly tight in New York the last time. It was a massive overdose and I have been rocky ever since.

I heard the other day of the death of J. M. Kennedy in London—influenza. An excellent man; his book on the United States told some hard truths. The war, of course, shut him off.

Yours in Xt.,
[*Unsigned*]

To Alfred A. Knopf
[AAK]

H. L. Mencken
1524 Hollins St.
Baltimore
December 13th [1919]

Dear Knopf:–

Put down the name of J. V. A. Weaver, Display Advertising Dept., Daily News, Chicago, as likely for your next year's poetry list. Weaver is gradually accumulating some excellent stuff, and it is very original. It represents an attempt to turn the common language of America into beauty. I think his book, when it's ready, will cause a lot of gabble. I'd be glad to do a preface for it. In the end, of course, it may turn out impossible, but meanwhile it might do no harm to get a sort of option on it.[3]

The sight of Schaff's check paralyzed my tongue. You forget that my great-great grandfather, Schmul Goldblatt, was a rabbi in Königsberg. It was like a beautiful widow showing me her appendicitis scar.

No news from Muir. Go ahead with the book. I have written to him, telling him that we could wait no more.[4]

I am asking Howe to send you a list of possible buyers.[5]

M.

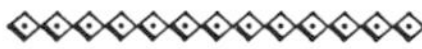

To Ernest Boyd
[OFP]

H. L. Mencken
1524 Hollins St.
Baltimore
December 20th [*1919*]

Dear Boyd:–

I have a notion that Huebsch will approach you with a proposal. His new weekly, at all events, has plenty of money—and Nock, the editor, is a good man.[6]

Thanks for the Athenaeum. The notice was not bad, and the spitball for Americanos in the last line rather tickled me.[7] It was a good phrase; I shall steal and use it. I'll be delighted to see the MacNamara stuff. His book, as you say, was second-rate, but he may have some good shorter things. Squire, it appears, has already engaged an American correspondent. His Solomon Eagle stuff I can't stomach. It is in the

---

[3] John V. A. Weaver was then assistant to the book editor of the Chicago *Daily News.* He wrote a book of verse prefaced by H. L. Mencken: *In American* (1921). Alfred A. Knopf was the publisher.

[4] The book: see note [5], p. 180.

[5] Howe: Edgar Watson Howe, the popular Kansas philosopher.

[6] His new weekly: *The Freeman,* edited by A. J. Nock (1920–4). Albert J. Nock (1872–1945): author, educator, editor.

[7] E. Boyd's notice: "Voices in the Irish Wilderness" (in *Athenaeum,* December 26, 1919).

orthodox causerie manner. Noff has reprinted a volume of it, and I am slating it in the S. S.

I have just received the New Witness for Nov. 28. In it is a gaudy article on me by Vincent O'Sullivan. It makes me larf to be greased in Chesterton's paper; he is one of my pet idiots. But the thing comes just in time to counteract some furious attacks at home. All the patriots are stirred up.

The other day Nathan and I had Dunsany to lunch. We couldn't escape it. He wrote saying that he would die unhappy unless he met his two American fathers. It turned out a great farce. It appears that he laps up in all eagerness the adulation of the social pushers. He told us, in fact, that the aristocracy of St. Louis was charming—Mrs. Baumgartner, the dowager Mme. Himmelheber, young Miss Katrina Oehlenschlager, etc. And then, in the midst of that blather, he outlined a new one-acter that he is writing—a genuinely beautiful thing. A curious fellow.

Dreiser is in Los Angeles. What he is doing there I don't know. He has no address; only a postoffice box. I have heard that he is being kept by some rich wench. If so, I envy him. I get idiotic letters from him. Both Lane and Liveright claim his new novel, "The Bulwark". He has collected advance royalties from both. How they will settle it I don't know.

Harper & Bros have been raided by the Comstocks for printing a book called "Madeleine", the autobiography of a girl of pleasure. It is silly stuff. The raid was engineered by Hearst. During the war, old Clinton Brainard, the head of the Harper firm, joined in the patriotic attempt to lynch Hearst. Hearst is now engaged upon paying up his enemies, one by one. I delight in the show. Brainard, an aged man and very respectable, is placarded daily as a pornographic monster. His sufferings must be fearful.

The anti-Woodrow movement grows steadily. Congress is now formally petitioned to impeach him, and there is a rising demand that he resign his office on account of his physical and mental incapacity. What ails him nobody knows accurately.[8] It is common gossip that he has paresis, but this is probably untrue. The country is being run, not by the cabinet, but by his secretary, Tumulty, a tenth-rater. House lurks in New York.

Erpf's new address is in care of the Kienzle Uhrfabriken, Schwen-

[8] Woodrow Wilson had suffered a stroke during a tour of the country in the fall of 1919.

ningen a. N., Württemberg. This is the second largest clock factory in Europe, and employs 3200 hands. Erpf says it is now working at full blast. He is engaged upon its advertising.

I salute you upon the birthday of Dr. Josephson. It will be very wet here. The dinner club will drink to you on the 28th.

Yours,
Mencken

To Edmund Wilson[9]
[OFP]

The Smart Set
25 West 45th Street
New York
December 20, 1919

Dear Mr. Wilson:

It seems to me that "The Devil" is still vague and inconclusive toward the end. The last part is undoubtedly better than it was, but it still leaves the reader wondering what the whole thing is about. In brief, you have no story. Why not try to work it up to some definite dénouement. Make something happen.

Some of the other stories interest us a good deal. If "A Student" were not a bit thin, we'd probably take it.

I have a feeling that sooner or late we will come to terms. If you care to take another hack at "The Devil", by all means let me see it.

Sincerely yours,
H. L. Mencken

To Fielding Hudson Garrison
[PT]

Baltimore, December 26, 1919

Dear Doctor:

Translating Nietzsche, I discover, is no child's play.[1] Now and then the old boy became so intoxicated by the exuberance of his own ver-

[9] Edmund Wilson (born in 1895), author and critic.
[1] Mencken was then translating Nietzsche's *Antichrist,* published in 1920 by Alfred A. Knopf as the third Free Lance book.

bosity that it is hard to make out precisely what he meant. But, despite interruptions, I am making progress. Any outrage that he overlooked will be cared for in my introduction. My present plan (still somewhat vague) is to make "The Antichrist" the first of a series of reprinted essays, with somewhat elaborate introductions. The second volume will be made up of Poe's critical essays.[2]

The news that the medical periodicals of England have discussed dead Germans with intelligence and fairness rather surprises me. That is surely not true of the general scientific literature. Only a few weeks ago I encountered an article by an English zoologist gravely proposing that all German contributions to the science be ignored. Moreover, I have actually read articles arguing that German music is second-rate.

The truth is that, standing on the outside looking in, I have been somewhat astonished by the effects of the war upon the Sassenach. Here in America the show has been superb. I have a stable loft half filled with newspaper accounts of mythical spy outrages, Liberty Loan speeches and so on, together with such amazing pamphlets as Hornaday's and the full files of the Creel Press Bureau in all languages. I don't know whether to attempt to boil all this down to a book, or to hand it over to some German pedant. He would spoil it. It needs good humor in the telling, not indignation.

Let your coming be soon. The finest malt liquor ever brewed in America is now on tap, but it won't last long. I am laying in case after case of synthetic wine from California. It is a poor dose, but it is surely better than Bevo.[3]

Sincerely yours,
H. L. Mencken

[2] The volume of Poe's essays was never published.

[3] Bevo: a nonalcoholic beverage, somewhat similar to "near-beer". See Mencken to L. Pound, April 23 [1920].

1920

◇◇◇◇◇◇◇◇◇◇◇◇◇◇◇◇◇◇◇◇

To LOUISE POUND
[PT]

Baltimore, January 14th [1920]

DEAR DR. POUND:–

I agree with you fully about poor Paula. She is my own favorite—an honest wife and noble woman, cruelly gnawed by a harsh and unintelligible destiny. Lucia, of course, is simply the orthodox blue-nose—the wife as policeman and drill sergeant. As for Dacia, she is no more than a cutie off a candy-box top. We put her in to prove the incurable imbecility of Helio—a man with many fine qualities, but still fundamentally a Schafskopf.[1] The play is full of Maeterlinckian subtleties. It is actually being considered by Max Reinhardt, though he'll probably decide against it. We have announced that it will not be offered for production in the United States until the backward culture of the country progresses to a point satisfactory to us. Result: five Jews are trying to buy it.

It surprises me to learn that I didn't send you the Prejudices book. A copy goes to you by this mail. With it is a copy of the new edition of my burlesques book. The latter contains one or two very fair things, particularly "Death: A Discussion" and "Panoramas of People". Also some very bad stuff. "Prejudices" has been very violently attacked by Stuart Sherman et al. But it has been treated politely by the Mercure

---

[1] Paula, etc.: characters in *Heliogabalus.*

de France, the London Times and the Athenaeum, and a whole article about it has appeared in G. K. Chesterton's paper, the New Witness. Much of the stuff in the book is a bit cruel. But in such combats it is necessary to give and take very heavy blows. I surely get my share.

I suspected Geheimrat of belonging to the Accursed Race because the unintelligent pundit is a very familiar German type. I have examples, in fact, in my own family. You must have a lot of fun observing the comedy. There is nothing more charming than to sit among dunderheads and watch them at their idiotic sports. This, in fact, is the one thing that makes life bearable. If you get the sharp-witted minority you get the best of the bargain. Think of the imbeciles that poor [X] must stuff! A beautiful system of natural selection works to your advantage.

Sincerely yours,
H. L. Mencken

◇◇◇◇◇◇◇◇◇◇◇◇◇◇

To GUY HOLT[2]
[UV]

[*J. B. Cabell's* Jurgen *had been declared obscene and indecent through the efforts of the New York Vice Society and had been withdrawn from the bookstores.*]

H. L. Mencken
1524 Hollins St.
Baltimore
January 20th [1920]

DEAR MR. HOLT:–

I am astounded to hear of the complaint against "Jurgen" by the Comstock Society. What can be complained of in the book I can't imagine. It is not only not a pornographic work; it is a very fine and delicate piece of writing—perhaps the best thing done in America in a dozen years. It is a pity that a work of art so earnest, so beautifully planned and so competently executed should be exposed to such mistaken attacks. If such things are permitted to go on, then it will be

[2] Guy Holt worked at Robert McBride & Co. He edited *Jurgen and the Law* in 1923, and *A Bibliography of the Writings of James Branch Cabell* in 1924.

simply impossible to print decent literature in America. The proceeding, like the Dreiser affair, will only cause the English to laugh at us as barbarians. What the French will make of it I hate to think.

Sincerely yours,
H. L. Mencken

To Guy Holt
[uv]

H. L. Mencken
1524 Hollins St.
Baltimore
January 24th [*1920*]

Dear Mr. Holt:–

If any chance offers to use the enclosed, use it as you please. And call on me for anything else I can do. I am sending a copy to Cabell.

Unluckily, all the decisions are against admitting critical opinion in evidence. The act was drawn up by Comstock, and it is a very deft piece of work.

I incline to think that the best defense will be simply to deny absolutely that there is any indecent significance in the book. Accuse the Comstocks of reading it into the text—in other words, put the burden on *them.* They are intolerable swine, but we are in America, and this is one of the things we must put up with.

Sincerely yours,
H. L. Mencken

To Ernest Boyd
[ofp]

H. L. Mencken
1524 Hollins St.
Baltimore
January 26th [*1920*]

Dear Boyd:–

So far as I can make out, Dunsany's "Tales of Two Hemispheres" is not yet published. I'll send you a copy immediately it comes out. I shall also send the Huneker autobiography. It seems to be in press. His pornographic novel will not be published until late in the year, if at all.[3] Liveright is planning to do it in a limited edition, but the Comstocks are in such fearful eruption that he may change his mind. I sent you a card announcing the seizure of Cabell's "Jurgen". Guy Holt, of McBride & Co., has been remanded for trial. He says that he will fight. All of them say it, but few do.

So "Heliogabalus" has not been beschlagnahmt. Noff thinks he will get away with it. It is published today, and he had sold out the whole edition last week. Several suspicious single orders have come to his office, but he is probably sharp enough to avoid filling them. If the book is seized, the booksellers will be the goats. Inasmuch as the proceedings will treble the value of their stocks of the book, they will not be greatly dismayed. "Jurgen" is now selling for $5, and going up. Max Reinhardt's New York agent has bespoken the Continental rights to "Helio" and is having the play translated into German and Hungarian at once. He says he thinks he can get an early production in Buda-Pesth. He probably lies. We have sent about 75 review copies to the Continent—shelling the woods.

The reorganization of The Sun is proceeding slowly, hence the delay in overtures to you. What can be done there eventually remains to be seen. The effort to create a Liberal newspaper is impeded by various things—chiefly by Adams' fidelity to Woodrow. Patterson is doing his damndest, but he is impeded by the fact that he can't find any men to substitute for the present incompetents. A first-rate journalist doesn't want to live in Baltimore. He has been in New York this week, scouting. My own connection with the paper is thin, and rather inconvenient to me. I'll probably pull out, once some sort of a new organization is completed. Have you heard from Huebsch or Nock? They are at work on their new weekly. Just how far they have got I don't know.

The present staff is timorous and futile. Two weeks ago it was headed for supporting Hoover—a most imprudent thing, in view of his vulnerability to chauvinistic attack. I went to the bat at once. But it is hard for me to think in Liberal terms. I grow more and more reactionary as I grow older. Some time soon I shall write an article for the New Republic, explaining why it is impossible to flock with the Liberals in America.

---

[3] The Huneker biography: *Steeplejack* (New York: Charles Scribner's Sons; 1920); his "pornographic" book: *Painted Veils.*

The growth of anti-English feeling is helping the Irish cause over here, despite the flabbiness of Valera. But the Irish leaders here seem quite unable to come to terms with the other factions that they need. For example, the Jew Socialists could give them very great help. But two-thirds of the Polizei who pursue and harass the Jews have such names as Flynn, Googan and O'Shea. The essential difficulty is that the Irish leaders are trying to posture as American patriots, and yet attack England. Official patriotism is still wholly English. The Irish must either change their tune, or wait until the gradual growth of anti-English feeling changes the definition of patriotism.

The letter in the Irish Statesman from an American Congressman (addressed to Shane Leslie) was sound doctrine. Woodrow is now almost forgotten. His collapse has been stupendous.

I am going through a dull period, and am unable to write. I must finish a new Prejudices by June.[4] Noff has sold 1700 copies of the First Series, and is printing another 1000; the book is quite out of print. I have some material blocked out, but the writing will be hard. On Democracy also waits. The American Credo will be out next week, and the first copy will go to you. Nathan's Comedians All has sold very well—probably better than any other book of dramatic criticism ever done here.

My sister-in-law is in the house, preparing to have her appendix taken out—if it turns out to need it. Your prayers are bespoken.

Yours,
Mencken

To THEODORE DREISER
[UP]

H. L. Mencken
1524 Hollins St.
Baltimore
February 2nd [*1920*]

DEAR DREISER:–

I think $75 or $100 would be a fair price for a short story ms. I am asking Liveright to send me some copies of the "Free" and "Twelve

---

[4] Mencken was then preparing a second series of *Prejudices.*

Men" pamphlets, and shall send them abroad. The future of both of us, I think, lies on the other side of the water. Next year I hope to do a book for publication in German only—on American literature and civilization. It will be sweet stuff.

Yours,
M.

Nathan and I often talk of the possibility of getting you into the magazine, but put it off for a simple reason. That is, we have gathered the idea that you think we drove hard bargains with you in the past, and so made an excessive profit on you. This is not true. You apparently share the general notion that we are full of money—another delusion. We have had a very tough struggle with The Smart Set from the start, and have kept it going without a cent of outside help. It has had to pay for itself. Well, the net result of all that effort is that, after 5½ years, it yet owes each of us 11 months of the smallest salaries drawn by any magazine editors in New York, and has not paid us a single cent in dividends. We have gone on with it for various reasons. First, we enjoy monkeying with it. Secondly, we like to dig up new authors and give them their chance. Thirdly, there is the sporting interest: it is pleasant to overcome difficulties. Fourthly, running the magazine gives us a certain prestige, and helps our books. Both of us have made a living by other devices, often onerous. I held a newspaper job until the middle of 1917, and have lately resumed it. Nathan has done a great deal of hard hack work. We started the Parisienne to get money, sold out to get rid of too much work—and are now starting another magazine.[5] The common view in New York seems to be that we got $100,000 for the Parisienne. I only wish we had. And what we got is nearly all gone. If it hadn't been for the fact that each of us has a small independent income, we'd have been down and out a dozen times.

All this for your private eye. I don't offer it as a reason why you should do any work for us. I go into it simply to purge your mind of any notion that you may harbor that we are Shylocks. We are sinful, but that is not one of our crimes. In my autobiography, announced by Knopf for the fall of 1950, I shall tell the whole story in detail, giving actual figures.

[5] Another magazine: *The Black Mask.*

◇◇◇◇◇◇◇◇◇◇◇◇◇

To THEODORE DREISER
[UP]

H. L. Mencken
1524 Hollins St.
Baltimore
February 3rd [1920]

DEAR DREISER:–

I have been in communication with Herman Scheffauer, who is now in Berlin, about German translations.[6] He is very friendly to both of us, and has gone to the length of approaching the Kurt Wolff Verlag, a very good publishing house, in Leipzig.[7] He says that he has been met with great friendliness: Wolff wants to introduce a few salient Americans of German blood to German audiences. I incline to go with Scheffauer as far as he chooses. He is a sound man and has had a good deal of experience. His suggestion is that you choose a couple of your books as most probably suitable for translation, send them to him in Berlin, and let him go on with the negotiations. What do you think of it? My own suggestions are Jennie Gerhardt and Twelve Men. I think the Germans would understand both. Or maybe substitute The Titan for Twelve Men. If you are interested, Scheffauer's full name and address follow:

Herrn Herman G. Scheffauer,
Cunostrasse 48, III,
Berlin-Grunewald,
Germany.

I am more and more convinced that we had better reach out for European audiences. The United States will go from bad to worse. Beginning with On Democracy all my books will be published in England simultaneously, and I shall make every effort to get them into German and French. It will be safe, I think, to allow Scheffauer to arrange terms. On account of the state of exchange, we'll get next to nothing from the first book or two, but after that we should get a fair royalty.

Yours,
M.

[6] Scheffauer lived in Berlin in the twenties. He advised German publishers about American books and translated some German books into English.

[7] Kurt Wolff had a large publishing house in Leipzig at the same time. During the Second World War he emigrated to the United States.

On second thought, The Titan is much better for the purpose than Twelve Men.

M.

To Ernest Boyd
[OFP]

H. L. Mencken
1524 Hollins St.
Baltimore
February 4th [1920]

Dear Boyd:–

[. . . . .]

The other day I had a note from Aldous L. Huxley, full of lofty compliments. My Prejudices seems to bemuse him. He wrote the Athenaeum notice.[8] Who is he? Somehow, I have a notion that he is a grandson of old T. H. Huxley. What has he done on his own account?

[. . . . .]

The prosecution of Cabell's "Jurgen" by the Comstocks is going unwept and unsung. I doubt that more than ten of us have gone to the rescue. The newspapers, as usual, give the Comstocks the better of it. Brainard, of Harper & Bros., has been fined $1,000 and denounced from the bench for publishing "Madeleine", a harmless vice-crusade document, with a preface by Judge Ben B. Lindsey. Hearst engineered the prosecution. Brainerd was among the patriots who accused him during the war. Now Hearst uses the Tammany judges to get revenge.

I am asking Upton Sinclair to send you a copy of his book on the American press. Hot stuff! [9]

Yours,
Mencken

---

[8] The *Athenaeum* notice, signed A. L. H., appeared on January 2, 1920.

[9] Upton Sinclair's book: *The Brass Check* (Pasadena, Cal.; The author; 1919), an indictment of journalism in America.

(1920)

To WILBUR CROSS[1]
[YU]

H. L. Mencken
1524 Hollins St.
Baltimore
February 5th [1920]

DEAR DR. CROSS:–

Perhaps the best plan would be for you to have your editors strike out the parts of the article that you object to, and then return it to me for patching.[2] Or, if it reads smoothly with the excisions, print it as it then stands. I do not object to changes. But I have a feeling that taking out the passages about the German and American professors will leave a gap. Instead of mentioning Northcliffe and Reading we could simply say "the sort of commercial and financial peers who come over to flatter and flutter Anglomaniacs".

Don't think that Comstockery is dead! It was never more potent. Brainard, of Harper & Bros., has just been fined $1,000 for printing a harmless vice-crusade document sponsored by Ben B. Lindsey, and another publisher is facing trial for printing James Branch Cabell's "Jurgen", perhaps the best piece of writing done in America in a dozen years. Every book publisher is terrified, and every imaginative author has to write with his sword over his head.

Sincerely yours,
H. L. Mencken

To LOUIS UNTERMEYER
[OFP]

H. L. Mencken
1524 Hollins St.
Baltimore
February 6th [1920]

DEAR LOUIS:–

I wrote to both Cabell and Holt two weeks ago, and have since tried to stir up the animals in various directions. But it is hopeless.

[1] Wilbur Cross (1862–1948): professor of English at Yale, dean of the Graduate School and editor of the *Yale Review,* governor of Connecticut (1931–9), ex-president of the National Institute of Arts & Letters.

[2] The article: "National Literature", by H. L. Mencken, in the *Yale Review* for July 1920.

For every man willing to do anything for Cabell, there are fifty glad to see him in difficulties. Some swine on the Chicago *News* actually printed a gloating attack on him. Are there any decent people in America? I begin to doubt it.

Incidently, I have been revolving a scheme for a small but effective organization of American authors. My proposal is that we start off with you, me, Dreiser, Cabell, Hergesheimer, Nathan, Cahan and maybe one or two others, and then gradually build up an offensive and defensive alliance, letting in new ones most carefully. It must be kept quiet. What do you think of it? Hackett ought to be in it, if an Irishman can be trusted. But not Huneker.

What of Aldous Huxley?

Yours,
Mencken

To F. C. PRESCOTT[3]
[CU]

H. L. Mencken
1524 Hollins St.
Baltimore
February 10th [*1920*]

DEAR MR. PRESCOTT:–

Thanks very much for your letter of the 5th, which has just reached me through Mr. Knopf's office. Your suggestions are excellent. I had much difficulty, when writing the book, in keeping a clear distinction between the English of educated Americans and the American of the populace. In various places, you will note confusions. I shall try to make the thing clearer when I revise the book, probably next year. It was my hope that someone competent to do it would study the history of American pronunciation, and that I'd get some help from professional philologists in the matter of the vulgate, but this hope has been disappointed. One very competent woman told me that her academic standing would be injured if she began toying with "I seen" and "I would have went".[4] It seems amazing. In all other countries the common speech is very seriously studied.

---

[3] Frederick Clarke Prescott: professor of English at Cornell University.
[4] One very competent woman: probably Dr. Louise Pound.

If any other suggestions occur to you I surely hope that you let me hear them. Meanwhile, my best thanks again for your letter.

Sincerely yours,
H. L. Mencken

To WILBUR CROSS:–
[YU]

H. L. Mencken
1524 Hollins St.
Baltimore
February 25th [*1920*]

DEAR DR. CROSS:–

Save in two instances the deletions seem to me to be quite all right. In the matter of the paragraphs on the professors I fear that cutting them out altogether would break the argument and so spoil the article. I suggest leaving in the attack on the American academic attitude, but omitting all reference to the German professors. What I say is surely not anarchistic. As a matter of fact, it has been said by no less a man than Prof. Gildersleeve, of the Johns Hopkins. The whole point of my article, in fact, lies in the attacks on the professors. If I leave them out my *intelligentsia* vanish altogether, and I am left hanging in the air.

The other point concerns the reference to the Comstocks. Here again it seems to me that I am on quite sure ground. Many men refused to sign the Dreiser protest for the reasons that I have given, but other men of equal reputation—for example, James Lane Allen, Bliss Carman, Winston Churchill, Ellery Sedgwick, Douglas Z. Doty, Robert Frost, Edgar Lee Masters, Booth Tarkington and E. A. Robinson—signed promptly, and with a full knowledge of the facts. I can't imagine discussing American literature without mentioning the evil influence of this unintelligent and often dishonest censorship. The matter is scarcely controversial. There is not the slightest doubt about the facts. A number of English authors, for example, W. L. George, have written about them. I myself devoted a whole chapter to them in my "Book of Prefaces", and my statements have never been challenged. So I hesitate to delete the references to the Comstocks in toto, though I have made some changes in them.

I dislike to appear to be arguing these points. As a matter of fact, if I could see any way of taking both subjects out of the article without destroying it I'd do so instantly. On all other points I go with you without question. I have revised the article in other ways and made such a mess of it that it must be recopied. I'll return it as soon as my stenographer finishes it. I think you will find it unobjectionable in its new form.

Sincerely yours,
H. L. Mencken

◇◇◇◇◇◇◇◇◇◇◇◇◇◇

To GUY HOLT
[UV]

H. L. Mencken
1524 Hollins St.
Baltimore
March 19th [*1920*]

DEAR HOLT:–

Your lawyers are probably right. But how are we going to tackle the law? I see no chance until there is a strong offensive and defensive alliance of authors, and there seems to be small prospect of forming it. Altogether, I begin to believe that the problem is hopeless. The only thing for a civilized man to do is to get out of the United States, and stay out. Once the Junkers come back, I shall get naturalized as a German.

Whenever you print a detective or adventure novel, send me a description of it in 150 words. I'll run it in the Black Mask, our new thriller.*

Yours,
Mencken

* Have you any at present?

◇◇◇◇◇◇◇◇◇◇◇◇◇◇

To ERNEST BOYD
[OFP]

H. L. Mencken
1524 Hollins St.
Baltimore
April 3rd [*1920*]

DEAR BOYD:–

Your letter of March 12th is just in. By this time, I suppose you have received my letter advising you to come out and take your chance. I still believe that you will encounter no difficulty. All sorts of opportunities present themselves. For one thing, I think Knopf could utilize you as adviser. Then there are the weeklies. Then there are newspaper chances. Finally, the magazines are wide open.

The cost of living over here, of course, is colossal. Nathan has been living at the Royalton for 10 years, and his rent for two small rooms and bath has gradually gone up to $80 a month. Now they propose to jump him to $175, and he must move. This leap of more than 100% is not uncommon. But I believe the end is in sight. In any case, there are much cheaper quarters and, in my opinion, much better. It is its location that makes the Royalton so expensive.

The moment I get the time I shall certainly write some stuff for the Athenaeum and the New Age. At the moment I am paralyzed by Prejudices II, which refuses to get itself written. I must deliver the ms. by June 1st and haven't 5,000 words on paper. It is largely a rewriting job—but rewriting jobs always torture me.

I am naturally much tickled by the news that you are to treat my merits in a piece for Murry. By a curious coincidence, I very lately advised Knopf to do Murry's book over here. It is full of good stuff. I think Knopf will bring it out in September.

Our new louse, the Black Mask, seems to be a success. But the paper famine may murder us at any moment. The thing has burdened both Nathan and me with disagreeable work. The Smart Set bonds fall due next year, and we must do some hard sweating to avoid bankruptcy. If we can stave off the bondholders we'll be safe thereafter. If not—but we have already devised a scheme to save the day, God willing. Such Geschäft keeps me in bad humor.

I am sending you copies of two new Free Lance books today.[5] The Baroja is still delayed. The Credo is getting very favorable notices, and is hence a great failure. I was counting on bitter patriotic denunciations. Instead, all the papers say that the work is full of sagacity, and so it is dying the death.

The Comstocks have just rated Hutchins Hapgood's "The Story of a Lover".

I have a suspicion that the next bugaboo over here will be John Bull Himself. If the Republicans nominate Hoover, Hearst will denounce him as an English spy—and convince nine-tenths of the plain

---

[5] Two new Free Lance books: Nietzsche's *Antichrist* (No. 3) and Edwin Muir's *We Moderns* (No. 4), both published in New York by Alfred A. Knopf in 1920.

people. In any case, the scramble for Russian trade is bound to make violent ill-feeling. The English press bureau deluges the country with tales depicting the Irish as a nation of murderers, but I doubt that the boobery is falling for the stuff.

Jews are still being jailed and I.W.W. meetings raided, but the Bolshevik scare begins to abate. Anti-Germanism is now confined to the old minority of social pushers. The proletariat now turns to other horrors. The Irish continue to maul one another, but rather less vigorously than in the past. A week or so ago, in fact, the factions called a peace conference. United, they could sweep the United States. But not with the Flynns and O'Googans playing detective on the Flahertys.

The other day I met, quite by chance, a very prominent American politician—one of the chief sponsors of a leading presidential candidate. He astounded me by launching into a tirade to the effect that the war was a huge mistake, that the United States should have helped the Germans, and that we must now undo the mischief. Well, I shall *not* volunteer. The eight wounds I got in the last war are not yet healed.

The anti-Prohibition movement is practically dead. The only states bawling for their beer are New Jersey and Rhode Island. All the rest acquiesce. Last night the Maryland Legislature killed a 3.5% beer bill. It is all over.

Yours,
Mencken

To ERNEST BOYD
[OFP]

H. L. Mencken
1524 Hollins St.
Baltimore
April 5th [*1920*]

DEAR BOYD:–

[. . . . .]

I rather doubt that my books would do well in England. They are horribly American. But Knopf is pursuing the matter in his slow way. I am banking on "On Democracy" next year. It will be written for the international trade, and there is a good prospect of getting translations. The Credo is a failure over here. All the notices are favorable. It would have been made by bitter patriotic attacks. As it is, everyone thinks it is sweet and harmless stuff.

Last night, being Easter, the dinner club celebrated the historic event in Palestine by staging a very wet dinner. In fact, the whole gang went over the top. Your health was drunk in a capital beverage made up of 50% rum, 25% Swedish punch and 25% Port. It sounds awful, but it reaches the spot. I am somewhat sour today.

In Xt.,
Mencken

To LOUISE POUND
[PT]

[*Dr. Louise Pound (1872–1958) was professor of English at the University of Nebraska; she edited various publications, mainly on linguistics.*]

Baltimore, April 5th [*1920*]

DEAR DR. POUND:–

Forget it, I prithee. No harm whatever is done. Nathan should be proud to join me in printing such stuff, and he knows it.

My grandfather was so violently anti-Semitic that I used to suspect him of harboring Jewish corpuscles. But an elaborate inquiry proved that he was pure. La Menken, I believe, was thoroughly Yiddish.[6] The family refuses to countenance her, but I have always had a sneaking sympathy for her. I regret that I was born too late to see her in "Mazeppa". Swinburne was mashed on her, and wrote her poems for her. Why doesn't someone write an honest biography of him? Imagine the book of Gosse—the perfect Presbyterian on the perfect infidel. Swinburne was a heavy and very hoggish drinker, and had a great liking for waitresses. Watts-Dunton imprisoned him at Putney to save him from scandal.

I sprained my arm lately, and have just got it out of the bandage. It looks to be as good as new.

Sincerely yours,
H. L. Mencken

[6] La Menken: Ada Isaacs Menken (1835?–68), actress, poet, author of *Infelicia* (Philadelphia, New York, etc.: J. B. Lippincott & Co.; 1868).

◇◇◇◇◇◇◇◇◇◇◇◇◇◇

To Louise Pound
[PT]

Baltimore, April 23 [1920]

Dear Dr. Pound:–

Thanks very much for the Stunts in Language reprint. As always, you have put together a great deal of interesting stuff. A couple of errors and omissions suggest themselves.

1. Can it be that you have never heard conductorette? It became almost universal in the East during the war, when many fair damsels took to robbing the fare-boxes. Here in Baltimore not a few conductorettes still survive.

2. -fest did not come in during the late war. It was very common ten or fifteen years ago—perhaps more common than ever since. It was suggested by Sängerfest and Schützenfest.

3. Some well-known examples of portmanteau place-names are Pen-Mar, Md., Mar-Del, Del., Penn-Yan, N. Y., and Norlina, N. C.

4. The o-termination for trade names originated in the cigar business before the Spanish war. Example: Cinco, a very well-known 5-cent cigar. My father was in the cigar manufacturing business, and had a great hand for composing brand-names in bad Spanish. The atrocity was imitated in other trades so long ago as 1895.

5. Bevo is simply Slavic, i.e., Polish-Ruthenian for beer. Cinco, of course, is Spanish for five.

But such inquiries are endless! Every time I think of rewriting my American Language tome I grow pallid and feeble.

Miss Cather dropped in at The Smart Set office the other day, and we had a long talk. She is off for Italy, to work on a new novel. She is leaving Houghton for my publisher, Knopf—a much better man for her. She told me some of the details of her heroic struggle against the Sherman metaphysic in literary criticism. A very interesting woman —a much finer artist than she knows. I bought a capital novelette from her.

I am at work on Prejudices II, and, as usual, cursing God. It is a rewriting job, but full of snares.

Sincerely yours,
H. L. Mencken

(Sent to Burton Rascoe with an Unidentified Letter)
[up]

[*Summer 1920?*]

Addendum on Aims:

If I have any definite purpose at the moment it is to get an audience wider than the home audience. This seems likely of accomplishment. Vincent O'Sullivan's brief references to me in the Mercure de France have opened the way for the possible French translation of On Democracy, and he has now printed a long article on me in the London New Witness (G. K. Chesterton's paper) for November 28.[7] The London Athenaeum has reviewed Prejudices favorably, and the London Times has noticed it. In Germany I have had a four column article in the Continental Times, and I am now in contact with various Germans who will introduce my ensuing books. In Denmark, Georg Brandes has read some of my books, and professed interest in them. E. A. Boyd told me that when he visited Brandes a year ago, B. told him that the three Americans who interested him most were Dreiser, E. W. Howe and me. (This is confidential.) I also have a good booster in South America, and he will do my On Democracy into Spanish.[8]

I believe, and have often argued, that the battle of ideas should be international—that is idiotic to expect any one country to offer hospitality to every imaginable sort of man. I do not fit into the United States very well. My skepticism is intolerably offensive to the normal American man; only the man under strong foreign influences sees anything in it save a gross immorality. The Sherman reaction is typical and quite honest.[9] If the notions of the right-thinkers are correct, then such stuff as mine (and particularly such stuff as I shall write hereafter) ought to be put down by law. I believe that, in the long run, it *will* be put down by law—that free speech is too dangerous to a democracy to be permitted. But I do not complain about this fact. If Knopf cannot print my books following On Democracy I shall print them in

[7] *Notes on Democracy* was not translated into French, unlike *In Defense of Women* and *Selected Prejudices*. Mencken was never too well-known in France. Vincent O'Sullivan's article: "La littérature Americaine", in the *Mercure de France* for January 16, 1919.

[8] A good booster: Isaac Goldberg (1887–1938), specialist of South American literature, and author of a book on Mencken.

[9] Sherman: Stuart P. Sherman.

Zürich or Leipzig. The Puritans have a right to determine the laws of their own country. And I reject the sentimentality that the minority also has rights.

Note on my relations to Nathan:

We are constantly accused of imitating each other. This is absurd. No two men could possibly be more unlike, in style and thought. Nathan detests philosophical questions, and particularly political questions; he sees life purely as idiotic spectacle. I delight in such questions, though I reject all solutions. Nathan aims at a very complex style; I aim at the greatest possible lucidity. Our point of contact is our common revulsion from American sentimentality. We are both essentially foreigners. But he is more French than anything else, and I am more German than anything else. We work together amicably because we are both lonely, and need some support. He dislikes the American Language book because it is full of of facts, and has never read it. I dislike his interest in the theatre, which seems to me to be an intellectual hogpen. But we come together on several essentials, e.g. our common disinclination to know authors or to belong to literary coteries, our lack of national feeling, and (perhaps most important) our similar attitudes toward money, religion, women, etc. We seldom disagree on literary judgments; it is very rare for either to exercise his veto in buying stuff for The Smart Set. Both of us think the same, for example, about Cabell, Dreiser, Cather, Dunsany, Conrad, Anatole France, etc. Both have the same (almost pathological) aversion to worldly failure; we dislike having anything to do with men who are so bad at their jobs that they can't live decently by them. Neither regards writing books as a job: it is the *reward* of a job. Both of us detest martyrs of all sorts.

My relations to Dreiser:

The common notion that I discovered Dreiser is bosh. He had written Sister Carrie before I ever met him. I probably helped him appreciably after Jennie Gerhardt, but it is not inconceivable that he would have been better off if I had never written a line about him. We remained on good terms so long as I was palpably his inferior—a mere beater of drums for him. But when I began to work out notions of my own it quickly appeared that we were much unlike. Dreiser is a great artist, but a very ignorant and credulous man. He believes, for example, in the Ouija board. My skepticism, and, above all, my contempt for the peasant, eventually offended him. We are still, of course, very friendly, but his heavy sentimentality and his naïve yearning to be a martyr make it impossible for me to take him seriously—that is, as man. As artist, I believe that he has gone backward—but he is still a great man. Think of "Twelve Men".

I know no other first-rate artist. I know Hergesheimer, but only slightly, and his rather gaudy vanity repels me. I have never met Cabell. I have met La Cather but once. Dunsany but once—he is an ass. I have never met Vincent O'Sullivan, who has written about me. I have never even seen such men as Howells, Herrick, Garland, etc. I know Ed Howe, and like him. He is the very best type of American—simple, shrewd and lively in mind. I mean the real American—not the Judaized New Yorker.

On Influences:

I have never consciously imitated any man save the anonymous editorial writer of the New York Sun. The man who made a critic of me was Robert I. Carter, an old New York Herald man, then managing editor of the Baltimore Herald, and my boss (circa 1912).[1] He taught me a lot, but particularly one thing—that the first desideratum in criticism is to be *interesting*. What has become of him I don't know. I haven't heard from him in years. Next to Carter, I learned most from Percival Pollard—particularly the value, to a critic, of concentrating on a few men. Pollard used Ambrose Bierce; I used Dreiser. I seldom read criticism. The work of such men as Brownell, More, Sherman, etc. seems to me to be simply silly—a dull emission of the obviously untrue.

I believe that the public likes criticism only in so far as it is a good show, which means only in so far as it is bellicose. The crowd is always with the prosecution. Hence, when I have to praise a writer, I usually do it by attacking his enemies. And when I say the crowd I mean all men. My own crowd is very small and probably somewhat superior, but it likes rough-house just as much as a crowd around a bulletin-board. All the favorable notices of Prejudices show an obvious delight in my onslaughts on Cobb, Veblen, Howells, Hamlin Garland, Sydnor Harrison, Shaw, etc. Such doings, of course, involve reprisals. I am myself attacked with great vigor. Not infrequently I am attacked unfairly, e.g., by the fellows who accused me, during the war, of German propaganda, which was just as unfair as accusing a man, in Catholic Ireland, of being an Orangeman. But such attacks do not annoy me.

---

[1] The date should be 1900.

I am skeptic enough to believe that some other fellow's notions of honor may be quite as sound as my own. Moreover, there is always a certain amount of truth in every attack, however dishonest.

Ethical note:

I have no superstitions about critical honor. I lean toward men I like and away from men I dislike. The calm, Judicial judgment makes me laugh. It is a symptom of a delusion of infallibility. I am often wrong. My prejudices are innumerable, and often idiotic. My aim is not to determine facts, but to function freely and pleasantly—as Nietzsche used to say, to dance with arms and legs.

Critical:

All of my work hangs together, once the main ideas under it are discerned. Those ideas are chiefly of a skeptical character. I believe that nothing is unconditionally true, and hence I am opposed to every statement of positive truth and to every man who states it. Such men seem to me to be either idiots or scoundrels. To one category or the other belong all theologians, professors, editorial writers, right-thinkers, etc. I am against patriotism because it demands the acceptance of propositions that are obviously imbecile, e.g., that an American Presbyterian is the equal of Ludendorff. I am against democracy for the same reason: it rests upon lunacy. To me democracy seems to be founded upon the inferior man's envy of his superior—of the man who is having a better time. This is also the origin of Puritanism. I detest all such things. I acknowledge that many men are my superiors, and always defer to them. In such a country as the United States, of course, few such men are to be encountered. Hence my foreignness: most of the men I respect are foreigners. But this is not my fault. I'd be glad to respect Americans if they were respectable. George Washington was. I admire him greatly. It seems to me that, within our own time, Germany has produced more such men than any other country. Next to Germany, England. Italy has not produced a single first-rate man in years, and France has produced very few since the fall of the Empire.

I detest men who meanly admire mean things, e.g., fellows who think that Rockefeller is a great man. I also detest poltroons—that is, men who seek unfair advantages in combat. In my gladiatorial days on the Baltimore Sun I never attacked a single man who was without means of hitting back. Often I insisted upon the paper giving him the means—I controlled space that was dedicated to anyone who wanted to attack me. No man was ever refused this space. My objection to Americans is that they like to fight with the enemy strapped to a board. Hence the persecution of Germans, lynching, the American Legion, the American Protective Association, the attack on Spain, the wars with Nicaragua, Santo Domingo, etc. This poltroonery is not essentially American; it is simply democratic; the inferior man always shows it. I never complain about an attack, however unfair.

As I say, all my work hangs together. Whether it appears to be burlesque, or serious criticism, or mere casual controversy, it is always directed against one thing: unwarranted pretension. It always seeks to expose a false pretense, to blow up a wobbly axiom, to uncover a sham virtue. My experience of the world teaches me that the best people are those who make no profession of being good—that all who do, absolutely without exception, are frauds. I regard Wilson as the archetype of the hypocrite—an incurable damned liar, utterly without honor.

My weapon is adapted to the enemy and the fight. Sometimes I try to spoof them, and sometimes I use a club. But the end is always the same. I have no general aim save this—that is, I do not aspire to set up any doctrine of my own. Few doctrines seem to me to be worth fighting for. I can't understand the martyr. Far from going to the stake for a Great Truth, I wouldn't even miss a meal for it. My notion is that all the larger human problems are insoluble, and that life is quite meaningless—a spectacle without purpose or moral. I detest all efforts to read a moral into it. I do not write because I want to make converts. In point of fact, I seldom make one—and then it is embarrassing. I write because the business amuses me. It is the best of sports. But all the fun is over by the time a book is printed. The reviews are seldom interesting. In particular, the favorable ones often depress me, for they credit me with purposes that I revolt against; they seek to make a Great Teacher out of me.

I am, tested by the prevailing definitions, a bad American. I do not believe the country has the glorious future that patrioteers talk of. It will probably remain second-rate for centuries—a mere milch cow for England. All of the American ideals, so-called, that I know of seem to me to be idiotic. If they were sound, I'd probably jump into the nearest river. The sort of country they conjure up would be simply a paradise of bounders—forward-lookers, right-thinkers, all sorts of stupid cowards. I do not believe that civilized life is possible under a democracy. Unless the Germans shoot all of their present democratic statesmen, Germany will sink to the level of the United States. But I do not care. No matter what happens, here or elsewhere, I shall be dead by 1950.

I am an extreme libertarian, and believe in absolute free speech, especially for anarchists, Socialists and other such fools. Once all those fellows were free to gabble ad lib., democracy would be reduced to an absurdity: the mob would go stark crazy. I am against jailing men for their opinions, or, for that matter, for anything else. I am opposed to all religions, because all of them seek to throttle opinion. I do not believe in education, and am glad I never went to a university. Beyond the rudiments, it is impossible to teach anything. All the rest the student acquires himself. His teacher merely makes it difficult for him. I never learned anything in school. As I look back, I remember but one teacher with pleasure. He saved me a whole year by insisting upon promoting me when all of the other asses were trying to teach me what I already knew.

It is my belief that democracy is inimical to literature, as to all other fruits of civilization, but this seems to me to be a fact of no importance. All it amounts to is this: that the artist in America can never have a large audience and must expect to encounter positive hostility—Comstockery, college-professorism, etc. But such handicaps are not fatal. They should merely spur on a genuinely good man. I believed every civilized American should help such men—not as a duty, but as a pleasure. Make it a duty, and it at once becomes dishonest.

My style of writing is chiefly grounded upon an early enthusiasm for Huxley, the greatest of all masters of orderly exposition. He taught me the importance of giving to every argument a simple structure. As for the fancy work on the surface, it comes chiefly from an anonymous editorial writer in the New York Sun, circa 1900. He taught me the value of apt phrases. My vocabulary is pretty large; it probably runs to 25,000 words. It represents much labor. I am constantly expanding it. I believe that a good phrase is better than a Great Truth—which is usually buncombe. I delight in argument, not because I want to convince, but because argument itself is an end.

Finally, I have no ambition to be praised by eminent professors. The reviews of my American Language actually made me sick. I don't want to get into the school literature books when I die. All I want is time to write half a dozen books that I have in mind. They will not deal with other books. In fact, I'll write very little about books hereafter. All my criticism is, at bottom, a criticism of ideas, not of mere books. But ideas—i.e., the follies and imbecilities of men—interest me. Blowing them up is the noblest of human occupations.

[*Unsigned*]

◇◇◇◇◇◇◇◇◇◇◇◇◇◇

To ERNEST BOYD
[OFP]

The Smart Set
25 West 45th Street
New York
July 19th [*1920*]

DEAR BOYD:–

I am happy to inform you that, after two all-night sessions, you have been unanimously elected a Knight of the Imperial and Royal (K.k.) Order of the Holy Ghost of Spain, first class. I enclose the K.k. ribbon of the order, blessed by His Holiness. It is worn like the red ribbon of the Légion d'Honneur. The duties of a knight are:

1. To protect innocence in all lands.
2. To foster the true faith.
3. To uphold all righteous laws.
4. To do battle for the Holy Sepulchre.
5. To seek the Holy Grail.

There are no dues.
God save us all!

[*M.*]

◇◇◇◇◇◇◇◇◇◇◇◇◇◇

To THEODORE DREISER
[UP]

H. L. Mencken
1524 Hollins St.
Baltimore
August 20th [*1920*]

DEAR DREISER:–

I shall come to the case of the old cow in due course. She is a dirty old slut.[2]

---

[2] The old cow, etc.: Mrs. Mary Hunter Austin, writer and contributor to the *Smart Set*. After declaring that she supported Dreiser against the Comstocks, she had refused to sign the protest.

That article on the American literary scene was a small part of a very long essay in Prejudices II—about 23,000 words. I'll send you the book when it comes out, in October. I made the index of the book the other day and found that, next to Jesus, Ludendorff and Liveright, you were mentioned in the text more than any other man. In one place I say flatly that you are a promising fellow, and will make a splash when you get your growth.

The Newspaper Days stuff interests me a great deal. You told me of it years ago. Is it ready?

I still cling to the notion that a lot of money could be made by reissuing The "Genius" with all of the passages complained of cut out of the plates, leaving white blanks, and with a special preface by the author. It would be easy to talk Jones into it. You could sell 5,000 in two months. The publicity would be enormous.

Boyd is in New York and I see him regularly. Send him a line of welcome. He is working for the Evening Post, and can be reached there. I have given him some beer. But not enough. The aim is to tease him and so keep him wild.

Yours,
Mencken

To THEODORE DREISER
[UP]

H. L. Mencken
1524 Hollins St.
Baltimore
September 2nd [1920]

DEAR DREISER:–

I'll drop in to see Jones the next time I am in New York, and find out what is in his mind. I had not heard of the suit in the Federal courts, though I knew that you were planning it. It offers a good way out. What boggles the whole situation is Jones' and Liveright's claims for royalties advanced. Both are poor sportsmen, especially Liveright. I was always in doubt about your alliance with him. He now has a great deal of money, obtaining from some new Jew backer. Confidentially, he is forever approaching Nathan and me, and lately he offered us a blank contract, including even 50% royalty. But we are too comfortable with Knopf. He gets out good-looking books—not abortions, like Jones and Liveright—, he pays royalties promptly, and he is a good drummer. Three years ago Jones printed my burlesques book. It got out of print and he let it die. Knopf bought the plates, and actually sold 50% more on a reprint than Jones had sold of the original edition. Lately Knopf has reprinted my Prefaces for the second time, though it is three years old, and such a book seldom lives two years. He is also in the third edition of Prejudices I, though it is an annual, and Prejudices II will be out in a month. But he couldn't afford to buy off Jones and Liveright. I have talked to him about it often. He sells books, but he lacks the capital for such enterprises. I have a feeling that both Harpers and the Century are sick. Of the two, I prefer the Century, on account of Tom Smith. But he may leave at any time.

I think your letter to Constable is rather sniffish, but on the whole you are right. It is, however, rather useless to ask a publisher to guarantee sales; he simply can't do it; he sells as many as he can. As you know, I am strongly against the advance royalty plan. It makes for rows inevitably. I know of no case in which it has failed. Constable is a reputable publisher, and if he had all of your books he should be able to do a lot with them. He is quite right to hesitate to go ahead without the novels. In the long run, they will outsell everything else. You got very small royalties from England on account of the sale-of-sheets system. It cuts royalties to pieces, and takes away all incentive to sell books. Fisher Unwin bought 500 sheets of my Nietzsche in 1908 and still has some of them. Meanwhile, the book has gone through four editions in the U. S.

Scheffauer writes that he has interested a German publisher in several of your novels. On account of the Heinecke arrangement I have advised him to write to you direct. German royalties, on account of the exchange situation, amount to little today. Indirectly, the results are excellent. For this reason, I am giving some of my own stuff to any German translator who will translate it and get it published. Already I have been in Jugend, Der Tagebuch, Die Glocke and other magazines. Don't say these indirect results are worthless. Until I got a few good notices in France and England, I was sneered at at home. Now they treat me so politely, in the main, that I am embarrassed. But this politeness sells books. My sales are now at least three times what they were a year and a half ago. The whole change began with a few favorable notices abroad. You yourself owe more to English notices than to American notices. Sister Carrie was made in England, and it was in England that the Genius suppression was converted into a celebrated case. Without English support, Cabell is dying of lack of interest.

E. A. Boyd is the name. In care of the Evening Post, edit. dept. I am down with hay-fever.

Mencken

I note that you still cling to your pickpocket's address. It is generally believed here in the East that you are being kept in Los Angeles by a fat woman, the widow of a Bismarck herring importer. The other day I was told that she had bought you a gold watch, fully jewelled, and a Ford painted blue. Congratulations.

If you want to, tell Gloom to send me Newspaper Days (collect). Every time I see her it costs me a bottle of absinthe cocktails.[3]

To THE EDITOR OF *The Nation*
(*Communicated by Carl Van Doren*) [4]
[PT]

September 6th [1920]

DEAR SIR:–

With the highest respect, my duty to my grandchildren impels me to protest against being shoved out of your ivory tower, as happens in your issue of September 4, page 263. I am no more a radical in letters than I am in politics, and I surely do not propose that the universities, such as they are, should cease teaching "Euripides and Lucretius, Montaigne and Voltaire, Kant and Goethe, Hazlitt (Hatzfeldt?) and Shelley (Scholle?)", and begin teaching Vachel Lindsay and Dreiser, Amy Lowell and George Sterling (a most immoral fellow: he refused the gilt-edged purple of the National Institute of Arts and Letters with scorn), Gerald Stanley Lee and Harry Kemp. All I ask is that they put a soft pedal upon Fenimore Cooper and James Russell Lowell, Edmund Clarence Stedman and Fanny Fern, Paul Elmer More and Hamilton Wright Mabie. If this is too much to ask, then God help us all!

In other words, the combat is not between the new men of today

[3] Gloom: Mrs. Estelle Kubitz, a friend of Dreiser's.

[4] Carl Van Doren (1885–1950) was then literary editor of the *Nation*. On September 4, 1920, the *Nation* had printed an anonymous article (written by Ludwig Lewisohn) entitled "The Ivory Tower", denouncing Mencken on the grounds that he despised the classics and showed no awareness of "the continuity of human culture".

and the indubitable classics, but between the new men of today and the bogus classics. In this combat I favor the new men, not because they are to be mentioned in the same breath with the indubitable classics, but simply and solely because, compared to the bogus classics, they are vastly more honest, interesting, ingenious, enterprising and alive. To go to music, the choice is not between Richard Strauss and Beethoven, but between Richard Strauss and Prof. Ludwig Blatz, instructor in harp, piano, violin, ukelele and theory in the Hannah More Academy for Baptist Young Ladies. I advocate all honest and diligent men, especially when they are against me. I am against all tripe-sellers and false-faces, let the chips fall where they may.

This letter is NOT for publication. I am decidedly opposed to vain discussions of what John Doe thinks and what is in Richard Roe's secret heart. But I read The Nation so diligently and admire it so enormously that you must permit me this private effort to avoid getting into its aviary of evil birds. If necessary, I'll kiss the First Folio Shakespeare, or give three cheers for Joseph Addison. But please don't try me with no bunk about George E. Woodberry being a greater poet than Lizette Reese, or Mrs. Humphrey Ward having it all over Dreiser.

Sincerely yours,
H. L. Mencken

To F. SCOTT FITZGERALD
[PU]

The Smart Set
25 West 45th Street
New York
September 9, 1920

DEAR MR. FITZGERALD:

Your suggestion is admirable. And if the Department of Justice ever forces me to abandon the title of "Prejudices", I shall adopt it.

Before you finish the novel we should have a secret conference.[5] There are certain episodes in Nathan's life that, while extremely

[5] This letter seems to confirm that Fitzgerald took George J. Nathan as his model for the character of Maury Noble. The story about Nathan and the "Schapiro girl" is, of course, pure invention and should be taken as a joke.

discreditable, are very effective dramatically and I'd like to impart them to you. There was, for example, the Schapiro case in 1904. I am surely not one to credit the Schapiro girl with anything approaching innocence, but, nevertheless, Nathan's treatment of her could not and cannot be defended. And no one sympathized with him very much when he was forced to leave town for two months and hide in Union Hill, New Jersey. La Schapiro was a typical Grand Street flapper. She has since married Irving Blumblatt, the lawyer.*

As soon as the hay-fever gets out of my eyes I am going to give "Flappers and Philosophers" a thorough reading. I suspect that it is a great deal better than you think it is.

The other day I had a letter from William Lyon Phelps referring to Scribner's use of his name and mine in their announcements of "This Side of Paradise" on the ash-cans. Phelps said that he was willing to refrain from legal proceedings if I was.

Sincerely yours,
Mencken

P.S. The pink pamphlet was actually written by Dr. Berthold Baer—a nom de plume for Huneker.

* The child was still-born. Sophia took Chichester's Family Pills.

To LOUISE POUND
[PT]

Baltimore, September 10th [*1920*]

DEAR DR. POUND:–

You scare me with your wallop.[6] I suppose that the ball went over the fence of the brewery and was lost. I grow so feeble, what with hay-fever and senile decay, that it becomes a labor to lift a knife-load of lima beans. As Ed. Howe says, all I have to do is to stretch my neck a bit to see the members of the Arion Gesangverein grouping themselves around the door of the crematory, the while the Herr Dirigent, Prof. Ludwig Batz, brings forth his tuning-fork from the tail pocket of his funeral coat. But such gloomy thoughts go with catarrhus estivus, which causes me to sneeze very little but to weep inwardly very copiously.

A secret: I actually *do* teach literature at Goucher (locally, Gouger, on account of its "drives"), though I receive no honorarium.

[6] Dr. Louise Pound was a State tennis champion.

One of my spies there once told me that all of the Jew gals (very few Christians are on the roll) hide The Smart Set under their pillows, along with Memoirs of My Dead Life and I, Mary MacLane. Worse, a professor of English there lately tried to sell me a short story—psychology à la Henry James—the Atlantic Monthly Complex. Nevertheless, if I entered the place the faculty would lock up the student body in the gymnasium and send for the fire department.

Sincerely yours,
H. L. Mencken

I'll try to get hold of a copy of the Yale Review. I have none by me. The article is part of a chapter in Prejudices II (very much expurgated). I'll send you the book when it comes out, about Nov. 1st.

M.

To THEODORE DREISER
[UP]

[*"Someday, if I ever find time to do* Literary Experiences, *you will find another angle of yourself suggested—no more—because I have never known you really". (Dreiser to Mencken, September 7th, 1920)*]

H. L. Mencken
1524 Hollins St.
Baltimore
September 13th [*1920*]

DEAR DREISER:–

If you ever put me into that book, all I ask is that you speak of me as one who loved God and tried to keep His Commandments. Please don't mention my beauty: it has been my curse.

Rascoe is a young fellow of much promise. He has a sound education and writes very well. Unluckily, he has a wife and children, and so it is hard for him to avoid newspaper slavery. The Tribune fired him a few months ago, and he is now rusticating in Oklahoma. But I think he'll be back in the mines before very long.

You say you have never known me really. No doubt you recall the story of the Irishman who dropped his sandwich in the gutter. "Mike", he said to his friend, "have you ever tasted horse-piss." "No", said the friend. "Well", said the sandwich-dropper, "you ain't missed much".

Huneker's autobiography is chiefly crap, but with some excellent spots.

Hay-fever has me by the ear.

Yours,
M.

To Carl Van Doren
[OFP]

H. L. Mencken
1524 Hollins St.
Baltimore
September 15 [1920]

Dear Mr. Van Doren:

I'd be delighted to do a review of the Huneker book, but I have just finished one for Canby and I must do another for The Smart Set. Worse, the thing is very bad, and I must give old James a wallop. To do it twice is bad enough; to do it three times would amount to persecution. The old rat has got respectable in his dotage, and is at great pains to prove that he is a God-fearing man and a 100% American. Some day or other I'll compose a piece on ivory towers, and what goes on inside them. The last time I entered, a large, florid, highly literate woman—

But that is for my autobiography. Surely we must meet in New York. Transporting ale is difficult, but I'll bring you at least one bottle, and another for poor Ludwig, poisoned by near-beer. I daresay his kidneys present a fearful spectacle.

Sincerely yours,
H. L. Mencken

To Carl Van Doren
[OFP]

H. L. Mencken
1524 Hollins St.
Baltimore
September 22nd [1920, or after]

Dear Mr. Van Doren:–

Goldberg is the man to do the article. As for me, I really know too little about Baroja, and every student of Spanish literature would detect my imposture. In doing the preface to the book, a very formal job, I was greatly aided by Underhill.[7] It is, in fact, little more than a restatement of his ideas.

Some day or other send me a medical book to review. I like to preach on pathology and therapeutics.*

Sincerely yours,
H. L. Mencken

* I always defend the faculty against the new thought.

To THEODORE DREISER
[UP]

[*On September 23, 1920, Dreiser had written to Mencken:*

The truth is that you are an idealist in things literary or where character is concerned and expect men to ring centre 100 times out of 100. Many of Huneker's earlier critical estimates and interpretations are excellent—quite generous and fascinating. What matter now if when he is old he dodders. Wait till you are 65 or 70—and see how you do. My quarrel with his earlier work was that in many cases he was the very last to discover certain people, especially Americans like Davies, and so far as I know, he never said a word about Inness until after 1910. I may be wrong. He waited until all the European reports were in and then generalized upon them—a safe bet. Despite that he was & is a fine writer, interpretive and illuminating. He was certainly very much needed over here. Beside you however—and I say it in all fairness—he is as a pop-gun to a howitzer. You blaze new trails—seek poor sprouts under the weeds and chop down all the choking vines for miles around. You almost kill the new things with sunlight. In addition you run into the offing and yell until a crowd collects. Excellent and wonderful. May your snickersnee grow heavier & sharper. But don't expect the bell to be rung every trip.

And remember Wright. In 1912 I warned you he was stealing your stuff—and revamping it. He had dropped a little tube into your well

[7] The book: the introduction to Pio Baroja's *Youth and Egolatry.* Underhill: Presumably John Garrett Underhill (1876–1946), playwright, critic, and producer; general representative of the Society of Spanish Authors in the United States. He translated many works by Spanish dramatists and edited them.

and was trying to siphon you out. He even assumed himself the larger figure—and began spouting to me until I threw him out. But to you—the idealist once more—he was a little tin Jesus. And now see.

Well it is your typical stunt & your typical experience. You will probably continue for years to come to bring in tin cans from the street and set them on the mantel. But in view of past flops—you might be careful—& not too hard on your idols once they are out in the street again. I like the Stuart Davis sketch of me very much. It makes me laugh.

Dreiser]

H. L. Mencken
1524 Hollins St.
Baltimore
October 1st [1920]

Dear Dreiser:–

Of course I don't believe that you would blab a confidential communication. But I saw a row looming up, and I have had a belly full of rows these last years. I am constantly tempted to throw up all literary business, buy a dog-house in Maryland, and live on $100 a month, writing one book a year. But by the time one mess is finished I am in another. I'll probably die in full regalia, wearing even a condom.

What you say of my high services to art is pleasant, but rhetorical. There is nothing much to do here save hatchet idiots. The country is irrevocably rotten. My work hereafter, if I keep on, will be a good deal more political than literary. In Prejudices II I skin Roosevelt's carcass. In Prejudices III I hope to tear out the cold bowels of Woodrow. A pox upon all such swine! May they sweat in hell forevermore!

The Wright episode was disagreeable, but I have no regrets. I got him every job he ever had in the East, supported him when he was in need, and stood up for him against the crowd. In reply he robbed me of money and lied about me. But consider his state today —full of drugs, hopeless, jobless and living by petty graft.

I read the newspaper book.[8] It is full of excellent stuff. Some of the newspaper chapters are gorgeous. The defect that I see in it is a certain flabbiness in form. Considering the great space given to the beginning

[8] The newspaper book: *A Book About Myself* (New York: Boni and Liveright; 1922).

of the S. W. episode, it seems to me that the thing is dismissed too briefly at the end. So with the Alice business. This objection, of course, would fade if the book were printed as one volume of a series—that is, if it were clearly understood that another volume would follow. Such a volume *should* follow. For this reason I think that Newspaper Days is a better title than A Novel About Myself.[9] If you use the latter, what will you call the succeeding and preceding volumes?

In places you philosophize, I think, at too great length. Again, I dislike the picking up of stuff from Twelve Men (the McCord episode). Yet again, the affair with the Bohemian woman is a bit wheezy—the sort of thing that all of us have at 22. It is true, of course, but it is also true that you shit your pants in 1884—and that is not mentioned. I don't think the Comstocks will bother the book. Changing a few words would stump them completely. Altogether, the book is a bit too long. It would be more effective if some of the thinner discourses were cut down. But there is enough good stuff in it to justify it.

You missed a fine chance when you didn't write a whole book about your brother. The idea dawned on me that day at San Francisco. We have biographies of all sorts of eighth-rate politicians, preachers, cheese-mongers, etc. Why not a full-length book on a genuine American original, what we Huns call a Kopf? I don't think the Twelve Men chapter has ruined it. What of his early days? How did he write his songs?

I don't object to Huneker growing senile; I object to him recanting so ignominiously. I enclose a tender review of his book. He deserved an attack with good German artillery. Also, I enclose a patriotic piece.

The Liveright letter is very amusing. A love affair, by God! He talks and talks.

I met W. L. George last night in New York. He will be in Los Angeles toward Christmas. Do you want to see him?

I returned the MS. to Gloom, and gave her a bottle of vermouth.

God save the Republic!

Yours,
M.

[*On October 8, 1920, Dreiser answered:*

Anent W. L. George. No—I don't want to see him. My experiences with literary men make me curse. I like a man anywhere—and if

[9] Mencken was to use the title later for the second volume of his memoirs.

he chances to be one—and really wants to see me, he will get in touch with me direct—and in the right spirit. Otherwise his books suffice. Thank god for private letter boxes, obscure neighborhoods & people who think you are in the real estate or insurance business.]

To FIELDING HUDSON GARRISON
[PT]

Baltimore, October 2, 1920

DEAR GARRISON:

I have been in New York all week, and so I have just got your letter. Let us meet soon, by all means. Ruhräh called me up last week and told me that he was going to Washington to see you, but the time he fixed fell during my visit to New York, so I couldn't come along. We have elected him to the old dinner club. Thus both of us will strive to haul you over some Sunday. We'll inaugurate him with solemn ceremonies on October 17th, if it so be God's will.

Hay-fever this year was short and mild. Wet weather delayed it nine days and it lasted less than two weeks. Toward the end of the first week I dropped in on Gottlieb in New York, and he gave me a horse doctor's dose of a new antitoxin, begotten upon two horses fortunately offered to him a few months ago. The next day I was quite free of the damned disease, but it came back. This return, however, was brief. I don't know whether to credit the antitoxin or the Blessed Saints. Mild anaphylaxis followed—a rash, urticaria, joint pains, etc. I incline to think that the antitoxin has possibilities, once it is concentrated and the dosage is determined. Gottlieb simply gave me all of the plain serum that would go into one arm; it seemed almost half a pint. I am a veteran laboratory animal. Find me in hay-fever season and show me a new label, and I'll take a dozen of the large bottles. I figure out that my left arm has had 100 injections of one sort or another in its time. The only permanent effect is pessimism. My one hope is that I am spared to die in battle, fighting for democracy.

The old Geheimrat seems a charming fellow. Like all Germans he is unduly depressed. Despair is the current cult over there. I have a friend in Berlin who writes to me regularly—one week a formal treatise upon the debacle of German industry and the next week a letter full of incautious boasts. The fact is that business is growing good, but with labor restless. I look for a bloody housecleaning in two or three years. The Jews are sowing the whirlwind, and so are the radicals. If ever the United States and England fall out, all parties in Germany will fall upon France overnight, and proceed to a colossal butchery. I have no belief in peace schemes. The late war was inconclusive and unsatisfactory. It left the victors too insecure to be generous, and hence merely exaggerated the old hatreds. I have been reading Treitschke. How history repeats itself!

I'll send you my new book in a few weeks. It is largely piffle, but with a poisonous chapter on Roosevelt, and a very long and partly intelligent discussion of the national letters. Also, there is a chapter on the South, deliberately aimed at the tender midriffs of the Macon Telegraph and Mobile Register. Huneker's autobiography, Steeplejack, is a curious mixture—half brilliant stuff and half drivel. The other day I read the MS. of one volume of Dreiser's autobiography. The same story. One chapter is gorgeous; the next is feeble bosh about some goatish love affair—once with a Bohemian charwoman. Imagine a man remembering all the loose gals of his youth!

I had dinner with W. L. George the other day. A naive fellow, very English; also very decent. He is being pawed by social pushers. They invite him to dinner, and then invite a mob of cads for a free show.

God save the Republic!

Yours,
Mencken

This is a hell of a long letter. Don't answer it. But DO come over to Ruhräh's initiation.

To THEODORE DREISER
[UP]

[*On October 8th, Dreiser wrote*:

Thanks for Huneker and "Star-Spangled Men". That last is certainly spangled satire. At times you remind me of an athlete leaping lightly from test to test, a devout Moslem whirling his sacred prayers, a scaly rattler fencing with a gopher. After all the gyrations of these lice for five years what fine comforting commentary. While I laughed

I thanked heaven for the blood being drawn. I actually hope you finish Woodrow. Why not a small brochure on that nobleman alone?]

H. L. Mencken
1524 Hollins St.
Baltimore
October 11th [1920]

Dear Dreiser:–

You take the Harris chapter too seriously.[1] After all, the general tone of it is very friendly. He puts you into a book on all fours with men that he regards as great, and elects you to the sodality. I begin to believe that *any* writing about a man does him good—that even when it is deliberately unfriendly it makes friends for him. Moreover, unfriendly stuff puts a man on his guard. This I know from my own experience: that I have learned more from attacks than from praise. In even the most vicious of them there is a touch or two of plausibility. There is always something embarrassing about unqualified praise. A man knows, down in his heart, that he doesn't deserve it. When he sees all his petty bluffs and affectations accepted seriously, the sole result is to make him lose respect for the victim. During the war I was belabored constantly by patriotic gents. Some weeks ten or twelve columns of denunciation would come in. Some of it was so violent that I began to look for libel, hoping to turn an honest dollar by entering some suits and then compromising. But the allegations (save the occasional charge that I was a Jew) were so sound that it would have been ridiculous to complain. The fundamental charge was always that I was a foul agent of German Kultur, seeking to poison the wells of the Republic. Well, this was true, at least in a general sense. The Puritans had a right to defend their country.

Harris is a quarrelsome fellow, with a mind full of suspicions. In Pearson's of this month he prints an attack on me by Middleton Murry. Well, what of it? The attack is apparently honest. Murry has printed two favorable articles about me in the Athenaeum and Harris once printed a long one. If the two of them think that I am wrong in the present case, maybe I *am* wrong. In any case, I am still alive, and able to work.

---

[1]The Harris Chapter: Frank Harris's *Contemporary Portraits* (2nd series) included a chapter on Dreiser (New York: The author; 1919).

So saith the preacher. I doubt that you have any reasonable complaint against Harris and company, or against the world in general. At fifty years you are not only permanently secure; you have become a sort of national legend. The younger generation is almost unanimously on your side. The professors have been beaten, and they know it.

George Sterling writes that he has laid in 4 barrels of grappo and 25 head of gals to entertain you. Beware! He dam near finished me in 24 hours.

Yours,
M.

◇◇◇◇◇◇◇◇◇◇◇◇◇◇

To THEODORE DREISER
[UP]

The Smart Set
25 West 45th Street
New York
October 12th [*1920*]

DEAR DREISER:–

You mistake me, my dear Emil. I don't cite Wright's collapse as a proof of the justice of God; I cite it as a reason why I can't wallop him. He is down and out. You begin to see moral banshees. This is three times within two months that you have accused me of being a Christian. I begin to have Freudian suspicions. You hear the whisper of Jesus in your own ear.

Thanks very much for the Hand of the Potter circular. I hope you send one to Nathan. The history of the play is particularly interesting.

If you can wait a bit I'll be very glad to go through *Newspaper Days* again and scheme out a few cuts. The best of it is so fine that it seems a pity to let the thing down here and there. I think that Gloom told me she was taking the MS. to Udall. In any case I'll get hold of her. I see no reason why the Bohemian woman episode should be cut out entirely. Maybe, on re-reading the MS., I'll conclude that it ought to stay in as it stands. As for McCord, wouldn't it suffice to refer to Twelve Men? Let the swine buy it.

I suppose George will try to find you. I have not mentioned the matter to him, but if he asks me flatly for a card to you I can't very well refuse. I am surely not one to cultivate these visitors. George, Walpole and Dunsany came to me. Walpole turned out to be a capital fellow, and George seems very decent. Dunsany is an ass. I have met none of the others, save Sassoon. I ran into him on the street one day, with Louis Untermeyer.

Write to Gloom, and tell her to send me the MS., or to leave it at the Smart Set office. I am in Baltimore.

God save the Republic!

Yours,
H. L. M.

The insurance business? Bah! They suspect you of being a swami.

M.

To LOUISE POUND
[PT]

Baltimore, October 22nd [*1920?*]

DEAR DR. POUND:–

Thanks very much for the ballad reprint. Like everything you do, it is interesting and valuable. I have a lingering doubt that even the simplest play-songs are ever invented by the great masses of the plain people. They represent, like negro music, merely blundering copies of songs originating higher up. To invent a word, they are nonsensicalized but not invented. A good many of the best German "folk-songs" were actually written by Friedrich Silcher. I have often noticed how children borrow popular songs, and sometimes change them so much that it is hard to recognize them.

I wish you had the task of rewriting "The American Language" —not because I wish you ill, but because you could do it much better than I. Material is pouring in from all parts of the world, and I have long since got beyond my very meagre knowledge of language. Why doesn't some one investigate the history of American pronunciation? And why doesn't some one else do a serious grammar of vulgar spoken American? I haven't either the time or the skill, and yet here is the publisher bawling for copy for a new edition.

Sincerely yours,
H. L. Mencken

I had a pleasant note the other day from Dr. Jespersen and he has sent me two of his books. I blush when I think how polite he is.

To SINCLAIR LEWIS
[YU]

H. L. Mencken
1524 Hollins St.
Baltimore
October 27th [*1920*]

DEAR LEWIS:–

I have just finished "Main Street", and hasten to offer my congratulations. It is a sound and excellent piece of work—the best thing of its sort that has been done so far. More, I believe that it will sell.

I'll review it in the January Smart Set, the first issue still open.

Sincerely yours,
H. L. Mencken

To CARL VAN DOREN
[OFP]

H. L. Mencken
1524 Hollins St.
Baltimore
October 27th [*1920*]

DEAR MR. VAN DOREN:–

Do whatever suggests itself with the Buck review.[2] I am the perfect contributor: I have absolutely no pride of authorship. What astonished me about Buck's book was that the Yale Press should have printed it. It is, in the main, childish stuff.

The news that Ludwig wrote the Ivory Tower piece surprises me.[3] The artful fox well concealed his tracks. A superb piece of hypocrisy. Tell him I say he would be more at home in a Bierkeller than in an Ivory Tower.

Sherman I have never met. It seemed to me that he aimed a bit below the belt during the war, but who am I to prattle of honor? Some day we must get hold of him and try to civilize him. He writes very well.

---

[2] The Buck review: probably a review of *The Budget and Responsible Government,* by Arthur E. Buck (New York: The Macmillan Co.; 1920).

[3] Ludwig: Ludwig Lewisohn.

Regarding American novels: as the Owen Johnsons slide down into the Saturday Evening Post, various tear-squeezers struggle to emerge. For example, Zona Gale, whose "Miss Lulu Bett" is excellent stuff. Again, Sinclair Lewis, whose "Main Street" is a genuine and very agreeable surprise. I am very eager to see your book.[4] When will it be ready?

Sincerely yours,
H. L. Mencken

To FIELDING HUDSON GARRISON
[PT]

Baltimore, November 4, 1920

DEAR GARRISON:

[. . . . .]

I am delighted that you like "The National Letters". The thing rather left me in doubt. A great deal of work went into it, but it seemed somehow flabby. I added the jazz chapters toward the end of the book to hold it up. Knopf has printed 3,000 copies. If he sells them, then the Jews deserve some respect. The formula of the Prejudice books is simple: a fundamental structure of serious argument, with enough personal abuse to engage the general, and one or two Rabelaisian touches. The Roosevelt chapter will get more attention than any other. The Roosevelt family, having tasted the preliminary blast in The Smart Set, is furious. In particular, the doctrine that Theodore was not an aristocrat is offensive to his heirs and assigns.

Anderson has written "Windy McPherson's Son", "Marching Men", "*Winesburg, Ohio*" and "*Poor White*", all fiction, and "Mid-American Chants", free verse. La Cather has written "Alexander's Bridge", "O Pioneers", "The Song of the Lark", "*My Antonia*" and "*Youth and the Bright Medusa*". I have only those underlined in red. I'll be glad to send them to you whenever you want them. Also any book of Cabell's. I have all of his except one.

The Solemn Referendum rather staggered me.

Yours,
Mencken

---

[4] Your book: *The American Novel* (New York: The Macmillan Co.; 1921).

(1920)

To THEODORE DREISER
[UP]

[*On November 14, 1920, Dreiser had written to Mencken:*

I don't know whether you are kidding me about an invitation to the P. D. ceremonials and I can't say that there will ever be any ceremonials—but if there are & you'd like to come—assuming that I'm invited—there's no one in the world I'd rather have by me all the way through for I certainly would need substantial intellectual support of some kind. As Duffy used to say—"one needs to acquire the power of simulating conviction". So if I go you go—if you will & I'll be very much flattered and Paul would be too, I know.

Someone suggests a Paul Dresser night out there with all his songs sung & it would be interesting—a gala occasion I bet.

Sterling says he is in doubt whether he will let you live in S. F.—that you're not worthy of its Bohemian resources—that you select impregnable virgins and cling to water as it were your heart's blood. How so? Come through?

Enclosed are two clippings sent on here—which please return. I note that your list—at last—is the one approved. You wield a big stick & no doubt of it. And looking at these things makes me think that this is as fit a time as any for me to acknowledge your services to yours truly. In his introduction to Erewhon Hackett (Francis) quotes Samuel Johnson as saying—"though it should happen that an author is capable of excelling, yet his merit may pass without notice, huddled in the variety of things and thrown into the general miscellany of life". And he adds: "It is even truer, as Dr. Johnson adds, that readers 'more frequently require to be reminded than informed' "—a very clear perception of a fact.

And looking back on myself I know now that except for your valiant and unwearied and even murderous assaults and onslaughts in my behalf I should now be little farther than in 1910. You opened with big guns & little & kept them going. The fact that a few white flags begin to appear is due to you & you alone. And now I sometimes wonder what more. The fireside & a limping old age. Hell.]

H. L. Mencken
1524 Hollins St.
Baltimore
November 20th [1920]

Dear Dreiser:–

1. I have asked Gloom to get the MS. from Yewdale as soon as he has finished with it, and to leave it at the Smart Set office to be forwarded to me. So far I have not heard from her, but she is always diligent in such matters.

2. Without the MS. by me, it is impossible to suggest chapters for serial publication. But a number of them are in the book, and I'll make a list when I go through the MS. again.

3. Are you set on chapter headings? Somehow, I have a feeling that they would not help the book. It seems to me that it needs relatively little changing. Now and then you got lost in your story, but not often.

4. I am quite serious about going to the Paul Dresser ceremony. The Baltimore Sun would be glad to pay my expenses. The concert of his songs would be superb; they are genuinely fine folk-music, and much better than you think. I shall try to give some help with an article in the Smart Set and one in the Sun. Let us buckle down to the thing, and we'll convert the celebration into a national affair. He deserves it, absolutely. A man who can do what he did that afternoon at San Francisco is extraordinarily rare.

5. Sterling is a low libeller. I drank alcohol each and every day I was in San Francisco, whereas he had to go on the water wagon and remained there six days running. It is true that I consorted with a virgin and that she is a virgin still, but that is simply because I was very tired and she was very amiable. Sterling announced months in advance that he had a boudoir companion for me—that all I'd have to do would be to go to her place and hang up my hat. But when I arrived she was non est, and so I had to scratch around on my own hook, seeking both sparring partners and a virgin to soothe me with her talk. I had a hell of a good time. George was superb, but history must record that he went on the water wagon. So much in simple justice to my honor. I would not have any reputable man think that I was actually sober in San Francisco. As a matter of fact, I came down with a severe alcoholic gastritis, and was ill in bed all the way home on the train—a ghastly experience. If you ever hear anyone say that I was sober, please call him a liar. I am touchy on such points.

6. You greatly overestimate my services to you. You were squarely on your legs before I came into contact with you or wrote a line about you, and you would have made the same progress if I had been hanged in 1902, perhaps more.

7. The combat of novelists is very interesting. If I had the list to make I'd leave out Atherton, a great fraud, and put in Hergesheimer, and maybe add a question mark to the name of Tarkington. Hergesheimer's Java Head is far better than any *novel* that Tarkington has done; his short stories—e.g., Beaucaire and the Penrod pieces—are something different. Atherton belongs to the Amelie Rives group; she lacks brains. Cabell has been made by the Jurgen case. He is tickled sick. Curiously enough, W. L. George does not like him. I see the reason: George is an implacable realist. Walpole, on the other hand, thinks that Jurgen is superb. George has asked me to do an article on him for Vanity Fair. When he reaches Los Angeles, take a look at him. He is not impressive, but he has a head on him.

8. The Writers' Club consists of contributors to Snappy Stories, the Parisienne, etc.

9. My apologies for this too long letter. Get right with God!

Yours,
Mencken

To LOUIS UNTERMEYER
[OFP]

H. L. Mencken
1524 Hollins St.
Baltimore
November 25th [*1920*]

DEAR LOUIS:–

You are quite right: the book, at bottom, is more serious than it appears to be.[5] More, it is an excellent piece of work, a triumph of technique. No one else that I know of could have done it half so well. My one doubt lies in a feeling that you have got a good deal beyond merely clever verse—that the thing is a child hatched by a mother close on 44. I think you see it yourself. You will escape from literary criticism, too, as I am trying to do. The wider field of ideas in general is too alluring. You could do a book on democracy, slapping your

[5] Untermeyer's book: *The New Adam* (New York: Harcourt, Brace and Howe; 1920).

honest opinions into it, that would make all the talked up tomes of Lippmann, Weyl, Croly u.s.w. seem silly. We live, not in a literary age, but in a fiercely political age. Your subconscious understanding of the fact explains your flirtations with the Liberator crowd. My impression is that you are not actually in accord with them, but simply sentimentally sympathetic. Well, so am I. The Liberator is one of the few magazines I read regularly—and I'd be glad to vote for Debs. But at bottom we are not democrats. Soon or late some one will start a weekly that we can write for. I shy at the New Republic because it is too damned superficial. True enough, it sometimes approaches truth-telling, but it never tells the *whole* truth. I suspect that Hackett, in secret, feels much as I do.

Nathan and I propose to print a confidential appendix to the Credo, embodying all the lewd ones.[6] It will start off with the doctrine that eating beans causes one to fart, and include the doctrine that coitus interruptus causes locomotor ataxia in the husband and adultery in the wife. Send me all you can think of. Your contributions to the main Credo reach me just too late, dammit. I passed the page proofs a week ago.

I have been through the Dell opus.[7] I fear he runs aground on a false assumption, to wit, that the average child is intelligent. The average child has no more intelligence than the average man—or cockroach. Teaching it must be done by main strength. Let its ego unfold spontaneously, and you will have, not a philosopher, but a stockbroker, a Methodist or a green-grocer.

Yours in Xt.,
Mencken

To BARRETT H. CLARK
[OFP]

The Smart Set
25 West 45th Street
New York
November 30, 1920

DEAR CLARK:

Nathan is down with some obscure senile disease and hence has been unable to read anything. My own inclination is against the

[6] The appendix to the *American Credo* was printed as a leaflet and distributed by the authors to their friends.
[7] The Dell opus: *Moon-Calf* (New York: Alfred A. Knopf; 1920).

Bernard play.[8] The simple truth is that the more I read the foreign stuff the more I am convinced that the native product is better for our great family magazine. Why don't you write a couple of one-acters for us yourself? You are a good deal better than any of the Frenchmen.

Yours,
Mencken

◊◊◊◊◊◊◊◊◊◊◊◊◊

To EDMUND WILSON
[OFP]

The Smart Set
25 West 45th Street
New York
December 1, 1920

DEAR MR. WILSON:

This story is very well devised, save for one thing. In the first part you raise an expectation that Bradshaw will meet the Captain again, and I think that it ought to be fulfilled. Why not have them come face to face at one of the raids—that is, in some ironical manner? The ending, as it stands, would not satisfy the average reader. The irony is a good deal too subtle for him: He must have it visualized in an overt incident. But the story is excellent and I'd like very much to have it.

I'll certainly be delighted to see the Army glossary. The Professor of English [. . .] compiled one, but it was the idiotic performance of a ninth-rate pedagogue. My book, of course, does not deal primarily with slang, but the manufacture of words during the War shows certain general tendencies worth studying.

Sincerely yours,
H. L. Mencken

◊◊◊◊◊◊◊◊◊◊◊◊◊

To THEODORE DREISER
[UP-CC]

[*This is a copy of a letter from Mencken to Dreiser, sent by the latter to his friend W. C. Lengel.*]

---

[8] The Bernard play: *Les Petites Curieuses,* by French playwright Tristan Bernard (Paris; 1920).

(1920)

1524 Hollins Street
Baltimore, Md.
Dec. 5, 1920

DEAR DREISER:

I have just finished "A Novel About Myself". It is full of excellent stuff, quite wonderful in places. Some of the newspaper chapters are gorgeous. The only defect that I see in it, as it stands, unedited, I presume, is a certain flabbiness of form. Here and there, in connection with the narrating of certain incidents, it tends to let down, but not so very much at that. All could be remedied by a few judicious cuts. And even if these were not made, the force of the work as a whole would not be invalidated. Rid of one or two weak spots it will certainly stand up among the best of your books.

Specifically, the things of which I complain, and which can and no doubt will be remedied in the editing, are as follows:

1. Considering the great space given to the beginning of the S.W. episode, it seems to me that the thing is dismissed too briefly at the end.

2. So with the Alice business.

Since the book is quite frankly a section of your life, and pretends to be nothing more, I can see how these objections would fade, supposing this volume were preceded by one relating your youth and were followed by another relating your subsequent experiences. These 2 volumes should be written.

3. In places you philosophize too much, or, at least, I think so. Yet these preachments can be easily reduced and I do not advocate their elimination by any means.

4. Again, I dislike the picking up of stuff from Twelve Men. (The McCord incident in particular.) Wouldn't it suffice to refer to Twelve Men. Let the swine buy that book.

5. Yet again, the affair with the Bohemian woman is a bit wheezy, —the sort of thing all of us do at 22. It is all true of course, but so is it that at some time or other you wore a celluloid collar or, that you contemplated small peculations. We all did. Yet these things are not mentioned. But again, this is not to say that I think that the episode should be eliminated. It may be that on rereading the book, I'll conclude that it ought to stay in as it stands. Cutting is probably what it needs. If you can wait a bit I will be very glad to go through the book again and scheme out a few cuts. The best of it is so very fine that it seems a pity to let the thing down here and there.

6. Now as to Lengel's argument that the book ought to be postponed for five years.[9] I cannot see that. I see no reason whatsoever, why it should not be published forthwith. Rid, as I say, of one or two weak spots, it will stand with the best of your books. He may be right when he says that it would have been better if you had postponed publishing The "Genius" for five years. If you had, it is possible that you would have changed it somewhat, and that these changes would have obviated the Comstock explosion. Nevertheless, it am thoroughly convinced that the Comstock explosion was, in the long run, very profitable to you, as a similar attack has been to Cable (sic). And how could you have had that explosion without publishing the book as it is? —and when you did really.

And anyhow, I am convinced that at the present stage of your life you can afford to print any book you please. I do not believe that Lengel (and some few others, perhaps), realize how you have grown, —that is, how thoroughly you have captured the imagination of the younger generation,—the tremendous color and appeal your personality and your viewpoint have for them. But as a critic reading manuscripts, I see it every day. You have followers and imitators on every hand. They expect the daring and the different from you. So it is that I say that you can publish what you choose.

I wish you would do a whole book about your brother Paul. It is not too late yet. After all that sketch in Twelve Men merely scratched the ground. There was a fellow, one out of many.

Henry L. Mencken

[*On December 6th, Dreiser answered:*

. . . As for Hey-Rub-A-Dub-Dub *will you believe it when I tell you it is outselling* Twelve Men *(?) I have to laugh when you speak of parts of it as unintelligible. I am convinced after long observation that you have no least taste for speculation. Years ago when I showed you a rough draft of "Equation Inevitable" you sent it back with the comment that you did not know what I was talking about. And I assume that you are still convinced that I do not know what I*

[9] W. C. Lengel: a New York friend of Dreiser's. Concerning this letter, he wrote Dreiser: "Mencken has it all wrong—My appreciation of you is and has been as great as if not greater than Mencken's and the only difference is that I have never deviated from my admiration, even if you do think I have been too frank in some of the things I have said. . . ." Dreiser told Mencken that he disagreed with Lengel and thought that the publication of *The "Genius"* had done much good to his reputation.

am talking about. Mere mumbling as it were. God—what a funny world. Yet we all have our blind spots. I will agree that I have mine. . . .]

◇◇◇◇◇◇◇◇◇◇◇◇◇◇

To HARRY RICKEL
[OFP]

H. L. Mencken
1524 Hollins St.
Baltimore
December 20th [*1920*]

DEAR RICKEL:

Send me the name of the baker's malt man, in God's name. Down here they would sell me only a barrel—about 300 pounds. Let me have the honest one's address—So far the malt hasn't arrived, but I have daily hopes. For all these things, infinite thanks.

I have a note from Graf de Rekowski, saying that he will be in Baltimore in January. It will be a great pleasure to meet him again.

Dreiser's conversation to Bolshevism doesn't surprise me. He will end a Methodist, as I have always predicted. The fellow is soft.

May you have a wet Christmas!

Yours,
Mencken

◇◇◇◇◇◇◇◇◇◇◇◇◇◇

To FIELDING HUDSON GARRISON
[PT]

Baltimore, December 31, 1920

DEAR GARRISON:

Keep the Huneker as long as you want it. Don't forget that I still have your Stendhal.

Let us investigate and anatomize the question of Southern Kultur when we meet here. I am getting a good many letters from Southerners. Nearly all of them agree with me, at least in general. One professor argues that I am unjust to Southern men in the matter of sexual vice; he says that they still venerate womanhood. Well, the most degraded bawdy houses in the world are in the South. For example, in New Orleans.

(1920)

I suspect that Huneker's heroine is chiefly Sibyl Sanderson, with touches of Olive Fremstad. Before the collapse of his glands he was in the intimate confidence of both of them. Today, having become non compos penis, he adores Mary Garden. But, after all, the heroine is secondary. The chief character is always Huneker. I had a long letter from him yesterday, explaining and apologizing for belonging to the National Institute. He also sent the enclosed ticket to be pasted in Painted Veils. The book's title, he says, should be Painted Tails. If you have a pot of paste handy, please stick it in.

1920 has been a bad year for me. I have got absolutely no work done. Prejudices II was a boiling of old bones. The cause was and is physical discomforts. Brown is to take a hack at me as soon as I get back from New York. I was foolish not to go to him a year ago.

The Black Mask is a lousy magazine—all detective stories. I hear that Woodrow reads it. Reading MSS. for it is a fearful job, but it has kept us alive during a very bad year. The Smart Set makes expenses, but very little else. It owes me nine months salary, but is now paying it off.

God help the Republic!

Mencken

1921

◇◇◇◇◇◇◇◇◇◇◇◇◇◇◇◇◇◇◇

To CARL VAN DOREN
[OFP]

H. L. Mencken
1524 Hollins St.
Baltimore
February 9th [1921]

DEAR MR. VAN DOREN:

I'll be delighted to do your book.[1] If you can get a set of sheets before it goes to the bindery, let me have it. I'll be in New York on Tuesday, at the Smart Set office. Are you ever uptown?

I have been tempted more than once to submit something to The Nation, but various considerations have held me back. One has been sheer lack of time for writing. The other has been a desire to expound a Realpolitik that would swear at the Nation's Liberalism. Merz, of the New Republic, induced me to do two articles. I hear that they caused a great moaning. At all events I was not invited to do any more. I have done nothing for the Freeman save a brief skit.[2] Nock and I are old friends.

But let us meet some time and discuss all this. I have a couple of

---

[1] In this letter, Mencken agrees to review Carl Van Doren's *American Novel.*

[2] Mencken had written "A Mysterious Matter" for the *Freeman* (May 12, 1920).

books in mind—one an attack with all arms upon democracy. The smell of it begins to offend me. I prefer either Kaiserism or Bolshevism.

Sincerely yours,
H. L. Mencken

To FIELDING HUDSON GARRISON
[PT]

Baltimore, February 11, 1921

DEAR GARRISON:

Like most quacks, I actually cure. My prescription is heavy physical exercise—not golf or any such frippery, but hard labor with pick and shovel. Try two days of it and you will be astonished. The liver and lights respond at once. I prescribe but do not practise. What with my sister-in-law on my hands, the office gone to hell and a great deal of unpleasant writing to do, including some political articles, I scarcely get time to shave. But when the Spring opens I'll resume my fence.[3]

Willa Cather has done nothing quite so good as My Ántonia, but all of her stuff is worth reading, particularly O Pioneers. Tom Smith, of the Century, told me the other day that she had lately sent him a very fine novelette, but that he had to pass it up because of some crim. con. in it. The Comstocks are in violent eruption, and the Century has been taking too many chances. Next month we are printing in the S. S. a very good novelette by a new writer. But there are two hoors in it, and I fear we'll have to sit in jail for a few weeks. Well, I am reconciled to it. Every civilized American will spend a few weeks of every year in jail hereafter.

La Cather, by the way, is a Swede so I do hear. She is remembered at the University of Nebraska, where she was pedagogued, for a revolt that she led against the way English was taught. The university text-book, by one L. A. Sherman, is almost inconceivably idiotic. Some time ago a member of the faculty (accidentally civilized) sent me a copy. I won't describe it: you'd never believe it.

My sister-in-law recovered from the appendectomy and the ex-

[3] The "fence" was in fact a brick wall that Mencken built in his backyard at 1524 Hollins Street over a period of several years.

ploration without incident. Now she faces the effort to drain her broken-down kidney—a nice mess.

Yours,
Mencken

To FANNY BUTCHER[4]
[OFP]

H. L. Mencken
1524 Hollins St.
Baltimore
February 20th [*1921*]

DEAR FANNY:–

Are you drinking again? I can't make out whether you are sending a woodcut print or the block itself. So far it has not arrived. In any case, my best thanks.

Keep your eye open for "Capitol Hill" by Harvey Fergusson, the first honest novel of Washington life ever written. I know Washington intimately, particularly the political side. Fergusson, who is a Congressman's son and a life-long Washington correspondent, describes the thing with the utmost accuracy. This Fergusson will be heard of later on.

My Confession must be very brief. I can't think of any books that I'd like to have written. I admire many books vastly, but even the best of them seems to me to have obvious defects. Words are veils. It is hard enough to put into them what one thinks; it is a sheer impossibility to put into them what one feels. Hence the air of unreality that hangs about all poetry, even the best. It is an effort to put feelings into words, which is just as absurd as trying to put them into stone. My own books are generally regarded as horribly frank, and, when I am praised at all, it is for clarity of utterance. Yet no reviewer of any of them has ever shown the slightest sign of understanding, or even suspecting, my feelings. Many of them actually set up the doctrine that I have none, which is an imbecility. Every man has feelings. Mine chiefly revolve around a concept of honor. This concept is incomprehensible to most Americans. They are a very moral people, but almost anaesthetic to honor.

---

[4] Fanny Butcher (born in 1890) was literary critic for the Chicago *Tribune*.

I'd rather have written any symphony of Brahms' than any play of Ibsen's. I'd rather have written the first movement of Beethoven's Eroica than the Song of Solomon; it is not only far more beautiful, it is also far more profound. A better man wrote it. Put the best of Shakespeare's sonnets beside a song by Schubert: at once it begins to smell of the lamp. I believe that Anatole France and Joseph Conrad are the best writers now living, but neither has written anything so good as the first act of "Der Rosenkavalier" or the last ten minutes of "Elektra". In music a man can let himself go. In words he always remains a bit stiff and unconvincing. Lately, after a patriotic abstinence of eight years and a half, I heard Wagner's "Tristan und Isolde". The love-song in the second act is full of plain defects, and they are made ten times worse by the presence of fat and puffing singers. Nevertheless, who ever encounters a love-song in mere words that was one half so eloquent and poignant?

I like your page very much. It is interesting and civilized.

Sincerely yours,
H. L. Mencken

To Guy Holt
[UV]

H. L. Mencken
1524 Hollins St.
Baltimore
February 24th [1921]

Dear Holt:–

Dr. F. Schönemann, formerly of Harvard, has gone to the University of Kiel to teach, and is undertaking to make a few Americans known in Germany and Scandinavia. He is a good man, and can accomplish a lot. Among the men he is most interested in is Cabell. I think it would be a good idea to send him the last three or four Cabell books, especially Domnei and Figures of Earth. He is in a position to open the way for translations. His address is Adolf Strasse 54, Kiel, Germany.

How are you?

Yours,
H. L. Mencken

◇◇◇◇◇◇◇◇◇◇◇◇◇

To Theodore Dreiser
[UP]

H. L. Mencken
1524 Hollins St.
Baltimore
March 27th [*1921*]

Dear Dreiser:–

I'll be careful about sending the MS. to Lorimer. Perhaps the best thing will be for me to saw out the articles here, and have my own girl copy them. This will save time. Schmidt still has the whole MS. I'll see him in New York during the coming week.[5]

I have a notion that you are unduly sensitive to criticism. Van Doren's article was certainly in the best of humor. What if he did call you a peasant? In a sense you are. I see nothing opprobrious in the charge. It is like saying that a man is a Swede or an Italian or an American. I am myself partly a peasant, and glad of it. If it were not for my peasant blood, the Mencken element would have made a professor of me. I always tremble on the brink of pedantry, even as it is. This heritage from the Gelehrten is my worst internal enemy. Thank God that my mother's grandfather was a Bauer, with all of a Bauer's capacity for believing in the romantic. Without him I'd have been a mere intellectual machine.

It seems plain to me that the most valuable baggage that you carry is your capacity for seeing the world from a sort of proletarian standpoint. It is responsible for all your talent for evoking feeling. Imagine Sister Carrie written by a man without that capacity, say Nietzsche. It would have been a mess. You say you are not striking at me when you complain of Van Doren. Well, why in hell *shouldn't* you strike at me, if the spirit moves you? When I write about you as an author I put aside all friendship and try to consider you objectively. When, as an author, you discuss me as a critic, you are free to do the same thing, and ought to do it. In this department I am a maniacal advocate of free speech. Politeness is the worst curse of the world.

Why don't you do an article some time on your critics, discussing them absolutely honestly and in detail? Young Farrar would be delighted to have it for the Bookman. It would make a sensation. Every idiot would be offended, but I believe that all competent men would

[5] Schmidt: Thomas R. Smith, editor, writer, managing editor of *The Century Magazine* since 1914 and literary adviser to several publishing houses.

like it. Or the thing might make a good chapter in your autobiography.

How long are you going to stay among the swamis? I wish we could have a palaver. I am in a bad state mentally, and begin to believe that I'll never do the books I want to do. One obligation after another keeps me penned in the brothel. I feel like a poor whore.

This Harper letter seems to me to be mainly slobber. The Harcourt business is too complex to discuss by letter. Harcourt simply saw an impossible MS. He is not idiot enough to lay his head on the Comstockian block. But why ask him to do it? Dell, in his "Mooncalf", gets away with an episode much worse than anything in "Newspaper Days". But he does it discreetly, without flinging the thing into their faces. The Comstocks are baffled by such tactics. But you simply play into their hands—bait and set the trap and then walk into it with hosannahs. They were never more active than they are today. A publisher who takes any unnecessary chances is not brave; he is simply silly. But, as I have said, "Newspaper Days" can be denaturized without changing 500 words. This is the United States, God's favorite country. The fun of living here does not lie in playing chopping-block for the sanctified, but in outraging them and getting away with it. To this enterprise I address myself. Some day they may fetch me, but it will be a hard sweat.

My arm is still crippled, but I can use the machine again. Stenographers always drive me crazy.

Yours,
Mencken

◇◇◇◇◇◇◇◇◇◇◇◇◇◇

To THEODORE DREISER
[UP]

[*In April 1921, John Macy, the critic, spread the rumor that Mencken was on the verge of marriage, or had been secretly married for years.*]

H. L. Mencken
1524 Hollins St.
Baltimore
April 23rd [1921]

DEAR DREISER:–

1. It is Euripides, not Euripedes. I blush for you.

2. I wrote to Kirah, but have had no reply from her.[6]

[6] Kirah: Mrs. Kirah Markham, a friend of Dreiser's.

3. Lorimer, the ass, says that the Newspaper Days chapters are not for him. Ditto Hovey, of the Metropolitan: he says he is using practically all fiction, save for Hard's stuff. The Hearst outfit looks unpromising. I am rather stumped. What do you suggest?

4. Hark, hark, thou comest back! I'll be delighted. When do you start?

5. I shall tackle the professors as they bob up. The fact is, they already show signs of demoralization. Most of them are now very polite to me. I had my best fun with them 6 or 8 years ago, when they were all full of gas.

6. Letters continue to come in as a result of the false report of my marriage, printed last week. Everybody laughs. But why should my marriage be ridiculous? I begin to grow indignant.

Yours,
M.

To LOUISE POUND
[PT]

Baltimore, May 11th [1921]

DEAR DR. POUND:–

Your prayers are unavailing! The American Language is making very poor progress. You will receive an early copy—but I begin to believe that the year will be out before it is ready.

Your ballad book is anything but monotonous and polemical. The form of it seems to me to be excellent. But I can't help thinking of poor Gummere. To spend a whole life-time cultivating a theory, to come to fame on the strength of it, and then to have it wiped out at one stroke. You leave nothing of it save a faint, delicate perfume.

I have joined the *Nation* as contributing editor. This is a joke, the significance of which rather escapes me. I have no duties and no honorarium. My politics are anything but Liberal. I am a kaiserliche-königliche Tory, believe in slavery, and await patiently the restoration of the Hohenzollerns and the new Vormarsch upon Paris. If the Japs ever land in the Chesapeake, I shall get up a bottle of Bernkasteler Doktor 1904, reserved for my death-bed, and drink it at a gulp.

Sincerely yours,
H. L. Mencken

◇◇◇◇◇◇◇◇◇◇◇◇◇◇

To LOUISE POUND
[PT]

Baltimore, May 18th [1921]

DEAR DR. POUND:–

Your athletic prodigies have always excited my envy. My own architecture is such that the only sporting enterprises that I am fit for are laying bricks (I do it very well), playing the piano and drinking beer (also talented here). You really cover an astounding territory. I shall come to the ceremony when you are installed, and make a speech. Meanwhile, I continue to shovel all of your hard work into "The American Language".

I have a suspicion that a good many professors read the *Smart Set;* every now and then one writes in to relieve his mind. But our chief customers, I believe, are of a different sort. In New York, at all events, all the Follies gals have turned intellectual, and keep the magazine on their tables. In fact, Nathan and I have long had a standing reward for anyone who could find a member of the superior half-world who didn't read it. Unluckily, they hold us in such high respect that they are too bashful to invite us to dinner.

My old paper has invited me to attend the Dempsey-Carpentier fight on July 2nd. I accept with joy.

Sincerely yours,
H. L. Mencken

◇◇◇◇◇◇◇◇◇◇◇◇◇◇

To EDMUND WILSON
[OFP]

[*Edmund Wilson had written an article on Mencken in the* New Republic *for June 1, 1921.*]

H. L. Mencken
1524 Hollins St.
Baltimore
May 26th, 1921

DEAR MR. WILSON:–

I need not offer my thanks. You have done me far more lavishly than any one else has ever done me, and with a far greater plausibility and eloquence. A little more, and you would have persuaded even me. But what engages me more, as a practical critic, is the critical penetration of the second half of your treatise. I think you have there told the truth. The brewery cellar, in these days, is as impossible as the ivory tower. For a while the show is simply farce, but inevitably every man feels an irresistible impulse to rush out and crack a head—in other words, to do something positive for common decency. Well, God knows what can be done. But it is certainly easier to do it with such a fellow as you are sitting in the grand-stand.

I drink to you in a large Humpen of prime malt. You must come down to Baltimore some time to try it.

Sincerely yours,
H. L. Mencken

To Louise Pound
[PT]

Baltimore, May 28th [*1921*]

Dear Dr. Pound:–

Who is the professor? He writes clearly and logically, and he ought to be drafted for the war on sorcery. I fancy that you will like "Civilization in America", a vast 36-barrelled gun that Harcourt is to publish in the Autumn.[7] Some of the stuff in it will be flabby, but I hear of some other things that should be good. My own share in it will be only a modest essay on the concept of honor in American politics. Lowie, the anthropologist, will be in it.

The University of Michigan row filled me with mirth. The Rankinistas were very indignant. Some day, when my troubles are over, I hope to tackle your learned colleague of the literary categories. Confidentially, we are soon to start a series in the Smart Set on American universities, beginning with Yale.[8] Each article will be done by a survivor who has undergone vocational rehabilitation.

I now have 750 bottles of prime ale in my cellar. Praise God, from whom, etc.

Sincerely yours,
H. L. Mencken

---

[7] *Civilization in the United States* (New York: Harcourt, Brace and Company; 1922), edited by Harold Stearns.

[8] The *Smart Set* series: "The Higher Learning in America".

(1921)

To LOUISE POUND
[PT]

Baltimore, June 14th [1921]

DEAR MISS POUND:–

Thanks for your very valuable corrections and notes and for the bibliography. I'll be delighted to have a copy of the monograph on blends. The discussion of nasals in *Englische Studien* is easier to get at. A file is in the Peabody Library here in Baltimore. Files of *Modern Language Notes* and *Dialect Notes*, of course, are also there.

The reviews, in the main, have been complimentary but stupid. Several of them hail me as a patriot eager to put American above English! But the notice of Francis Hackett in the *New Republic* was intelligent, and that in the Boston *Transcript* was excellent. Knopf, the publisher, tells me that the book will be sold out within a month. I shall not touch the revision for at least a year.

It has had the curious effect of making me respectable. The other day I was invited (a) to write for the London *Nation*, and (b) to join the Author's Club in New York. The former I accepted, but the latter I evaded. I shall return to the Bad Lands in my next book, "Prejudices". It will be devoted largely to making fun of the National Institute of Arts and Letters.

The photograph in *Current Opinion* rather startled me. It must have been exhumed from the morgue. It was made seven or eight years ago by a newspaper photographer. I have lost some beauty since, but have improved in sagacity.

I shall refer to Miss Hayden's article in the revision, and in general shall give a much better account of the material accumulated in *Dialect Notes*.

Sincerely yours,
H. L. Mencken

To Franklin Spier
[AAK]

The Smart Set
25 West 45th St.
New York
August 9, 1921

Dear Mr. Spier:

A young woman named Ruth Suckow at Earlville, Iowa has sent in to us a number of very remarkable short stories. She tells me that she is at work on a novel. I suggest that it would be a good idea to send her a friendly note, saying that I have told you about her and that you will be glad to read her manuscript when it is finished. I am convinced that she will do excellent work.[9]

Sincerely yours,
H. L. Mencken

To Alfred A. Knopf
[PT]

[*In a letter dated September 6, Knopf had proposed that a revision of* In Defense of Women, *then under way, be postponed until the Spring of 1922, because of post-war printing difficulties. The book was brought out in 1922 as Vol. VI of the Free Lance Books, a series edited by Mencken.* Prejudices: Third Series *was published in October, 1922.* On Democracy *was much delayed, and was not finally published until 1926, as* Notes on Democracy. *As to the second edition of* The American Language, *"revised and enlarged", it was published late in 1921.*]

Baltimore, September 7th, 1921

Dear Knopf:

You are the publisher; not I. I leave all such matters to your judgment. I hope to give you the MS. of Prejudices III by January

[9] Ruth Suckow (1892–1960) published many short stories in the *Smart Set*. The book referred to here is probably *Country People*, published in 1924 by Alfred A. Knopf.

1st, and that of On Democracy by next June. But all such things depend upon the whims of God.

All I ask is that you make The American Language good and thick. It is my secret ambition to be the author of a book weighing at least five pounds.

Yours,
M.

◇◇◇◇◇◇◇◇◇◇◇◇◇◇

To THEODORE DREISER
[UP]

[*Dreiser had sent a humorous letter to Mencken on September 26th.*]

H. L. Mencken
1524 Hollins St.
Baltimore
October 2nd [*1921*]

GENTLEMEN:–

I have to acknowledge your letter of September 26th, in re the death of the late Theodore Hermann Dreiser. Permit me to call your attention to the fact that you fail to give me his last words. If I am to write an obituary of him for the New York *Times* I must have them. Common rumor has it that he said "Shakespeare, I come!" But my extensive experience with moribund great men inclines me to doubt that he actually pulled such words. You will recall the case of the late Walt Whitman, another literary man. For years he practised the following last words: "My one regret is that I could not die on the field of honor, fighting for democracy". But his actual last words were: "Lift me up, Horace; I want to s—t".

A woman calling herself Delphine Hogan has gone into deep mourning here, and announces that she is one of M. Dreiser's widows. She says he overcame her maiden reluctance in the year 1893, and left her with twins. She is not destitute, but has made a fortune keeping a rooming house. She wants to erect a bronze equestrian statue to the memory of the late lamented.

Sincerely yours,
H. L. Mencken

To F. Scott Fitzgerald
[PU]

H. L. Mencken
1524 Hollins St.
Baltimore
October 7th [*1921?*]

Dear Fitzgerald:–

Let us, in God's name, drop honorifics. In any case, mine is not Mr. I prefer the Russian Knaiz, or Freiherr, or Mons., pronounced to rhyme with Ganz.

The Norris scheme is excellent and it goes without saying that I'll be glad to help it along. The impediment is the fact that most of the Norris books, if not all, are owned by Doubleday, Page & Co., a very lousy bunch. However, Charles Norris might be able to get control of them. A Man's Woman is bad stuff, but it ought to go into the series. So with the book of essays, The Responsibility of the Novelist. A good man to do the Blix preface would be George Sterling. He took me on a night-hack jaunt around San Francisco to visit its scenes. You ought to do one yourself.[1]

Tell Wilson I forgive him for his article. The other day Crowninshield asked me for a photograph. I sent him one that might be used as an advertisement for a rat-poison. A heavy frown. The face of a kill-joy.

But did Wilhelms tell you the sequel—how I locked him up in a room with a colored woman, and she worked her wicked will upon him?

Yours,
H. L. Mencken

[1] Mencken had been in San Francisco to cover the Democratic Convention in 1920.

◇◇◇◇◇◇◇◇◇◇◇◇◇

To ALFRED A. KNOPF
[AAK]

H. L. Mencken
1524 Hollins St.
Baltimore
November 21st [*1921*]

DEAR KNOPF:–

1. Scheffauer writes that a Russian countess, Gräfin Kleinmichel, has written her memoirs, and that it is a very interesting book. S. has just sold the German rights to Scherl. I haven't seen it myself.

2. The Krapp book is extremely interesting, but, despite its size, not exhaustive.[2] I have a feeling that it should be not one work in two volumes, but a series of volumes. The second volume, on American pronunciation, is complete enough as it stands, and I advise you to do it as a separate book, but the chapters on American literary style, American spelling, American proper names, etc., in the first volume are by no means as comprehensive as they might be. I think it would be a good idea to take the second volume, and to suggest to Krapp that he expand each of these chapters into a separate volume. This second volume, coming after my book, should arouse a good deal of interest in American English, and so pave the way for the others. Thus you would have a monoply on the subject. Krapp's stuff necessitates very few changes in my book. In many cases my treatment of the subject is more thorough than his.

3. I'll bring the MS. with me next week.

M.

◇◇◇◇◇◇◇◇◇◇◇◇◇

To SINCLAIR LEWIS
[YU]

H. L. Mencken
1524 Hollins St.
Baltimore
December 24th [*1921*]

DEAR LEWIS:–

I think you are quite right, and the fact ought to be set down.

[2] The Krapp book: *The English Language in America* (2 vols.), by George Philip Krapp (New York: The Century Co.; 1925).

Why don't you write an article on the subject, and send it to Canby for the Evening Post? Or somebody else? Nothing could be plainer than the collapse of the Walpole–Lawrence–Beresford group. All their late stuff is drivel. I can see nothing in France and nothing in Germany save Greenwich Village gone wild. But here there are plenty of youngsters who show great promise—Dos Passos, Fergusson, the "Zell" man, etc.[3] I lately unearthed a girl in Iowa, by name Ruth Suckow, who seems to me to be superb. I send you a Smart Set with two of her stories. She follows after you, Dreiser, and, to some extent, Anderson, but she is also a genuine original. She is now at work on a novel.

The land is filled with rumors about your own next opus. One day I hear that it is to be a romance of the American Revolution, and the next day that it is to be a Tendenz piece praising adultery—what is it actually about? My guess is that you are putting very good stuff into it. All I ask is that you say nothing against Woodrow or the War Mothers. Remember the ideals that Our Boys died for! We must Teach the World!

It is the day before Christmas, and I am on the water-wagon. Worse, on a strict diet. So to hell with you for mentioning your travelling bar. In my own cellar are bottles enough to keep me stewed for 15 years, yet I must swill milk, and eat eggs, zwieback and schmierkäse—a diet for sucklings. But I hope to get well before the ides of March.

Old Debs has been let out at last. Harding contrived to do the thing like a cad. The Disarmament Conference ends on the note of obscene farce. The English have simply backed Hughes into a corner, and pulled out his whiskers by the handful. The Japs are laughing themselves to death.

Sincerely yours,
H. L. Mencken

[3] "Zell": a novel by Henry G. Aikman (New York: Alfred A. Knopf; 1921).

1922

◇◇◇◇◇◇◇◇◇◇◇◇◇◇◇◇◇◇◇◇

To Amélie Rives, Princess Troubetzkoy
[YU]

H. L. Mencken
1524 Hollins St.
Baltimore
January 23rd [1922]

Dear Princess:–

Now Hergesheimer has gone into the West on a four months' trip and I am in such a low state of health and mind that I feel almost like jumping into the Chesapeake Bay! But Hergesheimer will return, and I'll recover, I certainly hope. In fact, I begin to feel better already. The cause, according to the Faculty, was too much work at the desk and too little exercise. Now I do hard physical labor daily from lunch to dinner, and it seems likely to be effective. Thus I still look forward to the pilgrimage!

Horses are old friends of mine, but increasing clumsiness forced me to give up riding long ago. Now I incline toward a safe Dayton wagon. But if I can no longer ride a horse, I can at least drive one. Hergesheimer, I believe, is a poor horseman. He uses a step-ladder to mount, and has to be strapped to the saddle. I went up to West Chester a couple of weeks ago to spend a day with him. He has a lovely old house, with a distillery on the top floor. I wonder how you like his "Cytherea". To me it seems very good stuff—in fact, the best thing that he has done.

Please remember me to the Prince.

Sincerely yours,
H. L. Mencken

To Sinclair Lewis
[YU]

H. L. Mencken
1524 Hollins St.
Baltimore
February 6th [*1922*]

Dear Lewis:–

I am sending your message to Miss Suckow. It should please her vastly. At last accounts she was still at work on her novel.[1] I told Knopf about her when she first bobbed up, and I believe he has bespoken her novel. But let Harcourt lay on!

Your plan looks to me to be excellent. The big city right-thinker seems to me to be even more typical of the Republic than the Main Street right-thinker. He is more influential. What he says and does today is imitated in the grass towns tomorrow. I have known and revered many such operators, and stood enchanted before their doings during the war, particularly in the matter of the Liberty Loan drives. In my old days here in Baltimore I invented the name of Honorary Pallbearers for them, and it still sticks, but only here. Did you ever notice that half of their time is given to acting as honorary pallbearers for one another? When you write to Harcourt, please tell him to let me have the sheets of the book as soon as possible. I'll be careful about the date of my review.

The death of the Sovereign Pontiff has filled me with sadness.[2] He was, I hear, an intelligent admirer of Pilsner beer. His predecessor, the late Pius, enjoyed the honor of my personal acquaintance. Some day, I'll tell you how we met.[3] My friends have kindly urged me to

---

[1] The Suckow novel: *Country People* (New York: Alfred A. Knopf; 1924).
[2] The Sovereign Pontiff: Benedictus XV.
[3] The account of H. L. Mencken's interview with Pius X will be found in *Heathen Days* (New York: Alfred A. Knopf; 1943).

stand for the vacancy, on the platform: "Rum, Romanism and Rebellion", but I can't bring myself to believe that my theological talents are sufficient for the job. As I write, it seems certain that some wop will get it.

I have been down with a chronic belly-ache, and unable to do any work except routine. But prayer seems to be bringing me relief. Let your confessor put in his oar.

Sincerely yours,
H. L. Mencken

To LOUISE POUND
[PT]

Baltimore, March 7th [*1922*]

DEAR DR. POUND:–

Thanks for the clipping. Ah, that I could attend one of those annual conferences and observe the lovely carnations and dahlias! I dedicate "Dianthus Caryophyllus" to the club, and forbid anyone to read it elsewhere.[4]

"The American Language" brought me a pleasant note from Jespersen this morning, and the German philologs are writing in for review copies. The book will kill me yet. It is still full of errors, and I must make another revision before the plates are cast. Knopf has sold about 2,200 copies so far, and expects to clear off 3,000 before the thing is stereotyped. This is fairly good for a $6 book.

I inform you confidentially that I am preparing to make my bow as a college lecturer. One of the clubs at Goucher has invited me to preach on journalism. I have accepted on condition (a) that the harangue be delivered outside the college bounds, in a private house, (b) that only one member of the faculty be admitted (to maintain a decent decorum), and (c) that no report of the proceedings be printed in the college paper. I shall advise the gals to get married as soon as possible, and so forget journalism. It is no trade for a lady.

Sincerely yours,
H. L. Mencken

---

[4] "Dianthus Caryophyllus" is the title of a newspaper article by Mencken.

(1922)

To WALTER F. WHITE[5]
[YU]

[*Baltimore?*]
March 13, 1922

DEAR MR. WHITE:

This play looks to me to be hopeless. The long speeches in the first episode would drive an audience out of the theatre and the climax at the end of the last episode would make it laugh. The suggestion of the minstrel show is far too insidious to be resisted. Moreover, I doubt that the fundamental idea is plausible. That is to say, no such thing has ever happened nor could it conceivably happen. In fiction, it is not sufficient merely to convince the reader that an episode is possible, it is also necessary to convince him that it is probable. He will believe a story on the front page of a newspaper that would make him laugh even in the Argosy Magazine.

Let me see the other pieces that you have in mind. After you have finished half a dozen of them, you may find a way to go back to this one and save it.

Sincerely yours,
[*H. L. Mencken*]

To THEODORE DREISER
[UP]

[*In his letter of April 18, 1922, Dreiser had criticized Mencken's assertion that puritan censorship was on the way out.*]

H. L. Mencken
1524 Hollins St.
Baltimore
April 22nd [1922]

DEAR DREISER:–

With all due respect, Tush! Even Doubleday would print Sister Carrie today; Briggs, of Harper's, told me not two weeks ago that they

[5] Walter F. White (1893–1955): The Negro author and leader.

would be glad to have The Titan. *Some* progress has been made, and maybe a damned sight more than you suspect. You are shut off from human society, and apparently read nothing. Worse, you are befogged by your weakness for The "Genius". I could get it past Sumner easily, with not a dozen changes, all of them unimportant. But while it was on the stocks I'd be hot for cutting out whole reams of words. There we would quarrel.

The air is again filled with rumors that the Second Coming of Christ is at hand. Once I thought that Woodrow was the man, but this seems to have been an error. Maybe it is Will H. Hays.[6]

Yours,
M.

To Edmund Wilson
[OFP]

The Smart Set
25 West 45th Street
New York
May 17, 1922

Dear Mr. Wilson:

I note that your letter is dated May the 12th. It seems to have been touring the various postoffice sub-stations for four days.

I doubt that a dialogue between Brooks and Fitzgerald would be for us. It would inevitably collide with the somewhat numerous dialogues between Nathan and me that we printed last year. It is possible that the latter may be resumed before the end of the present year. But we'd be delighted to have some short pieces from you. The chances are that they would fit admirably into our new department, "The Nietzschean Follies".

I don't know what the Baltimore Sun folks are doing nor what their plans are for covering the Federation of Labor convention. Certainly they'll cover it in some more or less careful way. I suggest that you write forthwith to J. Edw. Murphy, managing editor of the Evening Sun. The stuff that you have done for the Sun has been printed in the evening edition, and I think that it would be better to deal with Murphy. The only jobs worth having done there involve

[6] Ex-Postmaster General of the U. S., then president of Motion Picture Producers and Distributors of America, Inc.

living in Baltimore, which you told me that you were disinclined to do. Nevertheless it might be possible eventually to evolve something that would avoid this difficulty. Why don't you run down to Baltimore some time and meet the chief functionaries of the Sun? I'll be glad to arrange it at any time convenient for you.

I changed the meaning of the word "jejune" eight or ten years ago. That is to say, I added a new special meaning, to wit, that of youthful feebleness. This new meaning you will find in all of the latest editions of the international dictionaries.

Sincerely yours,
H. L. Mencken

To SINCLAIR LEWIS
[YU]

H. L. Mencken
1524 Hollins St.
Baltimore
July 25th [*1922*]

DEAR LEWIS:–

I have just finished "Babbitt". It is absolutely first-rate stuff. My very sincere congratulations. You have not only kept up to "Main Street"; you have gone far beyond it.

Yours in Xt.,
H. L. Mencken

[*In a letter dated January 21 (1923?) Sinclair Lewis recognized his debt to Mencken in the matter of* Babbitt; *it was Mencken, he wrote, who had helped him decide between several projects he had in mind, and had suggested doing a portrait of the city booster.*]

To SINCLAIR LEWIS
[YU]

August 13th [*1922*]

DEAR LEWIS:–

I enclose a proof of my review of "Babbitt" for the October Smart Set, out on the day of the book's publication. I am also doing a notice for the Baltimore Evening Sun. This is written on the high seas, and in a few days I shall land at Plymouth and kiss the soil of the Motherland. A week or two in London will be enough. Then for Pilsen, Munich, Kulmbach, Dortmund and the rest of the beer towns. I doubt that I'll see any literati in London, save perhaps Walpole and Huxley.

This ship, the Reliance (i.e. a new Hamburg–American liner falsely flying the Stars and Stripes) is very comfortable, with large rooms, good victuals, and an excellent bar, but the passengers are the damndest morons I have yet encountered on earth. I have been aboard five days, and have yet to speak to a soul. To look at them (and overhear them) is enough. Babbitt's brother-in-law, Frank J. Thompson, is aboard with his new wife. I suspect that she was on the musical comedy stage but recently; worse, I can't put away a horrible feeling that she probably lived at the Ansonia, and under the protection of Stanley Mandlebaum.

God help us all!

Sincerely yours,
M.

To THEODORE DREISER
[UP]

H. L. Mencken
1524 Hollins St.
Baltimore
October 28th [1922]

DEAR DREISER:–

I hear from New York that you are thinking of doing an unexpurgated edition of "The 'Genius'" next year. Is this true? If it is, I'd like to know it in advance, so that it may not appear to Sumner that I was fooling him about the cuts. He acted very decently and I don't want him to think that I was stringing him.

What are you doing?

Yours,
M.

To PERCY MARKS[7]
[OFP]

H. L. Mencken
1524 Hollins St.
Baltimore
December 2nd [*1922?*]

DEAR MR. MARKS:–

You astonish me. Now and then I get a letter from an undergraduate or a clipping from an undergraduate paper (usually a comic paper), but it never occurred to me that I had any considerable body of readers in the universities. If you are right, then I'll certainly write the book I have had in mind for a long while, to wit, "Advice to Young Men", a frank, realistic, unsentimental treatise on such things as politics, education, business, sex, etc., revolving around the doctrine that the most precious possession of man is *honor.* Honor has been neglected in American ethics. I have never seen any public reference to it, save, of course, by such cads as Wilson.

A man is always surprised by his readers. I had always been under the impression (quite sincerely) that the *Smart Set* was largely read by women of a superior intelligence but perhaps inferior virtue—among them, by the higher ranges of kept ladies. But last week, for the first time, I took a look at the subscription list. The first subscriber I encountered was an Elks' Club! And further on I found a great many very solemn dodoes, including even some clergy.

I wish I could take "Hail, Friend!" but it is too much like the *Red Book* story. The sentimental situation is the same in both. But let me see the other story you mention. You write very well.

I doubt that you are right about the "Higher Education" series. Most of the articles were sentimental and favorable. The only genuine slating was in the one on the University of Michigan. [. . .]

We shall follow the series with one on the principal prisons of the Republic, also by graduates.

Sincerely yours,
H. L. Mencken

[7] Percy Marks (1891–1956) was the author of *The Plastic Age* (New York: Grossett & Dunlap; 1924). In a letter addressed to Julian P. Boyd (July 29, 1942), Mencken writes: "Advice to Young Men has never been finished. But I still have 30 lbs. of notes and hope to put it through some day". His intention, however, was never carried out.

◇◇◇◇◇◇◇◇◇◇◇◇◇

To PHILIP GOODMAN
[EPL]

Baltimore, Md.
December 3rd [1922]

DEAR PHIL:

Bloodgood's illness turns out to have been somewhat serious. I find, in fact, that he is still in bed, and that his quacks have ordered him to stop all work for 3 or 4 months. He proposes to go to Egypt as soon as he can navigate. So it is useless to try to make an appointment with him. Moreover, there is no need for it. Mrs. Goodman is quite well. I have asked various men here about the lameness in her arm. They all say that persistent exercise of the arm will overcome it—that enough muscles are always left to make all the ordinary motions. This is also Bloodgood's view. I have heard him say so a dozen times.

I am lecturing at Goucher College tonight: an annual affair. The audience consists of 250 virgins. I begin on the subject of national literature, but at 8.35 modulate gracefully into the Old Subject in F sharp minor. I always advise them to marry early, as, after all, the most sanitary and economically secure way of life for a Christian girl. The college was established by rich Methodists. The committee on my lecture consists of the Misses Krause, Connolly, Levine, Epsteen and Katzenstein.

Yours,
[*M.*]

◇◇◇◇◇◇◇◇◇◇◇◇◇

To SINCLAIR LEWIS
[YU]

H. L. Mencken
1524 Hollins St.
Baltimore
December 22nd [1922]

DEAR AND REV. BROTHER:

Well, then, we'll postpone the party until you get back. I'll be here certainly between January 1st and 4th. Let me know the precise date of your arrival, so that I may get my stomach into condition for a session.

(1922)

Your plan for the bacteriological novel is the damndest nonsense I have heard for years. Your next one must be a full-length picture of an American college president. De Kruif is in the pay of the Turks.

If you want to have the guard turned out when you get to the Hun Inferno next year, send a few dollars to Dr. Arthur Eloesser, Schutzverband Deutsche Schriftsteller, Schoeneberger Ufer 25, Berlin W. 35, for his fund for starving literati. Some of the older boys over there are living on rye bread and coffee substitute, with no heat in the house.

I hope you escape leprosy, botts and the blind staggers in 1923.

Yours,
Mencken

1923

To JIM TULLY[1]
[OFP]

The American Mercury
730 Fifth Avenue
New York
January 21st [1923]

DEAR MR. TULLY:–

Lay on, and do your damndest; I'll certainly go as far with you as any editor in this great Christian Republic. Blink is worth far more than one story; there is a whole book in him.

I suspect that "The Man Who Knew God" is your pet child, and that you love it beyond reason. The plain fact is that, rereading it, I can't get away from the feeling that it doesn't come off—that somehow it seems a bit false. The machinery, perhaps, works too slickly; at all events, the ending somehow seems magaziney to me. Moreover, there are weaknesses in the central theme. It is far too easy to make a crazy man say or do anything. Altogether, I gather the conclusion that it is not up to what you can do. Keep it to admire in secret. Every man has a pet.

If you write any more tramp sketches like those in "Beggars" or

[1] Jim Tully (born in 1891): a former farm laborer, who had become a writer. He had already published *Emmett Lawler* (New York: Harcourt, Brace and Company; 1922) the year before, and was preparing *Beggars of Life* (New York: A. & C. Boni; 1924).

"Life" I hope you give me a chance at them. But don't write what I like, or what anyone else likes; write to please yourself. The magazines are a curse to authors. A magazine is never quite a free agent, save in its last number. But an author ought to be absolutely.

Sincerely yours,
H. L. Mencken

To CARL VAN DOREN
[OFP]

H. L. Mencken
1524 Hollins St.
Baltimore
February 20th [1923]

DEAR VAN DOREN:–

God will both forgive you and reward you! Speaking as one professor of the black art to another, I hope I may not be suspected of prejudice if I say that, in your "Smartness and Light" article, you have achieved a couple of pieces of very sound and penetrating criticism.[2] Imprimis, that the war greatly improved trade for me. Why has no one ever noticed that before? I hate to think of it, but it is so. Zum zweiten, that I have been doing the thing a bit too violently, with too little regard for human feelings and public decencies—especially with too little regard for good intentions and honest hopes. I'll reform next year! First, I must get "On Democracy" on paper—or asbestos!

Herewith a souvenir of a perfect day. Old Johann died in 1732, and yet there are whole passages in his book that I might have written. A curious case of atavism: I never saw a copy until long after my own tune was set. Don't tell me that you don't read Latin! What is to become of us? Neither do I! I had a decayed priest translate it for me.[3]

My infinite thanks!

Sincerely yours,
Mencken

---

[2] Your article: in the *Century* for March 1923.

[3] Johann Burkhard(t) Mencken (1674–1732) was the author of *De Charlataneria Eruditorum* (1715), which H. L. Mencken edited in English (New York: Alfred A. Knopf; 1937). In 1923 a bad translation of the book in English was already in existence.

(1923)

To Percy Marks
[OFP]

H. L. Mencken
1524 Hollins St.
Baltimore
February 23rd [1923]

Dear Mr. Marks:–

My apologies. A slip of the machine and eye. *Would* should have been in the place of *you.*

My scheme, in brief, is to canvass all the American authors (in belles lettres only) who are in "Who's Who in America", and determine their racial ancestry. The four grandparents will suffice. Then separate into groups—those born before 1860, those born between 1860 and 1870, and so on. The inquiry would show, I believe, that there has been a steady displacement of the Anglo-Saxon strain.[4]

I have myself gathered some materials, and I'd go on with the thing if I had the time. But I simply have not. If you want to tackle it yourself, or know of anyone who does, I'll be delighted to assist. It would be very easy to sell the final monograph.

Pattee is a noble old Assyrian. I hear he wears pulse-warmers and reads Whittier.

Sincerely yours,
H. L. Mencken

To Edmund Wilson
[OFP]

H. L. Mencken
1524 Hollins St.
Baltimore
March 4th [1923]

Dear Mr. Wilson:–

Georg Müller, the German publisher, has asked me to choose 12 modern American short stories for translation by Franz Blei, with an

[4] The investigation mentioned was never made.

introduction by me. I plan to select stories by Cabell, Lardner, Gouverneur Morris, Edna Ferber, Willa Cather, Ben Hecht, Ruth Suckow, Thyra Winslow, etc. Obviously, "The Death of a Soldier" ought to be included: it is the papa of the whole "Three Soldiers" school. May I use it?

Müller will pay the usual royalties on this collection, but they will come in marks. Divided among 12 or more writers and translated into dollars, they will amount to nothing. I am therefore suggesting to all hands that the whole sum be handed over to Eloesser, of the German Authors' League, for his fund for old and disabled authors. Many of them are starving.

If you agree will you please send me a brief biographical sketch to run with the translation, covering these points:

Education

Date and place of birth

Ancestry, i.e., birthplace and nationality of all four grandparents.

Sincerely yours,

H. L. Mencken

To THEODORE DREISER

[UP]

H. L. Mencken
1524 Hollins St.
Baltimore
March 9th [*1923*]

DEAR DREISER:–

I agree with you. Anderson's short stories often give me a great kick (as Scott Fitzgerald would say), but his novels usually seem a bit confused and muddy. I doubt that he has the sheer power needed to swing a long book. But his details are often superb.[5]

I am laid up with a severe laryngitis, and can't speak. It is a mercy. I am in training for my last days as a Trappist.

Yours,

M.

---

[5] Anderson: Sherwood Anderson.

(1923)

◇◇◇◇◇◇◇◇◇◇◇◇◇

To THEODORE DREISER
[UP]

The Smart Set
25 West 45th Street
New York
March 20, 1923

DEAR DREISER:

There is a special publishers' rate for advertisements in The Smart Set. I enclose a rate card. It is 36¢ an agate line a month straight. They tell me here that your advertisement would work out to about $75 a month. In addition, we run a page of small book advertisements. A one inch space on this page costs $12.50 a month straight.

I think your advertisement is very effective typographically, but some of the text seems to me to be rather silly. For example, the paragraph beginning "Mr. Dreiser is the only American novelist who rises to heights of cosmic sublimity". This is nonsense. Again, under the title of "The Bulwark", I am credited with the following sentence: "In 'The Bulwark' especially the big power of Dreiser's massive impetus is evident". I never said anything of the sort. If I did, I was drunk. The fact is, as you know, I have never seen the manuscript of "The Bulwark". Otherwise, it seems to me the advertisement is very effective. I enclose the proof.

Sincerely yours,
M.

To GEORGE STERLING
[PT]

The Smart Set
25 West 45th Street
New York
[*March 22, 1923*]

DEAR GEORGE:

Nathan reports that no verse is to be bought at the moment: too much in type. But next month!

I defy you to do your damndest with your "Sceptic's Fate".

Skepticism, in fact, is the only comfortable philosophy. One is never disappointed. But very good verses.

New York grows better and better. All of the most respectable restaurants—for example, Delmonico's—are now booting. God knows where it will end. I begin to despair of public virtue.

I have been laid also, along with my whole family. But God has delivered us all.

Ys.
[*Unsigned*]

◇◇◇◇◇◇◇◇◇◇◇◇◇◇

To THEODORE DREISER
[UP]

[*Dreiser had apologized because Liveright had used an apocryphal recommendation signed Mencken in order to promote the sales of* The Bulwark (*March 21, 1923*).]

H. L. Mencken
1524 Hollins St.
Baltimore
March 23rd [*1923*]

DEAR DREISER:–

I'm sorry if you thought I was peevish about that matter of "The Bulwark". The fact is that I scarcely ever pick up one of the weeklies without finding an advertisement crediting me with something I have never said. I long ago gave up protesting. As for Liveright I shall punish him by having 20 anonymous letters written to Sumner, complaining that "The Story of Mankind" is obscene.

The "cosmic sublimity" stuff is simply garbage. What in hell does it mean, if anything? I hope you make Liveright cut it out. If you don't, some comedian will notice it and poke fun at it. Incidently, I discovered in New York after writing to you that the Smart Set could not print the advertisement. A complex and unintelligent matter, too long to explain. In brief, an idiotic contract with a wholesaler of advertising prohibits the magazine selling any book advertising direct save the small $12.50 boxes that I mentioned. Every full page advertisement must go into *all* of this wholesaler's magazines, not the Smart Set alone. Who made this contract I don't know. It seems insane to me.

My whole family has been ill, but everyone is now recovering. I met Gloom on the train coming down this afternoon. She was on the way to New Windsor to see her mother, who has had a stroke of paralysis and is very ill.

The word "ad" is one of my abominations, along with "alright". I pray God every night to send the great pox to every man who uses either. It is a harsh prayer, but that is the way I feel about it. God knows why. A silly prejudice, that is all.

Liveright called me up the other day and said he was hatching another bawdy lunch-party. I told him that I'd be delighted to honor him. He gives good parties.

Look at the enclosed (which please return). The old boy seems to be much disturbed. It goes without saying that I never said what I am accused of saying. Who starts such imbecile lies? In this case I suspect a woman who has vowed to have me deported from the United States because I once refused to pander to her baser appetites. As a matter of politeness I would have been glad to roger her, but at the moment I happened to be too drunk.

Yours,
M.

To PERCY MARKS
[OFP]

H. L. Mencken
1524 Hollins St.
Baltimore
April 24th [*1923 or 1924?*]

DEAR MR. MARKS:–

Thanks very much for the view of the Tall Cedars.[6] I shall have it enlarged and hang it in my consulting-room.

By a curious piece of bad luck I happened upon a capital bomb for use against La Atherton after my review of her was on the press: [7] a quotation from Hrdlicka, the highest authority, to the effect that the

---

[6] "The Tall Cedars of Lebanon, a recreational association within the Freemasons. They are to the Shriners as the Lions are to the Rotarians. They dress up idiotically and march in parades". (Note by H. L. Mencken)

[7] The Atherton book: *Black Oxen* (New York: Boni and Liveright; 1923).

coons are the most steadily dolichocephalic Americans.[8] I shall have to drag it in somehow later on.

Sinclair, in many ways, is impossible. His malady is a credulity complex. But it seems to me that his book, on the whole, will do some good.[9] Here in Baltimore it has already set up an active discussion of the Johns Hopkins, which is fast going to hell under Goodnow.

When are you coming to New York again?

Sincerely yours,
H. L. Mencken

To GEORGE JEAN NATHAN
[CU]

H. L. Mencken
1524 Hollins St.
Baltimore
May 3rd [1923]

DEAR GEORGE:–

The trouble with your revision of the memorandum I drew up is that it goes both too far and not far enough. The third paragraph I find it impossible to agree to. It would tie me up disagreeably and uselessly. I might want to change the Table of Contents page completely. I must be free in all such matters. But I agree freely to the essential thing: to print your name exactly as my own is printed.

So with your Paragraph 1. I am disinclined to make any hard and fast agreement regarding make-up. I must be free to change it, when necessary. I will agree to the essential thing: to print Clinical Notes when you write them, and to let you stop whenever you want to.

On reflection, I object to "Editorial Associate". I'll agree to what you suggested first, "Contributing Associate". If you dissent, then we are unable to agree, and "Contributing Editor" must be used under the contract.

The salary agreement (Paragraph 4), as it stands in your draft, is worthless. I want to get rid of negotiations, not open the way for more of them. Name your percentages now, and I'll say yes or no to them. If we can't agree, let us strike out the paragraph altogether.

---

[8] Hrdlicka (1869–1943): an anthropologist.
[9] The Sinclair book: *The Goosestep* (Pasadena, Cal.: The author; 1923).

My last paragraph was suggested by your request regarding stationery. I can't accede to this request. We must get rid of the chance of such dissensions arising in future. I don't want to discuss the magazine at all, once we are set. I propose,—in fact, that we agree between us to avoid the subject absolutely, once we have come to terms. And if we can't come to terms, to avoid it in the same way.

I assume that you still have a copy of the letter you drew up. I enclose my proposed substitute. I'll be at the office Tuesday morning. Let us settle the business at once.

[Unsigned]

[*Mencken and Nathan already thought of publishing a new magazine to supersede the* Smart Set.]

To George Sterling

[PT]

The Smart Set
25 West 45th Street
New York
May 23, 1923

Dear George:

I have put your name down for the Arnold committee and shall send you your certificate of manuscript and silk rosette anon. The Hon. Charles Evans Hughes has consented to serve as Honorary Chairman and we hope to include a number of the Anglo-Saxon Chauvinists, especially Otto Kahn, Henry Morgenthau, Oscar Straus, Rabbi Stephen S. Wise, Horace B. Liveright and Judge Brandeis. I'll see that you receive bulletins of news from time to time.

What you say about the Poetry Department has not failed to make its impression upon me. As a matter of fact, we are planning to reorganize the whole magazine in various ways. We took to the sweet and lovely stuff eight or nine years ago at the height of the free verse movement, and for several years The Smart Set was the only magazine in [America] printing any actual poetry. But now even the free verse fellows have begun to snuffle and sob, and so I rather incline to letting them in. But that they write any actual poetry, I deny absolutely. There is no more poetry in the whole published work of Bodenheim than you will find in any average college yell.

Nathan is going abroad next week, and I'll have to sit on the job here in New York. A very powerful yearning to come out to the coast again is upon me. I'd be willing to serve twenty extra years in Hell if I could only hop a train tomorrow. Maybe I'll do it when he gets back.

Yours in Xt,
[*Unsigned*]

To ALFRED A. KNOPF
[AAK]

H. L. Mencken
1524 Hollins St.
Baltimore
May 30th [*1923*]

DEAR ALFRED:–

1. The MS. of the architecture book has reached me from Scheffauer, and most of the illustrations should be here in a few days. I somehow gather the notion that you and he are not in accord about it. Is this true? If so, why waste any time debating it? Let me send it to someone else. The matter looks very good, but, as I say, I have not yet seen the pictures.

2. Miss Emily Clark, 1008 Park Avenue, Richmond, Va., is at work on a book of Virginia sketches that has some excellent stuff in it. Hergesheimer and Cabell are both interested in her. It might be a good idea, if you haven't done it already, to write her a polite note.[1]

M.

To THEODORE DREISER
[UP]

H. L. Mencken
1524 Hollins St.
Baltimore
May 31st [*1923*]

DEAR DREISER:–

I think you waste your time quarreling with such a hollow fellow as Burgess, or with the Authors' League.[2] The organization is frankly

[1] Emily Clark (d. 1953) was then on the staff of the Richmond (Va.) *News Leader;* she was the founder and one of the editors of *The Reviewer* (1921–5). She wrote *Innocence Abroad* (New York: Alfred A. Knopf; 1931) and *Stuffed Peacocks* (New York: Alfred A. Knopf; 1927).

[2] F. Gelett Burgess: an author and humorist.

devoted to protecting the business of movie authors, and has no possible concern with artistic questions. I resigned from it five or six years ago, and have since exposed its stupidity several times, notably in Prejudices II. You might as well carry on a debate with the American Legion or the Lambs' Club. Some time ago Beach asked me to sit on his movie committee.[3] I, of course, refused instantly. But my name was published, nevertheless, as a member of the committee. A gang of cads.

You say in your letter to Burgess that you have always fought "The 'Genius'" battle single-handed. With all due respect, you lie like an archbishop. Young Hersey sweated for you like a bull, and there was a critic in Baltimore who, as I recall it, laid out $300 in cash to round up the authors of the United States on your side. Most of them, true enough, ratted, but that was surely not his fault.

How are you, anyhow? I am thinking of giving up literature and returning to the cigar business.

Yours,
M.

To MAX BROEDEL
[OFP]

H. L. Mencken
1524 Hollins St.
Baltimore
July 30 [1923]

DEAR MAX:

God knows I wish I could come up in August, but the fact is that I am preparing to assassinate the *Smart Set* about that time and to start a new magazine—something far grander and gaudier—in brief, a serious review, but with undertones of the atheistic and lascivious. Knopf is to be the publisher. This business burdens me with very hard work, and the chances are that I'll forget hay-fever. It is my hope to horn into politics, economics, the sciences, etc., as well as into the fine arts, and to stir up the animals. A special department will be devoted to theological idiots. Altogether, the prospect makes me young again.

You are missing some very refined evenings, and the club is miss-

---

[3] Rex E. Beach was the president of the Author's League of America.

ing you. Hildebrandt has opened a rathskeller in his cellar—a superb room. The first evening he had 6% beer, and the club got unanimously tight. I hope that, in at least one of your pictures of Cullen's churches, you insert a small view of a dog voiding upon it. Or put in a Hackenkreuz in honor of Flexner.

My best regards to the family. My niece is here, recovering from tonsillectomy. Hazlehurst took them out day before yesterday. She bore it very well, and is now preparing to eat again.

Yours,
M.

To ELLERY SEDGWICK
[OFP]

[*In his letter of July 27, 1923, Ellery Sedgwick had congratulated Mencken on his influence on the young writers of the day; he also asked him for an article about "The standards of taste—literary and social—of the people who are coming on very fast to take our places".*]

H. L. Mencken
1524 Hollins St.
Baltimore
July 30th [*1923*]

DEAR SEDGWICK:–

I wrote to you some time ago, but got no reply. Afterward I heard that you had been in South America. I surely hope that you have fully recovered your health. It is a pity that we meet so seldom. Don't you ever come down into this region?

At the moment I am engaged on plans for setting up a new review. The Smart Set is too trivial and I have been trying to get rid of it for five years. Now the chance seems to be at hand. Just what the new one will be I don't know, but I shall try to cover a pretty wide field—politics, economics, the sciences, etc., as well as the fine arts. If all goes well the first number should be ready toward the end of the year. Knopf is to be the publisher. Please say nothing about this for the present.

I'll be delighted to do an article for you, once I get rid of my current harsh labors. Perhaps a good subject would be a sort of general consideration of the national scene by a non-Anglo-Saxon American—that is, how the thing looks to a man who feels himself wholly American, and yet necessarily cannot subscribe to the prevailing view that whatever is not Anglo-Saxon is foreign and accursed. Curiously enough, this has never been done. There have been plenty of treatises by enthusiastic immigrants, but none by a native. I think I could do the business within the bounds of decorum, and yet manage to shake up the animals a bit. The question of new standards of taste, which you raise, would enter very naturally.

My feeling is that, in so far as I have got any following among the young writers of the country, it has been obtained by sticking to the offensive—that is, by constantly carrying the war into Africa. One of the appalling results of that strategy is that I have been set up as a sort of professional enemy of professors. The other day, in the interest of science, I began counting up the professors on my family tree—men from whom I am directly descended. I counted 24 and then stopped. It is a peculiar and sardonic fate!

When will you be in New York? I'd like very much to see you. I'll probably be there every week or two for the next three months.

Sincerely yours,
H. L. Mencken

To Gamaliel Bradford
[ofp]

H. L. Mencken
1524 Hollins St.
Baltimore
August 7th [1923]

Dear Bradford:-

I am making plans to set up a new monthly review toward the end of the year—something a great deal livelier and more amusing, I hope than anything now existing. Knopf is to be the publisher, which insures first-rate printing, and there is enough money to go on indefinitely. It will attempt to cover the whole field—politics, economics, the sciences, etc., as well as the fine arts.

Needless to say, I hope to get you into it. Have you anything in hand that is not otherwise bespoken? It occurs to me that some sketches of *living* Americans might interest you. Or what else have you in mind?

Politically, we'll be conservative, but with some attempt to preserve a sense of humor. No fawning over Judge Gary and company, à la the *Independent*. The thing will probably be called the *American Mercury*, but it will be a great deal less pedantic than the *London Mercury*—more, in fact, like the *Mercure de France*.

Sincerely yours,
H. L. Mencken

◇◇◇◇◇◇◇◇◇◇◇◇◇◇

To THEODORE DREISER
[UP]

[*Dreiser had congratulated Mencken on his project for a new review, and volunteered his own contributions (August 8, 1923).*]

H. L. Mencken
1524 Hollins St.
Baltimore
August 10th [*1923*]

DEAR DREISER:–

The new one is not to be a weekly, but a monthly along the lines of the Mercure de France and the London Mercury, but very much more violent, and, I hope, amusing. Its main aim will be to shake up the Anglo-Saxon. Physically, at all events, it will be very fine. Knopf is spreading himself. God knows when the first number will be out—probably toward the end of the year. I must first get rid of the Smart Set, which has been a fearful nuisance for five years past, what with its narrow field, smelling history and lack of money.

Let me see the poems, by all means. It is not yet decided finally whether the new monthly is to print poetry, but I am eager to see the stuff anyhow. The article you mention embodies an excellent idea. Why not write it? My agents report that you have some unpublished woman sketches. What do you want for them? May I see them? [4]

Yours,
M.

---

[4] Unpublished woman sketches: the nucleus of *A Gallery of Women.*

(1923)

To SARA P. HAARDT[5]
[PT]

Baltimore, August 17, 1923

DEAR MISS HAARDT:–

I have a feeling that the center of gravity of the story wobbles—that it is about the mother one minute and the daughter the next minute. Take a minute and prayerful look at it, and see if you can't pull it together better.[6]

Incidentally, get yourself cured of the quotation-marks disease: you have quoted every fourth phrase in some paragraphs. It is a clumsy device, and unnecessary. Ruth Suckow had it, and I had to use an axe on her to cure her.

I am working day and night on the new review. Knopf is to be the publisher, and it will be very sightly. Why not send me some ideas for it? Anything that interests you—the South, the American University, the Anglo-Saxon, anything. Our aim is to set up an organ of educated Toryism, avoiding the chasing of Liberal butterflies on the one hand and the worship of Judge Gary on the other. I hope, in an early number, to print an article denouncing Abraham Lincoln.

Sincerely yours,
H. L. Mencken

To PERCY MARKS
[OFP]

H. L. Mencken
1524 Hollins St.
Baltimore
August 19th [1923]

DEAR MR. MARKS:–

It seems to me that "Cream of the Earth" is very well done, and I see no reason why you should have the slightest difficulty disposing of it. Its chief defect, to me, is that its standpoint is rather vague—that

---

[5] Sara Haardt (1898–1935), who became Mrs. H. L. Mencken in 1930.

[6] The story mentioned here is probably "Rebecca", which Mencken finally rejected. Mencken had met Sara Haardt at one of his annual lectures at Goucher College, where she was an instructor of English.

you tell the story without throwing much illumination upon it. Causes and motives are too much taken for granted. I am not advocating, of course, thesis fiction, but I believe that a novel is improved when it shows a certain drive and prejudice. However, this lack is not enough to spoil the story. I think you have done a very good piece of work.

The only way to get it printed is to send it to the publishers. I doubt that Knopf would be interested in it; it is rather too placid for him. But Houghton and Mifflin would probably take it. Or Holt. Or Appleton. Or Doran.

I am returning the MS by this mail.[7]

Sincerely yours,
H. L. Mencken

The chapter on yellow paper is quite harmless. Put it back, by all means.

To CARL VAN DOREN
[OFP]

H. L. Mencken
1524 Hollins St.
Baltimore
August 20th [1923]

DEAR VAN DOREN: [8]

Literary intelligence: I am leaving the Smart Set to launch a new review, with Knopf as publisher—something grander and gaudier, I hope, than anything ever seen in the Republic. Probable name: the American Mercury. First issue: January, 1924. Contents: any damned thing that seems amusing, including especially politics. Knopf will spread himself on the format and printing.

In brief, the scheme is to drive a wedge between the Liberals and their chasing of butterflies on the one hand and the New York Times Conservatives and their worship of Otto Kahn on the other. There must be many young fellows in the country who balk at Liberalism and yet can't go the pace of the North American Review. The college

[7] Mencken wrote about this letter: "I haven't looked into *The Plastic Age* since it came out, and have pretty well forgotten it" (July 29, 1942). "Cream of the Earth" was the original title of the book.

[8] Carl Von Doren had left the *Nation* for the *Century* in June 1922.

faculties, I suspect, are full of them. Well, I hope to bring them out, and to set them to performing.

Can't you do something for us? I certainly hope so. We gray-haired veterans must set the pace. Have you anything in hand, not otherwise bespoken? I leave the subject to you. It may be literary, or it may be political, or it may be simply the state of the human race.

Incidentally, if you ever happen upon stuff that is too wild for the Century I hope you whisper the news to the authors. You owe me something for stealing Ruth Suckow. But do not gloat! I have laid up for the first number the best short story she ever wrote.[9]

Sincerely yours,
H. L. Mencken

To UPTON SINCLAIR
[OFP]

H. L. Mencken
1524 Hollins St.
Baltimore
August 24th [*1923*]

DEAR SINCLAIR:–

"The Goslings", unluckily, finds me in an unexpected situation. I am leaving the Smart Set next month to start a new serious review, and hence cannot buy a serial for the former. And the new review probably will not begin before January, and so it could not use any substantial part of "The Goslings" before the publication of the complete book. The Los Angeles section, as it stands, would make, of course, far more than one instalment, and in view of the plan upon which you have written it I see no way to cut it materially without grave damage to it. So the whole scheme seems to blow up. The enclosed stuff is excellent. I have read every word of it, and with constant interest.

Now to the new review. Knopf is to be the publisher, and it is to be a genuinely first-rate monthly, well printed on good paper. I shall try to cut a rather wide swathe in it, covering politics, economics, the exact sciences, etc., as well as belles lettres and the other fine arts. I

---

[9] The Suckow story: "Four Generations", in *The American Mercury* for January 1924.

have some promises of stuff from men who have something to say and know how to write, and I hope to stir up the animals. In politics it will be, in the main, Tory, but *civilized* Tory. You know me well enough to know that there will be no quarter for the degraded cads who now run the country. I am against you and against the Liberals because I believe you chase butterflies, but I am even more against your enemies.

Nothing would delight me more [than] to have a roaring article from you in the first number. I go further, and suggest a subject. Why not a sort of reminiscent and autobiographical chapter, "aus meinem Leben", rehearsing realistically your adventures as a reformer—not the objective facts and struggles, but the psychological adventures and observations. Isn't it a fact that the majority of people, even those who are most obviously oppressed, are quite devoid of any comprehension of liberty—that they are contented in their wallow? Haven't you, as a matter of actual experience, found them apathetic and even hostile? It is my own observation that liberty seems dangerous to all ordinary men—that respect for it and love of it are confined to small classes. Think of the doings of the American Legion!

But maybe this notion doesn't appeal to you. If not, what other ideas have you? I needn't point out that this new review would get you before an entirely new audience—a cynical one, perhaps, and impatient of exhortation, but nevertheless one with a keen relish for wit and a decent attitude toward opponents. Give the matter your prayers.

Yours,
Mencken

To Howard Parshley[1]
[OFP]

H. L. Mencken
1524 Hollins St.
Baltimore
August 28th [*1923*]

Dear Dr. Parshley:–

Let me see it, by all means. The subject looks enormously interesting.

---

[1] Howard Parshley was an assistant professor of zoölogy at Smith College and frequently contributed to *The American Mercury.*

Would you care, incidentally, to do us a short article now and then on current progress in zoölogy, or in general biology—not a bald summary, but a more or less detailed account of some salient investigation? Also, there is the matter of book reviews. We'd like to review all important books in all fields—not the whole mass of them but the best (or worst) ones.

Incidentally, if you know of anyone else who has an interesting MS in hand I'll be delighted to hear of it. Better still, tell the authors yourself to send their stuff to me. I shall read everything myself, and am eager to find new men.

Sincerely yours,
H. L. Mencken

To THEODORE DREISER
[UP]

[*Dreiser did not like the title of* The American Mercury; *why not "H. L. M.", or "Mencken and Nathan", he suggested.*]

H. L. Mencken
1524 Hollins St.
Baltimore
September 10th [1923]

DEAR DREISER:–

1. The title is changed to Proteus.

2. Phil Goodman writes that his first week's takings with his new piece were $12,000. I am suggesting to him that he give us a bang-up party in gratitude for God's beneficence.

3. The names you suggest would give the thing away. What we need is something that looks highly respectable outwardly. The American Mercury is almost perfect for that purpose. What will go on inside the tent is another story. You will recall that the late P. T. Barnum got away with burlesque shows by calling them moral lectures.

Yours,
M.

(1923)

◇◇◇◇◇◇◇◇◇◇◇◇◇

To Howard W. Odum[2]
[OFP]

H. L. Mencken
1524 Hollins St.
Baltimore
September 10th [1923]

Dear Dr. Odum:–

I have read the *Journal of Social Forces* from cover to cover—perhaps a sufficient tribute to its interest from a man who shares the common journalistic prejudice against the uplift in all its forms! If, as a practical journalist, I may offer any criticism of its general tone, it must be this: that there is rather too much mere glow and eloquence and too little practical information. Such an article as that of Mr. McAlister on "Selling, But Not Selling Out the Kingdom" seems to me to be sheer rhetoric; the same vague and blowsy stuff is printed in all the denominational papers. And such things as Miss Mudgett's "The Use of Advanced Students in Field Work" are simply sophomoric attempts at the professorial manner. But then I turn to Mr. Branson's "Farm Tenancy in the South", and at once encounter sound and useful information, intelligently presented. It seems to me that this is what is needed now, above all things. Social work is constantly being crippled by theorists who set up their theories before they are sure of their facts. Before anything of permanent value may be even so much as attempted, there must be an exhaustive study of the clinical facts; it will take time and labor, but they will be well spent. One reason why your study of the negro stands above all others of its kind lies in the simple circumstance that it is realistic and discreet—that it confines itself to what is demonstrable. It seems to me, for that reason, to stand clearly above any other study of the negro ever made. As one brought up among blacks, I recognize its truth in every line. But when I read most other treatises on the negro I seem to be listening to some preposterous sentimental clergyman or chautauqua orator.

What a chance the South offers for field work! Its problems have

---

[2] Howard Odum (1884–1954) was a professor of sociology at the University of North Carolina. He was also director of the Institute for Research in Social Science there. In 1930 he became president of the American Sociological Society. Interracial problems were his special field of research.

been discussed endlessly, but never investigated. Johnson's article on the Ku Klux Klan leaves many of the most important facts unmentioned. What the South suffers from, even more than from the negro question, is the rise to power of the poor white trash of an earlier time —in brief, the gradual solidification into custom and law of the ignorance and prejudice of a very low grade of Caucasians. The people described by Branson, as he points out, are almost undistinguishable from the negroes. Yet it is such people who, in most Southern states, set the tone of politics and religion. I believe that the the best way to break down their power is to describe them realistically.

I suppose you have heard of the American Mercury. Johnson, of Greensboro, is going to write for it. Why don't you do something for it yourself?

Sincerely yours,
H. L. Mencken

To PHILIP GOODMAN
[EPL]

New York
December 28, 1923

DEAR PHIL:

All of your remarks are full of justice, truth and sagacity. I made some of them myself anterior to the receipt of your esteemed communication. But the truth is that such matters are in the hands of Knopf and that I had so many troubles of my own that I had no steam left for fresh combat.

Laugh if you will, but the fact remains that we are actually on the press with the second edition of the first number. We have word this morning that the subscription department was 670 subscriptions behind—that is, behind in entering them up. Knopf has bought 30 new yellow neckties and has taken a place in Westchester County to breed Assyrian wolfhounds.

I waited on you yesterday at your show-house and was informed that you were giving a dance at the Ritz.

Your statement that you are going abroad on January the 12th still fails to convince me.

Yours,
[*M.*]

1924

To GAMALIEL BRADFORD
[OFP]

The American Mercury
220 West Forty-second Street
New York
January 2nd [1924]

DEAR BRADFORD:–

You are, I think, quite right. More, I don't think I am as far from your position as you assume. Both points that you make, in fact, are covered in that editorial. On the one hand, I admit that I fear my own variety of truth is often not actually true, and on the other hand I offer to hear and print all proponents of antagonistic truths, so long as they are neither doctrinaire or sentimental. So I doubt that you will have anything to complain of, save perhaps some axe-work now and then. In that department I crave your indulgence! God hath made me so. I can withstand almost any temptation, including even that of alcohol, but when a concrete Methodist bobs up in front of me in his white choker I must simply fall upon him or bust. So I warn you that you may expect some brutal slaughter of holy men. But maybe not often.

I am delighted that you like the looks of the American Mercury. Knopf put a great deal of hard work into it. I was in some fear, when it was still a dummy, that the Garamond type would be a bit Frenchy, but in the actual magazine it looks very well.

Which recalls the fact that Nathan and I live in hope that every mail will bring your Greeley, or something else from you.[1] The day it

[1] Gamaliel Bradford published "Horace Greeley", later reprinted in *As God Made Them* (Boston and New York: Houghton Mifflin Co.; 1929), in the *Mercury* for April 1924.

comes in we shall celebrate in the Christian manner with a libation.

The best of luck in 1924!

Sincerely yours,
H. L. Mencken

To HOWARD PARSHLEY
[OFP]

H. L. Mencken
1524 Hollins St.
Baltimore
February 4th [1924]

DEAR DR. PARSHLEY:

I am sending to you today, by Reichpost, "The Philosophy of Friedrich Nietzsche" and "Pistols for Two". Of the other books you list I have but one copy each, and I am afraid to trust them to the mails. But there is nothing in them worth reading. The Shaw book is an early work and "Europe after 8.15" is trivial. All that was worth reading in "A Little Book in C Major" is now in "A Book of Burlesques". "A Book of Calumny" is twelfth-rate. So, with the Knopf books, you now have everything.

My first act as boss of Baltimore is to order all the saloons closed for half an hour today in memory of the late Woodrow Wilson. His passing affects me greatly. He was unquestionably the greatest man since Munyon.[2]

Sincerely yours,
H. L. Mencken

To UPTON SINCLAIR
[OFP]

H. L. Mencken
1524 Hollins St.
Baltimore
February 17th [1924]

DEAR SINCLAIR:–

The sheets of "The Goslings" have just come in. I beg to remark:

"The Goslings" is a valuable and excellent successor to "The

---

[2] Munyon was a medical quack, well known at the time.

Goosestep". It is the fruit of a long and painstaking investigation of the public schools of the United States, and the facts that it presents are of the utmost importance. They show clearly how opinion is deliberately manufactured in the Republic—how the standardization of ideas is managed in its primary stages. The story is told with humor, and has a racy, picaresque color. I have read the book with great delight, and shall read it again.

We moved in New York yesterday and I am down with housemaid's knee.

Yours,
Mencken

◇◇◇◇◇◇◇◇◇◇◇◇◇

To THEODORE DREISER
[UP]

[*On May 12th, 1924, Dreiser had agreed to write an article on the contemporary novelists for* The American Mercury *and had set forth his views at some length. He had also asked Mencken to read his piece, "The Mercy of God", which was published in the* Mercury *for August 1924.*]

H. L. Mencken
1524 Hollins St.
Baltimore
May 13th [1924]

DEAR DREISER:–

1. My prejudices against literary clubs is so violent that what I say about the P.E.N. outfit probably must be discounted. I can only tell you that I refused absolutely to join it myself and have since refused to go to any of its dinners. It contains some excellent fellows, notably Carl Van Doren, but I believe that most of its members are selling-platers. It has a strongly Anglomaniacal tinge. It would do you no good to join, and it might embarrass you greatly. All sorts of third raters would use you as a stalking horse to get publicity.

2. What you say about the young novelists would make a capital article. You would offend no one save the fakes, and they are against you anyhow, and ready to devour your carcass the moment you founder. Simply take them up one by one, setting forth your ideas about them simply, and then finish with some general observations on the present state and probable future of the American novel. Certainly,

the article should be written. The novel is constantly discussed, but very seldom by a novelist. I hope you tackle it.

3. My best thanks for the Haldeman-Julius first edition. Julius is a truly amazing fellow. I met him some time ago with Upton Sinclair. He talks and acts like a Rotary Club go-getter, but he prints many good books.

4. I don't know "The Mercy of God".[3] Has it been published? If not, I'll be delighted to get a whack at it.

5. Name the day and I'll be on hand for your soirée. All I ask is that you invite a few clergymen.

6. My hoof is still lame, and the quacks apparently don't know how to cure it, but I have not yet lost my faith in divine Providence. I have just finished "Prejudices IV", in which you appear in the light of a patriot and Christian. Now I must do a great mass of writing for the Mercury against my absence in June at the two national conventions.

Yours,
Mencken

◇◇◇◇◇◇◇◇◇◇◇◇◇◇

To SHERWOOD ANDERSON
[PT]

[*1524 Hollins Street*
Baltimore, Maryland]
August 19th [*1924*]

DEAR ANDERSON:–

I received the MS. from Liveright on Saturday and read it Sunday. I am eager to do a chapter from it; the one thing to find out is whether it is technically possible. If Huebsch publishes the book in October we'll have to get that chapter into our October number—and it is already set up and ready to be made up. Nathan is looking into the matter. I hope he is able to manage it.

The best of luck with the new novel. I hope you make a bootlegger the hero of it. If you do, call him T. Herman Dreiser.

God is punishing me for my sins. I am lame, have hay-fever and am also enjoying lumbago.

Sincerely yours,
[*Unsigned*]

Your handwriting is improving. I can now read 40% of it.

[3] "The Mercy of God" had been printed in *Chains* the year before (New York: Boni and Liveright; 1927).

To STANTON B. LEEDS[4]
[PT]

Baltimore, September 5th [1924]

DEAR STANTON:

I am just out of hospital, and on crutches. Moreover, hay-fever has me by the coccyx. But I should be all right in ten days. The operation was trivial—removal of a tumor that had been making me gradually lamer and lamer for six months. It turned out to be a harmless wart. What started it, God alone knows.

Harris is such a liar that I doubt his whole story. His denunciations of Conrad, Mark Twain and Dreiser have only made him ridiculous. I get letters from him pretty regularly. He is always after money. But, for all his faults, a most interesting man.

The Davis campaign seems to have blown up. I believe that Cal will be elected. What La Follette will do is very uncertain. If the election were tomorrow he would probably carry ten States. But third parties are always strongest at the start. They disintegrate as the campaign wears on, mainly because their factions quarrel. Hundreds of labor leaders have already sold out to the Republicans.

Come back to the Republic before it is too late. I believe that God will take a hand in the farce before long.

Yours,
Mencken

To ALFRED A. KNOPF
[AAK]

H. L. Mencken
1524 Hollins St.
Baltimore
October 13th [1924]

DEAR ALFRED:–

I agree with you in general, and always refuse requests to reprint whole articles. But the Coolidge article presented a special case.[5] I gave permission to reprint it to both the Democratic National Committee and the La Follette organization. At least a million copies have

[4] Stanton B. Leeds was a journalist and an author.
[5] See the next letter.

been distributed. They have got an enormous amount of notice in the newspapers, and have been worth a great deal as advertising—more than a thousand paid ads. If the impression has got about that we are partisan in the matter of Coolidge, and vigorously against him, it is true and will do us good. Try to imagine any Coolidge man reading the Mercury. Two numbers would set him to flight. We'll never get anywhere trying to woo the Babbitts.

All political printing is bad. It is let out to union shops as graft. I never saw a political pamphlet that was well printed. But the people such things reach do not notice printing—that is, they are used to the kind on tap.

I'll see you next Tuesday.

Yours,
M.

To George Jean Nathan
[cu]

[*It was not long before Mencken and Nathan disagreed on the editorial policy of the* Mercury; *George Jean Nathan cared nothing for politics, and Mencken cared less and less for art. On February 19, 1925, Nathan ceased being co-editor and became contributing editor; but it was not until 1930 that he left the magazine entirely. The following letter throws some light on what the public long considered a mystery.*]

The American Mercury
October 19th [*1924*]

Dear George:–

What I am thinking of is the future—two, five or ten years hence. In particular, I am thinking of my own future. As things stand, I see nothing ahead save a round of dull drudgery, with no chance to lift the magazine out of casualness and triviality and to make it of solid dignity and influence. Its present apparent success, I believe, is largely illusory. It is appealing mainly to a superficial and unstable class of readers. Their support is not to be depended on. They buy it at the news-stands, and gabble about it intermittently, but they are not permanently interested in ideas. What the magazine needs is a sounder underpinning. It must develop a more coherent body of doctrine, and maintain it with more vigor. It must seek to lead, not a miscellaneous and frivolous rabble, but the class that is serious at bottom, however much it may mock conventional seriousness. There is great significance, I believe, in the fact that the most successful thing we have ever printed, and by long odds, was the Kent article on Coolidge. It proved that the civilized minority, after all, *does* take politics seriously.[6]

You mention The Smart Set, and say that I was wrong about it. I believe, on the contrary, that I was right every time. The Smart Set went to pot because it was too trivial—because it interested intelligent readers only intermittently, and then only when they were in trifling moods—when they were, so to speak, a bit stewed intellectually. Eventually, many of them tired of it—because it got nowhere. Their reading of the magazine became irregular, and so its circulation declined. As you will recall, I proposed at least a dozen times that we put more solid stuff into it. We could never agree as to the character of this solid stuff, and I thus lost interest in it. During its last three or four years I certainly put no hard work and thought into it. I simply slopped along. I don't want to do this with The American Mercury. Too much is at stake in it. On The Smart Set we could hide behind the obvious handicaps—the absurd name, the wretched printing, the imbecility of Warner, and so on. But now we are out in the open, with the harsh sunlight on us.

I believe that either of us, convinced of all this and with a simple and vigorous policy, could make The American Mercury something very much better than it is, and give it eventually the solid position of the Atlantic, or even a better position. Its chances are not unlike those which confronted the Atlantic in the years directly after the Civil War: it has an opportunity to seize leadership of the genuinely civilized minority of Americans. But I doubt that the job thus presented is one for two men: divided councils make for too much irresolution and compromise. In particular, I doubt that you and I could carry it off together. Our interests are too far apart. We see the world in wholly different colors. When we agree, it is mainly on trivialities. This fundamental difference was of relatively small consequence on The Smart Set, for neither of us took the magazine very seriously: the presence of Warner made it impossible. But it is different with The American Mercury. I see no chance of coming close together. On the contrary, I believe that we are drifting further and further apart. I cite an obvious

[6] The Kent article: "Mr. Coolidge", by Frank R. Kent, in the August 1924 *Mercury.*

proof of it: we no longer play together. Another: when we sit down to discuss the magazine itself we are off it in ten minutes.

What is to be done I don't know. But I believe the matter ought to be talked out. I can see clearly only what is ahead for myself. My current job tends to irritate me. I am tied to routine, and much of it is routine that shouldn't be thrown on me—for example, watching the printer, and especially the make-up man. Page 374 in the November issue is in point. If I get out of contact with the office for three days my desk is in chaos. All this makes it a practical impossibility for me to do what I ought to do, and what Sedgwick does—that is, track down ideas, manuscripts and authors. I have duties that are antagonistic, and that kill each other. If I go on, I'll slide inevitably, in self-protection, into the easier of them. In other words, I'll do precisely what I did on The Smart Set. I could work with a competent slave, but I can't work when I must be that slave myself.

But I don't want to make this a roster of grievances. You have your own troubles, and some of them are worse than mine. All I suggest is that we sit down and look at the situation realistically, and try to remedy it if it can be remedied. It goes without saying that I am willing to go on as now until a remedy can be found. But nothing is to be gained by evasions. It ought to be clearly understood by all hands that I am dissatisfied with the present scheme, and that its continuance is bound to make me less and less useful to the magazine. Look at my December book article: it is dreadful stuff. I therefore propose a palaver. Why should we quarrel? Either I am right or I am wrong. If I am right, I assume that everyone will agree. If I am wrong, I engage to shut up.

[*M.*]

To GAMALIEL BRADFORD
[OFP]

The American Mercury
730 Fifth Avenue
New York
October 24th, 1924

DEAR BRADFORD:

What is there mysterious about it? You show all of the qualities that I admire in a writer: sound and extensive knowledge, patient and yet unpedantic industry and perfect clarity.

I certainly have no objection to the Puritan philosophy per se—what I object to is the perversion by Methodists, Rotarians and other such vermin.[7] Down in Maryland, I get on very well with the native gentry, but the bogus intellectuals pain me severely. The virtue of the gentry lies in the simple fact that a back-ground is behind them. That is also the virtue of the genuine Puritan of New England. In such matters, I am extremely reactionary. I believe that a man's great-great grandfather influences him enormously more than the people he ordinarily meets with in this life.

Your dialogs are excellent, particularly the one between the two J. C.'s.[8] Curiously enough, I met Hartman for the first time last night and have never met Mark Van Doren at all. His brother, Carl, I know very well—a capital fellow; very logical and yet full of human juices. Mark, judged by his writings, seems to me to be very pedantic. Hartman made no impression on me whatever, probably because he was very tight.

Let me hear of it by all means when you head this way. I am in New York only irregularly, but I'll surely try to be here when you come.

Sincerely yours,
H. L. Mencken

To ALFRED A. KNOPF
[AAK]

H. L. Mencken
1524 Hollins St.
Baltimore
November 17th [*1924*]

DEAR ALFRED:–

1. I forgot to tell you that James Weldon Johnson, the chief man in the Association for the Advancement of Colored People, is preparing

[7] In a letter dated October 18, 1924, Gamaliel Bradford had admired Mencken's "joyous capacity for belief" and described him as "the real Puritan, the simon pure thing, the man with an ideal". He had furthermore expressed his surprise that Mencken should have treated him so politely despite his "conservatism and antidiluvianism".

[8] The dialogues mentioned here were imaginary conversations recorded by Gamaliel Bradford in his diaries, one of them being a discussion between two Jesus Christs.

to write his reminiscences. He has had a very remarkable career and writes very well. You will get the book automatically. I may be able to use parts of it in The American Mercury.[9]

M.

To Ellery Sedgwick
[OFP]

H. L. Mencken
1524 Hollins St.
Baltimore
December 7th [*1924*]

Dear Sedgwick:–

Have you such a thing as a Style Sheet for The Atlantic? If not, what authority do you follow? The magazine always looks clean and well edited. I have been wobbling along since The American Mercury began in a sort of day to day manner, but now I think we ought to try to formulate some rules. If you can suggest any workable authority I'll be very greatly obliged.

I hope you let me hear of it some time when you are in New York. I'd like very much to see you.

Sincerely yours,
H. L. Mencken

To Upton Sinclair
[OFP]

H. L. Mencken
1524 Hollins St.
Baltimore
December 10th [*1924*]

Dear Sinclair:–

I like the Jack London chapter very much, but its onslaughts upon alcohol make it impossible for us. We are committed to the revival of

[9] James Weldon Johnson (1871–1938) wrote two volumes of reminiscences: *The Autobiography of an Ex-Coloured Man,* published in Boston by Sherman, French and Co. in 1912, then in New York by Alfred A. Knopf in 1927; and *Along This Way* (New York: The Viking Press; 1933). This probably refers to the second edition of the first book.

the saloon, exactly as it was. America misses it, and is much the worse for the lack of it. London, sober, would have written nothing worth reading. Alcohol made him.

The other chapters seem to me to be feebler. In fact, most of them, e.g., the ones of Clemens and Howells, say only what has been said before, and is obvious. I am holding the MS. at your order.[1]

The news that The American Mercury is "lacking in constructive points of view" is surely not news to me. If any such points of view ever get into it, it will only be over my mutilated and pathetic corpse. The uplift has damn nigh ruined the country. What we need is more sin.

Twenty barges in tow of five tugs set out from the Bahamas for Baltimore last Tuesday. It will be a Christian Christmas. God's hand is in it!

Yours,
Mencken

To HERBERT PARRISH
[OFP]

H. L. Mencken
1524 Hollins St.
Baltimore
December 16th [*1924?*]

DEAR MR. PARRISH:–

Of course there is no objection to tragedy per se. The trouble with the Russian story is that it is suddenly injected, without dramatic preparation, into light comedy. The result is a dissonance at the close.

Rule No. 1: Fiction always has to be made more plausible than fact. Stories based upon fact are usually weak for that very reason. The author proceeds upon the assumption that their truth justifies them. But what is really needed is an *air* of truth—a quite different thing.

Don't give up so easily! You'll sell 'em yet.

Sincerely yours,
H. L. Mencken

---

[1] The book was *Mammonart,* by Upton Sinclair (Pasadena, Cal.: The author; 1925).

◇◇◇◇◇◇◇◇◇◇◇◇◇

To William Feather[2]
[OFP]

The American Mercury
220 West Forty-second Street
New York
December 19th [1924]

Dear Mr. Feather:–

I think this is now excellent stuff—all except the epilogue. There you suddenly change the key; there ought to be a return to the tonic. That is, I think you ought to return to Patterson's influence on the salesmanship of today, and describe it again in a humorous way, as in the opening. Don't try to estimate it: simply describe it—the sales conventions, the parades, the go-getting, the he-man stuff, the Advertising Clubs of the World, the idiotic speeches, the Kiwanians, the Rotarians—in brief, the New Business.

My apologies for making so many suggestions. But I think the article is on the verge of being very fine stuff, and I don't want to let it get by with a false note in it. It won't do to say flatly that Pattersonism has been overdone. Let the fact shine out of the record. And pile up the record as much as you can!

I trust that you will not go dry at Christmas.

Sincerely yours,
H. L. Mencken

The title is wrong. It should be "The Prince of Pep" or something of the sort. Or "Jazz among the Babbitts".

To Upton Sinclair
[OFP]

The American Mercury
730 Fifth Avenue
New York
December 22nd [1924]

Dear Sinclair:–

So long as you represent me as praising alcohol I shall not complain. It is, I believe, the greatest of human inventions, and by far—much greater than Hell, the radio or the bichloride tablet.

[2] William Feather (born in 1889): president of the William Feather Co., printers and publishers in Cleveland.

Sterling is not to be heeded. If it were not for alcohol he'd still be working in that pants factory, and the world would be short a poet. He could no more write on well water than he could sleep without a fair one to warm him. His blood is thin.

Free speech? To hell with it! I am a 100% American, and loathe it. Next week, in fact, I am to harangue the Baltimore Rotary Club against it.

Good luck in 1925!

Sincerely yours,
Mencken

◇◇◇◇◇◇◇◇◇◇◇◇◇◇

To EDGAR LEE MASTERS
[OFP]

H. L. Mencken
1524 Hollins St.
Baltimore
December 30th [1924]

DEAR MR. MASTERS:–

My doubt about taking any more of these Lichee-Nut Poems at the moment lies in this fact: that we can run but one piece of verse a month, and we already have enough in type to last about 12 months. I thus fear that if I took on the whole book we might get bogged, and unable to work off the stuff before the publication of the book. True enough, the number of poems used each time might be augmented, but I believe that it would be bad practise to augment it greatly—that the selections are more effective when they run to a few pages only. Thus I am somewhat stumped. The first batch is in the magazine for January, but the second is not scheduled until April or May. I did not know when we took the two batches that you proposed to go on. I therefore propose this: that you offer the remaining stuff, so much of it as you may write, wherever you please, and let me see whatever is left of it, say, on April 15th. And then again, say, on September 15th. I hope this will solve the problem.

I'll be delighted to see you at the end of the month. You say you are to lecture on January 24th. That is a Saturday night. I propose that we meet on Friday the 23rd instead of on the day before. We can have dinner together and put in the evening in spiritual exercises. On the morning of the 24th you can have your clothes boiled, visit a chiropractor, and so get yourself ready for the dinner with the pastor's family and the lecture in the evening. Unless you veto it, I'll invite one or two honest Christian men to victual with us—say Raymond Pearl, of the Johns Hopkins, and one other.[3] On Saturday afternoon I shall have myself incarcerated in the city jail, so that there will be no danger of kidnapping me and taking me to the Poetry Society dinner. I advise you to wear smoked glasses at your lecture. If you get one good look at some of the lady poets you will come down with asthma.

Is my first paragraph clear? In brief, I release you from any claim that The American Mercury may set up to the whole series of poems, but agree to take new whacks at them as circumstances permit—that is, to those not disposed of otherwise.

Yours in Xt.,
H. L. Mencken

◇◇◇◇◇◇◇◇◇◇◇◇◇◇

To HARRY KEATING
[PT]

Baltimore, December 31, 1924

DEAR MR. KEATING:

Sherman is very amusing. He has been wobbling for several years, and lately sent an emissary to me and invited me to review his new book in his paper. I refused on the ground that, while I had no objection to his book, I could not enter upon personal relations with a man whose conduct during the late war was not that of a gentleman. Now he calls me a proletarian! Shades of my learned and bewigged forebearers! That this dreadful charge should come from an Iowa Methodist! [4]

I shall apply for membership in the Third International at once.

Sincerely yours,
[*H. L. Mencken*]

---

[3] See note [9] on p. 286.

[4] Sherman's new book: *Points of View* (New York [and] London: Charles Scribner's Sons; 1924); his paper: the New York *Herald Tribune* Book Section, for which he wrote occasional reviews. The one Mencken objected to here was "A liberating sword" in the issue for November 30, 1924, or possibly "Mr. Brownell and Mr. Mencken" in the January 1925 issue of the *Bookman*.

1925

◊◊◊◊◊◊◊◊◊◊◊◊◊◊◊◊◊◊

To Sara P. Haardt
[PT]

[*Sara Haardt's health was never very good; at the time of this letter, she was under treatment in a Maryland sanitarium for tuberculosis of the lungs.*]

H. L. Mencken
1524 Hollins St.
Baltimore.
January 22, 1925

Dear Sara:–

You tell me too little about yourself. How do you feel? I don't preach patience to you so much as cynicism: it is the most comforting of philosophies. You will get over your present difficulties only to run into something worse, and so on until the last sad scene. Make up your mind to it—and then make the best of it. If you can't write a book a year, then write one every two years.

I believe that life is a constant oscillation between the sharp horns of dilemmas. I work like a dog, and accomplish nothing that really interests me. Once I gave up all routine work and devoted myself to a book: I was sick of it in six months, and went back to answering letters and reading MSS.

Nevertheless, life remains livable. Biological necessities keep us going. It is the feeling of exerting effort that exhilarates us, as a grasshopper is exhilarated by jumping. A hard job, full of impediments, is thus more satisfying than an easy job. When I get letters from Germ. *Gelehrten,* complaining that they are having a hell of a time, I always congratulate them. They will do good work, and enjoy it. The men at the Rockefeller Institute, with money to pay for everything they want, are unhappy, and the place is full of intrigue.

But I run on *à la* Polonius. Please excuse poor pen.

Yours,
M.

◇◇◇◇◇◇◇◇◇◇◇◇◇◇

To Percy Marks
[OFP]

H. L. Mencken
1524 Hollins St.
Baltimore
February 3rd [*1925?*]

Dear Mr. Marks:–

Just when I'll get to New York I don't know. I'll call you when I do. Maybe it will be next week. Don't worry about the Four Roses. My cellar is still holding out.

My explanation of Puritanism, as of democracy, is that it is founded upon hatred of the fellow who is having, or seems to be having, a better time. The Puritan is simply one who, because of physical cowardice, lack of imagination or religious superstition, is unable to get any joy out of the satisfaction of his natural appetites. Taking a drink, he fears that he is headed for the gutter. Grabbing a gal, he is staggered by thoughts of hell and syphilis. Observing that other men do such things innocently, he hates them. The more innocent they seem or pretend to be, the more he hates them.

I have exposed this idea at various times and at great length, but never, so far as I can recall, in a formal essay. It will be at the bottom of my projected book on democracy. Democracy, as I see it, is simply the organized hatred of the lower orders. That hatred explains all of its phenomena; nothing else does.

Sincerely yours,
H. L. Mencken

(1925)

To F. Scott Fitzgerald

[PU]

The American Mercury
730 Fifth Avenue
New York
May 26th [1925]

Dear Fitz:–

When are you coming back to the Republic? You are missing a superb show. In a few weeks I am going down to Tennessee to see a school-teacher tried for teaching Evolution.[1] Match that in your decayed principalities if you can! William Jennings Bryan is to prosecute, and Clarence Darrow and Dudley Field Malone are for the defense.

I am very eager to see the new novel. But two years is a hell of a long while. I hope you find time by the way to compose a piece for the above great family magazine. Why not a treatise on the very subject you discuss in your letter, i.e., novel-writing? It is much belabored, but seldom by anyone who has ever actually written a novel. La Wharton's fulminations in Scribner's scarcely constitute an exception. Her ideas are those of a high-school teacher.

As Law Enforcement grows rigider and rigider, New York grows wetter and wetter. Baltimore is now knee-deep in excellent beer. I begin to believe in prayer.

Sincerely yours,
H. L. Mencken

To Jim Tully

[OFP]

H. L. Mencken
1524 Hollins St.
Baltimore
May 27th [1925]

Dear Tully:–

May God guide your hand! I only hope you make it plain that I am a baptized man and a strict monogamist. It is 20 years since I last

[1] The trial here mentioned is, of course, the celebrated Scopes trial at Dayton, Tenn., where Mencken was sent as reporter for the Baltimore *Evening Sun.*

went to bed with two women at once, and then I was in my cups and not myself.

I enclose the autographs. What books of mine do you lack? Let me know: I'd like to send them to you.

Boyd's book is charming stuff and he is a sound critic, but I think he rather misses me.[2] The trouble is that he is purely a literary critic himself, and so sees me mainly as one. But I am nothing of the sort: I am far more of a politician. As for Goldberg, he tries to fit me with a moral purpose. But both of them are sharp fellows, and get into my viscera more than once.

Lent nearly floored me. I am still suffering from the fasting.

Yours,
H. L. Mencken

To ISAAC GOLDBERG
[PT]

July 28th [*1925*]

DEAR GOLDBERG:–

It is manifestly impossible for me to judge your book as criticism: you disarm me constantly by a tremendous generosity. But if you thus overrate what I have done, you at least come very close to what I have tried to do. For the rest, I can only congratulate you sincerely on a very remarkable piece of research. It is easy to anatomize the dead; the living are far harder. You strip me of false face, dickle, underwear and fig-leaf, and turn me out upon the public street. The figure I make is surely not heroic. But I believe that any human being, so turned inside out, should be interesting and instructive to other human beings. Let us hope so, anyway. Your facts, so far as I know them, are exactly accurate. So the cadaver gives three cheers for the medical student!

Sincerely yours,
H. L. Mencken

---

[2] Ernest Boyd's book: *H. L. Mencken* (New York: Robert M. McBride; 1925), still the best study to date on Mencken's personality and significance.

(1 9 2 5)

◇◇◇◇◇◇◇◇◇◇◇◇◇◇

To Ernest Boyd
[ofp]

H. L. Mencken
1524 Hollins St.
Baltimore
August 30th [*1925*]

Dear Boyd:–

I have now read the book three times, and come to this conclusion: that you have done a damned fine job.[3] It is, in fact, a quite extraordinary piece of synthesis; you organize all that immense material superbly, and separate what is essential from what is not essential almost perfectly. If I were attempting a summary of my own case I'd use almost precisely the same quotations. You make them hang together, you keep the thing moving, and you come very close to the basic facts in the end.

In particular, I am delighted with your very clear statement of my divergence from the Liberals, and your discussion of my motives as a literary critic. The latter have been much misunderstood. For a long while I was looked upon as a sort of crusader for Dreiser—even, I suspect, by Dreiser himself. The fact is that Dreiser simply gave me a good chance to unload my own ideas, which were seldom identical with his. Nor had I any interest in the aesthetic gabble that went on in 1908. It seemed to me to be mainly buncombe. I have, in fact, no respect for aesthetic theories. They are always blowing up. More and more I incline to the notion that every first-rate work of art, like every first-rate man, is sui generis. When I hear a theory I suspect a quack.

So far as I can make out, I believe in only one thing: liberty. But I do not believe in even liberty enough to want to force it upon anyone. That is, I am nothing of the reformer, however much I may rant against this or that great curse or malaise. In that ranting there is usually far more delight than indignation. Such things interest me, as gastric ulcers interest pathologists. I think you have made all of this plain enough. My affection for Baltimore is largely mere laziness. I dislike being disturbed. Here it is possible to live through three or four days on end without being bothered. In New York I am beset day and night.

---

[3] See note p. 280.

But all this is beside the point. The main thing is that you have done an excellent piece of criticism. More, it is a fine piece of writing. The sentences roll off capitally. It is readable in every line, and it is full of shrewd observations and effective phrases. God, in his infinite mercy, will reward you. He has me, at the moment, by the snout. A fair, windy day! I am almost fit for religion.

A few errors: On pp. 28 and 29 the y and the i are interchanged in Dyonisian. On p. 41, in the second paragraph, are the errors that you have already noticed yourself. On p. 44 the The in front of Sturm should be roman and lower case.

I had hoped to get to New York during the coming week, but travelling will probably be impossible. In that case I'll come up next Sunday.

Yours,
Mencken

◇◇◇◇◇◇◇◇◇◇◇◇◇◇

To SARA P. HAARDT
[PT]

[*Mencken had refused an article by Sara Haardt for the* Mercury.]

Baltimore, August 31, 1925

DEAR SARA:–

Don't get impatient about your writing. You are doing it better month by month. The hard labor of the past years will come home to roost, so to speak, later on. At 35 my income from books was $200 a year. Now, if I had the time to write more, I could live on them.

Boyd's book is certainly not bad. But he overlooked two things. First, the fact that my whole body of doctrine rests upon a belief in liberty. Second, that I am far more an artist than a metaphysician.

Yours,
M.

◇◇◇◇◇◇◇◇◇◇◇◇◇◇

To BLANCHE KNOPF
[AAK]

[*On September 16, 1925, Mrs. Alfred A. Knopf had written to Mencken:*

Dear Henry,

I spoke to George Gershwin last Friday about an article on INSTRUMENTATION OF JAZZ. *He said he'd like to do it but at present he is fearfully busy and added that a man by the name of Russell Bennett could do it infinitely better than he. However, he suggested that probably what we wanted to use was his name—Gershwin's. I think that is rather good, don't you? However, he is coming in this week sometime to talk about it.*

Sincerely,
(B. W. K.)]

H. L. Mencken
1524 Hollins St.
Baltimore
September 17th [*1925*]

DEAR BLANCHE:–

1. Thanks for seeing Gershwin. If Bennett does the article, perhaps Bennett had better sign it. But the signature is not important. What I want is a good article, explaining exactly how the effects of jazz are obtained. Tell Gershwin that we can use any number of illustrations in music type.

2. Cain will be at my house Sunday. He has ideas for several books. I'll keep in contact with him.[4]

Yours,
M.

◇◇◇◇◇◇◇◇◇◇◇◇◇◇

To GAMALIEL BRADFORD
[OFP]

The American Mercury
730 Fifth Avenue
New York
October 3, 1925

DEAR BRADFORD:

I fear that we are on opposite sides of the fence, but that only proves that it has two sides. Somehow the stuff in "Americana" tickled

[4] See note 8, p. 422.

me immensely.[5] I roared over it as it came in, and it even made me laugh when I read it again in proof. Most of it, I am convinced, is not satire at all, but pure humor. It is raw material awaiting another Mark Twain. Think of "The Gilded Age" and then figure out old Mark's reaction to Kiwanis!

I am reading "Wives" and enjoying it immensely. It contains some of the best stuff ever done.[6]

Sincerely yours,
H. L. Mencken

◇◇◇◇◇◇◇◇◇◇◇◇◇◇

To CARL VAN VECHTEN
[YU]

H. L. Mencken
1524 Hollins St.
Baltimore
October 10th [1925]

DEAR CARL:–

The Widow Saltus' book is a horrible thing.[7] Coming so soon after Mrs. Arnold Bennett's exposure of Bennett, it makes me thank God that I married an illiterate colored woman, who doesn't know what my trade is, and never wants to meet and scare my friends. I am reviewing it for the Tribune syndicate next Sunday. As you know, I put Saltus himself lower than you do. Lately I reread five or six of his books. All save "Imperial Purple" seemed amateurish to me. Did you ever know, by the way, that "Imperial Purple" inspired "Heliogabalus"? A curious bibliographical detail.

I'll believe in Johnson's article on jazz when I see it. He promised it to me in the Autumn of 1893.[8]

Yours,
Mencken

---

[5] *Americana* was a section in *The American Mercury* dealing with indigenous imbecilities in the form of quotations, mainly from newspapers, alphabetically arranged by States.

[6] *Wives:* by G. Bradford (New York and London: Harper & Brothers; 1925).

[7] The Widow Saltus's book: *Edgar Saltus, the Man* by Marie Saltus (Chicago: Pascal Covici; 1925).

[8] Johnson: James Weldon Johnson.

(1 9 2 5)

To Sherwood Anderson
[PT]

H. L. Mencken
1524 Hollins St.
Baltimore
November 16th [1925]

Dear Anderson:–

I am glad the notice didn't disgust you. A lot of hard work went into it. The book is solid and it will last. You have come to such a position in a few years that not all the professors will ever be able to shake you out of it.

Don't you ever come East any more?

Sincerely yours,
[*Unsigned*]

To Fielding Hudson Garrison
[PT]

Baltimore, December 2nd [*1925 or after*]

Dear Garrison:

I liked "The Constant Nymph" very much. One defect, it seems to me, is in it: the people are not completely musicians, but simply generally dispersed artists, so to speak. There is little of what might be called musical local color. But the whole thing is very well imagined and briskly written.

Whenever I hear Hofmann I think of old Rafael Joseffy's anecdote about him. When Josef was 17 or 18 his father worked him like a slave and gave him no money. In consequence the girls would not look at him, and he had to resort to manual pleasure a cappella. "Back to Bach!" Joseffy would say.

I hope the tooth-pulling can be escaped. A hell of a nuisance. But I begin to believe that only oxen are absolutely well. Last night I had dinner with two clergymen, and they put on such a feast that I feel like a vinegar barrel today.

Yours,
Mencken

To Raymond Pearl[9]

[OFP]

H. L. Mencken
1524 Hollins St.
Baltimore
December 3rd, 1925

Dear Pearl:–

My best thanks for the reprints and for the autobiographical note. The last is superb. Why not expand it? It would make a capital book. Soon or late you must do it. Why wait, as usual, until you are a mere garbage can of disintegrating colloids, with teeth gone, thirst gone and memory gone? I think every man should put down his recollections of this obscene world before he is 50. I have a lot of notes for mine, and shall compose it as soon as I finish three more books. The Goldberg, of course, is mainly applesass. Goldberg is a very moral fellow, and the truth would have scared him off.

Forget not that we meet at my house on Saturday. The pastors sent me to the bicarbonate can yesterday. What a gorge!

Yours in Xt.,
Mencken

To Alfred A. Knopf

[AAK]

H. L. Mencken
1524 Hollins St.
Baltimore
December 12th [*1925*]

Dear Alfred:–

Thanks for your note. My mother seems to be a bit better today, but she is still very ill, and I may not be able to get to New York on Monday as arranged. If so, I'll telegraph Angoff in the morning, and he will notify you. If I am not heard from it will be a sign that I am on my way.[1]

[9] Raymond Pearl was professor of biometry, biology and vital statistics at the Johns Hopkins University.

[1] Charles Angoff was then assistant editor of *The American Mercury.*

The enclosed MS. is by Nancy Hoyt, a sister to Elinor Wylie. It seems to me to be excellent stuff, and well worth printing. There is some melodrama in one spot, but I think it could be dug out. The general atmosphere is very charming, and the thing is very well written. My opinion is that Nancy, in the long run, will turn out to be better than Elinor.[2]

M.

To SHERWOOD ANDERSON
[PT]

The American Mercury
730 Fifth Avenue
New York
December 22, 1925

DEAR SHERWOOD:

When you were in Baltimore there was no opportunity to open the question of doing something for the above great family magazine. This note is simply to say [that] since our last transaction the amount of money in the drawer has somewhat increased and that I am now in a position to negotiate with you in a strictly business manner. If you have anything in hand or in mind, I hope you give me a chance on it. Put your price on it and I'll pay it if it is at all possible.[3]

I assume that by this time you have completed your tour of the open spaces.

Yours,
[*Unsigned*]

[2] Nancy Hoyt (b. 1902) wrote a number of novels published by Alfred A. Knopf, among them: *Roundabout* (1926) and *Unkind Star* (1927).

[3] Sherwood Anderson was soon to contribute "Death in the Woods" to *The American Mercury* for September 1926, and several other pieces later on.

1926

◇◇◇◇◇◇◇◇◇◇◇◇◇◇◇◇◇◇

To THEODORE DREISER
[UP]

[*Relations with Dreiser were beginning to deteriorate. There was no further exchange of letters between the two men for about nine years. The following incident seems to have brought about this estrangement: Dreiser has asked Mencken to use his influence to obtain for him permission to visit the Sing Sing death house. Acting through acquaintances he had at the New York* World, *Mencken was able to secure this permission for Dreiser, but some unpleasantness subsequently developed between the latter and the editors of the* World *over financial matters, a fact which greatly indisposed his friend. Moreover, when Mencken's mother died in December 1925, Dreiser happened to be touring Florida and did not have a chance to offer his condolences until February 2nd, 1926. This delay Mencken attributed to indifference and, whether he really understood its true cause or not, he decided to have no further communication with Dreiser.*]

H. L. Mencken
1524 Hollins St.
Baltimore
February 5th [*1926*]

DEAR DREISER:–

Thanks for your note. I begin to realize how inextricably my life was interwoven with my mother's. A hundred times a day I find myself planning to tell her something, or ask her for this or that. It is a curious thing: the human incapacity to imagine finality. The house seems strange, as if the people in it were deaf and dumb. But all life, I begin to believe, resolves itself into a doing without.

Are you back in New York for good? If so, let us have a session very soon. I am performing upon you without anaesthetics in the March Merkur, but *with* reservations.[1] I think the trial and execution of Griffiths goes beyond anything you have ever done. But the first volume made me shed some sweat.

I hear the book is selling very well.

Yours,
M.

To RICHARD J. BEAMISH[2]
[PT]

Baltimore, February 23 [1926]

DEAR BEAMISH:

My best thanks for the review. But what would you? Goldberg is full of anti-Christian prejudice, and so suppressed all mention of my theological studies. He is a leader in the Ku Klux Kohn, and is sworn to put a kike in the White House. God help the Republic!

I have a resident spy at Dayton, Tenn., and get regular news from thc front. A high-powered, bean-burning go-getter, with a salary of $300 a month, has come to town to promote the Bryan Fundamentalist University. More than 60 Baptist preachers have already applied for the presidency. Old Judge McKenzie, as you no doubt know, was taken with a jug ten days ago, and fined $50. The Widow Jackson, back in the hills, is pregnant again, and again by the Holy Ghost. Old Mrs. McPherson is dead at 97½. Wildcat Creek has overflowed its banks. Jud Taylor is planting 40 acres [of] Lima beans.

How are you, anyhow?

Yours,
Mencken

---

[1] In the March 1926 *Mercury,* Mencken wrote a violent review of *An American Tragedy.*

[2] Richard J. Beamish (1869–1947?): a lawyer, writer, historian; he was connected with the Philadelphia *Enquirer.*

◇◇◇◇◇◇◇◇◇◇◇◇◇◇

To A. L. S. Wood
[YU]

H. L. Mencken
1524 Hollins St.
Baltimore
April 2nd [*1926*]

Dear Mr. Wood:–

I suppose you have heard that Chase has raided the April Mercury, alleging that the Asbury article is "immoral". Obviously, he is seeking revenge for your operation upon him last September.[3]

Confidentially, we hope to show malice in his action. Have you heard anything from him about your article? Or do you know anyone to whom he has expressed dissatisfaction and a desire for revenge? If so, will you please let me have a brief outline of the facts at the Copley-Plaza Hotel, Boston? I shall be there Monday morning. We have engaged Arthur Garfield Hays and propose to make a fight to a finish. But don't mention our defense to anyone. If we could find a witness to whom Chase has uttered a threat against us the testimony would be very valuable.

On second thought, don't write to me at the Copley-Plaza, but in care of Leo R. Goulston, 80 Federal Street, Boston. He is our Boston lawyer.

Sincerely yours,
H. L. Mencken

[3] J. Frank Chase, secretary of the Boston Watch and Ward Society since 1907, had found the April *Mercury* objectionable because of Herbert Asbury's article "Hatrack", the story of a prostitute. Chase had previously been incensed by a series of pieces more or less directed at the Boston censorship, and seized this occasion for revenge. A. L. S. Wood, of the Springfield (Mass.) *Union*, had written "Keeping the Puritans Pure", an article exposing the methods of Chase's society, for the September 1925 *Mercury*.

(1926)

◇◇◇◇◇◇◇◇◇◇◇◇◇◇

To F. Scott Fitzgerald
[PU]

The American Mercury
730 Fifth Avenue
New York
April 8, 1926

Dear Fitz:

I'd have used the article instantly if it were not for the fact that it discussed me. You know what our rule is. It goes without saying that I hope you do something else for our great magazine.

When are you coming home? Let me hear of it in advance. I shall be very glad to have a parley with you.

I suppose you have heard of the raid on the April American Mercury by the Boston Comstocks. I went to Boston on Monday, accepted responsibility for the magazine, was arrested at the order of the Comstock student, tried and was triumphantly acquitted by a learned and Christian judge. I am now entering suit for heavy damages against every Methodist north of Westport, Conn.

Sincerely yours,
H. L. Mencken

◇◇◇◇◇◇◇◇◇◇◇◇◇◇

To A. L. S. Wood
[YU]

The American Mercury
730 Fifth Avenue
New York
April 8, 1926

Dear Mr. Wood:

Thanks very much for your letter and your telegram. If you hear anything regarding Chase's threats and other fulminations, I hope you'll let me have news of it. Our victory over him is complete and we are beginning a suit in the federal court in Boston on Monday. This suit raises very interesting questions of law and will be pushed with the utmost vigor. We hope by the time it is finished that we will have completely destroyed the power of the Watch and Ward Society to attack and damage the property of innocent men.[4]

Sincerely yours,
H. L. Mencken

To HAMILTON OWENS[5]
[PT]

Baltimore, April 25, 1926

DEAR HAMILTON:

Here is a chance for the Free State Association to function. The City Club swine invited Countée Cullen to their party, and then stood by without a protest when he was kicked out of the Emerson.[6] I am informed that he did not come to eat with them, but simply to talk to them. That the Emerson has a rule forbidding coons to *talk* in the hotel is outrageous. It would be hard to match it in Mississippi. Moreover, the City Club cads, knowing very well that Cullen was a coon, should have looked into the matter at length before inviting him. The net effect of their poltroonry was that their guest was insulted, and Maryland was made ridiculous. I hope to lambast them, and make a big case of it. I called up the *Sun* today and gave the city desk some information that I had. This morning's story was very feeble.

---

[4] This letter was written three days after Mencken's arrest on the Boston Common. The judge at the Boston Central Municipal Court was James P. Parmenter. Mencken was defended by Arthur Garfield Hays. On April 14th Judge James M. Morton, Jr., of the Circuit Court, granted the *Mercury* an injunction to restrain Chase from further interference with the April issue, and sustained Mencken's $50,000 dollar damage claim. Hays then filed suit in Federal District Court against Horace J. Donnelly, solicitor to the Postmaster-General in Washington who, after Chase's intervention, had instructed New York's Postmaster, John J. Kiely, to forbid the mailing of the April *Mercury*.

The injunction against Kiely was granted Mencken on April 28. The Government appealed of this decision, and in May 1927 the Circuit Court of Appeals found for the Post Office Department. Thus, Mencken was beaten in the end, although on a largely academic question, since the *Mercury* for April 1926 had been mailed as early as March 20, 1926, with no interference from the postal authorities. But the Watch and Ward Society was weakened by the trial, and a useful precedent was created; it was often invoked afterward in similar cases and Mencken became a symbol of the freedom of the press.

[5] Hamilton Owens (born in 1888): the editor of the Baltimore *Evening Sun.*

[6] The Baltimore City Club is now extinct. The Emerson is a Baltimore hotel. Countée Cullen: the Negro poet.

It was a great party last night. I have consumed two whole cans of bicarbonate since breakfast, and feel like a yearling stallion. I am off to N. Y.

Yours,
M.

◇◇◇◇◇◇◇◇◇◇◇◇◇

To CARL VAN VECHTEN
[YU]

The American Mercury
730 Fifth Avenue
New York
May 1, 1926

DEAR CARL:

Thanks very much for your note. Frankly, I rather hesitate to approach La Glasgow. Her recent compositions have seemed to me to be poor stuff and I doubt that her article will be as good as she says it will be. If I ask for it and it turns out to be bad, I'll be in a dreadful position. She is, as you know, a personal friend of the Knopfs. But I am still in prayer upon the subject. My very best thanks.[7]

I am hard at work gathering evidence for use against the Comstocks. We have started a suit against the Postmaster General in the Federal Court at New York and shall presently fall upon the wowsers in Boston with a suit for damages.

Sincerely,
Mencken

◇◇◇◇◇◇◇◇◇◇◇◇◇

To UPTON SINCLAIR
[OFP]

The American Mercury
730 Fifth Avenue
New York
May 29, 1926

DEAR SINCLAIR:

You are up to your old business of confusing the artist with the propagandist. I question very seriously that Wells will be remembered

[7] La Glasgow: Ellen Glasgow (1874–1945), novelist. She wrote *Vein of Iron* (New York: Harcourt, Brace and Co.; 1935).

in fifty years. Shaw may be, but if so, it will be for his earlier plays and for his uncommonly excellent criticism. MacDonald and Sidney Webb I believe are merely transient figures.[8]

Why don't you come East sometime? I'll take you to Washington and introduce you to Coolidge. Next to Rabbi Stephen S. Wise, he is probably the greatest living American. Merely to look at him makes me tremble. The effect, indeed, is almost precisely that of getting off a train at Munich and sniffing the first zephyrs from the breweries.

Sincerely,
H. L. Mencken

To PHILIP GOODMAN
[EPL]

Baltimore, Md.
June 15th [*1926*]

DEAR PHIL:

I give you Article No. 1: "Clowns". In brief, a review of all the comiques who have made your bones shake since your nonage. Their tricks and devices. Why you prefer A to B. The fundamental principles of buffoonery. Why the failures fail. What is the most comic scene you have ever witnessed? Give names and dates. Mention the clowns in practise today, white and black. How does each excel? What have you seen of foreign buffoons? How all of them, like the juggler of Notre Dame, serve God. Notes on gags and wheezes. This is a superb idea: I give it to you free.

No. 2: Max Schoenefeld. You have already blocked out his life at Tribschen. But you forgot his secret nostalgia. Why does he long for the United States? What, precisely, does he miss? His sentimental reminiscences of Philadelphia waiters. Finally, the three reasons why he'll never come back. Two are cultural. The third is a widow in Kensington. Her lawyer is waiting for him with papers.

No. 3: The old-time saloons. Not the gaudy Knickerbocker hells, but the actual saloons. If you want to, confine it to Philadelphia. Big Karl and Little Karl. Schemm's beer. Old Schemm's rules and peculiarities. What was the best beer ever served in America? I vote for

[8] Sidney James Webb, Baron Passfield (1859–1947): a British economist, sociologist, and politician. He was governor of the London School of Economics and wrote numerous books.

the Franziskaner Bock at the old Füchshole in Baltimore. Fuchs, the Wirt, wore a goatee of the 70's. Failing in the picture-frame manufacturing business as the old walnut frames went out, and he found himself stuck with $18,000 worth of plush rope, he opened his place opposite Lexington market, and soon had the trade of all the German intelligentsia. I have seen eight professors and ten doctors at his tables at once.

Out of this should flow No. 4: "Light Wines and Beer". Reminiscences of noble brews and vintages. The rising difficulty of getting them under Prohibition. Saloons that have risen and fallen since 1920. An interlude of free lunch in the old days. The celebrated delicacies.

Give these your prayers. You are the only man who can do them. And they should and must be done.

Yours,
[*M.*]

We visited Gunther's brewery last night, for a crab party in the cellar. The Braumeister, Herr Borghardt, was in personal attendance. A noble Helles—that is to say! They got out an old 32 ounce goblet for me.

◇◇◇◇◇◇◇◇◇◇◇◇◇◇

To UPTON SINCLAIR
[OFP]

H. L. Mencken
1524 Hollins St.
Baltimore
September 9th [*1926*]

DEAR SINCLAIR:–

Your questions are easy. The government brings my magazine to you only unwillingly. It tried to ruin my business, and failed only by an inch. It charges too much for postal orders, and loses too many of them. A corporation of idiot Chinamen could do the thing better. Its machine for putting out fires is intolerably expensive and inefficient. It seldom, in fact, actually puts out a fire: they burn out. In 1904 two square miles of Baltimore burnt down. I lost a suit of clothes, the works of Richard Harding Davis, and a gross of condoms. The Army had nothing to do with the discovery of the cause of yellow fever. Its bureaucrats persecuted the men who did the work. They could have done it much more quickly if they been outside the Army. It took years of effort to induce the government to fight mosquitoes, and it does the work very badly today. There is malaria everywhere in the South. It is mainly responsible for the prevalence of religion down there.

You shock me with your government worship. It is unmanly. Today I got word from a friend who lately had a session with a Department of Justice moron. The moron told him that I was on the official list of Bolshevik agents, and that the American Mercury was backed by Russian money. What do you make of that! I am tempted to confess.

Yours,
Mencken

To BLANCHE KNOPF
[AAK]

[*On October 14, 1926, H. L. Mencken and Paul Patterson had left Baltimore for a ten-week tour across the "Bible Belt" to the Pacific coast.*]

New Orleans, October 23rd [*1926*]

DEAR BLANCHE:–

I am having a swell time, seeing the points of [interest in] this progressive region. Every town has been swell, and I am having a swell time. Everyone has treated me swell. If my gizzard holds out I'll return to New York. Meanwhile, I am fleeing into the wilds of Texas to get some sleep. I have averaged less than 5 hours a night since I left Baltimore. This whole region is bone dry. Especially Atlanta.

Yours,
M.

1927

To BLANCHE KNOPF
[AAK]

H. L. Mencken
1524 Hollins St.
Baltimore
February 10th [*1927*]

DEAR BLANCHE:–

I have read three chapters of a quite unusual book on life in prison. Maybe you will want to see it when it is finished. The author is Robert Joyce Tasker, Box [38862?], San Quentin, Calif.[1]

Yours,
M.

To JIM TULLY
[OFP]

H. L. Mencken
1524 Hollins St.
Baltimore
May 4th [*1927*]

DEAR TULLY:–

You will find a long account of my family in "The Man Mencken", by Isaac Goldberg. I'd send you a copy at once, but you say you want

[1] See note on p. 302.

to tackle the article at once, and it is my experience that it takes 2 or 3 weeks for a book to reach the Coast from here. If there is no copy in the Hollywood bookshop kept by the German (I forget his name), there is probably one in the Los Angeles Public Library. It is full of gaudy detail. Goldberg is a learned man, but has no humor.

I am credited with discovering many writers who actually discovered themselves. Among those I whooped for in their earliest days are James Joyce, Ruth Suckow, James Stevens, Eugene O'Neill and Dreiser. I also did a lot of writing about Joseph Conrad and Lord Dunsany when they were new to this country. But what I did for all these, and the rest likewise, was really very little. I was looking for good copy, not for orphans to rescue.

You ask if I feel lonely here. My belief is that all authors are essentially lonely men. Every one of them has to do his work in a room alone, and he inevitably gets very tired of himself. My mother's death, in December, 1925, left me at a loss. My sister is keeping house but the place seems empty. It is hard to reorganize one's life after 45.

Give Jannings my best regards: he knows his trade. And thanks very much for being so kind about Tarovsky. Is Cruze coming to New York? If he does so, I certainly hope to see him, and his wife.

Yours,
H. L. Mencken

To EDGAR LEE MASTERS
[OFP]

H. L. Mencken
1524 Hollins St.
Baltimore
May 24th, 1927

DEAR MASTERS:

This is an excellent article indeed but I carry away the fear that The American Mercury is not the place for it. It is too long and too serious. It really ought to go into such a publication as the Yale Review. I thus return it with the greatest regret, for nothing would delight me more than to have you in the magazine again. But I hesitate to step outside our proper field. We like to deal with personalities more than with history. True enough, this has plenty of personality in it, but it lies under the general stream of the narrative.

Sincerely,
H. L. Mencken

To FRANK HARRIS
[PT]

The American Mercury
730 Fifth Avenue
New York
July 19th [1927]

DEAR HARRIS:

The third volume of your autobiography has reached me through your New York agent and I also have a copy of the play.[2] Needless to say, I'll fall upon both of them at once. I am in New York for a couple of days tackling some long delayed office work, but I hope to get back to Baltimore before the end of the week.

The moral snifflings prevailing in the Republic grow worse and worse. I assume that you have heard of the uproar in Boston. A long list of books has been put under the ban there. There are, in fact, so many upon it that Bostonians are now doing all their book buying in New York. The other day some local postmaster or other barred Sinclair Lewis's latest book from the mails. The solicitor of the postoffice decided that while the other postmasters were not bound to follow suit, the local postmaster was well within his rights. In other words, we now have 27000 new censors, for every village p.m. is barring books at will. This seems incredible, but it is a literal fact.

I have been worked to death during the past six months and shall have to keep on until the end of the year. But I have a scheme to spend Christmas on the ocean and if it works out, I'll see you before the new year.

I hear from various sources that you are in excellent condition and enjoying life immensely.

Yours,
H. L. Mencken

---

[2] Frank Harris's play: *Joan la Romée;* (New York; 1926).

To Ernest Booth[3]
[OFP]

The American Mercury
730 Fifth Avenue
New York
July 26, 1927

Dear Mr. Booth:

I am sorry indeed to hear of your accident and only hope that you are making a good recovery. What a dreadful adventure! I am asking the office to look into the matter of the check. No doubt it has already gone forward to you. If it is held at San Quentin, it certainly won't be there long. No one can cash it without your signature. If you write to me about it again, please address your letter to Mr. Charles Angoff, my assistant in The American Mercury office. I am leaving Baltimore in a couple of days for the South and shall not be back for ten days.

Don't bother about the photograph. We'll print the sketch without it. "The Texas Road Gang" will probably be published in the October issue. Though of this I am not yet certain. If it misses October it will be printed in November.

There is excellent stuff in the enclosed article but it seems to me that as it stands it is rather badly planned. I suggest that there ought to be a somewhat general introduction with the various episodes following. That of Yvonne, the story of Red's two girls, and several of the smaller episodes are excellent. But I think that the story of Georgie and episode #9 should be omitted. I also suggest that the title be changed to something like "Ladies of the Mob". The present title is too vague. In brief, I think there should be some generalization in the article. Take your time with it. We can't use it in any case until December.

Please note that there is no such word as "alright". The correct form is "all right", two words.

Sincerely yours,
H. L. Mencken

---

[3] Ernest Booth was serving a life sentence in Folsom Prison, Represa, California, for armed robbery. His "Ladies of the Mob" was published in *The American Mercury* for December 1927.

◇◇◇◇◇◇◇◇◇◇◇◇◇◇

To Ernest Booth
[OFP]

The American Mercury
730 Fifth Avenue
New York
September 27, 1927

Dear Mr. Booth:

This is excellent stuff and I am eager to use it. But as it stands, it seems to me that there are two defects in it. In the first place, I believe that the use of the present tense is feeble and ineffective. It is constantly employed by bad writers and so has become somewhat threadbare. The story would be better if it were put into straight narrative throughout.

In the second place, there is the matter of your prepared defense and the unexpected appearance of the witnesses who blew it up. As the text stands, you make it plain that your attorneys were well aware that your defense was false. I fear that printing this would be libel. The lawyers might be identified and they could very easily make a great deal of trouble by bringing suit for damages.

Wouldn't it be possible to change the narrative to make it appear that they believed in your prepared defense and that they were disconcerted when you confessed to them in the courtroom that the unexpected witnesses would blow it up? That would make their conduct perfectly proper.

Let me see the slang material at your leisure.

I believe that Hardy is a perfectly reliable man and that he should be able to sell a great deal of stuff for you.

Yours,
H. L. Mencken

◇◇◇◇◇◇◇◇◇◇◇◇◇◇

To Jim Tully
[OFP]

H. L. Mencken
1524 Hollins St.
Baltimore
September 30, 1927

Dear Tully:

Thanks very much for your two immensely interesting letters about Booth. I am very eager to do whatever is possible for him. But, like you, I am in some doubt about the best way to proceed. If you say so, I'll write to George Hearst direct and also to Fremont Older. But if you think it would be better to tackle the Shanleys, I'll do so. What is the precise name and address of the principal Shanley? I don't believe that it would do much good to write to the Chief of Police at Berkeley. If he is intelligent, the present authorities probably hate him already. Booth's attempt to escape from San Quentin, of course, raises up difficulties of the first calibre. The warden there would undoubtedly protest against receiving him again. Nevertheless, if we are patient, I believe that something may be done.

You are quite right about Tasker.[4] He is much lighter stuff than Booth. Nevertheless his book on his experiences at San Quentin contains a great deal of excellent stuff and I believe that Knopf will do it. There has even been an inquiry about it from an English publisher. Getting Tasker out ought to be relatively simple. I had a long palaver a week ago with one of his old pals, recently liberated. This man is now living in Baltimore and he has promised to find out for me just what man I should approach. If necessary, I shall get a letter from the Governor of Maryland to the Governor of California and so try to get a pardon for Tasker before he comes up for final sentence. I think it is extremely unlikely that, in case he is liberated, he will ever engage in crime again. He has had enough.

I am sending Booth half a dozen copies of the magazines containing his two articles. One of them is out, as you know, and the other will appear in November. Meanwhile, I am writing him by this mail. You make him one hundred times as real as he ever was before.

My very best thanks again for your two letters. What an article you could write yourself about your various visits to the two prisons!

Miss Haardt, of whom I wrote to you sometime ago, left for Hollywood yesterday. I hope you find it possible to see her. She was brought up in Montgomery, Alabama, and is still extremely shy. The life of Hollywood will probably shock her half to death. I think you'll like her very much. She is immensely amiable. Moreover, she has a great deal of talent. She is in Hollywood simply because the Jews offered her a chance to get some easy money.

Yours,
Mencken

---

[4] Robert J. Tasker: another convict; he was serving a five-year sentence at San Quentin for robbery. He wrote contributions to *The American Mercury* and a book on his prison life: *Grimhaven* (New York and London: Alfred A. Knopf; 1928).

◇◇◇◇◇◇◇◇◇◇◇◇◇◇

To GEORGE S. SCHUYLER
[OFP]

The American Mercury
730 Fifth Avenue
New York
October 11, 1927

DEAR MR. SCHUYLER:

Thanks very much for your good offices in the matter of the "Tips" article. Naturally, I'd much prefer to have you go over it. The one thing I want to keep out is ranting against the tipping system. What I am interested in is not its evils, but its technique. Certainly, an old hand must know many dodges for squeezing money out of suckers. It seems to me that getting it in this way is quite as honest and decent as getting it, say, by serving in Congress, or preaching the Word of God. If your candidate fails, I'll certainly turn to Mr. Lewis. My very best thanks again.

Unluckily I fear to do an article on the A.M.E. Church. During 1926, I devoted the magazine very largely to religious follies, and I have a feeling that I probably exhausted the interest of its readers in that subject. For that reason I have been avoiding it this year. Maybe I'll go back to it later on.

Sincerely yours,
H. L. Mencken

◇◇◇◇◇◇◇◇◇◇◇◇◇◇

To ERNEST BOOTH
[OFP]

The American Mercury
730 Fifth Avenue
New York
October 18th [*1927*]

DEAR MR. BOOTH:–

The literature of criminology now runs to two or three hundred five-foot shelves, and practically all of its books deal more or less with psychology. That is, they discuss the question, why do men commit crime. But not one of them, so far as I know, gets anywhere. Have you ever given any thought to the matter yourself? And would you care to do an article on it? If so, it goes without saying that I'll be very glad to see it.

I think such an article ought to discuss the chances of escape from punishment, as a professional lawbreaker sees them and estimates them. And the rewards of the trade, as he knows them. And the influences that bring men into it. And why they quit, when they do. And why they stay at it, when they refuse to quit.

Tully believes that it should be possible to have you retransferred to San Quentin, and is launching a plan to that end. I needn't add that I'll give it whatever help is possible.

"Ladies of the Mob" is in the forms for December. I have just re-read it in proof. It is very fine stuff.

Sincerely yours,
H. L. Mencken

◇◇◇◇◇◇◇◇◇◇◇◇◇◇

To George S. Schuyler
[OFP]

The American Mercury
730 Fifth Avenue
New York
October 19th [*1927*]

Dear Mr. Schuyler:–

I am sorry indeed that you put in any work on this, for I fear it won't do as it stands. The introduction is rather too long and obvious, and there are too few illuminative anecdotes. It would be better, indeed, if it started with an anecdote. The reference to Terre Haute, again, might be developed into an amusing discussion of regional liberality. In brief, the thing shows some good material, but it jogs a bit, and so is not effective. I scarcely know whether to advise reworking it or scrapping it. And I am sorry that I put you to trouble about it.

I discover that the clipping bureaux do not clip the Negro papers. This seems astounding. But it offers a good chance to set up a Negro clipping bureau. If you know anyone who wants to make the venture, tell him I'd like to be his first customer.

Sincerely yours,
H. L. Mencken

"Our White Folks" will lead the December number.

To CHARLES GREEN SHAW[5]
[PT]

H. L. Mencken
1524 Hollins St.
Baltimore
December 2nd [1927]

DEAR CHARLES:–

A few notes:

1. I bought some brown shoes six or eight years ago, and have worn them off and on ever since. I have also taken to brown oxfords.

2. I have now seen about twelve movies, four or five of them to the end. I liked them all pretty well, but am not tempted to go back.

3. My favorite drinks, in order, are: beer in any form, Moselle, Burgundy, Chianti, gin and ginger-beer, and rye whiskey. I use Swedish punch only as a cocktail flavor. I dislike Scotch, and seldom drink it. It makes me vaguely uneasy. I also dislike Rhine wine, save the very best. I never have a head-ache from drink. It fetches me by giving me pains in the legs. When I get stewed I go to sleep, even in the presence of women and clergymen.

4. Curiously enough, I greatly dislike the common American dirty stories, and avoid the men who tell them habitually. They seem dull to me. I love the obscene, but it must have wit in it.

5. As for politics, I always go to national conventions, and have missed very few in 28 years.

6. Of my inventions I am vainest of Bible Belt, booboisie, smut-hound and Boobus americanus.

7. I have been in the Johns Hopkins Hospital but once, and then

[5] Charles Green Shaw (born 1892) was preparing a book of information on leading personalities, *The Low-Down* (New York: Henry Holt and Co.; 1928), for which he also used Mencken and Nathan's *Pistols for Two* (New York: Alfred A. Knopf; 1917).

it was for medicine, not for surgery. I think all of the Baltimore hospitals are good, but prefer those run by nuns.

8. I changed my collar to a lower level two years ago.

9. I never use mullen on my hair. Nothing but soap and water ever touches it. George has gone gray greasing his hair.

10. I believe in marriage, and have whooped it up for years. It is the best solution, not only of the sex question, but also of the living question. I mean for the normal man. My own life has been too irregular for it: I have been too much engrossed in other things. But any plausible gal who really made up her mind to it could probably fetch me, even today. If I ever marry, it will be on a sudden impulse, as a man shoots himself. I'll regret it bitterly for about a month, and then settle down contentedly.

11. I believe in the advocate monogamy. Adultery is hitting below the belt. If I ever married the very fact that the woman was my wife would be sufficient to convince me that she was superior to all other women. My vanity is excessive. Wherever I sit is the head of the table. This fact makes me careless of ordinary politeness. I don't like to be made much of. Such things please only persons who are doubtful about their position. I was sure of mine, such as it is, at the age of 12.

12. Pilsner should be in Roman type, and begin with a capital.

13. I usually lie to women. They expect it, and it is pleasant to watch them trying to detect it. They seldom succeed. Women have a hard time in this world. Telling them the truth would be too cruel.

14. I am completely devoid of religious feeling. All religions seem ridiculous to me, and in bad taste. I do not believe in the immortality of the soul, nor in the soul. Ecclesiastics seem to me to be simply men who get their livings by false pretenses. Like all rogues, they are occasionally very amusing.

15. I can't get rid of certain superstitions, and suspect that there must be some logical basis for them. My mother and father both died on the 13th.

16. I am always in trouble around Christmas, and usually about a woman. The fact makes me dread the season.

17. I have another superstition: that all men who try to injure me die. It happens almost invariably. Of the six bitterest enemies I had two years ago, five are dead, all suddenly and unexpectedly.[6]

18. My belief is that happiness is necessarily transient. The nat-

[6] Among Mencken's enemies alluded to here: Stuart Sherman, William J. Bryan, J. Frank Chase.

ural state of a reflective man is one of depression. The world is a botch. Women can make men perfectly happy, but they seldom know how to do it. They make too much effort: they overlook the powerful effect of simple amiability. Women are also the cause of the worst kind of unhappiness.

19. I have little belief in human progress. The human race is incurably idiotic. It will never be happy.

20. I believe the United States will blow up within a century.

21. Being an American seems amusing to me, but not exhilarating. But I am very proud of the fact that I am a native and citizen of the Maryland Free State. I like to believe that I have had a hand in keeping it free.

22. I hope to write at least one good book before I die. Those that I have done are all transient and trivial: they will be forgotten in 25 years. I have ideas for five good books, but shall be content if I manage to write one.

23. I live pretty well, but am careful about money, and greatly dislike extravagant persons. I believe that it is discreditable to be needy. Economic independence is the foundation of the only sort of freedom worth a damn.

24. Most people regard me as very energetic. I am actually very lazy, and never work when I don't want to. On most days I take a nap. I also take frequent short holidays. But I dislike long ones.

25. I drink exactly as much as I want, and one drink more.

26. I never lecture, not because I am shy or a bad speaker, but simply because I detest the sort of people who go to lectures, and don't want to meet them. So with the fools who go to public dinners.

27. I have been reported engaged during the past year to six women. It consoles me to reflect that all were charming, and that all save five were beautiful. Their total net worth ran to $2500.

28. I dislike receiving presents, and never accept them if I can get out of it. But I like giving them to women and children. Many a worthy gal has lost a handsome beau by giving me something nifty.

29. My apologies for inflicting so long a letter upon you.

Yours,
Mencken

1928

◇◇◇◇◇◇◇◇◇◇◇◇◇◇◇◇◇◇◇◇

To GAMALIEL BRADFORD
[OFP]

The American Mercury
730 Fifth Avenue
New York
January 27, 1928

DEAR BRADFORD:

Thanks very much for your most generous letter. I was in fear that you'd think my review of your Moody was rather hastily written.[1]

Unluckily I confess to a dreadful prejudice in such matters. It is almost inconceivable to me that any evangelist should be anything save a fraud. I have known all the principal ones in my time and I have yet to meet one who was not. But Moody, as you say, was probably above the general level. I remember well what an uproar he caused in Baltimore in my early youth. Even my father, who was a professional atheist, went to his meetings and was considerably impressed.

It goes without saying that I'll be delighted to see your new book. It sounds immensely interesting.

I have just got in from Havana, where I went to cover the Pan-American Conference for the Baltimore *Evening Sun*. Unfortunately the protesting Nicaraguans lost their courage after taking aboard 15

[1] Your Moody: *D. L. Moody—A Worker in Souls* (New York: George H. Doran Company; 1927), by Gamaliel Bradford.

to 20 Havana cocktails, and so, for our purposes, the Conference blew up and all the *Sun* men save one returned.

Yours,
H. L. Mencken

To IRITA VAN DOREN[2]
[OFP]

H. L. Mencken
1524 Hollins St.
Baltimore
May 22nd [*1928*]

DEAR IRITA:–

My best thanks. Poor old Dreiser has been going about New York saying that I rushed my review of "An American Tragedy" into The American Mercury in order to get ahead of Sherman, and so poison the wells. It is, of course, nonsense. My review didn't come out until the March, 1926, issue—i.e., February 25, 1926—, five weeks after Sherman's. It was not even written when Sherman's was printed. But Dreiser, I fear, is a bit ratty.

I'll be in New York week after next, but probably only for a day, for I must start for Kansas City June 8th.[3] I hope you let me see you when I get back.

Yours,
H. L. M.

To BENJAMIN DE CASSERES
[OFP]

H. L. Mencken
1524 Hollins St.
Baltimore
May 25, 1928

DEAR BEN:

I'll be delighted to have you dedicate the book to me. But I warn you that it will be dangerous. Red Lewis dedicated "Elmer Gantry"

[2] Irita Van Doren: Mrs. Carl Van Doren, editor of the weekly book review of the New York *Herald Tribune.*

[3] Mencken was going to the Republican Convention in Kansas City.

to me and at least four-fifths of the reviews denounced him for it. I am seldom mentioned in any American newspaper without being abused.[4]

Yours,
H. L. Mencken

◇◇◇◇◇◇◇◇◇◇◇◇◇

To GEORGE S. SCHUYLER
[OFP]

Baltimore,
August 15th, 1928

DEAR MR. SCHUYLER:

It seems to me that this piece is still full of holes. Furthermore, I believe that the fundamental scheme of it is wrong. Why start with the argument that there is no sexual antipathy between the races? The fact is known to everyone. It seems to me that the whole article should be based on a study of actual interracial couples and that you ought to go into the matter further than you have. That is to say, you ought to examine a number of such couples at length and find out precisely why they were married, what difficulties they encountered and how they are getting on now. As it is, you generalize without sufficient data and so the whole thing becomes a bit literary and dubious.

You also introduce a number of irrelevancies, including a reference to such men as Dumas. I don't think the subject has anything to do with your main theme.[5]

Let us have a session the next time I am in New York. Just when that will be I don't know. Hay fever has begun to tease me and travel is painful. But I'll certainly be there again before the middle of September. I believe a detailed study of mixed couples would be really valuable. Can't you do it by correspondence? Certainly it ought to be easy to get into contact with forty or fifty of them.

Have you any other ideas?

Sincerely yours,
H. L. Mencken

---

[4] Benjamin De Casseres thus dedicated his *Superman in America* (Seattle: University of Washington Book Store; 1929): "To H. L. Mencken, the Fabre of the American Insect."

[5] French novelist Alexandre Dumas was partly of Negro ancestry.

1929

To J. B. DUDEK[1]
[PT]

Baltimore, January 2, 1929

DEAR MONSIGNOR:

That editorial made me bust into sobs. It was indeed a bitter blow of fate that put Woodrow's birthday so near Christmas. Nevertheless I believe that it will be celebrated in the coming years. He was a great man and died for humanity.

By the way, what is the best current book of Catholic doctrine? I want to find out precisely what the church teaches on all the salient points of the faith. Sometime ago I had such a book in the form of a series of questions and answers, but unfortunately I lost it. No, I am not preparing to disgrace the church as a convert. I simply want to get at some facts for an article I am planning.

Sincerely yours,
H. L. Mencken

[*The editorial, according to Msgr. Dudek, was from the* Daily Oklahoman, *Oklahoma City, and proposed making Woodrow Wilson's birthday a public holiday.*]

---

[1] J. B. Dudek: a prelate of Czech descent, who was writing a book on the Czech language in America. He contributed to *The American Mercury.* Mencken was preparing his *Treatise on the Gods* (New York: Alfred A. Knopf; 1930).

◇◇◇◇◇◇◇◇◇◇◇◇◇

To Madeleine Boyd
[pt]

H. L. Mencken
1524 Hollins St.
Baltimore
January 15, 1929

Dear Madeleine:

Very good. I'll present myself at your house at 7 p.m. on the 22nd. It will be an immense pleasure to see you again. It seems at least forty years since our last session.

I am delighted to hear the news about Wolfe. If he has anything that would fit into The American Mercury I surely hope you give me a chance at it.[2]

Miss Haardt is at the Algonquin. If you happen to be there will you look her up? She is in New York on literary business, wrestling with editors. She'll probably return before I get there.

Tom Smith will go down into history as one of the greatest villains ever heard of. I match him against Raskob, John Wilkes Booth and Torquemada.

Yours,
M.

To Fielding Hudson Garrison
[pt]

Baltimore, April 10, 1929

Dear Garrison:

The two reprints came in this morning, and I shall read them at once. My very best thanks. They look very interesting.

I only hope that you are not forgetting the article that you had in mind for The American Mercury. I'd be delighted to see you in the magazine again. The last time, you will recall, you were an innocent

---

[2] Mencken had only a modicum of admiration for the work of Thomas Wolfe. Charles Angoff and Sara Haardt, however, held it in high esteem, and would have liked to see some of it published in *The American Mercury.*

bystander in the Boston massacre. I am sorry for it, but the net result of that transaction was very salubrious. The Boston publishers, stirred to action at last, immediately prepared a new and more liberal obscenity act. A few weeks ago, after a long struggle, they got it passed by the lower house of the Massachusetts legislature. Unfortunately, the Senate killed it by a small vote, but I hear that they hope to pass it at the next session. Thus the uproar over "Hatrack" was not in vain.

Yesterday I received an invitation from the Boston Book Sales Association to come up and speak at a banquet. When I was there in 1926, they were afraid to give me any help. I have, therefore, invited them to go to Hell.

Sincerely yours,
Mencken

To GEORGE S. SCHUYLER
[OFP]

The American Mercury
730 Fifth Avenue
New York
May 15 [*1929*]

DEAR MR. SCHUYLER:

I think your questionnaire would make an excellent article, and what you say about the future of the Negro would make an even better one.[3] On the latter subject, an immense amount of bilge is being written. The plain fact is that neither the whites nor the blacks know where they are heading. I have read as much about the matter as most men and yet I can never formulate a plausible picture of the relation of the races say fifty hears hence. If you care to deal with the subject realistically, I'll certainly be delighted to do the article.

My best thanks for your help in the matter of the Northwestern questionnaire. If you can find it, I'll be delighted to have it.

Sincerely yours,
H. L. Mencken

---

[3] The questionnaire was sent out by George Schuyler to get data for a piece he was writing on Racial Intermarriage in the U. S. G. Schuyler wrote "A Negro Looks Ahead" for the February 1930 *Mercury*.

To JIM TULLY
[OFP]

H. L. Mencken
1524 Hollins St.
Baltimore
May 18, 1929

DEAR JIM:

Sara is in hospital under observation. Just what is the matter with her the doctors are trying to determine. She is in considerable pain and visiting her, for the present, would be imprudent. I'll let you know more as soon as I hear from her doctors. I saw her yesterday, but only for a few minutes.

Miss Baker writes that you and Marna were immensely hospitable to her. She will cover a whole page in the Birmingham *News* with a story of your virtues.

Unluckily, I have no means of reaching Hindenburg, and my relations with the Kaiser are such that I'd hesitate to give you a letter of introduction. It would only serve to have you kicked out. Behind this there is a longish story which I'll tell you when we meet. The fact is that you don't need letters at all. Simply, announce that you are an American journalist and you'll find a considerable hospitality. My feeling is that both the Kaiser and Hindenburg are hardly worth seeing. You will get nothing out of them save dull platitudes.[4]

Yours,
M.

[4] Wilhelm II, the former Kaiser, was appreciative of Mencken's work. After the publication of *Notes on Democracy*, he sent Mencken two inscribed photographs of himself. In 1922 Mencken had visited the Kronprinz in Holland, but declined to see the Kaiser, whom he did not admire.

1930

To Blanche Knopf
[AAK]

H. L. Mencken
1524 Hollins St.
Baltimore
March 13th [*1930*]

Dear Blanche:–

George tells me that he wants to use the title, "Clinical Notes", on a book to be published by some other publisher.[1] I have asked him to hold up the business until Alfred gets back. The title is my invention, and I regard it as the property of The American Mercury. I may want to revive it later on, with someone else doing the stuff. Altogether, I am against transferring the copyright unless it is made clear that the title belongs to the magazine, and that it will not be used on a book. I see no reason why we should give George anything for nothing.

I'll be on hand April 4th, swelly garbed.

Yours,
H. L. Mencken

To Herbert F. West[2]
[OFP]

[*Alfred A. Knopf had just issued* Treatise on the Gods.]

[1] George: George Jean Nathan.
[2] Herbert F. West (born in 1898): a professor at Dartmouth College.

The American Mercury
730 Fifth Avenue
New York
March 29, 1930

DEAR MR. WEST:

Thanks very much for your friendly note. It goes without saying that I am delighted to hear what you tell me. The book is doing fairly well, but the reviews, in the main, are naturally hostile. This week one of the Catholic weeklies devotes three full pages to it.

Sometime soon I hope to do an article on Dewey. He has always interested me immensely, though I confess frankly that I have never been able to read him. Thus what I know about him is largely at second hand. Time and again I have tried to get through his books, but without success. His capacity for being uninteresting really amounts to genius.

Sincerely yours,
H. L. Mencken

[*On the subject of Dewey, Mencken wrote to Benjamin De Casseres on July 24, 1931:*

As for John Dewey, I hesitate to tackle him. He is perhaps the most dreadful writer ever heard of, but he is also a well-meaning old man, and I hate to knock him about.]

To HAMILTON OWENS
[PT]

[*The Free Lance was the column that Mencken had conducted daily on the editorial page of the Baltimore* Evening Sun *from 1911 to 1915. Hamilton Owens, then editor of the paper, had suggested reviving it for one day to mark the 20th anniversary of its foundation.*]

Baltimore, April 15, 1930

DEAR HAMILTON:

After putting in hours trying to concoct a Free Lance column, I am forced to give it up as hopeless. It is simply impossible to recover the mood. In those early days I was young, and full of gas. Today I am an aged and somewhat solemn man. If I sent you the stuff that I wrote it would disgrace both of us. The idea of reviving the column is excellent, but executing it turns out to be impossible.

Yours,
M.

◇◇◇◇◇◇◇◇◇◇◇◇◇◇

To HERBERT F. WEST
[OFP]

The American Mercury
730 Fifth Avenue
New York
April 17, 1930

DEAR MR. WEST:

An article on Blunt's estate would fall outside the scheme of The American Mercury. And so would one on Cunninghame Graham. The magazine is very strictly confined to the American scene. As for a treatise on myself, it would be barred by the rule that I am not to be mentioned in my own magazine.

This leaves Henry Adams. Certainly I'll be delighted to see anything you do about him. He was a most curious and baffling fellow, and deserves to be studied at length.

Sincerely yours,
H. L. Mencken

◇◇◇◇◇◇◇◇◇◇◇◇◇◇

To BENJAMIN DE CASSERES
[OFP]

The American Mercury
730 Fifth Avenue
New York
April 28th [*1930*]

DEAR BEN:

I am still uncertain about the department, but have not forgotten it. More about it after my prayers have been answered. My hesitation in the matter is due simply to the fact that the drama happens to be uninteresting to me personally. I believe it is bad policy to put anything into the magazine that I don't like myself.

Yours,
M.

◇◇◇◇◇◇◇◇◇◇◇◇◇◇

To PHILIP GOODMAN
[EPL]

Baltimore, Md.
June 13, 1930

DEAR PHIL:

I certainly hope you do the piece. It sounds very amusing. Please don't forget to note that oboe-players always end in lunatic asylums; that horn-players are excessive beer-drinkers, and that clarinet-players always have unfortunate love affairs. In fact, it is pretty safe to assume that every clarinet-player's wife, soon or late, will run away with some other man. Often it is with the trombone-player or kettledrummer. Thus, the poor clarinet-player not only suffers injury, but also gross insult. He is commonly a Belgian or a Frenchman, and not infrequently he is a good amateur cook, or writes poetry on the side. All first violins, as you may know, are ambitious to be composers, and nearly everyone of them has done two or three symphonies. The bull-fiddle players, on the other hand, never write anything—not even letters. In fact, it is common for them to be completely illiterate.

The session Wednesday night was perfect. That is precisely the sort of thing I enjoy. You can have the Ritz if you like it. Give me Scheffel Hall!

Yours,
[*M.*]

◇◇◇◇◇◇◇◇◇◇◇◇◇◇

To PHILIP GOODMAN
[EPL]

Baltimore, Md.
June 27th [1930]

DEAR PHIL:

You will be astounded to hear that I am to make a trial of connubial bliss, beginning as of August 27th, Eastern Standard Time. The bride, of course, is Sara Haardt. Now tell me you knew it all along! You knew nothing of the sort. The formal announcement will shock humanity next Sunday. Keep it to yourself meanwhile—that is, to your self and Lily's self, and Ruth's.

Sara is the grandest of girls, and will help me in my chosen art.

As for me, I have promised to behave with relative decency. I am to be allowed five sessions at Schellhase's a week, not counting the anniversaries of the great German victories. More details anon. I count on your advice. But don't tell me I am too young!

The nuptial high mass will be very quiet. I am even now convassing the local clergy for a seemly officiant. We shall follow the rite of the Church of England—after all, a very high-toned ecclesiastical organization, say what you will. I have rejected all evangelical bids.[3]

No Wedding Presents. This rule is polizeilich.

My love to Lily. When is she going abroad?

Yours,
[*M.*]

◇◇◇◇◇◇◇◇◇◇◇◇◇

To Dorothy Hergesheimer
[OFP]

H. L. Mencken
1524 Hollins St.
Baltimore
July 28th [*1930*]

Dearest Dorothy:–

If any scandal-mongers call you up and try to make you believe that Sara and I are to be joined in connubial bonds on August 27th don't deny it, for it is a fact. The solemn announcement will issue from Confederate G.H.Q. at Montgomery in about a week. Your congratulations I take for granted, for you know Sara, and so you know what a lovely gal she is. If you write to her please say nothing about my heavy drinking, or about the trouble with that girl in Red Lion, Pa., in 1917. I still maintain that I was innocent of any unlawful or immoral purpose.

The wedding will be very pianissimo, in view of my great age and infirmities. We are taking a swell apartment in Baltimore, overlooking Mt. Vernon place and very close to Schellhase's kaif and several other excellent saloons. Wedding presents are absolutely forbidden, on penalty of the bastinado. I shall continue my book-writing business as usual. Sara also proposes to engage in literary endeavor, but I suspect

[3] The clergyman who married Mencken and Sara Haardt was Herbert L. Parrish, a former Baltimore rector, and a contributor to *The American Mercury*. H. L. Mencken's marriage surprised many people, and the press made more or less ironical comments on the occasion.

that cooking, washing and ironing will take up a lot of her time. Her novel, by the way, has been taken by Doubleday, and will be published shortly. Thus in one year she gets launched as an author and marries the handsomest man east of Needles, Calif.

I was so sorry to hear of your mother's death. I had met her only a few times, but that was enough to show how very nice she was. You will go on missing her. I still miss my own mother every day, though she died in 1925. It is a fact that I often catch myself planning to tell her this or that. Well, we are now of the oldest generation. But life is still interesting.

I had a disturbing letter from Gertrude Carver yesterday. She is in a sanitarium at Palisade, N. J., and scarcely able to sit up. Worse, her paralysis is beginning to affect the muscles of respiration. It is really dreadful.

I kiss your hand. Recall me to the Mister.

Yours,
H. L. M.

◇◇◇◇◇◇◇◇◇◇◇◇◇◇

To BLANCHE KNOPF
[AAK]

H. L. Mencken
1524 Hollins St.
Baltimore
July 28th [*1930*]

DEAR BLANCHE:–

I am writing to Miss Lustgarten and to Angoff, breaking the news.[4] For the rest keep it quiet. The announcement will be hurled to a breathless world next Sunday. It will take the form of a communiqué of the Confederate General Staff. I only hope it gets us some subscriptions to the Mercury in the South.

Enemies have told the bride that I am a beer-drinker. I am having a hard time putting down this slander.

Please don't forget that wedding presents are absolutely forbidden on penalty of fine, imprisonment and loss of civil rights.

If you want to write to the bride her address is 704 Cathedral Street, Baltimore. That will be mine also after the obsequies.

Yours,
M.

---

[4] Miss Lustgarten was Mencken's secretary at *The American Mercury.*

(1930)

To BLANCHE KNOPF
[AAK]

[*Henry and Sara Mencken were spending their honeymoon in eastern Canada.*]

The Lord Nelson
Halifax, Canada
September 4th [1930]

DEAR BLANCHE:–

The weather in the St. Lawrence valley was infernal, so we came down here. Certainly I never expected to see Halifax in this life. It turns out to be a small but very pleasant town, with a good hotel and all the latest fillums on view nightly. The sky is a clear blue, there is a breeze from the ocean, and the temperature is perfect. How long we'll stay here I don't know—probably a few days. Then for St. John, N. B., and the Maine coast. If hay-fever doesn't fetch me as we move southward we may be in N. Y. in a week. Sara is out buying hand-painted sea-shells, carved toothpicks, and other souvenirs. I have spent the afternoon writing an article for the Evening Sun on the malt liquor situation in Quebec. I found real Pilsner in Montreal; also Münchner Hofbraü. You shall have the details when we meet.

We got off from Baltimore without being discovered, but the newspaper brethren routed us out in Montreal and made some appalling pictures. In one of them Sara looks like a Japanese piewoman, and I appear to be an arctic explorer, brought home after 30 years.

I am henpecked, but am getting used to it. It begins to seem that I'll make a perfect husband.

Yours,
H. L. M.

To BENJAMIN DE CASSERES
[OFP]

H. L. Mencken
704 Cathedral St.
Baltimore
September 30, 1930

DEAR BEN:

I challenge you to meet me on the subject of Emerson before any recognized sporting club. I'll take you on for ten rounds. The man was actually a Methodist of the worst type. All of his radicalism was so much hooey. I don't object to his personal conventionality. After all, he was wise to keep comfortable. What I object to is his intellectual shiftiness. Don't forget the Whitman case!

Yours,
M.

◇◇◇◇◇◇◇◇◇◇◇◇◇◇

To UPTON SINCLAIR
[OFP]

H. L. Mencken
704 Cathedral St.
Baltimore
September 30, 1930

DEAR SINCLAIR:

That notification episode is really superb. I saw nothing about it in the Eastern papers, though perhaps Duncan Aikman sent the story to the Baltimore *Sun*. Unfortunately, I was out of contact with the *Sun* for three weeks, during my trip to Canada.

It is good news that you have induced Darrow to join you in the debate. He'll give an excellent show. Unfortunately, I find it simply impossible to believe in thought transference. I am not unfamiliar with the subject, for I made experiments more than thirty years ago. At that time I was acquainted with a telegraph operator who seemed to show an extraordinary gift, but the more I investigated the matter the more I was convinced that ordinary causality could account for everything that he did. The interest of Einstein seems to me to be of slight importance, despite his eminence. It is a well known fact that physicists are greatly given to the supernatural. Why this should be I don't know, but the fact is plain. One of the most absurd of all spiritualists is Sir Oliver Lodge. I have the suspicion that the cause may be that physics itself, as currently practised, is largely moonshine. Certainly there is a great deal of highly dubious stuff in the work of such men as Eddington. I'll read your book again, and give it my prayers.[5] Maybe our Heavenly Father will lead me to the light.

Sincerely yours,
M.

---

[5] Your book: *Mental Radio* (London: T. Werner Laurie, Ltd.; 1930). Sir Arthur S. Eddington (1882–1944): British physicist and philosopher, author of *Science and the Unseen World* (London: G. Allen & Unwin, Ltd.; 1929).

To Upton Sinclair
[ofp]

H. L. Mencken
704 Cathedral St.
Baltimore
October 17, 1930

Dear Sinclair:

The word *wowser* does not, necessarily, mean a preacher. It simply means one who devotes himself to interfering with the private pleasures of his fellow-men. Thus, a prohibitionist is a perfect wowser. And the man who advocates strict Sunday laws is another. All sorts of censors belong to the clan. The origin of the word is doubtful, though I believe that it is derived from one of the Australian native languages. I have consulted various Australians on the point, but they differ so greatly that it is hard to arrive at the facts. The word was brought to Europe by the Australian soldiers during the war, and adopted by the English. It had a considerable vogue in England for a year or two, but then dropped out. I tried to introduce it in America about 1918. It has made some progress, but is still rather a stranger.

If you put me into "The Eighteenth Amendment", I only hope you make it plain that I am a baptized man and hope to sit upon the right hand of God, post-mortem. This is a point that is frequently overlooked by publicists who denounce me.[6]

The phenomena you point to, even though they may not be explicable by ordinary causality, may, nevertheless yield to ordinary probability. The influence of coincidence upon human beings has never been adequately discussed. One night last week an aunt of mine, in Baltimore, dreamed that something dreadful had happened to the family lot in Loudon Park cemetery. Arising with the lark, she awakened her daughter, boarded a high-powered car and rushed to the place. She found the gates ajar and the lot covered by crosses and wreaths. No one in the family had put them there. They were, apparently, deposited by error and probably belonged to some poor Odd Fellow's funeral. My aunt is enormously impressed by her dream. What she forgets is that she had probably dreamed the same thing forty times before.

[6] The Upton Sinclair book mentioned here is probably *The Wet Parade* (New York: Farrar & Rinehart, Inc.; 1931).

Years ago I had traffic with a telegraph operator who pretended to be able to name the numbers written on a sheet of paper. The paper, of course, was concealed from his direct gaze. For a long while he greatly impressed me but, in the end, I came to the conclusion that natural causes were sufficient to account for his trick. Though he could not see the letters written, he could hear the pencil scratching. He simply learned to differentiate between different scratches.

Let us have a session some time and discuss that book of letters. It sounds very interesting. Aren't you coming Eastward in the near future? Certainly you are missing a great show by staying in California. Hoover gets better every minute. It wouldn't surprise me at all to see him sprout wings.

Yours,
Mencken

◇◇◇◇◇◇◇◇◇◇◇◇◇◇

To Alfred A. Knopf
[AAK]

H. L. Mencken
704 Cathedral St.
Baltimore
November 19th [*1930*]

Dear Alfred:–

The only reason why I ever objected to advertising George's books in The American Mercury is that he forbade the use of The American Mercury announcement on their slip-covers. If he will withdraw this prohibition, not only with respect to his new book but also with respect to all his other books, my objection will fall down. In any case, it is only an objection. The advertising department is in your hands, and I'll agree to any decision you make.

Let us discuss the Lambek business when we meet next week. I agree with you that Lambek looks like a nuisance.

I go on a diet Sunday morning, to prepare for Kaplan. Unluckily, Sara is not coming along. She will have visitors here, and can't get away.

Yours,
M.

1931

◇◇◇◇◇◇◇◇◇◇◇◇◇◇◇◇◇◇◇◇

To JIM TULLY
[OFP]

H. L. Mencken
704 Cathedral St.
Baltimore
February 14, 1931

DEAR JIM:

I think you are on the trail of a good book here. But as the stuff stands, I don't believe that either of the two chapters fits into the scheme of The American Mercury. The first one, it seems to me, is still somewhat vague. You don't define all of your terms sufficiently, and so the average reader would probably find it hard to make out precisely how chains are fabricated. I suggest that you describe the whole process in detail, showing how the rod is cut and bent, and then welded. For one thing, you don't explain why the chain-maker needs to use his small hammer. I assume, of course, that it is in order to rectify the work done by the large sledges, but that is by no means clear in the story.[1]

The second chapter is an interesting character sketch, but it seems to me that there is too much God in it for the Mercury. Its general tone, indeed, is somewhat sentimental. If you care to let me have any part of the book, I'd rather have a chapter or two dealing with more

[1] Jim Tully had been a chainmaker and a Government chain inspector during the First World War.

racy and comic characters. You know the sort of stuff I mean. If the book goes on as it has begun, I think you'll have a very good one. It will strike indeed a region never before traversed by an author.

Sara has been dreadfully ill with some sort of violent flu. Her temperature has been extraordinarily high, but it is now falling, and she begins to feel comfortable again. For several days her condition was somewhat alarming, but I now believe that she will recover smoothly and quickly.

When are you coming Eastward again?

Yours,
M.

◇◇◇◇◇◇◇◇◇◇◇◇◇◇

To ALFRED A. KNOPF
[AAK]

[*On March 4, 1931, Alfred A. Knopf had written to Mencken:*

DEAR HENRY,

Sinclair Lewis is just back and I see that it is now public news that he is leaving Harcourt. He has not signed up anywhere else. Are you still quite certain that we should not, under any circumstances, take him on? He made violent love to me in London and I was really more embarrassed than I ever have been with an author because I simply could not respond in any sort of hearty way after our first meeting. He talks of Ben Huebsch, Doubleday Doran and Harrison Smith. It may be too late to get him now in any case and I am quite willing not to make any further effort if you are absolutely satisfied that I shouldn't. The terms I cabled were, of course, a wild maximum and I don't honestly believe that a publisher would have any difficulty with Red over finances. But for him to camp on your doorstep and talk endlessly would, of course, be quite another matter.

I am sorry you couldn't get up this week. I am terribly anxious to see you. By the way, the Bach festival takes place on May fifteenth and sixteenth. To protect us I have secured tickets and room reservations at the Bethlehem Hotel.

My best to Sara.

Yours always,
A. A. K.]

H. L. Mencken
704 Cathedral St.
Baltimore
March 5th [1931]

Dear Alfred:–

It seems to me that the Lewis business resolves itself into a matter of advances. The more you give him, the more he will drink and loaf, and the less likely you'll be to get a good book out of him. I see no reason why at the moment he should want any advance at all. He has plenty of money, he has had a long rest, and if he can't do a book without further sugaring then he'll never do one at all. I am convinced that, in any case, he'll never do another "Babbitt", but all the same he may produce a saleable book. I suggest offering him a reasonable advance, *payable when he completes his* MS. If you don't make that condition he may never complete it at all.

There would be some advantage, obviously, in taking on another Nobel Prize winner. And Lewis, I believe, is a decent fellow and will not try to rook you. But his weakness is his weakness, and must be considered. You couldn't get his earlier books away from Harcourt—that is, at a plausible price. You'll have to depend on what he does hereafter. I think you should proceed on the cautious assumption that what he does will probably earn much less than what he has done.

A letter from Harrison Smith indicates that he is shopping around. Have you see Harcourt? I believe it would be worth while to find out why Harcourt is letting him go.

I hope to get to N. Y. some time next week. Sara's illness has greatly upset me and I am far behind with my work. She is making good progress, but it will be weeks before she is quite normal again. Pleurisy is a bad business, especially in a patient with her history. She feels very well, but a slight fever persists, and she must stay in bed until it subsides. I hate to leave her while there is any chance of a relapse. The last time I had to rush home to take her to hospital.

I note what you say about the Bach Choir. Let us go to it this year, by all means.

Read the enclosed in full. It is an amazing story, and shows precisely what sort of knave Hoover is.

Yours,
M.

[*On March 6, 1931, Alfred A. Knopf replied:*

DEAR HENRY,

I had lunch yesterday with Brace, of Harcourt Brace, whom I really know very well and after a long talk with him, I really think we would be unwise to attempt to do any business with Lewis. I don't think it's a question of money, for there, I am satisfied he would, in the end, be reasonable. But it is three years since he turned in the last manuscript of a novel, he has shown no signs yet of settling down, and I think the Nobel Prize award has had a most unfortunate effect on him. I could learn nothing from him as to why he left Harcourt beyond curses and a general dissatisfaction with what Harcourt has done. Brace tells me that his complaint was not enough advertising and not enough sales, which, of course, is utterly idiotic.

I hope to see you soon and would come to Baltimore were it not that I am behind in my work too. I hope Sara will be well enough for you to get up next week as we have much to talk about. I know how tough pleurisy is with that slight fever that seems to persist so long. My best to her.

Yours,
A. A. K.

P.S. I don't intend to close the door here to Lewis except perhaps by implication. I simply won't approach him and I rather doubt if he will approach me again.]

To ROSCOE PEACOCK
[OFP]

H. L. Mencken
704 Cathedral St.
Baltimore
April 30, 1931

DEAR PEACOCK:

It seems to me that you are generalizing from very small evidence. Certainly it would be absurd to say that the kind of Jews you met aboard ship were the only kind in existence. Some of the most intelligent people in America are Jewish, and not only some of the most intelligent, but also some of the most charming. My own feeling indeed is, that taking one with another, Jews average much higher than Americans. However, I agree with you that the unpleasant ones are unpleasant almost beyond endurance.

Sincerely yours,
H. L. Mencken

◇◇◇◇◇◇◇◇◇◇◇◇◇◇

To James T. Farrell
[UP]

H. L. Mencken
704 Cathedral St.
Baltimore
June 1, 1931

Dear Mr. Farrell:

"The Open Road" tempts me but, in the end, I find myself with certain doubts, mainly revolving around the fact that I have printed several other articles of the same general character within recent months. So I am sending the manuscript to *Scribner's* as you ask.

Worse, I find myself with doubts about the projected article on the dance marathon craze. The subject has been heavily belabored in the newspapers. I surely hope you have something else in hand in mind. It would be a pleasure indeed to print you. Will you please send all manuscripts to me as above?

Sincerely yours,
H. L. Mencken

◇◇◇◇◇◇◇◇◇◇◇◇◇◇

To George S. Schuyler
[OFP]

H. L. Mencken
704 Cathedral St.
Baltimore
June 15, 1931

Dear Mr. Schuyler:

Needless to say, that story is a lie out of the whole cloth. I was never in Norwich, Connecticut, in my life, and I haven't delivered a lecture for at least twenty years. Such fictions are constantly in circulation. I suspect that the report that I have turned Ku Kluxer emanates from a certain gentleman in Baltimore. I don't think he is important enough to get any notice.[2]

Last week Floyd Calvin telegraphed to me asking for an expression of my opinion on the crusade against Amos and Andy. I told him what I have been preaching for years past—that all such crusades seem to me to be ill-advised and dangerous. I can imagine nothing more tedious than the Amos and Andy dialogues, but I certainly see nothing libelous in them. Such Negroes as they depict are as common as flies. I think the Negro people should feel secure enough by now to face a reasonable ridicule without terror. I am unalterably opposed to all efforts to put down free speech, whatever the excuse. The Jews have been greatly damaged in America by professional agitators, and I am afraid that if the Amos and Andy crusade goes on the Negroes will suffer in the same way. Worse, they will suffer in vain, for I believe it will be completely impossible to stop the Amos and Andy show. In brief, the net result promises to be that the race will be made ten times as ridiculous by its own efforts as it is now made by Amos and Andy.

What are you up to? I read in the Pittsburgh *Courier* that you were ill. I surely hope that you are completely recovered, and that some good ideas are entertaining you.

Sincerely yours,
H. L. Mencken

◇◇◇◇◇◇◇◇◇◇◇◇◇◇

To GEORGE S. SCHUYLER
[OFP]

H. L. Mencken
704 Cathedral St.
Baltimore
June 19, 1931

DEAR MR. SCHUYLER:

I think a story of the American Negro who went to Liberia, and was then robbed and driven crazy, would be excellent for the American Mercury. I'd also like to do a general article on the country, but I suggest that it had better wait until after you have printed your newspaper stuff.

---

[2] Charges of racism have been made against H. L. Mencken at various times; a debate on this question was held in the columns of the *New Republic* and the London *Times Literary Supplement* in 1957 and 1958.

I assume that you picked up malaria in Africa. If so, please do not be uneasy. I had it myself as a boy of 16, but got rid of it completely. A perfect cure is now possible. I surely hope that you have put yourself into the hands of a good doctor.

The Pittsburgh *Courier's* crusade seems to me to be very ill-advised. Naturally enough, it has not printed the protest that I wrote for Mr. Calvin. My feeling is that any such crusade is bound to fail, and that its failure will react very seriously upon the whole Negro people. It is always a foolish thing to undertake hopeless and useless wars. Such stuff as the Amos and Andy dialogues seems to me personally to be dreadfully stupid, but I think it is absurd to call it libelous. I have known many such Negroes. They were almost idiotic, but I must add that they were usually amiable fellows. Just as many are to be found in the white race. The other Negro papers, so far as I have observed, do not seem to be taking any interest in the *Courier's* fight. Probably some of the more intelligent of them will eventually oppose it. The *Courier,* of course, is not to be blamed too harshly. All magazines and newspapers make errors now and then. I have heard of much worse ones.

Sincerely yours,
H. L. Mencken

To Alfred A. Knopf
[AAK]

H. L. Mencken
704 Cathedral St.
Baltimore
July 10, 1931

Dear Alfred:–

I think this Harris book should cover the whole history of surgery from prehistoric days (there are plenty of archeological evidences) down to the present.[3] There should be chapters on Egyptian and Greek surgery, and on the great advances made in the Middle Ages and thereafter, for example, by Ambroise Paré. Then he should come down to modern times, with chapters on anaesthetics and asepsis, and plenty of stuff about the men who brought them in. The history of the

[3] The book was never published.

principal operations of today should be told—appendectomy, the Billroth breast operations, tonsillectomy, etc. The history of cutting for the stone will naturally fall into its place. At the end there should be some discussion of the different schools of surgery. Of late there have been three main movements—toward reducing hemorrhage, toward the use of block anaesthesia to cut off shock, and toward the careful handling of exposed tissues. I think the book should be illustrated, and that it should mention as many concrete surgeons as possible. Every advance had a beginning in a different man.

Yours,
M.

◇◇◇◇◇◇◇◇◇◇◇◇◇

To ALFRED A. KNOPF
[AAK]

H. L. Mencken
704 Cathedral St.
Baltimore
July 15, 1931

DEAR ALFRED:

I don't think it would be worth while to do a biography of George Sterling. His life, after all, was relatively uneventful, and his writings were scarcely important enough to justify dealing with him at length. Every few weeks I receive a note from some woman offering to sell me a series of his love letters. He wrote them by the thousands, and sent them apparently to hundreds of women. Very often he sent the same poem to as many as a dozen women. One of those who got a long series was Upton Sinclair's present wife. Sinclair is such an ass that he did not know Sterling's habits with women, and so he solemnly printed the letters in a book after Sterling's death. They made his wife look a bit ridiculous.

Wolfe is an energetic and ambitious young man, but he has yet to learn to write. I spent a great deal of time patching up his rubber article. If he ever produces anything fit to print I'll make sure that you see it.

Yours,
M.

(1931)

To Philip Goodman
[EPL]

Baltimore, Md.
August 29th, 1931

Dear Phil:

Well, we are now in our second year. So far it doesn't seem to differ materially from the first. I still have my free say about everything. If, in the end, we follow Sara's ideas, then it is only because they are logically persuasive. She never uses coercion on me—that is, never in an obnoxious manner. I have seen no reason to mistrust her judgment—save maybe in a few cases, and in those it was always too late to follow my own plan. In marriage, as they say, there must be give and take.

Please don't let your faux pas in the matter of Guggenheim worry you. Even the best surgeons lose patients. I tried him on you simply because he was hard. I'd never think of bothering you with easy problems. The brief account of his Lebensbahn is from the Café News, the same paper which printed his portrait. I confess frankly that I'd have put him in some learned profession: he looks to me like a painless dentist or a highly reformed rabbi.

I am willing to be convinced about that new beer. But it must wait until hay fever liberates me. We'll probably be with you for the Brooklyn opening. Do you want the flowers sent to the theatre or to your office?

Yours,
[*M.*]

To Blanche Knopf
[AAK]

H. L. Mencken
704 Cathedral St.
Baltimore
October 21st [*1931*]

Dear Blanche:–

I'll leave Monday evening open, and shall count on you for lunch on Tuesday. Tuesday night I'll be stuck, and on Wednesday I want to start home if possible, for my book is much delayed, and I am hard at it.

My prices on O'Neill:[4]
For going to the performance: $10,000
For seeing one act: $1750
For listening to the plot: $3,500
For reading the reviews: $200

Yours,
M.

To FIELDING HUDSON GARRISON
[PT]

[*Dreiser was then in Kentucky where, as Chairman of the National Committee for the Defense of Political Prisoners, he investigated the working conditions which had led to a bloody strike and to the bullying of union sympathizers by the authorities. After he had given a courageous, outspoken interview to the* Knoxville News-Sentinel, *he was soon to make himself unpopular with the local right-thinkers, who sought to extradite him after his return to New York on charges of adultery and criminal syndicalism.*]

Baltimore, November 6, 1931

DEAR GARRISON:

I seize the opportunity to wish you many happy returns of the day. You are the youngest man at 61 that I have ever encountered. My prediction is that you will live to be 90 at least. I surely hope your difficulty with your eyes is only a passing nuisance. Every now and then my own get on a rampage, but if I give them a reasonable amount of rest they quickly recover. Despite the horrible ill-usage that they commonly get, I was told by Alan Wood six months ago that they were substantially perfect.

My feeling about Dreiser is that all of his best work was done before he became successful. Like most peasants, he is bearing money very badly. This morning's paper says that he is down in Kentucky

---

[4] *Mourning Becomes Electra,* by Eugene O'Neill, was then beginning its career in New York.

heading a gang of so-called authors, and engaged upon a so-called investigation of the mining situation. Of all the men that I have ever known he is the least fitted to carry on any such inquiry intelligently. When he went to Russia he was taken in by the Bolsheviki with the greatest ease. He will come home with a silly report, and do more damage than benefit to the people he is trying to help.

You are quite right about Mark Twain's "The Mysterious Stranger". It was written many years before he published it. In fact, before his wife died. While she lived, of course, he didn't dare to print any such thing, and for years after she died he was still under the influence of her qualms.

Dreiser's "American Tragedy" seems to me to be a very poor piece of work. My feeling is that his best book was "Jennie Gerhardt", with "The Titan" following closely after it.

Yours,
M.

To Fielding Hudson Garrison
[PT]

Baltimore, November 12, 1931

Dear Garrison:

I refuse absolutely to spread your farewell on my minutes. A pox upon it! You and I will go on heaving dead cats at each other, I hope, until the end of the chapter. But it will be time enough to quarrel when we meet in the dissecting-room. The idea that I have high-hatted you really makes me larf! Go ask anyone to whom I have poured out my dithyrambs on your tremendous learning and capital style—for example, Phil Goodman. I gave him the last edition of your History of Medicine to read as a piece of writing: he is not interested in medicine, and, in fact, gets the botts every time he sees them mentioned in print. Well, he sat up two nights reading it, and mentions it every time we meet.

As for Dreiser, what annoys me is the way he is succumbing to all sorts of exploiters, especially Greenwich Village Bolsheviks. They are making a dreadful fool of him, and taking him off his work. True enough, he can't write, but nevertheless he is a great writer, just as Whitman was. But now, instead of doing another "Jennie Gerhardt"—and he could certainly do a better one now than he did in 1910—, he wastes his time clowning. The Bolsheviks kept away from him while he was poor. Now that he is well heeled they discover that he is a great moral leader, travel about the country at his expense, and lap up his booze. He and I used to sit all evening over one 40 cent bottle of California wine. I have no animosity to him, but he has become too tragic to be borne. Seeing him would be like visiting an old friend who had gone insane, or had both legs cut off. When I say he is a peasant, I don't mean that *all* peasants are damned fools. I simply mean what I say: that he is a peasant.

Has Col. Blakely the permission of Cajal's Spanish publisher to print those epigrams in English? If so, I might be able to use a few pages of them in the A.M. And introduce Blakely to Knopf. I can't make out from your letter what the exact state of affairs is.

You must have misunderstood my wife. I haven't been to any public meeting save one for 25 years. I'd almost rather go to church. I must have been at the Sun office. I'm sorry I missed you.

If I put on a Bierabend, beginning at 10 P.M., will you come? That is the precise hour when the liver and lights begin to crave malt. I suggest getting together 6 or 8 head of sound-money Democrats. I'll be in New York next week, but after that I'll be here indefinitely.

John Ruhräh actually believes that you are one of the noblest bucks ever fashioned by Yahweh. He has told me so often.

Yours,
Mencken

To BENJAMIN DE CASSERES
[OFP]

H. L. Mencken
704 Cathedral St.
Baltimore
November 28, 1931

DEAR BEN:

I have so little interest in the theatre myself that I hesitate to print anything about it in The American Mercury. Thus I fear I must pass up the proposed article on O'Neill. Of all the dramatists of any importance, in fact, he interests me the least.

Your book is here, and I shall give it an earnest reading tomorrow, which is the Sabbath day.

Yours,
M.

1932

To Albert G. Keller[1]
[OFP]

H. L. Mencken
704 Cathedral St.
Baltimore
January 5, 1932

Dear Dr. Keller:

Thanks very much for your most generous and friendly letter. I needn't assure you that it has delighted me. Your interest in my writings is more than matched by mine in yours, for I have read you for many years, and have the new edition of your "Societal Evolution" on my desk at this minute. The books of your old chief, Dr. Sumner, made a powerful impression on me when I was young, and their influence has survived. I only wish that such things as "The Forgotten Man" could be printed as circulars in editions of millions. The obscurantists flood the country with their literature, but the works of sensible men have relatively small circulation. I have long cherished a plan to deluge my own State of Maryland with tracts against the prevailing Methodism. That such treatment is needed is shown by the fact that we had a lynching a couple of weeks ago in the remote part of the

[1] Albert Galloway Keller (1874–1956) was professor of the science of society at Yale University. His *Societal Evolution* (New York: The Macmillan Co.) had been published in 1915.

State.[2] However, I have never been able to interest any man of money in the project.

Do you ever come to New York? If so, I surely hope you let me hear of it. I'd like very much to see you. At the moment I am preparing to go to the West Indies for a brief holiday, but I'll be back in harness by the end of January. My wine supply in New York is excellent, and we might have lunch in quiet at my hotel.

It goes without saying that I am in hopes that you'll be able to write something for The American Mercury. I can imagine nothing more pleasant than printing you.

Meanwhile, my best thanks.

Sincerely yours,
H. L. Mencken

To PHILIP GOODMAN
[EPL]

S. S. Columbus, near Jamaica,
Jan. 19 [*1932*]

DEAR PHIL:–

The trouble with you and me is that we are never serious. As people say, we make a joke about everything. I suppose you have had the experience many times of having everyone swallow what you said in jest. Well, here is another case. I warn you so that you won't swallow the enclosed yourself. I hear that the Captain did. He told the passengers who told other passengers who told me that, after working for the Lloyd for 35 years, and going through 175 horrible storms, each and every one of which was the worst in his experience, he was still learning something about the history of the line.

The Pilsner not only holds out, but also holds up. I got down three or four big ones last night, and the last was as caressing as a first kiss. The effect on the viscera, of course, is somewhat over-exhilarating. One retires more often than on land. But what else is there to do? And what could be more comfortable than a N.-D. Lloyd toilet-seat? I suppose you know that the new ones have armrests and reading

[2] The lynching mentioned in this letter took place on December 4, 1931, at Salisbury on the Maryland Eastern Shore. Mencken's articles in the *Evening Sun* ("The Eastern Shore Kultur", December 7, and "Sound and Fury", December 14, 1931) aroused considerable emotion among the local people.

lamps. As for the paper, I can do no better than send you a specimen. You will find it within. Rub it between your fingers, hold it up to the light. Test its solubility in water, alcohol and acetone. It is yours to keep. Don't bother to return it.

I have not seen Jamaica for 27 years. No doubt there have been great improvements. At the time of my last visit there were no automobiles. It seems hard to believe. Well, I suppose the next time I come down this way we'll all be traveling by airplane, and television will be perfected.

Yours,
[*M.*]

◇◇◇◇◇◇◇◇◇◇◇◇◇

To EDGAR LEE MASTERS
[OFP]

H. L. Mencken
704 Cathedral St.
Baltimore
February 13, 1932

DEAR MASTERS:

God knows what has come over poor Dreiser. I have not seen or heard of him for more than six years, and get news of him only occasionally and indirectly. My suspicion is that the money which poured in upon him a few years ago augmented his happiness very little. He is not the sort of fellow to enjoy a lavish and gaudy life. I think he greatly prefers living very simply, and that his season as a Broadway celebrity and literary host actually bored him. His new book is just here. It looks rather depressing, but I suppose I shall have to tackle it.[3]

I am just putting into type an article on Lindsay by a college professor named Hazelton Spencer, now at the Johns Hopkins University. He edited the volume of Lindsay's Selected Poems a year or two ago.[4] It seems to me to be excellent stuff. There is a mention of you in it, wholly favorable. For this all I ask is that you leave me one of your Bibles when you are translated to Heaven.

Yours,
Mencken

---

[3] Dreiser's book: *Tragic America* (New York: H. Liveright; 1931).
[4] Masters himself wrote "The Tragedy of Vachel Lindsay" for the July 1933 *Mercury.*

(1932)

◇◇◇◇◇◇◇◇◇◇◇◇◇◇

To Wilbur Cross
[yu]

H. L. Mencken
1524 Hollins St.
Baltimore
March 11 [*before 1931?*]

Dear Dr. Cross:–

I have a feeling that you get at the truth exactly without putting it into set terms, to wit, that novels are, after all, third-rate things. For a year or two past I have found it almost impossible to read them. Probably fifty reach me every month. I pick up one after another, unable to get beyond the first few pages. Now and then one interests me. But just why I seldom know.

Maybe it is true that my arteries are hardening, though the Johns Hopkins reports that they are not. As for the *Evening Post* piece it reminds me somehow of the poor harlot who was taken before a J. P. by the Polizei. She was prepared for a lecture and thirty days, but when the learned jurist leaped down from the bench, threw his arms around her neck and kissed her, she died of the shock.

I begin to suspect that criticism, after all, may not be an exact science. Canby's janissary accuses me of knowing no music since Brahms'—after all my struggles for Richard Strauss! And of having no palate for style per se—after my laborious importation of Dunsany!

Sincerely yours,
H. L. Mencken

◇◇◇◇◇◇◇◇◇◇◇◇◇◇

To James T. Farrell
[ofp]

The American Mercury
730 Fifth Avenue
New York
March 21st [*1932?*]

Dear Mr. Farrell:

Here again it seems to me that you fall considerably short of your own best work. The idea of the story is excellent, but it somehow seems pumped up. That is to say that there is no apparent reason, at the end, why the boys should backslide so promptly. Another defect lies in the dialogue. Certainly you cannot tell me that Chicago boys use the

Chimmie Fadden dialect that you put into the mouth of Slug. Here I refer to the first page of the MS., but the dialogue later on seems to me to be almost as wooden. All the spontaneity that was in "Helen, I Love You" is missing.

I hate to be making this report, but such are my prayerful convictions. You know how to make your characters real, but I don't think you have been doing it in the last couple of MSS. I have seen.

Sincerely yours,
H. L. Mencken

To PHILIP GOODMAN
[EPL]

Baltimore, Md.
April 11 [1932]

DEAR PHIL:

So you have fallen for the O'Neill play? [5] Let me now have a note saying that "Of Thee I Sing" is great satire, and I shall believe that they got you down in Hollywood, and filled you with paraphenylene-diamine. Next you will be telling me that Charles Hanson Towne is a great lyric poet. And that *Vanity Fair* prints swell fiction. And that there is nothing like a good old American meal to put meat on a man's ribs.

I had a burst of industry the other day, and wrote 5000 words in four hours. This was the first time anything of the sort had happened since 1903. I must be winding up for the final leap into Gehenna.

I hope to be in Gotham next Monday, the 18th. What of a session at that miraculous Bierstube? I scoffed at it when you reported it, but reflection makes me curious. Can it be that you are right?

Yours,
[*M.*]

To PHILIP GOODMAN
[EPL]

Baltimore, Md.
May 5th [1932]

DEAR PHIL:

I confess that when you cleared out I had an uneasy feeling that it

[5] The O'Neill play was *Mourning Becomes Electra.*

would be a long while before we met again. I predict formally that you will find your heart going out to the heroic French people, and that you will stick among them for at least a year. Well, I don't blame you. The United States grows increasingly uninhabitable, and especially New York. Now that you are away I actually don't know what to do with myself there. Twice, on my last visit, I turned in at 10 P.M., to read the *News of the World*. The parties are ghastly and the public shows are worse. One evening I caught a bad bluefish at Nick's, returned to the hotel to empty it, and then drank two scotches *alone*, something I had not done for 25 years. Nick's red meat is edible, and his beer is the best I have found, but the pissoir smell is beginning to fetch me. It appears that he has to use disinfectants heavily because so many patrons bring their dogs, and the dogs void upon the table-legs. Also, some of the chiselers piss themselves when they see a big shot enter.

I concluded some time ago that Red was hopeless, and made up my mind to avoid him. Nothing could have been in worse taste. Moreover, it was obviously suggested by Nathan, whose operations along the same lines have been going on for a long while. Well, let us not expect too much. It takes more than one generation to breed out the stigmata of Sauk Center. I begin to have a great respect for Gracie. She had her faults, but I think she at least steered Red in the right direction. His present lady, I fear, has made a sad mess of him. I shall not read his new book if I can help it. I can imagine what dreadful stuff it is, and it would be unpleasant to have to do execution upon it.[6]

I have killed The American Mercury editorials, and resumed work on my book. The magazine is in very fair shape, considering the times. By dint of magnificent sacrifices in the cause of art we have kept the budget balanced, and at the moment actually show a small profit. But it will remain very small until there is a general turn upward. God knows if that will ever come. I begin to believe, in fact, that we are in for a whole Era of Low Living.

I wrote to Ruth last week, telling her confidentially why you were coming abroad. I'll never forget that night you got tight in my room, and began telling me how happy it would make you to dance your little grandson, Julius Abarbanel, on your knee. Well, I do not hold it

[6] Sinclair Lewis's new book: *Ann Vickers* (New York: Doubleday, Doran & Co.; 1933); Gracie: Grace Livingston Hegger, Sinclair Lewis's first wife. His present lady: Dorothy Thompson, whom he married in 1928.

against you. Such things are human. I enclose a few cards for use if there is ever any need for them.

I'd be at home in Dooveel. It looks exactly like Rehobeth Beach, Del. I have put on so much weight since January 1st that I begin to be somewhat uneasy. I actually weigh 192 pounds in my pajamas. But reducing is a bitter business, and I hate to try it. Imagine living without bread! Maybe the next Jap war scare will bring me down to 180.

I look forward without much joy to the new national conventions. They will be bawdy shows, but I have seen it all before. They are two weeks apart, so I'll probably return home in the interval. Think of *four* trips between Chicago and Baltimore, each of 22 hours! Next week I am going to Bethlehem with Alfred Knopf. Such little jaunts are pleasanter. The beer is likely to be very good. After that, a week-end with Hergy.[7] Then to my book for the Summer. It is hard stuff to write, but it is turning out very well. You will like it.

My best to Lily, Ruth and Gus. Ruth writes that Gus is also putting on weight. Tell her to forget it. It is natural for a German gentleman to be larger in the middle than a 100% American. He has longer, sturdier and wider bowels.

I am taking another course in hay-fever vaccines. They will do me no good, but it pleases the quacks.

Yours,
[*M.*]

◇◇◇◇◇◇◇◇◇◇◇◇◇◇

To ALFRED A. KNOPF
[AAK]

H. L. Mencken
1524 Hollins St.
Baltimore
July 8th [1932]

DEAR ALFRED:–

1. The Newman article on Verdi is a book review, and so I think we had better pass it up. But let us watch his later pieces. I think we should be able to get him into Music. I have made an article out of part of his introduction to the Wagner book.

2. At your house last week I picked up a small encyclopedia of

[7] Hergy: Joseph Hergesheimer.

chamber music. Will you please let me know who wrote and published it?

3. I believe a compilation to be called, say, The Agnostic Handbook might do well. It should include Huxley's essay on the value of witness to the miraculous, and extracts from Haeckel, Wheless, Paine, Ingersoll, etc. There should also be sections on the contradictions and absurdities in the Bible. Much of this last stuff has been assembled by the American Association for the Advancement of Atheism. There should also be summaries of the butcheries during the Inquisition, extracts from the New England Blue Laws, and so on. Angoff would be a good man to do the book. Maybe he'll want to take a holiday from his history of American literature when he finishes Vol. II.

Yours,
M.

◇◇◇◇◇◇◇◇◇◇◇◇◇◇

To JIM TULLY
[OFP]

H. L. Mencken
704 Cathedral St.
Baltimore
August 3, 1932

DEAR JIM:

I am glad you liked the Bradley article. If it is in your heart to write a brief note to Bradley himself, in care of The American Mercury, I am sure that it will pick him up immensely. He has been trying to make a living by free lancing, and I gather from him that he has not been very successful. I have another article by him in the next number on Jim Farley, the Irishman who put over Frank Roosevelt.

Your news about our San Quentin friend doesn't surprise me in the slightest. It makes the record complete. Every one of the convicts I tried to give a hand to three or four years ago has turned out badly. One of them, arrested in New Jersey for burglary, tried to make it appear that he was driven into the crime by the failure of some unnamed magazine to pay him promptly, and the inference was that it was The American Mercury. As a matter of fact, I had bought nothing from him for more than a year, and all of his checks in the past had reached him within six days. Another sweet gentleman came out of San Quentin and announced that I had hailed him as the greatest author ever heard of. I had, of course, done nothing of the sort. I begin to believe that it is unwise to fool with such babies. They are all scoundrels.

I ran into Mayfield in the lobby of the Algonquin one day last week, but had only a few minutes talk with her. What she is up to I don't know.

Yours,
M.

To F. Scott Fitzgerald
[PU]

H. L. Mencken
704 Cathedral St.
Baltimore
September 12, 1932

My dear Scottie:

I think your poem is excellent, though I confess that it seems a bit irrelevant. However, that is no objection in poetry. Your rhymes are very good, and your count of syllables is sufficiently accurate for all practical purposes.

Now and then stamps come in from Finland. I'll send them to you hereafter.

I am sorry indeed to hear that your father has been ill. He called up yesterday, but didn't say a word about it. Please remember me to your mother.

Sincerely yours,
H. L. Mencken

To Fielding Hudson Garrison
[PT]

Baltimore, September 12, 1932

Dear Garrison:

I have an uneasy feeling that you have made a really brilliant diagnosis. Undoubtedly, there has been something within me that has worked against the book. I now begin to believe, following your suggestion, that it is a deep-lying conviction that ethics is a delusion that is scarcely worth writing about. Whatever the fact, I am certainly eager to get rid of the book and, once it is off my hands, I'll never go back to the subject. Curiously enough, the manuscript looks pretty good. That is to say, it is relatively amusing stuff, despite the imbecility of the fundamental theme. I have been plowing into the byways of morals, and finding some instructive curiosities.

My next book will be something enormously different, probably a volume of reminiscences dealing mainly with the literati, and showing that four-fifths of them are insane. That is really an underestimate. What I should say is that all of them are insane, and that nine-tenths are also criminals.

For the first time in years, I am really free of hay fever. It is toying with me, but it is certainly enormously milder than ever before. I have been taking a vaccine made by Dr. Robert A. Cooke in New York. Four or five times in the past I took other vaccines, but without result. This time I am really getting some relief. Perhaps prayer has also had something to do with it.

When are you returning to Baltimore? We meet far too seldom.

Sincerely yours,
Mencken

To ROSCOE PEACOCK
[OFP]

H. L. Mencken
704 Cathedral St.
Baltimore
September 24, 1932

DEAR PEACOCK:

Thanks very much for the letter.[8] It goes without saying that I'll be glad to print it in The American Mercury. Certainly you deserve the book, and it is a pleasure to send it to you.

I haven't a file of the articles on Hill that have been printed, but certainly there have been a great many of them.[9] In fact, he was discussed at enormous length in the advertising journals only a couple of years ago. As I recall it, he refused absolutely to make any defense of

---

[8] The letter from Peacock in the December *Mercury* was entitled "Gasoline on the fire", and criticized over-production in agriculture.

[9] Hill: probably George Washington. Hill, president of the American Tobacco Co.

himself. He would undoubtedly make an excellent hero for a novel, but I don't think that Kaufman is the man to do it. Sinclair Lewis would be far better, but Lewis, at the moment, seems to be turning himself into a glad writer.

The theory that I am in a low and senile state always amuses me. The truth is that I feel better than ever before, and hope to do a couple of books within the next five years that will be better than anything I have ever done in the past. I begin at last to believe that a man actually learns something as he grows older. If I had my early books to do over again, I'd certainly make them better.

My belief is that all advertising men are quacks. Hill is rather more picturesque than the average, but he is certainly not more dishonest. If I could find somebody to do a series of articles on the frauds and imbecilities of the advertising business, I'd certainly be delighted to print them.

Sincerely yours,
H. L. Mencken

To FIELDING HUDSON GARRISON
[PT]

Baltimore, September 28, 1932

DEAR GARRISON:

Thanks very much for the loan of the two books. I have been dipping into the Lichtenberg, and find it immensely interesting.[1] I shall go through it in detail and make some extracts from it for a book of quotations on which I have been working for years. Some time ago, incidentally, I did some liberal borrowing for that book from your pamphlet of medical aphorisms. I hope you will forgive me, as God has.

I am glad you liked the Masters poem.[2] Printing so long a piece of verse involves a considerable editorial risk. Three readers out of four damn it without reading it at all. My feeling is that the poem is one of the finest things Masters has ever done. This morning, curiously enough, there came in a letter from William Lyon Phelps of Yale, in which he says that very thing. Phelps, of course, is anything but a professor of poetry, but he certainly represents a large section of civilized

[1] The Lichtenberg: "*Reflections*", by G. C. Lichtenberg (1799).
[2] The Masters poem mentioned here is: "Beethoven's Ninth Symphony and the King Cobra", printed in *The American Mercury* for November 1932.

opinion. Masters has been hard at work for six months past on the life of Vachel Lindsay. As you may know, Lindsay was a very curious fellow, and full to the neck with complexes. I have seen Masters' manuscript. It is pretty good stuff, and I hope to print a chapter or two from it in The American Mercury.

I'll pass on what you say about your publishing situation to Knopf. Please bear in mind that he'll be eager to do you at any time you have anything that seems suitable. I sent him your "History of Medicine" three or four years ago, and he has been talking about it ever since.

I am still at work on my treatise on morals. It is going slowly, but it is nevertheless going.

I'll return the Lichtenberg and the other book within a week.

Sincerely yours,
H. L. Mencken

To Fielding Hudson Garrison
[PT]

Baltimore, October 5, 1932

Dear Garrison:

As always, you put me in your debt. Your essay on "The Literary Tradition in English Medicine" is a charming piece of work indeed, and one of the best things you have ever done. I have been reading it with great pleasure.

All of the dictionaries of quotations that you mention are already on my shelf. There is some merit in every one of them, but I agree with you that they show a certain dull sameness. My hope is that the volume Angoff and I are at work on will be measurably better than any of them. However, I am not too sure.[3]

The notion that a man goes through a sort of crisis every seven years is one that has always seemed to me to be reasonable. My own experience is that at intervals of about that length I find myself feeling tremendously out of sorts, and almost unable to work. Usually I rush to the brethren and demand to be examined, but they never find anything. After a while the storm passes off, and I am back on an even keel. I have just got through such a period.

I hope to see Masters in New York in a short while. When I do

[3] Mencken's *New Dictionary of Quotations* was not published until 1942 (New York: Alfred A. Knopf).

so I'll tell him what you say about his poem. It will delight him immensely. Curiously enough, he gets very little praise. The quacks who pretend to be poetry critics have been trying to cry him down ever since the Spoon River Anthology. Unfortunately, he has given them plenty of ammunition.

Sincerely yours,
Mencken

To George S. Schuyler
[OFP]

The American Mercury
730 Fifth Avenue
New York
October 5, 1932

Dear Mr. Schuyler:

Here again, it seems to me you spoil a good story by showing too much indignation. The missionaries are depicted with such hostility that in most cases they become mere caricatures. Thus the general effect of the article is considerably diminished, and I find myself hesitating to take it. In such writing, it seems to me that the really effective weapon is irony. The moment you begin to show indignation you weaken your whole case.

Sincerely yours,
H. L. Mencken

To James N. Rosenberg
[AAK]

[*Having received this telegram from the office of* The American Mercury:

PLEASE INFORM ME IMMEDIATELY WHO IS YOUR LAWYER ON WHOM I CAN SERVE PAPERS IN MANDATORY INJUNCTION SUIT TO COMPEL YOU TO RESUME WRITING EDITORIALS IN THE MERCURY I ALSO WANT TO INCLUDE ACTION FOR HEAVY PUNITIVE DAMAGES AGAINST YOU PERSONALLY WHAT

DO YOU MEAN BY OMITTING TO WRITE EDITORIALS INDIGNANTLY YOURS JAMES N ROSENBERG

Mencken wired back:]

October 11, 1932

The mandamus referred to in you esteemed favor was issued by the Supreme Court of the United States yesterday. Mencken is now in the custody of the marshall of the court, and will be on bread and water until he finishes his November editorials. No beer. No gebratene Gans.

Goldfarb? Hohenzollern, Mussolini & Flaherty
Attorneys of record for the American Mercury Charter Subscribers Protective Association

To BENJAMIN DE CASSERES
[OFP]

H. L. Mencken
704 Cathedral St.
Baltimore
November 5, 1932

DEAR BEN:

I am sorry indeed that we can't agree. I have read this article twice more, and still find myself in such doubt about it that it would be folly for me to print it. Obviously, even the greatest minds must sometimes clash. This seems to have happened with us in the present case. Let us console ourselves by remembering that it has happened very seldom. God knows what is to be done with the article. I see nothing ahead save to keep on offering it. You'll probably sell it unexpectedly, and get an enormous honorarium for it.

I am looking forward to your book with great interest. Spinoza seems to me to have been one of the worst scoundrels who ever lived in the world. I rank him indeed with Abraham Lincoln and Henry Ward Beecher. Nevertheless, I am willing to be convinced, and if you can convince me God will reward you.[4]

Yours,
H. L. Mencken

[4] Benjamin De Casseres was a collateral descendant of Benedict de Spinoza on his father's side; he was preparing a book on that philosopher.

(1932)

To Louis Untermeyer
[OFP]

H. L. Mencken
704 Cathedral St.
Baltimore
November 9, 1932

Dear Louis:

I can't get rid of a feeling that this piece is rather too casual and superficial as it stands. I think it would be enormously more effective as a straight article.

Incidentally, it probably should answer a couple of questions that will naturally occur to the reader. One is, Why are so few decent poets produced in America? Another is, Why do the good ones tend to appear in clumps? Eight or ten years ago a great deal of really interesting stuff was being concocted in this country, but of late there has been almost none. At least a ton of poetry passes across my desk every year, but it is most unusual for me to find any of any merit whatever. The reason for this probably lies concealed in the will of God, but you are precisely the man to penetrate it.

I voted for Roosevelt yesterday and now feel almost ashamed, for he is the first candidate of my choice ever to win.

Sincerely yours,
M.

To Alfred A. Knopf
[AAK]

H. L. Mencken
704 Cathedral St.
Baltimore
November 23rd [1932]

Dear Alfred:–

I have a feeling sometimes that we don't do enough blowing. We used to do it in our first days, but of late we have not. It would probably do some good, and help to keep up our own spirits.

I suggest that we might print a very effective announcement in January or thereabout, saying that, almost alone among American magazines, the A. M. has closed 1932 without showing a loss. We could say that our annual subscribers have stuck to us in larger proportion than those of any other magazine, and that our news-stands returns are lower than those of our chief competitors. And we could say that this has been achieved without offering cut-rates, without employing any solicitors, and without any premium scheme.

The moral for advertisers is plain: we reach a large class of Americans able to pay 50 cents for a magazine, even after three years of the Depression, and they stick to us faithfully. We can admit that we have lost circulation, but say that we have lost less than the other fellow. I believe that an ostensible frank announcement to this effect would do some good. Perhaps the place for it is As I See It. I see no objection to your discussing the magazine there.

M.

To EZRA POUND
[EPT]

H. L. Mencken
704 Cathedral St.
Baltimore
November 26, 1932

DEAR POUND:

I know nothing whatever about the *American Spectator*, and have not seen or heard from Nathan for more than a year. Boyd I see at very long intervals, and then only briefly. The truth is that I seldom read any other magazine. It is labor enough to get through the dreadful manuscripts that pour into The American Mercury office. Far from reducing their number, the depression has actually tripled it. Every third American out of a job tries to recoup his fortunes by turning literatus. I am actually receiving manuscripts from former stock brokers, kept women, and even actors.

The utter collapse of Hoover gave me great delight. For some reason or other the fellow is unbearably offensive to me. I hate to look at him, or even to think of him. Why this should be I simply don't know. Roosevelt is a weak sister, but he'll be better than Hoover. I look for a circus during the next year or two. Once the country discovers that it has been saddled with the whole war debt there will be Hell to pay.

What are you up to yourself. Why don't you do your recollections of the literary life? They would make a very amusing book. When I turn fifty-five I shall probably sit down in some quiet spot and begin pouring out my recollections as a Christian.

Yours,
Mencken

To ALFRED A. KNOPF
[AAK]

H. L. Mencken
704 Cathedral St.
Baltimore
December 2nd [1932]

DEAR ALFRED:–

1. A letter from E. W. Howe says that he thinks your department in The American Mercury is swell. Well, so do I. I begin to believe that it ought to be printed less like a display advertisement.[5]

2. My memorandum was clumsily drawn. I didn't mean to argue that we should tell advertisers that we reach the Nation audience of Bolsheviks. What I had in mind was simply to show that *even the Nation* duplicates more of our circulation than Harper's and the Atlantic, and to argue therefrom that we reach an audience that can't be reached by those magazines.

3. I certainly don't enjoy listening to the woes of advertising men. But I think they should be allowed to come in if they want to. If it accomplishes nothing else, it at least gives them some notion of what I am driving at. But this is in your hands.

4. I agree with you that we should refuse all requests for reprinting rights while we hold the copyright. We are in the business of selling magazines. But I assume that an author who wants 50 or 100 copies will be able to get them at a considerable reduction from the news-stand price.

5. I think you should choose the articles for display on the cover—that is, if you care for the job. My own judgment in the matter is apt to be biassed by the fact that a given article falls a great deal short of

[5] Your department: an advertisement, sometimes written by Alfred A. Knopf, and sometimes about him, and called the *Borzoi Broadside*.

what I tried to make it. In brief, I am rather too close to the woods to judge the size of the trees.

6. I suggest that the two topmost display lines on the cover might be made somewhat blacker. They look thin to me. I am in favor of putting some real display at the top on occasion—if necessary, with a border. The date line can always go at the bottom, next to your name, or split in the middle, on the two sides of mine.

7. I'll get to the office on Monday afternoon, the 12th. I have put down Tuesday for lunch with the advertising men.

Yours,
M.

◇◇◇◇◇◇◇◇◇◇◇◇◇◇

To JIM TULLY
[OFP]

H. L. Mencken
704 Cathedral St.
Baltimore
December 8, 1932

DEAR JIM:

Thanks very much for the revision of the yegg story.[6] I think you have done an excellent job, and I'll be glad to embalm it in The American Mercury. The manuscript as it stands now runs to 31 pages, which is somewhat long, but I believe I can make a few cuts without doing the argument the slightest damage. It seems to me that you made a capital job of the rewriting. The article is now perfectly clear.

It may be that I'll have to shade the price a bit in view of the advertising situation, but I'll try to hold as closely as possible to the old standard. We are getting through the depression very fortunately, but it is naturally at the cost of a relentless carefulness. I suspect that The American Mercury is the only magazine of its class that is actually closing 1932 without a loss. As you know, I am strongly opposed to endowed magazines. The moment The American Mercury showed a loss I'd shut it down. So far, we have not only survived but maintained our rate of payment better than any other magazine I know of, not excluding the *Saturday Evening Post.*

Your new place looks almost perfect. I am sorely tempted to come

---

[6] The yegg story: "Yeggs", in the April 1933 *Mercury.*

out to California and drink you out of house and home. Unfortunately, I fear the movie people would drive me crazy with offers to play heroic parts.

Yours,
M.

To PHILIP GOODMAN
[EPL]

Baltimore, Md.
December 29, 1932

DEAR PHIL:

The Paulaner Bock sign came in safely. My very best thanks. It is the noblest bock beer sign that I have ever seen, and Sara insisted at once that we hang it on the wall in our hall. There it is on display at this minute, and as the brethren come in one by one it brings tears to their eyes.

I have just finished reading "Ann Vickers". On the whole, I was pleasantly disappointed. I expected something truly appalling, but what I found was simply a bad novel, with a few bright spots. There are, in fact, places which show a good deal of Lewis's old skill, especially the scenes in the girls' school and in the suffragette headquarters. The worst parts, of course, are toward the end. I believe that it would be unjust to put the whole blame on Dorothy. After all, Ann Vickers is not really her kind of uplifter. My belief is that Red imagined the thing himself, and that Dorothy's influence, if she had any, was probably for the good quite as much as for the bad. I have done a review of the book for The American Mercury, telling the truth about it.[7] Under Dorothy's influence Red will undoubtedly do the Dreiser act soon or late, so I see no reason why I should do any lying for him now. He is a man of good instincts, but dreadfully weak.

I put in the usual dull Christmas. On Christmas eve we had a bowl of eggnog, and my brother August and I drank about a gallon of it. This made us sleep well, but brought us up on Christmas morning with a certain gloom in our hearts. During the day I got down three glasses of beer—nothing else. I tried to work in the afternoon, but quickly fell asleep.

---

[7] *Ann Vickers* was reviewed by Mencken in *The American Mercury* (March 1933).

The American Mercury is getting through 1932 with a profit of a little over $5000. It is probably the only American monthly that shows any profit at all. However, I am not too hopeful about 1933. The decline in advertising continues, both for magazines and for newspapers, with no sign that it is going to stop in the near future. The big papers during December have been forty per cent. under their 1931 mark, and 1931 was certainly not a good year. They are printing no more than one-third of the business that they carried in 1928–29. Some of the loss, of course, has been taken up by a drastic reduction of expenses, but certainly not all.

The *Sun* directors have once more decided to maintain salaries. There are only two newspapers in the United States that have done so —the *Sun* and the Washington *Star*. I should add, of course, the New York *Daily News,* but it is not commonly counted as a newspaper. All of the other New York papers have made at least one heavy cut, and most of them have made two or three.

Let me hear about your Christmas journey. If you relented at the last minute and went to Vienna to see Red, please don't tell me of it. It would convince me that you had turned mashuggah at last.

Yours,
[*M.*]

1933

To PHILIP GOODMAN
[EPL]

Baltimore, Md.
January 15 [*1933*]

DEAR PHIL:

Ha, ha! He, he! Hi, hi! Ho, ho! Hum, hum! Did I or did I not predict that you would succumb to the Lewis siren and march on to Vienna? I asked you, as a friend, to keep me ignorant of it if you did, but you had to blurt it out. Well, I believe in looking on the brighter side of things, and making the best of them. What I want you to do is to send me frequent and copious bulletins on all important European affairs. You are now hep to the lowdown, and I can use it in my business as a journalist. Let me hear confidentially *precisely* what Schleicher is up to. On this side we get only the reports of journalists who have no access to the front office. But you will now be admitted to secret circles, and I rely upon you to pass the dope on.

In the midst of the cheap skates who swarm in Vienna you will find one very intelligent and pleasant fellow, Fodor, correspondent of the Manchester Guardian. Give him my regards when you see him. Also, if you encounter one Fedor Juhasz, tell him that I still pray for him. He translated a book of mine into Hungarian, and must have made at least $3 by the job. Like Fodor, he is a civilized man. But the journalists who have desks at the foreign office are mainly ninth-rate reporters from Greenville, Ill. You will wonder, when you meet them, how such persons get their jobs. They get them by roving Europe on their own, and waiting for some previous correspondent to get drunk, fall down on a big story, and be canned. Then they cable in for the post, and often get it. For to a news editor any reporter on the spot is better than none.

I have done the best I could by Red in my review of "Ann Vickers". There is some good in the book, and I have made as much as possible of it. But another such botch will ruin him. I await the reviews almost in trembling. (The book is not yet released.) It will be praised as a masterpiece by William Lyon Phelps. Worse, Red will believe that it *is* a masterpiece.

I see little trace of Dorothy in it. She may have given Red some of his materials, but I believe she is too shrewd to have been responsible for the general tone of the book. It might have been written by Fannie Hurst. And the next will probably be even worse.

We go downhill very fast over here. The full impact of the Depression is just beginning to be felt. Until lately, thousands of people were able to get along on their savings, but now their savings begin to vanish. Every savings-bank in Baltimore lost both depositors and deposits during 1932, chiefly during the last half. The cities are going broke one and one, and most of the States have reached the limit of their borrowing. I doubt that the big railroads will last beyond the Spring. The only securities that show any strength are the Government loans, a few of the State bonds, and the public utilities. But even the public utilities begin to crack. The industrials have all gone to hell, and so have the mortgage bonds.

For the first time in my life I begin to give serious thought to money: it is a new experience for me. But so far I have been extraordinarily lucky. I'll lose something when the railroads bust, but not much. The American Mercury, of course, will make little if anything in 1933, but it is not likely to show any heavy loss. Knopf has done an excellent job with it. The Sun is still paying full salaries. And Sara is working hard, and selling her stuff. So I hope to continue to eat.

What are your plans in the Larger Sense? That is, how long do you propose to remain abroad? You say nothing about your play. Is Harris to put it on? I crave light.

Yours,
[*M.*]

◇◇◇◇◇◇◇◇◇◇◇◇◇◇

To Jim Tully
[OFP]

H. L. Mencken
704 Cathedral St.
Baltimore
February 3, 1933

Dear Jim:

I am inclined to say no to this letter. That, of course, is not because it is not good stuff. In truth, it is very excellent stuff. But I think it would be a disservice to you to let you tackle your critics with so much heat. My very thorough conviction is that an author *should never show any such heat.* Cabell has almost ruined himself by bellowing against the men who don't like him. Rewrite the letter in a more serene tone, leaving out all reference to Rascoe and other such fools, and I'll be delighted to print it. You are far too competent a writer to let such fellows upset you in the slightest.

Sara is in bed with a degree of fever. Apparently, it is an attack of flu. She bears such things badly, and I fear she'll be laid up for a week or so.

Yours,
M.

◇◇◇◇◇◇◇◇◇◇◇◇◇◇

To Alfred A. Knopf
[AAK]

H. L. Mencken
704 Cathedral St.
Baltimore
February 4, 1933

Dear Alfred:

1. Unfortunately, Sara will be unable to travel Monday. She is running a degree of fever, and Louis Hamburger insists on keeping her in bed. I'd hesitate to leave her alone until she is up. I therefore propose that our meeting be postponed two weeks instead of one. This will put me into New York on February 21st, and so I can sit in at the directors' meeting. I assume that we can take on the ad-

vertising men the same day. If we see them at one o'clock, there will be time enough for the directors' meeting later in the afternoon.

2. I have serious doubts about the booze law pamphlet. To print it with a critical introduction by a lawyer would involve us with troublesome obligations, and cause a considerable delay. If what has happened in Baltimore is any gage of what would happen in the country in general, I think it is plain that printing it would be very unprofitable. The local discussion has been very meagre, and no person of any sense has shown any interest in the projected law. All of the letters received by the *Evening Sun* have been from the usual moronic contributors to the letters column.

3. You will recall that I suggested a popular book on pharmacology by Macht. It might be worth while to write to him about it. I'd hesitate to tackle him myself, for he is one of the most active and offensive bores on my local staff, and I'd very likely quarrel with him if I began negotiations.

4. If Mr. Reubens can close with Brewton for $200, without making any admissions embarrassing to Dr. Wade, I am in favor of letting him do it.[1]

5. The question of Angoff's compensation is in your hands, not mine. It was fixed from time to time by your father. If it must be reduced, then it must be reduced. It might be well to remember that Nathan has got into contact with Angoff and may be trusted to pump the news out of him and spread it. He apparently visits my office in my absence.

6. The value of Smith's projected annual review of politics would depend wholly upon the skill of the editors engaged. Of those he mentions, I believe that Broadus Mitchell would be likely to do the most effective job. Beard is too busy to fool with it, and I know too little about the others to have any confidence in them. In general, I have some doubts about such annuals. Unless they are done really well, they blow up very quickly.

7. Substantially, the same thing may be said about the proposed biography of Wilson. Its chances will depend wholly upon who writes it. I assume that both Bowers and Nevins have publishing arrangements. Bowers would write a long and windy book, but it would probably have a fair chance. I doubt that Nevins' life of Grover Cleveland really did well.

[1] This probably refers to a threatened suit for plagiarism or libel against *The American Mercury*.

8. I know too little about Crozier's work to be able to offer an opinion on him. I have learnt by bitter experience that scientists who do original work are seldom able to describe it in a manner suitable for public consumption. I believe that it might be well to ask Pearl what he thinks of Crozier.

9. His opinion would also be worth more than mine in the matter of the book on experimental embryology. I am wholly unacquainted with this work, and hence have no useful views about it.

10. A good book on diet was published two or three years ago by Dr. McCallum of the Johns Hopkins and one of his associates. It covers the ground that Smith describes, and has been a considerable success. There is, however, always room for another book on diet, for immense numbers of people are dieting at all times.

11. Tolman seems to be an active pressagent of the school of Millikan. Whether his scientific work is really sound I don't know. He has lately appeared in the newspapers as an advocate of technocracy. If he could be induced to do a book I think he could be trusted to whoop it up, maybe with the aid of Millikan.

12. Paul de Kruif is not the man to do a biography of Jacques Loeb. He would make it too romantic. Just who would do it better I don't know.

13. Postgate's suggestion about Neurath sounds interesting indeed. I see no reason why the printing of the charts should not be done at a reasonable expense. Neurath seems to be a very intelligent man, and I think he could be trusted to avoid extravagances. A good many of his charts indeed might be very well printed in one color.[2]

Yours,
M.

To Harry Leon Wilson
[PT]

Baltimore, February 9, 1933

Dear Wilson:

You will be rewarded post-mortem for your very generous letter. It reached me on a day when I was beset by a flood of manuscripts from world-savers, a bad cold in the head, and a notice from my bank

[2] Alfred A. Knopf published *Modern Man in the Making* by Otto Neurath in 1939. Nothing written by Crozier or Tolman was printed by Knopf.

that two more bonds had folded. But I had not got to the bottom of the first page before I was cured. Little did I reck when the American Mercury was started how hard it would work me. The *Smart Set* was easy, for it dealt only with the practitioners of Beautiful Letters, but the Mercury also attracts publicists, sane and insane, and so I linger on a hot spot. For two years now I have been trying to do a book, and it is still only half done.[3] Soon or late I must invent some way to get from under this load.

My best thanks for your invitation to the Grove play. God knows I wish I could say that I'll be on hand, but unfortunately I have some doubts about it. If I get any holiday at all this Summer I'll probably take my wife on a long-promised trip to Europe.

Don't you ever come Eastward any more? I certainly hope you let me hear of it the next time you are in these latitudes.

I saw Sam Blythe at Chicago, and we got down several pleasant drinks together. He is a grand fellow. Thayer is still flourishing in Westport, Connecticut. The last time I heard from him he was engaged in practise as a typographical counsellor. I gather that he has lost a good deal of his money, but that he has enough left to live.

Sincerely yours,
H. L. Mencken

To PHILIP GOODMAN
[EPL]

Baltimore, Md.
February 24, 1933

DEAR PHIL:

The Hugo Wolf and Beethoven portraits and the Schubert cards reached me safely. God will reward you. They are lovely, and I am delighted to have them. The mustard and cheese came in long ago, and I wrote to you at the time saying so. The plain fact is that you never read letters, and I begin to believe that you also evade the reading of magazines. I refuse absolutely to send you any more copies of The American Mercury. You have received two copies every month since you left, and yet you complain that they have not reached you. I have also sent you clippings of my *Sun* stuff from time to time.

[3] Mencken had for some time been working on his *Treatise on Right and Wrong* (New York: Alfred A. Knopf; 1934).

Whatever Red says about it today, he will be believing in a few weeks that "Ann Vickers" is really a masterpiece. The effects of notices upon novelists are well known to psychiatrists. Before he gets back to the United States he will be agreeing with all of the critics that "Ann Vickers" is his greatest work, and that printing "Elmer Gantry" was a great mistake.

Setting up a new magazine really costs nothing. The big printers are so short of work that they will trust anybody, and so are the paper men. There remains only the cost of manuscripts, and in most cases this can be evaded also. I could get out a 128 page magazine at a cash outlay of no more than $500. As a matter of fact, Nathan and I did it in the case of the *Black Mask,* and that was fifteen years ago. Today the printers and paper men are much more accommodating. You will observe that the average new magazine lasts about six months. This means that the printer becomes uneasy at last and clamps down. The moment he does so there is an end of the happy dream.

Sara and I are leaving tonight for the Georgia coast. There is an excellent hotel down there on an island, and we are going to try it for a week. We are quite recovered, but need a few days of loafing and sunshine. After that we'll work our way through Alabama and return home.

Yours,
[*M.*]

To ALFRED A. KNOPF
[AAK]

H. L. Mencken
704 Cathedral St.
Baltimore
April 6th [*1933*]

DEAR ALFRED:–

My thought has always been that with the advent of Hazlitt, or any other new editor, I would clear out altogether. It would probably embarrass him to have me hanging about. If, on the contrary, he depended on me to any extent, I'd still have the magazine on my mind, and it would be difficult for me to do the other work I want to tackle. In all my negotiations with Hazlitt I have told him that he would have a free hand.

But on this point we had better hear him. If you see him alone you can find out precisely what he thinks. In case he believes that I should clear out, and that we should make my clearing out plain, he may hesitate to say so in my presence. What he thinks about my editing of the magazine I don't know. He may believe that I have made a mess of it, and may plan radical changes in it.

In case we come to terms with him he should take over the office not later than the end of September, so that he will have plenty of time to prepare the January issue, which must be made up November 15. There will be some stuff in type, of course, that he can use, but probably not much, and he will want to add enough of his own stuff to flavor the whole. There is thus plenty of time ahead of us. It is possible, if we make a deal with Hazlitt, that he may find someone to buy the magazine, but that is unlikely and unnecessary.

My plan, if I can get loose, is to finish my morals book at once (it is two-thirds done), and to follow it with another and smaller book. After that I propose to rewrite The American Language, probably making two volumes of it. This is a rather large programme, but in addition I'll have to do some magazine articles to keep the pot boiling. However, I think I could get good enough prices to make it unnecessary to do many. The Evening Sun has a standing offer, on very good terms, for any additional time that I can give it, but I don't want to take it if I can help it. But I would like to do an occasional job for The Sun, now impossible.

I am opposed to displacing Angoff for the present. If we make a trade with Hazlitt, he will need Angoff badly, at least for his first four or five months. And if we fail, I'll need him myself. He is of little use for ideas or at conferences, but he does the routine work of the office very well. That is precisely what he was hired for.

Yours,
M.

◇◇◇◇◇◇◇◇◇◇◇◇◇◇

To PHILIP GOODMAN
[EPL]

Baltimore, Md.
May 1, 1933

DEAR PHIL:

[. . . . .]

What are you up to? I often wonder how you put in your days. It would drive me frantic to have nothing to do, and all day to do it in. Why don't you spit on your hands and write something for The American Mercury? We are sweating blood at every pore, but seem likely to survive. Our loss so far this year is very slight. Unfortunately, it catches Knopf at a time when his revenues are enormously diminished. The sales of books in the United States are running below 40% of the sales of a year ago. The whole publishing business, in fact, is paralyzed. There is probably not a solvent bookseller between Maine and California.

The situation of the magazines is quite as bad. Circulation has fallen off at least 40%, and advertising revenues are scarcely 25% of what they were three years ago. The only magazines that seem to be making any real money are the women's magazines, and among them the competition is almost cannibalistic. As for me, I am not worrying. Sara, whose chief market is the women's magazines, has sold more stuff within the last month than she had ever sold before in a whole year. Moreover, she is beset with orders. Thus I hope that she'll earn enough by 1934 to support me in reasonable decency. If so, I shall retire from the public service and devote myself to writing the history of metaphysics.

Yours,
[*M.*]

To Ernest Boyd
[OFP]

H. L. Mencken
704 Cathedral St.
Baltimore
May 5th [1933]

Dear Boyd:

Has the Boyd family gone mashuggah? Some time ago Madeleine wrote to me, hinting that I was lying awake at night and beating my breast over The American Spectator, and now you throw out the same suggestion.[4] What could be more fantastic? I fear you have got a whiff

[4] *The American Spectator,* founded in November 1932, was under the joint editorship of Ernest Boyd, Van Wyck Brooks, Theodore Dreiser, and Eugene O'Neill until 1935, then passed under the editorship of Charles Angoff and ceased publication in 1937.

of one of poor George's complexes. If so, put it out of your mind. I can recall discussing the magazine only once, and then it was to defend a little article written by Angoff. I am surely not going to tell you that Dreiser's monographs thrilled me, but they at least gave me some innocent amusement. I renew my prophecy that the old boy will end in a font of holy water. I incline to believe that you took in too many contributors, and had to put up with too much waste-basket stuff. The magazine would have been much better if you and George had written all of it. Ed Howe shows the right way. He is still going strongly after twenty years.[5]

You are in error also about our exchanges. The last communiqué that passed between us was a note from me to you. I forget what was in it, but if it did not end with Christian sentiments then I must have been in my cups when I wrote it.

Yours,
M.

To ERNEST BOYD
[OFP]

H. L. Mencken
704 Cathedral St.
Baltimore
September 29, 1933

DEAR BOYD:

After a long and expensive investigation, I discover that that wireless was actually sent from the ship by a passenger whose name seems to be Hyman Ulrich, or something of the sort. He sent it to shore and ordered that it be sent back to you. What was in it I simply don't know. I only hope that it fell well within the limits of Christian decency.

Incidentally, I hear that the same person inserted the following in *L'Action Française* for September 14: [6]

---

[5] Ed(gar) *Howe's Monthly* was published in Kansas from 1912 until 1933.

[6] *L'Action Française:* a rabidly reactionary, monarchist periodical founded by Léon Daudet and Charles Maurras in 1908. It is now extinct. Mencken was so delighted with this canard that he had it printed on cards and sent to his friends. The article reads:

"Un Prophete Americain de la Monarchie

La revue de critique l'American Mercury, que dirige le *Juif* Mencken, est, de l'avis de M. Bernard Fay, spécialiste des choses d'Amérique, 'l'une des plus vivantes, des plus pittoresques, des plus typiques des [Etats]—Unis,' en même temps 'qu'une des forces d'opinion les plus solides' ".

I seem to be going up in the world.

Yours,
M.

To Albert G. Keller
[OFP]

H. L. Mencken
704 Cathedral St.
Baltimore
October 4, 1933

Dear Dr. Keller:

Your letter of last week put me on a hot spot. The truth is that I have been trying for a year past to detach myself from The American Mercury. I'll have completed ten years of service at the end of this year, and I want to get rid of my editorial routine and devote myself to a couple of books. The arrangements for my escape have been made at last, though they have not been announced. I make this proposition to you: let your subscription stand for two numbers after my departure. If you then find the magazine uninteresting let me know, and I'll see that you get your money back. But I think that you'll like it, for the new editor is a very competent fellow.[7] I am leaving, of course, under the friendliest of circumstances, and shall continue as a director in Alfred A. Knopf, Inc. I simply find it impossible after six or eight hours a day of hard editorial work to do the kind of writing that I have in mind.

An American Prophet of Monarchy

Mr. Bernard Fay, the specialist of American affairs, states that *The American Mercury*, edited by the Jew Mencken, is "one of the most lively, colorful and typically American periodicals" as well as "one of the most influential on public opinion in the States".

[7] Henry Hazlitt, who became the editor of *The American Mercury* when Mencken resigned in 1933.

I hope you let me hear of it the next time you are in New York.

Some time ago I sent Ed Howe a copy of "The Forgotten Man". It seems to have made a powerful impression upon him, as you will see by the enclosed clippings.

Sincerely yours,
H. L. Mencken

◇◇◇◇◇◇◇◇◇◇◇◇◇◇

To EUGENE F. SAXTON
[PT]

Baltimore, October 9, 1933

DEAR GENE:

Thanks very much for your note. I feel as happy and care-free as the boy who killed his father. The job has been a lot of fun, but I needn't tell you that it has carried a dreadful burden of routine. My true business, after all, is writing books, not editing magazines, and I concluded after long prayer and soul-searching that I had better get to it before it was too late.

Curiously enough, my next book will probably contain a considerable discussion of St. Alphonso Liguori, whose name, by the ways, is always set by the printers as Liquori. I'd hesitate however to do a whole treatise on him, despite my great admiration for his moral ingenuity, but surely it ought to be done.

When are you heading this way again? The club is now beautifully set at Schellhase's Palace Cafe, and the music is louder and better than ever.

Yours,
M.

◇◇◇◇◇◇◇◇◇◇◇◇◇◇

To ELLERY SEDGWICK
[OFP]

H. L. Mencken
704 Cathedral St.
Baltimore
October 9, 1933

DEAR SEDGWICK:–

Thanks very much for your note. I'd have cleared out a couple of years ago, but first the depression landed on us, and then Samuel

Knopf died.[8] After hard struggles, we have got the magazine on what seems to be a safe and even keel again, and so I can depart with a clear conscience. Hazlitt is an excellent fellow. He will, of course, make some changes, but on the whole I believe that they'll be good ones.

I enjoyed the job more or less, but in the last few years its routine has somewhat oppressed me. After all, I am an author rather than an editor, and I think I had better return to my proper trade before it is too late.

Don't you ever get down into these latitudes any more? I'd certainly like to see you soon.

Sincerely yours,
Mencken

To Alfred A. Knopf
[aak]

H. L. Mencken
704 Cathedral St.
Baltimore
November 2, 1933

Dear Alfred:

Needless to say, my collection of wine labels is at Mr. Taylor's disposal. As soon as he lets me know what he wants especially I'll send him specimens. I suggest that a good title for his book might be "Handbook for Wine-Bibbers".

Williams' poems in the main fatigue me severely.[9] Nevertheless, he undoubtedly has a large following, and inasmuch as most of his existing books are inaccessible, I believe that a comprehensive collection of his work will have a chance. He would certainly do a lot of loud whooping for it himself, and he might get some effective aid from the other writers of advanced verse.

Ulman's proposed book on criminology looks very promising.[1] He confessed to me that he had never read any other book on the subject, but that fact is really an advantage, for most of them are dull masses of pedantry. I told him that I thought he ought to base his book on the

---

[8] Samuel Knopf: Alfred A. Knopf's father.

[9] William Carlos Williams, poet and novelist, born in 1883.

[1] Alfred A. Knopf published one book by Joseph N. Ulman: *A Judge Takes the Stand* (New York, 1933).

case system, and try to keep it as far away as possible from the general plan of the other texts. He writes so well that I think he'll make it interesting no matter what he puts in it. He is now toying with a scheme to put down lynching in Maryland. I tried to convince him that it would fail, but he seems determined to go on.

Yours, *M.*

◇◇◇◇◇◇◇◇◇◇◇◇◇

To Harry Leon Wilson
[pt]

Baltimore, November 7, 1933

My dear Wilson:

Considering the fact that Salter is or has been a clerk in Holy Orders it seems to me that his book on Nietzsche is very good stuff.[2] It is, in the main, strictly accurate and though some of its conclusions are probably faulty it is certainly anything but absurd. My own book, done early in life, is an extremely vealy thing. Whether or not it is still in print I don't know, but I am inquiring, and if I can scare up a copy I'll send it to you anon. Please remember that it was written long before I attained to my present unparalleled wisdom, and that I have never had a chance to revise it.

I agree with you thoroughly about metaphysics. Who was it that said that a metaphysician is a blind man searching a dark cellar for a black cat that is not there? [3] Nietzsche, like most young Germans of his class and education, fell under the spell of metaphysics in his youth, and so wrote a great deal of feeble stuff. In later years, however, he became more and more the realist, and toward the end of his life, as, for example, in "The Anti-Christ", he was writing clearly and very vigorously. Have you ever read, by the way, my own translation of "The Anti-Christ"? If not, let me know and I'll send you a copy. I put a great deal of labor into it, trying to reproduce Nietzsche's blistering German in English. I probably failed, but nevertheless I came considerably closer to success than the other translators of the book, all of whom converted it into an essay by Emerson, with corrections by Bruce Barton.

---

[2] W. M. Salter's book: *Nietzsche the Thinker* (London: Cecil Palmer and Hayward; 1917).

[3] The definition of the metaphysician is ascribed to Baron Bowen of Colwood by Mencken in his *Dictionary of Quotations.*

I hope the osteopaths soon lift their ban on coffee. I have to avoid it myself, but somehow manage to drink tea. If they ever take me off beer I'll climb to the top of Al Smith's building and leap into space, hoping to hit Rabbi Stephen S. Wise, or at all events Bishop Manning.

Yours,
H. L. Mencken

To HARRY LEON WILSON
[PT]

Baltimore, November 28, 1933

DEAR WILSON:

A good many of Nietzsche's books are explained on the ground of his early training. He was brought up in an extraordinarily narrow and uncomfortable household. As he grew up he could never quite throw off the ideas thus rammed into him, and in his most florid revolts there was always a touch of prissiness. His glorification of mere strength was in large part a reaction from his own feebleness. He had a bad gizzard, and suffered horribly from headaches and other rather womanish complaints. A number of German critics insist that he died a virgin, but there are others who defend him vigorously against this charge. Certainly the women he showed any interest in were almost unanimously homely. The worst of them was Cosima Wagner, but there were others almost as bad. Once or twice he seems to have been flustered by a cutey as Ibsen was, but he apparently never got very far along the path of sin. Altogether, he was an odd fellow, and in reading his books it is necessary to remember that fact, and not to assume that they are the works of a normal man. He had a considerable bitter wit, but almost no sense of humor.

The Free Will controversy is endless and maddening. I have had to write a couple of thousand words about it for my new book. The job took me weeks, and reduced me to a frazzle. Obviously, your own disposition of it is the correct one. There is not the slightest evidence that man has any actual free will, but his illusion that he has is so powerful that he simply couldn't live without it.

I am taking the liberty of telling George Milburn that you like him.[4] It seems to me that he is the most talented fellow of his years

[4] George Milburn was a junior at the University of Oklahoma when he began contributing to *The American Mercury* in 1929; the notice described him as a "hobo and newspaper writer".

now on view in America. Unfortunately, he lately married and became a father, and in consequence he is now forced into kinds of writing that will do him no good. His wife seems to be a very sensible girl, and in the long run she'll help him, but I am firmly convinced that the cares of a family are not good medicine for a young author.

Yours,
H. L. Mencken

1934

◇◇◇◇◇◇◇◇◇◇◇◇◇◇◇◇◇◇◇◇

To ALFRED A. KNOPF
[AAK]

H. L. Mencken
704 Cathedral St.
Baltimore
January 6, 1934

DEAR ALFRED:

My belief is that the only kind of history of Christianity that would have a chance must be rather agnostic in tone—that is to say, it must describe Christianity completely objectively, and without any pious qualms. There are thousands of good histories done by Christians, and even better ones by mild skeptics. What is needed is a book that gets rid of the religious prejudice altogether. I don't mean a slating, of course, for a large part of the history of Christianity is not discreditable, and all of it is immensely interesting. But the general tone of the book ought to be that of Huxley, not that of Bishop Manning.

Sara and I had to be vaccinated and to take typhoid vaccines, and the combination floored both of us. Thus I lost two days of precious time. However, I am on the last section of the book, and barring further jokes of Yahweh, hope to have it in your hands by the last day of the month. As soon as I do so, I'll come to New York. I'll let you know a week or so in advance. I can imagine nothing more pleasant than meeting Woolsey, Cather and Pforzheimer.

Yours,
M.

◇◇◇◇◇◇◇◇◇◇◇◇◇

To Ernest Boyd
[ofp]

H. L. Mencken
704 Cathedral St.
Baltimore
April 14, 1934

Dear Boyd:

Coming down the gang-plank I walked into a sea of troubles, and so escaped to Baltimore as soon as possible.

That radio scheme sounds interesting indeed. Unfortunately, I am at the moment in negotiation with the N.B.C. on another project, and I can't say either yes or no until I find out how the latter proceeds. The next time I get to New York I'll discuss the business with the N.B.C. brethren at length. As you know, they always have ideas of their own, and it is difficult to move them in any other direction. My private belief is that a dialogue would be much more effective than any conceivable solo. I am to do a short harangue at the end of next week, but that will be merely a casual job. What subject I'll discuss I don't know yet, but it will probably be the sorrows of the time.[1]

I have a valuable souvenir for you from the Holy Land, and shall place it in your hands when we meet. It is a gall-stone passed by Abraham back in the year 1700 B.C. It has been cherished as an heirloom in the Margolis family in Jerusalem, and was presented to me by the present head of the house, J. Lloyd Margolis.

Yours,
M.

◇◇◇◇◇◇◇◇◇◇◇◇◇

To Roscoe Peacock
[ofp]

H. L. Mencken
704 Cathedral St.
Baltimore
April 24, 1934

Dear Peacock:

If I really believed that I had Left a Mark upon my Time I think

---

[1] H. L. Mencken spoke over the N.B.C. radio network (April 27, 1934) on "What is Ahead", a warning to the Brain Trust that the country might eventually rise against it. On February 21 of the following year he delivered another "Address on the Brain Trust".

I'd leap into the nearest ocean. This is no mere fancy talk. It is based on the fact that I believe the American people are more insane today than they were when I began to write. Certainly the Rotarians at their worst never concocted anything as preposterous as some of the inventions of the Brain Trust. They were harmless fools, seeking to formulate a substitute for the Christianity that was slipping from them. But the Brain Trusters, at least in large part, are maniacal fanatics, and will lead us down to ruin if they are not soon suppressed. I believe seriously that if they go on for another year there'll be a march on Washington.

Your renewed arguments in the matter of "Convention City" begin to shake me. Maybe I'll take a look.

Sincerely yours,
H. L. Mencken

To F. Scott Fitzgerald
[PU]

H. L. Mencken
704 Cathedral St.
Baltimore
April 26, 1934

Dear Scott:

I am sorry indeed that you won't be here the rest of the week. Let me hear of it as soon as you get back, and we can have a session. I'll probably have to go to New York myself next week, but if so it will be only for a few days. I hate the town and never go near it if I can help it.

I hope you don't let yourself be upset by a few silly notices. The quality of book reviewing in the American newspapers is really appalling. Reviews are printed by imbeciles who know nothing whatever about the process of writing, and hence usually miss the author's intentions completely. I think your own scheme is a capital one, and that you have carried it out very effectively in the book.[2]

My "Treatise on Right and Wrong" is getting the usual violent denunciations, but it seems to be selling fairly well and I am confident

[2] In a letter to Mencken dated April 23, 1934, F. Scott Fitzgerald had complained that the critics had misunderstood his intentions in writing *Tender Is the Night;* the motif of the "dying fall", he said, was not a result of his own waning dynamism, but it was a deliberate intention throughout.

that it will make its way. My books always start off badly, but usually they keep on selling for a long while.

Please remember me to Zelda. I surely hope that she is making good progress.[3]

Yours,
M.

To ROSCOE PEACOCK
[OFP]

H. L. Mencken
704 Cathedral St.
Baltimore
April 28, 1934

DEAR PEACOCK:

That Nebraska letter is really capital stuff. I have never seen the case stated with more effect. Lorimer is now printing at great length what I was printing in The American Mercury almost a year ago.[4] While I was abroad I happened upon a copy of the *Saturday Evening Post* containing three editorials. It is a literal fact that every one of them took the position that The American Mercury was taking last Summer, and that the arguments of all of them were substantially our arguments. But this, of course, only proves that Lorimer is a man of sagacity.

Sincerely yours,
H. L. Mencken

To RICHARD J. BEAMISH
[PT]

Baltimore, July 7, 1934

DEAR DICK:

There is a rich harvest awaiting Pastor Gardiner in the Maryland Free State. We have not had a genuine spiritual revival for years, and the damned are moaning for hope. I think I could guarantee the Pastor

[3] His wife Zelda Sayre Fitzgerald was in the hospital under treatment for a psychopathic condition.

[4] George H. Lorimer: the editor in chief of the *Saturday Evening Post.*

a net revenue of at least $15 a week for a three weeks' campaign. To be sure, this is not what evangelists used to take, but the times are hard for them as well as for us.

I see nothing ahead in Germany save more disorders. My guess is that Hitler himself will be bumped off very soon. In the long run the Junkers are bound to come back. They have a genuine talent for war, and the means to make it are in their hands. Soon or late they'll clean out all the political quacks and restore the monarchy. My belief is that every really intelligent German longs for them to cut loose. Germany has suffered much more from politics since 1919 than it did from the war during the five years preceding.

The weather in these latitudes is really infernal. I haven't sweated so much since the days when I was studying the catechism.

Yours,
M.

To HARRY LEON WILSON
[PT]

Baltimore, August 23, 1934

MY DEAR WILSON:

Six or eight years ago the London correspondent of the Baltimore *Sun* collected four or five hundred clippings from English papers on the subject of American vulgarity and infamy. He made a little article of them and I printed it in The American Mercury. It showed some extremely amusing things. The truth is that the English have a sneaking fear of the United States, and thus hate it. It is rare indeed for them to mention any American book without sneering at it. I have in my files a great many examples. Even when they can't find anything to sneer at they sneer at the fact that there is nothing to sneer at.

In the next edition of my "The American Language" I shall reply to their libel of Miss Cather by printing a few specimens of English surnames. Some of the hyphenated ones are really almost fabulous. My own relations with the Mother Land have always been rather pleasant. The English reviewers denounce my books, but otherwise they treat me very politely. I know a good many of them, and have boozed with most of them in London. The common belief that Englishmen are hypocrites is probably inaccurate. They are really rather frank fellows, and their dislike for the United States is never concealed. Only the politicians over there pretend that it doesn't exist.

I'll never write another book like "Treatise on Right and Wrong". The materials I collected were so enormous that I was lost in them several times and had to be rescued by police radio cars. At the end I heaved overboard at least twenty pounds of notes. My fear is that the book shows this strain. Maybe I'll go back to it in a few years and try to smooth it out a bit.

What are you up to? The weather here all Summer has been really infernal. The temperature reports tell only half of the story. Almost every day the relative humidity has been higher than the temperature. Fortunately, there is a tremendous supply of really good beer, and so I have managed to survive.

Yours,
H. L. Mencken

◇◇◇◇◇◇◇◇◇◇◇◇◇

To ALFRED A. KNOPF
[AAK]

H. L. Mencken
704 Cathedral St.
Baltimore
September 13, 1934

DEAR ALFRED:

I am loose at last, and am proceeding to North Carolina. When I'll get back I don't know, but it will certainly be before the end of next week.

I think I'd hesitate to read Joe's manuscript without his knowledge. I therefore suggest that you propose to him that it be sent to me. If he says yes, I'll go through it as soon as I get back. I gather from his own account of it that it is somewhat heavy going. My suspicion is that Lorimer is correct in his criticism. Certainly those parts of "The Foolscap Rose" that I have read contained too many characters, and the relation between them is not sufficiently established.[5]

My best thanks for your telegram. At first sight the signature puzzled me, and I thought that one of the New Deal agencies was trying to flirt with me. I put in the day rather miserably, for there was a little flare-up of hay fever. However, it was enormously milder than my old bouts, and so I retain my confidence in the vaccines.

Yours,
M.

---

[5] Joe: Joseph Hergesheimer.

To Marvin Chauncey Ross[6]
[YU]

H. L. Mencken
704 Cathedral St.
Baltimore
September 24, 1934

Dear Mr. Ross:

My apologies for this delay in replying to your note of September 18th. I have been in the South and have just returned.

Unluckily, my view of Miss Stein's genius is somewhat low, so I fear it would sound falsetto for me to do any whooping for her. Her lecture should be a success here, for she is an old Baltimorean and must have a great many friends in the town. I have never met her myself.

Sincerely yours,
H. L. Mencken

To Harry Leon Wilson
[PT]

Baltimore, October 29, 1934

Dear Wilson:

You will enjoy a rich reward in Heaven for sending me so heartening a letter. Both of the books got immensely unfavorable notices, and not a few eminent authorities denounced them with tremendous violence. They fall, of course, between two stools. On the one hand they are completely unsatisfactory to Christians, and on the other hand they don't go far enough to soothe the more militant skeptics. Thus they appeal only to fair men, and fair men are not numerous. Nevertheless, they have done pretty well. "Treatise on the Gods" sold 13,000 copies during its first year, and has been moving along slowly but steadily ever since. The other book did less well, but considering the horrible state of the publishing business it was still on the right side. I'll probably never do another of the same sort. The labor is too dreadful. I am still hauling out the books that I accumulated for "Treatise on Right and Wrong".

John Adams Thayer seems to be still alive. I hear from him at

[6] Marvin Chauncey Ross managed Gertrude Stein's lecture tours.

irregular intervals. Usually he reports that he is engaged in some new scheme that will make him rich. I haven't seen him face to face for five or six years. He is still living at Westport, Connecticut, and a letter sent to him there, without any street address, will reach him.

It is not at all improbable that I may see you on the Coast before the end of 1935. I haven't been there for seven or eight years, and I am eager to see what the repeal of prohibition has done for San Francisco. If Sinclair is elected I'll surely come out on a newspaper enterprise.[7] Four years of him would be certainly too rich. I fear I'd laugh myself to death.

Yours,
H. L. Mencken

◇◇◇◇◇◇◇◇◇◇◇◇◇◇

To THEODORE DREISER
[UP]

[*In his* Smart Set Anthology, *Burton Rascoe had written that Dreiser had refused to help Mencken by sending him contributions for his magazine. Dreiser had immediately written to Rascoe, asking him to retract his accusation, and on the same day (November 20th, 1934), he had also written to Mencken in order to clear himself of the charge. This letter marks the resumption of their correspondence.*]

H. L. Mencken
704 Cathedral St.
Baltimore
November 21st [*1934*]

MY DEAR DREISER:—

It goes without saying that I never suspected you for an instant of saying anything of the sort. Putting aside the wanton libel on Alfred Knopf and the distress I knew it must have given you to be involved in it, the pamphlet gave me a loud laugh, rare enough in these last days before the Second Coming.[8] The source of some of Rascoe's more grotesque statements is only too obvious. The poor fellow is himself a

[7] Upton Sinclair was then running for governor of California on the Democratic ticket; he was eventually defeated after an animated campaign.

[8] The pamphlet: *A History of The Smart Set,* an introduction to *The Smart Set Anthology* (New York: Reynal and Hitchcock; 1934), by Groff Conklin and Burton Rascoe, later reprinted separately.

ridiculous object. He got a stout kick in the pants, and now he is running around rubbing his backside and complaining that it hurts. He has been silly before, and he will be silly again.

I am seriously thinking of doing my literary and pathological reminiscences, probably in ten volumes folio. This is my solemn promise to depict you as a swell dresser, a tender father, and one of the heroes of the Argonne.

My best thanks for your letter. It was decent of you to go to the bat so promptly. The libel on Knopf—perhaps the squarest man in money matters ever heard of—was really filthy and disgusting.

Yours,
Mencken

To HARRY LEON WILSON
[PT]

Baltimore, December 7, 1934

DEAR WILSON:

Whenever I see advertisements like that canary announcement I begin to pine and moan for the old Americana department of the *American Mercury*. Why it has been abandoned by my heirs and assigns I simply don't know. It used to bring in an enormous mail, and was apparently diligently read by thousands of readers.

The other day I had a long letter from Thayer. He is much upset by some idiocies published by one Burton Rascoe. Rascoe has got out a so-called Smart Set Anthology. He tried to stick me up for an introduction and for permission to reprint a lot of my own stuff. When I refused him flatly, he determined upon a schoolboy revenge. His introduction actually depicts me as a peasant standing in awe of the aloof aristocracy of George Nathan! The document is amusing, and I shall certainly not complain of it, for Rascoe gives away his grievance in every line. He included in the original draft a gross libel of Alfred Knopf, and his publishers had to withdraw it. Thayer is also handled somewhat roughly; hence his letter to me. I have advised him to say nothing about it. He seems to be in good health and spirits.

I am going to Washington Saturday night to make a speech at the Gridiron Club dinner. This is a dreadful ordeal for me, and I bespeak the prayers of all Christian people.

Yours,
H. L. Mencken

To THEODORE DREISER
[UP]

H. L. Mencken
704 Cathedral St.
Baltimore
December 8, 1934

MY DEAR DREISER:

Under another cover I am returning your memorandum in the Edwards case. Needless to say, I have read it with the greatest pleasure. As always, you make the drama of the courtroom extremely vivid. The newspaper stories of the trial were naturally confusing and misleading, but as you present it I can see the issues clearly and also gather something of the drama.

In general I agree with you, though a couple of doubts suggest themselves. For one thing I question that the social forces which shape such a boy as Edwards are peculiar to America. As a matter of fact, exactly similar crimes occur in England and on the Continent. In the second place I have some doubt that setting up special courts to try such fellows would accomplish much good. Our whole system is so corrupt that in a little while such courts would be monopolized by professional gangsters. The truth is that society is probably fundamentally wise in putting its Edwardses to death. After all, they are decidedly abnormal, and when they live their careers are commonly very costly to the rest of us.

Hundreds of boys confront a situation exactly analogous to that which faced Edwards, yet they do not resort to murder. My guess is that Edwards himself, if he were liberated tomorrow, would turn out to be incurably unfit to live in the society he was born to, and that soon or late he'd be in the hands of the cops again.

As for the peculiar prejudices of Wilkes-Barre, I see no way to dispose of them. After all, every community is entitled to its own mores. In such matters I am in favor of local self-government. Edwards was born in the place and knew what the penalties were for his acts. I don't think anyone would have molested him if he had simply seduced a few town girls. The thing, in fact, goes on all the time and at a wholesale rate. But he went a shade too far, and so the local morons fell back upon their theology and sent him to the stake. If he had not killed the girl they'd have been proud of him for his prowess. Here I seem to describe a lunatic moral system, but I needn't argue with you that most moral systems are precisely that.

You may recall that you showed me the other night a Japanese book in which there was a chapter on me. I'd like very much to get a copy of it, but I assume that it would be impossible to make a memorandum of the title page inasmuch as it is in Japanese. Could I bother you to lend me the book long enough to have a photostat made? I could then send the photostat to a Japanese book-seller and get the book. My apologies for bothering you, but I'd like to have the book for my files, if only in the hope of impressing the coroner.

My apologies also for a too long letter. Your manuscript should reach you along with this.

Sincerely yours,
M.

◇◇◇◇◇◇◇◇◇◇◇◇◇◇

To EDGAR LEE MASTERS
[OFP]

H. L. Mencken
704 Cathedral St.
Baltimore
December 15, 1934

MY DEAR MASTERS:

The effects of theology upon the female psyche deserve a great deal harder study than they have got. Your reminiscences encourage me to make some notes myself. I once had a curious encounter with a Dunkard girl from Red Lion, Pennsylvania. This poor creature, after a trivial slip with her beau, came to the conclusion that there was nothing ahead of her save to lead a life of shame. So she borrowed $3 and an old dress-suit case and came packing to Baltimore. A polite hackman at Union Station hauled her to Nellie Henderson's old public house. When she told her story Nellie bust into laughter and locked her up in an upper chamber. That evening the late Percy Heath and I were summoned for consultation, and we listened to the poor gal's story. It appeared that the prospect of resorting to harlotry horrified her almost unendurably, but she assumed that her pastor knew his business and that there was no other recourse for her after her sin.

Old Nellie and Percy and I spent three hours trying to convince her that the pastor was wrong, but she stuck to his doctrine. Finally,

Nellie gave her a stiff drink of what the printers used to call hand-set whiskey, and under its influence she was packed in another hack, hauled back to Union Station, and started home for Red Lion. What became of her after that I don't know; nor do I know how she explained her absence to her people and the town gossips.[9]

I have been making notes about the Christian Scientist. She was a strange creature indeed. I haven't heard from her for years, and don't know what has become of her.

Yours,
M.

[9] The anecdote recounted in this letter is told at great length in *Newspaper Days* (New York: Alfred A. Knopf; 1941).

1935

To Theodore Dreiser
[UP]

[On January 3rd, Dreiser asked Mencken if he advised him to join the National Institute of Arts and Letters, as H. S. Canby had suggested. Dreiser eventually declined the honor, but in 1944 he accepted the American Academy of Arts and Letters Award of Merit.]

H. L. Mencken
704 Cathedral St.
Baltimore
January 4, 1935

My dear Dreiser:

Canby's letter offers you a great honor, and if you were a man properly appreciative you'd bust into tears. The National Institute of Arts and Letters includes all of the greatest authors of the country. Prominent among its members are: Louis Bromfield, Stephen Vincent Benét, Struthers Bart, Owen Davis, Edna Ferber, Herman Hagedorn, Don Marquis, Ernest Poole and Agnes Repplier. One of the most eminent members is Hamlin Garland, whose efforts to put down "The 'Genius'" you will recall. These great men and women now propose to lift you up to their own level, and I think you should be full of gratitude.

Seriously, I can't imagine any sensible man joining any such organization. When Red Lewis was elected five or six years ago he refused instantly. Masters, so far as I know, has never been a member, and neither has Anderson nor Cabell. The chief hero of the club ten years ago was Stuart Pratt Sherman.

There is a superior branch of the Institute, known as the American Academy of Arts and Letters. You must yet go a long way, of course, before you are eligible to it. Its leading light is Robert Underwood Johnson, and among its other luminaries are John H. Finley of the *New York Times,* the aforesaid Garland, Judge Robert Grant of Boston, Owen Wister and Paul Elmer More.

Here's hoping that you are lucky in 1935. Christmas in my house was a horror. My wife's mother died on December 23rd and was buried down in Alabama on Christmas morning.

Yours,
H. L. M.

◇◇◇◇◇◇◇◇◇◇◇◇◇◇

To THEODORE DREISER
[UP]

H. L. Mencken
704 Cathedral St.
Baltimore
January 15, 1935

MY DEAR DREISER:

I suggest that the easiest way to deal with the German business will be to write to Karl von Wiegand, Hearst correspondent in Germany. I think he can be reached at the Adlon Hotel, Berlin. If he is not there the New York American office will tell you where he is. I assume that you know him. If not, it is immaterial. He'll be glad to be of any service to you. If for any reason you hesitate to tackle him, I suggest Guido Enderes, Berlin correspondent of the New York Times. He, too, may be reached at the Adlon.

God knows what the Nazis are up to. They seem to be a gang of lunatics to me. I hear that I am also on their Blacklist. Whether they suspect me of being a Jew I don't know. Every now and then I am listed among Jews in some European paper. When this happened a year ago I had the enclosed cards printed and circulated them at large. I have, of course, no means of reaching the Nazis directly. I don't know a single man among them, and all of my friends in Germany seem to be in opposition—that is, all save a few damn fools who I'd hesitate to approach.

Let us discuss all of this when we meet. I'll wait on you at the Ansonia at about 7 P.M. on Wednesday, January 24th.

Yours,
M.

◇◇◇◇◇◇◇◇◇◇◇◇◇

To B. W. HUEBSCH
[OFP]

H. L. Mencken
1524 Hollins St.
Baltimore
January 28th [*1935*]

DEAR BEN:–

My recollection is that I sent the Anti-Censorship Council $10 last year, and so I enclose a check for the same amount. If I am wrong, please ask the treasurer to correct me. I have just concocted a violent protest against the Comstocks' raid on Farrell's "A World I Never Made", a really fine book. But in a lunatic country such things will probably go on forever.

The radicals, as usual, are wrong. I am still against quacks of all sorts, and especially against radicals. Stalin seems to be swindling them in the grand manner, and I am naturally delighted. The pious mind was made to be rooked, whether by the religion of Jahveh or the religion of Marx.

I begin to believe seriously that the Second Coming may be at hand. Roosevelt's parodies of the Sermon on the Mount become more and more realistic. The heavens may open at any moment. Keep your suitcase packed.

Yours,
M.

◇◇◇◇◇◇◇◇◇◇◇◇◇

To BLANCHE KNOPF
[AAK]

H. L. Mencken
704 Cathedral St.
Baltimore
January 28, 1935

DEAR BLANCHE:

Did I tell you the other day that Edgar Masters is at work on his autobiography? I incline to think that the book might have possibilities.

He has, so far as I know, no publishing arrangements at the moment. Nor will he undertake to make any until the manuscript is finished. I suggest making a memorandum about this against Alfred's return. It will be time enough along in March to bring Masters to the office. Tackling him at the moment would probably do no good.

Yours,
M.

◇◇◇◇◇◇◇◇◇◇◇◇◇◇

To JIM TULLY
[OFP]

H. L. Mencken
704 Cathedral St.
Baltimore
February 12, 1935

DEAR JIM:

Thanks very much for the copy of *Rob Wagner's Script*, with your article. It seems to me that, as always, you have done an excellent piece of work. The so-called row with Nathan is completely imaginary. So far as I can recall, I have never had any words with him, and certainly the last time I encountered him he was immensely cordial. We seldom meet simply because the friends of each do not interest the other. Nathan plays with a gang of rich nonentities who seem to me to be extremely tiresome, and I suppose my own friends look pretty much the same to him. The American Mercury business in 1924 apparently left him with some unhappiness, but it simply couldn't be helped.

George Howard was very fond of putting his enemies into stories.[1] He once wrote a piece about Armstrong that was full of bitter stuff. Paul's reply was to put George himself in a one-act play in the character of a hop-head. I knew both of them intimately, and used to enjoy their rows immensely. Howard was much cleverer than Armstrong, but Armstrong was the heavier slugger.

Is there any chance that you'll be in the East in the near future? I surely hope so.

Yours,
M.

---

[1] George Bronson-Howard (1884–1922): writer and playwright.

To ALFRED A. KNOPF
[AAK]

H. L. Mencken
704 Cathedral St.
Baltimore
April 11, 1935

DEAR ALFRED:

I was unfit for writing yesterday, and so managed to get through both of the books. It seems to me that they are of very high merit, and especially Guignebert's "Jesus". Certainly you must do it.

"The Origins of Religion", by Karsten, is also an excellent book. It clears off a great deal of buncombe and presents a completely rational and plausible theory. I may be prejudiced against it because that theory is substantially the one I set forth in "Treatise on the Gods", but Karsten, of course, maintains it with enormously more learning. The pity is that such a book would probably have a very small chance of selling. I therefore don't recommend it specifically, but merely say that it is a really fine work.

The Guignebert is quite as good as his earlier book printed by you—in fact, it is better. There has never been to my knowledge a more competent summarization of the known facts about the history of Jesus.

Both sets of proofs are going back to you by parcels post today.

I have written to Ben saying that I'll be delighted to dine with him any night during the week of April 29. If he sets the 29, let us meet on the 30. If he sets the 30, let us meet on the 29. Will that fit in with your plans?

Sara is making excellent progress, and if the weather would only become reasonably decent she could come home.

Yours,
M.

(1935)

To George S. Schuyler
[OFP]

H. L. Mencken
704 Cathedral St.
Baltimore
May 7, 1935

Dear Mr. Schuyler:

As usual, you blow the quacks 10,000 feet into the air.[2] However, I am not too sure that you have actually butchered them. The scheme to set up a separate State is so magnificently idiotic that it is bound to win customers. My belief is that the Negro wizards of the past, like the whites, have always made the mistake of underestimating the imbecility of their customers. The great masses of the plain people are much dumber than even politicians have ever suspected.

I have been reading with great interest and pleasure your articles in the *Courier* on your Southern tour. In particular, I have been cheered by your reports from Mississippi. Nevertheless, I continue to believe that it will take 200 earthquakes, 50 foreign invasions and the second coming of the Twelve Apostles to lift up that sorry state to the level even of Bridgeport, Connecticut.

Sincerely yours,
H. L. Mencken

To F. Scott Fitzgerald
[PU]

H. L. Mencken
704 Cathedral St.
Baltimore
May 23, 1935

Dear Scott:

Sara's illness distracted me from the Stein book, but I have now finished reading it.[3] I agree with you thoroughly that there is some

[2] George S. Schuyler writes: This possibly refers to some blast I made at the Communist "Self-Determination for the Black Belt" which was then much fancied by the Leftist crackpots. I have an idea that he refers to a piece I wrote in the *Crisis* (official NAACP magazine) for May 1935, entitled the "Separate State Hokum" which was a three-way debate between an advocate of a 49th State for Negroes, a Communist defender of the "Self-Determination" blague, and myself.
[3] The Stein book: *Three Lives.*

excellent stuff in it. In all three of the stories La Stein shows an excellent feeling for character, and some of her minor observations are extremely astute. However, I still hold to the doctrine that her writing is bad. Some of the English in "The Good Anna" is really dreadful, and more than once she forgets on one page what she has written on some previous page, and so falls into transparent contradictions and other absurdities.

At bottom, of course, such things as "The Gentle Lena" are simply sentimental tales of a familiar sort. Nevertheless, she brings something new to them. I believe that if "The Good Anna" and "The Gentle Lena" had reached me in my editorial days I'd have printed them. But I don't think I'd have printed them without sending them back for a few repairs.

Carl Van Vechten's enthusiasm is hardly to be taken seriously. Carl is a great fan for literary oddities, and whenever he happens upon delicatessen of that sort he starts beating the drums. To be sure, he has thus made some propaganda for really first-rate authors, but I think it is only fair to say that he has also whooped up some duds.

The fact that La Stein greatly impressed Sherwood Anderson is completely irrelevant. On all this earth there is no more unreliable literary guide than Sherwood. His estimates of his own stories are usually wrong, and his estimates of the work of other men are even worse.

Sara was making good progress when she succumbed to what seems to have been a mild flu. She has been in bed ever since. I hope, however, to take her northward about the first of June. The Baltimore Summer is too hot and muggy for her, and I am thinking of settling her in the Adirondacks until September.

Are you still on the water-wagon? If you ever slip off far enough to indulge yourself in a few rounds of beer I hope you let me hear of it. I'd like very much to have a sitting.

Yours,
M.

To Ellery Sedgwick
[OFP-MS]

[*On May 31 Sara Mencken died of tubercular meningitis. She was 37.*]

(1935)

H. L. Mencken
704 Cathedral St.
Baltimore
June 7th [1935]

My dear Sedgwick:

Thanks so much for your note—My marriage lasted less than five years, but it was a beautiful adventure while it lasted. Now I feel completely dashed and dismayed. No sensible work is possible, so I am going abroad for a few weeks with my brother, who has been ill. What a cruel and idiotic world we live in!

I hope I'll be seeing you soon.

[Yours,]
H. L. M.

To Benjamin De Casseres
[ofp]

H. L. Mencken
704 Cathedral St.
Baltimore
July 25, 1935

Dear Ben:

I am sending my staff psychoanalyst, Mr. Ralph Schmittkind, to see you. I begin to believe seriously that the hot weather and the evils of the time have made you mashuggah. Go back to beer and you will feel better. Seriously, I am still convinced that the uproar being made by the Jews in this country is doing them far more harm than good. A very definite anti-Semitic movement is gathering force behind the door, and whenever a convenient opportunity offers it will bust out. At that time you may trust me to mount the battlements and holler for the Chosen. Meanwhile, all I can say about Hitler is that he seems to me to be an idiot. That all other Germans are idiots I doubt gravely.

Yours,
M.

To Benjamin De Casseres
[ofp]

H. L. Mencken
704 Cathedral St.
Baltimore
August 3, 1935

Dear Ben:

The peculiar aspect that you note in Germans is not due to sin but to idealism. They are the most talented of human metaphysicians, and it is thus natural that they should look somewhat groggy. If you will go to Columbia University and observe the philosophical faculty you will find that they all look the same way, the Yids along with the Goyim. Give yourself this pleasure some day and you will thank me.

I often marvel that some one doesn't write a really scientific book on anti-Semitism. I have read at least a dozen treatises on the subject, but all of them are bilge. Those written by anti-Semites accuse the Jews of crimes that are palpably imaginary, and generalize as idiotically as a Baptist evangelist. On the other hand, those written by Jews are full of sentimental blah. My belief, often expressed, is that the Jews probably deserve their troubles, but if you ask me to say categorically *why* they deserve them I can't answer you. Go into prayer on the subject and let me hear what your own theory is.

I was told in London that what will amount to an offensive and defensive alliance between the English and Hitler is in the making. The English have apparently concluded at last that the French are quite impossible. Thus you may find yourself toting a musket for Hitler in the next war, for the United States is certain to go into it on the English side—in fact, the English assume that to be the case as a matter of course. They simply don't bother to discuss it.

Yours,
M.

To H. L. Davis[4]
[OFP]

H. L. Mencken
704 Cathedral St.
Baltimore
August 13, 1935

Dear Mr. Davis:

Needless to say, I'll be delighted to have that embellished copy of your book. So far it has not come in from Harper's, but I assume that it will arrive shortly.

I have concocted a florid review for the book section of the *New York Herald Tribune.* I'll stake my oath on every line of it. "Honey in the Horn" seems to me to be the best first novel ever printed in this country, and I incline to believe that it is the best novel of any sort since "Babbitt". You are probably too close to it to see how good it is. I gave it to my brother to read and it set him to yelling. Ordinarily, he dodges fiction assiduously.

When the book comes out it will probably get a rousing reception. The proletarian brethren, of course, will denounce it, but the more intelligent critics are bound to praise it. I was told by Alfred Knopf the other day that he liked it so much that he is writing a blurb for Harper. This is something unusual in publishing. Ordinarily, every publisher devotes a large part of his time to secret whispering against his competitors' books. But Knopf is different.

My most sincere congratualtions. You have done a grand job!

Sincerely yours,
H. L. Mencken

◇◇◇◇◇◇◇◇◇◇◇◇◇

To Benjamin De Casseres
[OFP]

H. L. Mencken
704 Cathedral St.
Baltimore
September 7, 1935

Dear Ben:

It delights me to see you falling for that French bunk. The notion that the French are intelligent is really almost fabulous. They are im-

[4] H. L. Davis (born in 1896): author and contributor to *The American Mercury;* his book *Honey in the Horn* won the Pulitzer prize in 1936.

mensely amusing, but certainly not intelligent. The only really intelligent people on earth are the English. They have no graces and their selfishness is brutal and undisguised, but they can think at least four times as fast as the French and ten times as accurately. Observe what happens in the present situation. In the end the English will have all of the cards and the French will be ready to go on the German block.

I hear that Hitler has offered the Governor-Generalship of Palestine to Streicher, but that Streicher has declined.

Yours,
M.

◇◇◇◇◇◇◇◇◇◇◇◇◇◇

To JIM TULLY
[OFP]

H. L. Mencken
704 Cathedral St.
Baltimore
September 28, 1935

DEAR JIM:

The brethren who are celebrating my funeral may have a surprise in store for them. As soon as I clear off the revision of "The American Language" I'll probably do a number of magazine articles, and in them I hope to tell some plain truths. You are quite wrong about "The American Language". It is worth every moment of time that I put into it. It will long outlast anything else that I have ever written.

It seems to me that the Davis book is a really fine piece of work. All of the objections that the moron critics raise to it are really arguments in favor of it—for example, the objection that it has no plot. Neither has "Tom Jones" any plot, nor "Huckleberry Finn". I asked Romeike to send me all of the reviews of the book, and I have been reading them with great interest. They reveal in a most amusing manner the imbecility of some of the idiots who write reviews for the newspapers.

August and I are preparing to spend a couple of days in the high mountains of western Maryland. I have never been there, and I am very eager to see them. The whole region is very primitive, and cannibalism is still practised in its more remote parts. The rest of the people are violent Baptists and frequently drown a neophyte when they immerse him. I shall wear a bullet-proof vest and carry a machine gun, borrowed from one of the Baltimore bootleggers.

Yours,
M.

To H. L. DAVIS
[OFP]

H. L. Mencken
704 Cathedral St.
Baltimore
October 7, 1935

DEAR MR. DAVIS:

It doesn't surprise me to hear that you are finding a scattering of sensible people in Tennessee. I made that discovery some years ago in the course of a journalistic joint through the South. It is astonishing how many really interesting men and women are hidden in God-forsaken and apparently hopeless towns. I have never been in one that didn't provide civilized society. Often, of course, it had to be enjoyed behind closed doors with the blinds down, but invariably it was there.

Fadiman made a dreadful ass of himself, and the fact will pursue him unpleasantly hereafter.[5] The rest of the Communist brethren were apparently so overcome by the book that they forgot their undying principles. Thus my scheme to write an article on the reviews failed for lack of effective material. I am, however, keeping them, and may have some fun with them in one way or another a bit later on. The standard magazines that turned pink are now paying the penalty. All of them, I hear confidentially, have suffered heavy losses in circulation. Unfortunately, their editors seem to be too stupid to see what an opportunity confronts them. The country is fairly panting for a Tory magazine done with lively humor. Very few Americans are actually Communists at heart. The Red outfits are composed almost wholly of various varieties of recent immigrants. Sometimes those immigrants sport such names as Montague, Jefferson and Smith, but if you run along their family trees for no more than one generation you'll find very strange fruit.

---

[5] Clifton Fadiman was editor at Simon and Schuster. He had been book editor for *The New Yorker* since 1933. He edited *I Believe* in 1939, and is generally a prolific author, as well as a radio and T.V. commentator.

I hope your travels will bring you this far East. I'd be delighted to see you in Baltimore and show you what remains of a medieval city in the last stages of arterio-sclerosis.

Sincerely yours,
H. L. Mencken

P.S. Here is a letter that I sent to you at San Francisco. It was returned by Jim Farley this morning.

To THEODORE DREISER
[UP]

H. L. Mencken
704 Cathedral St.
Baltimore
October 7, 1935

DEAR DREISER:

It is good news that you are returning to the East. I surely hope that the chance offers for a meeting soon after you get to New York. I'll be there off and on all Winter and ready for any deviltry, so long as it remains refined in its main outlines.

I have been grinding away at the rewriting of "The American Language" and have come pretty close to the end. I began it a year and a half ago, but my wife's illness and death interrupted it dreadfully, and it has only been since September that I have put in hard licks on it. The book will be enormous in size—indeed, it will probably make "An American Tragedy" look like a college yell. But the material in hand was so interesting that I simply couldn't resist it.

I haven't read the Carrel book, but it is on my desk and I hope to tackle it shortly. I hear from all competent persons that it is dreadful bilge. Carrel has apparently gone over to Holy Church. Well, this is nothing new. There is a kind of scientist who inevitably weakens in the long run. I give you Millikan and Whitehead as examples. Unfortunately, the real scientists seldom write books dealing with religion, so their position is not known. I have been urging some of my friends among them to form a national association for putting down such Presbyterians as Carrel.

Once I clear off "The American Language" and one or two other small jobs, I'll probably tackle the first four or five volumes of my autobiography. There will be very little news in it, but I am hoping to make parts of it at least amusing. The first volume will deal with my sufferings on the immigrant ship coming over from Poland, and the second will describe my career at Harvard.

Yours,
M.

◇◇◇◇◇◇◇◇◇◇◇◇◇◇

To HAMILTON OWENS
[PT]

Baltimore, October 17, 1935

DEAR HAMILTON:

Unluckily, I know too little about the more recent Irish literature to do that piece. In the early days of the Talbot Press I used to read all of its publications, but that was twelve years ago. The Irish stuff is predominantly gloomy, and after sweating through it for two or three years I finally gave it up. The current Irish, I believe, are turning toward Holy Church. Boyd tells me that the priests now really run the country.

Yours,
M.

◇◇◇◇◇◇◇◇◇◇◇◇◇◇

To VICTOR THADDEUS[6]
[OFP]

H. L. Mencken
704 Cathedral St.
Baltimore
December 17, 1935

DEAR MR. THADDEUS:

Thanks very much for your two letters, and for the enclosure. Despite the speed with which you wrote the story, it reads beautifully, and I have been going through it with the greatest pleasure.

The other day I wrote a little piece for one of the Hearst papers mentioning your incarceration, and arguing that a few weeks in jail would make excellent medicine for every American author. Its tone is jocose, and I hope that you won't be offended. In all seriousness, I believe that the quiet of jail life has its compensations. Now and then, when my telephone is buzzing and the letter-carrier is arriving with fresh heaps of trouble, I long for thirty days in the House of Correction

[6] Victor Thaddeus, an old contributor to the *Smart Set,* refused to pay a one dollar fine for a row with a neighbor, and was jailed for one day.

at Jessops, Maryland. It is a better place than most of the Maryland country clubs. For one thing it is more sanitary, and for another the society is more civilized.

Sincerely yours,
H. L. Mencken

To H. L. DAVIS
[OFP]

H. L. Mencken
704 Cathedral St.
Baltimore
December 27, 1935

DEAR MR. DAVIS:

Typhoid is a God-awful infection, and it doesn't surprise me to hear that Mrs. Davis has had those complications. I surely hope that they have cleared up, and that she is beginning to pick up weight. It used to be the belief in Baltimore, when typhoid was epidemic here, that an attack, if survived, was a life insurance policy. The patient usually grew stout and hearty, and it was most unusual for any of the sequela to be serious. You were lucky to escape yourself. Moral: never drink any water.

It is too bad that you are not getting some money from Harper. Why not ask him to make a payment on account of royalty? It is quite usual for a publisher to do so, and certainly you have earned enough to be treated politely. My guess is that the book will sell steadily much longer than the average novel.

The decay of Red Lewis is tragic indeed. I haven't seen him for several years, and don't want to. My guess is that his present political monkeyshines are largely due to his wife. She is a violent anti-Nazi, and has sound reasons for being so, for the Nazis apparently do not admire her. So far I haven't read "It Can't Happen Here", but I am planning to do so in the near future.

It is grand news that you will be coming to Baltimore with Saxton. He drops in every now and then and we have a pleasant evening. I can show you some durable victuals and the best beer in the Western hemisphere.

Sincerely yours,
H. L. Mencken

1936

To Victor Thaddeus
[OFP]

H. L. Mencken
704 Cathedral St.
Baltimore
February 1, 1936

Dear Mr. Thaddeus:

I'll certainly be delighted to see your pieces about Mrs. Arlt. Let them come to me as above. I'll be away from Baltimore during next week, but after that I'll be here continuously for at least a month.

When my own reminiscences come to be done there'll certainly be a couple of chapters on the old *Smart Set.* The apparent influence of the magazine always amazed Nathan and me. We ran it as a sort of lark, and never took it quite seriously. But it brought us contacts with many charming and ingenious people, and we were lucky enough to bring out a number of writers who have since done extremely well.

Some of these days I must drop off in Wilmington to see you and Mr. Martin. The only other acquaintances I have there are young Alfred duPont and his wife. They are a very amusing couple. A week or so ago they passed through Baltimore and I saw them for a few hours. DuPont, as you probably know, is not in the family business. He is practising as an architect, and is apparently doing very well.

Sincerely yours,
H. L. Mencken

(1936)

To Roscoe Peacock
[OFP]

H. L. Mencken
1524 Hollins St.
Baltimore
March 31, 1936

Dear Peacock:

Journalism is far from an exact science, and McIntyre proves it now and then like all the rest of us.[1] The only dispute I ever had with Nathan was about the conduct of the *American Mercury*, and it ended amicably enough. I seldom see him for the simple reason that the people he is interested in and the things that he regards as important—for example, the theatre—seem to me to be tiresome. But when we do meet we are surely on amiable enough terms. If he were condemned to death tomorrow I'd take him cigars, chocolates and Bibles to the death-house, and I incline to believe that he'd do the same for me.

Sincerely yours,
H. L. Mencken

To J. B. Dudek
[PT]

[Baltimore,] April 30, 1936

Dear Monsignor:

Your review of "The American Language" really overwhelms me.[2] I was frankly somewhat uneasy about it. The trouble with doing so large a book is that one almost inevitably gets lost in the midst of it. I was in fear that I had done that, and that the result was a vast accumulation of undigested materials. But your notice reassures me, and I needn't add that I offer my most profound thanks. It is not only very generous, it is also an excellent piece of writing, and if Canby is really a good editor he'll print it in full.

I was amazed the other day to receive a copy of *America*, a Jesuit

---

[1] Oscar O. McIntyre (born in 1884) had been writing "New York Day by Day" for syndicated newspapers since 1912.

[2] J. B. Dudek reviewed Mencken's *The American Language* in *The Saturday Review of Literature* for May 16 under the title "A Philological Romance".

weekly, containing a flaming advance notice of the book. Who wrote it I don't know. Hitherto *America* has treated me with great suspicion as an enemy of the True Faith and a corrupter of youth. I have always got along very amiably with the *Commonweal,* but not with *America.* Now, however, it gives me its imprimatur, and I begin to suspect that in the end I may really die in the odor of sanctity.

The weather down here is getting warm and work begins to be difficult. I am up to my ears in a history of the Baltimore *Sun,* which will be 100 years old next year.[3] Unfortunately, I have been horribly beset for two weeks past by visitors, many of them strangers who have bothered me without amusing me. This happens at intervals, and apparently can't be helped. Most of my callers have been political propagandists, with new schemes for ending the Depression. I begin to suspect that there are many more lunatics at large in America than in lunatic asylums.

Sincerely yours,
H. L. Mencken

To Upton Sinclair
[OFP]

H. L. Mencken
1524 Hollins St.
Baltimore
May 2, 1936

Dear Sinclair:

I can see nothing unfair or insulting in that somewhat jocose but still quite reasonable speculation. When you proposed to become the savior and boss of California, and then of the United States, you invited the opinion of every citizen as to your qualifications, and with them, of your probable course of action in office. If my own views in that direction differ from your own it may be only because I am a better psychologist than you are. It seems to me that you are a professional messiah like any other, and would perform precisely like the rest if you got the chance. Once in power, you would certainly not be too polite to the money-mad widows and orphans whose stocks and bonds now haunt your dreams.

[3] The book Mencken was then preparing: *The Sunpapers of Baltimore* (New York: Alfred A. Knopf; 1937).

I admit that you have done more or less hollering for free speech, but how much of it did you do during the war, when free speech was most in danger? My recollection is that you actually supported Wilson. If I am right, then you also gave aid and comfort to A. Mitchell Palmer. Well, so did every other Socialist in this great Republic—every one, that is, save a handful. The handful went to jail—for example, Rose Pastor Stokes and Gene Debs.

Your frank disapproval of my controversial technic induces me to say with equal frankness that I think your own is much worse. You have spent your life making reckless charges against all sorts of people—some of them, as when you alleged categorically that the *American Mercury* was financed by unnamed "men of wealth," completely false—and yet you set up a horrible clatter every time you are put on the block yourself. It seems to me that a world-saver ought to be more philosophical, not to say more sportsmanlike.

I am against the violation of civil rights by Hitler and Mussolini as much as you are, and well you know it. But I am also against the wholesale murders, confiscations and other outrages that have gone on in Russia. I think it is fair to say that you pseudo-communists are far from consistent here. You protest, and with justice, every time Hitler jails an opponent, but you forget that Stalin and company have jailed and murdered a thousand times as many. It seems to me, and indeed the evidence is plain, that compared to the Moscow brigands and assassins, Hitler is hardly more than a common Ku Kluxer and Mussolini almost a philanthropist.

If you will denounce the orgy of sadistic fury that has gone on in Russia in terms at least as violent as those you have applied to your political opponents for years past, then I'll be glad to print your denunciation, and to hail you with joy as a convert to fair play. And if you will acknowledge publicly that your quack friend, Dr. Albert Abrams, was a fraud, and that your support of his spondylotherapy was idiotic, then I'll engage to cease mentioning it. But you can't ask me to stop discussing you freely, and speculating about your political and other hallucinations so long as you keep on trying to get on the public payroll, trafficking with (and being gulled by) such obvious demagogues as Roosevelt, making whoopee out of the pathetic hopes and illusions of poor and miserable people, and reviling everyone who shows better taste and better sense than you do.

In political controversy there is such a thing as give-and-take. If you want to speak your mind freely, you must let your opponents speak their minds freely, even when what they have to say collides with your vanity and violates your peculiar notions of the true, the good and the beautiful, whether in politics, theology or pathology. It seems to me that you fail here. You are far, far better on the give than on the take. No man in American history has denounced more different people than you have, or in more violent terms, and yet no man that I can recall complains more bitterly when he happens to be hit. Why not stop your caterwauling for a while, and try to play the game according to the rules?

Yours,
Mencken

◇◇◇◇◇◇◇◇◇◇◇◇◇◇

To EDGAR LEE MASTERS
[OFP]

H. L. Mencken
1524 Hollins St.
Baltimore
May 5, 1936

DEAR MASTERS:

Sometimes I begin to doubt seriously that Boyd is really right with God. Like you, I frequently meet him in saloons, but I can't recall ever seeing him entering a house of worship. His whiskers, I often suspect, are a deliberate libel on our Redeemer.

My belief is that Whitman's talk about illegitimate children was all hooey. I doubt that he ever had anything to do with women. I doubt equally that he was actually a homosexual. He was really probably a nomo, if I may be permitted by the faculty to coin a word. There are many such men, and I could give you a long list of them. They seem to be completely devoid of sexual enterprise, though many of them show a considerable interest in the subject. Indeed, the number of male virgins in the world is enormously greater than most people appear to believe. Some of these days I hope to do an article on the subject.

By this mail I am sending you an account of the exorcism of a demon from a poor Christian in Iowa. You will laugh when you look at the title page of the book, but before you have read ten pages your eyes will be bulging. Down here in Maryland the powers and principalities of the air are still in full function. I know at least thirty people who have been bewitched. At this very moment, indeed, one of the leading clergymen of Baltimore shows plain signs of demoniacal possession.

Yours,
H. L. M.

To Roscoe Peacock
[OFP]

H. L. Mencken
1524 Hollins St.
Baltimore
May 7, 1936

Dear Peacock:

Communists have no more humor than Christians. No man who believes in apocalypses can possibly bring himself to laugh. But though he can't laugh himself, he is a constant source of mirth in others. My belief is that the Communists constitute the best bit of comic material on tap in America since the disappearance of the Single Taxers. If the chance offers after the campaign gets under way, I certainly hope to give them a few licks.

My reference to Upton Sinclair in the *American Mercury* for May offended him gravely, and he has demanded space to answer me. Paul Palmer is giving it to him, but he is also allowing space for me to answer Sinclair's answer. This combat promises to give me some pleasant entertainment.

Sincerely yours,
H. L. Mencken

To Upton Sinclair
[OFP]

H. L. Mencken
1524 Hollins St.
Baltimore
May 12, 1936

My dear Sinclair:

You duck artfully, but not enough to get out of range. *Exemplia gratia:*

1. You protested when the late A. Mitchell Palmer jailed Reds,

but all the while you supported his boss, Wilson. In other words, you objected to the St. Valentine's Day massacre, but certified to the virtue of Al Capone.

2. The American Mercury was *not* backed by "gentlemen of wealth". Every cent of the small sum it took to launch it was supplied by its publisher, Alfred Knopf. In a few months the magazine was paying its own way. When I showed your nonsense to Knopf, he laughed, and in The American Mercury for February, 1928 I laughed too, as all sensible men laugh at palpable imbecilities.

3. The difference between Abrams's spondylotherapy and his electronic vibrations was the difference between tweedledum and tweedledee. Both were bald and shameless frauds. If you will produce evidence that Lord Horder, or any other reputable medical man, ever said that either would cure syphilis and cancer, which is what Abrams claimed for both, I'll stop mentioning your childish belief in his *bona fides.*

You evade the question of your political sword-swallowing. What is to be thought of a great lover of the down-trodden who ran for Congress as a Socialist in 1920, for the United States Senate as a Socialist in 1922, for Governor of California as a Socialist in 1926, and then popped up in 1934 as a life-long Democrat, and entered upon negotiations with such professional politicians as Franklin D. Roosevelt and Jim Farley, and incidentally, was taken for a ride? What is to be thought of him save that he has learned, like any other chronic job-seeker, to rise above principle? What is to be thought of him save that the itch for office has got him down, and is burning him up?

According to news items reaching the East, you were lately running for something or other again. The people of California, it appears, turned you down, along with your brother messiah, Dr. Townsend. With the utmost friendliness, I can only say that I think they showed sound judgment. They have had plenty of chance to estimate both you and Townsend, and they prefer anybody else, including even Hoover. They refused to follow you as a Socialist, they refused to follow you as a Prohibitionist, they refused to follow you as an electronic vibrator, they refused to follow you as a thought transferer, they refused to follow you as a Democrat, and now they refuse to follow you as anything whatsoever. The rule is that three strikes are out. To the bench, Comrad; to the bench!

Yours,
Mencken

[*This letter, as well as that of May 2nd, 1936, was printed in the "Open Forum" of* The American Mercury *for June and July 1936.*]

To UPTON SINCLAIR
[OFP]

H. L. Mencken
1524 Hollins St.
Baltimore
May 26, 1936

DEAR SINCLAIR:

I observe that Palmer has printed our first exchange of letters in the current *American Mercury,* but that the second pair is missing. Whether he proposes to print them next month I don't know. Readers, I take it, enjoy such debates. In any case, your enemies will be pleased by what I say of you and mine will be pleased by what you say of me.

Rather curiously, it took very little money to start the *American Mercury.* The printer offered credit for the first few numbers, and by the time they were off subscriptions began to roll in so fast that the magazine almost financed itself. At various times later on Knopf made investments in the magazine, chiefly in an effort to improve it. But it really supported itself from the start. Many other successful magazines have been launched with just as little money. The amount put into *Time* must have been very small—in fact, magazines that start off with fat treasures seldom do very well. What the moral of this may be I don't know.

In a couple of days I shall send you a Maryland madstone, examined and passed by the State Board of Examiners. As an old Marylander, you will know how to use it.

Sincerely yours,
H. L. M.

(1936)

To CARL VAN DOREN
[OFP]

H. L. Mencken
1524 Hollins St.
Baltimore
September 1, 1936

DEAR CARL:

I have just written a brief review of "Three Worlds" for Joe Krutch. I am only sorry that it isn't better. Unfortunately, I found so many pleasant references to myself that I was somewhat wobbled, and so when I seized my pen in hand the flow of swell ideas was somewhat impeded. I read the book with the utmost pleasure. It is full of interesting and amusing stuff, and it is a beautiful piece of writing. I make a suggestion at the end of my review that I hope you will heed.

There is one slight error. It has to do with my old feud with Sherman. My objection to Sherman was not that he denounced *me* as pro-German. As a matter of fact, I was on the best of terms with various men who had done the same thing. Until the United States got into the war and free speech was cut off, I was writing politics in the Baltimore *Evening Sun* almost daily, and my arguments in favor of the Germans were certainly not pianissimo. It seemed to me, therefore, to be quite fair for anybody to denounce me for what I had done. My objection was to Sherman's denunciation of *Dreiser.* Dreiser had written nothing about politics, and was hardly interested in the subject. The accusation that he was pro-German was made without adequate evidence and had the obvious effect of greatly damaging him at a time when he surely had enough other troubles. It seemed to me that in the heat of controversy Sherman hit below the belt, and that's the reason I refused to have anything to do with him. But I certainly never complained about what he wrote about *me.* As a matter of fact, I have always made it a point to take such things lightly. And, as I have said, I got on very well with some of the patriots who belabored me violently during the war. I should add, of course, that as soon as my hands were free I did my best to cave in their literary skulls.

We meet far too seldom. Don't you ever get into these latitudes? I have spent the whole Summer following the politicoes for the Baltimore *Sun,* and having a roaring time. The Townsend and Coughlin conventions at Cleveland were really magnificent. Nothing more completely idiotic has been seen on earth since the Scopes trial.

Yours,
H. L. M.

To HUNTINGTON CAIRNS[4]
[OFP]

H. L. Mencken
1524 Hollins St.
Baltimore
October 19, 1936

DEAR MR. CAIRNS:

Thanks very much for that copy of the London *Times Literary Supplement.* It was kind indeed of you to think of me.

I met Miller when he was in New York last Spring.[5] His books have always impressed me most favorably. To be sure, the stuff he is now writing can't be printed in America, but nevertheless it seems to me to be quite serious in intent, and extremely competent in execution. He is a wild fellow, and his political ideas are probably mainly fantastic, but he has a really diabolical talent for getting character on paper. His new book, dealing largely with the customers of his father's tailor shop, is full of capital stuff.

I begin to doubt that there will be any war at all. It is a pity.

Sincerely yours,
H. L. Mencken

To J. B. DUDEK
[PT]

[Baltimore,] November 13, 1936

DEAR MONSIGNOR:

That letter by Oscar Henshaw of the Southwestern Teachers College in the *Daily Oklahoman* is really most astonishing. He says: "The right to free speech in America is indeed threatened by such an

---

[4] Huntington Cairns (born in 1904) is a lawyer and a writer, now treasurer and general counsel of the National Gallery in Washington, D. C.

[5] Miller: Henry Miller, the novelist; he was on friendly terms with Mencken.

attitude as Henry Mencken assumes toward Earl Browder".[6] As you will recall, the only thing I wrote about Browder was a denunciation of the cops who interfered with him in Terre Haute. In other words, I argued that he should be given the same right of free speech that everyone else is supposed to have. Despite that fact, this imbecile pedagogue now denounces me as an enemy of free speech.

I begin to believe seriously that large numbers of the American people are completely incapable of understanding English. Whenever I write anything that sets up controversy its meaning is distorted almost instantly. Even the editorial writers of newspapers seem to be unable to understand the plainest sentence. I ascribe all this to the public schools. They have been debauching the American mind for years and they are chiefly responsible, it seems to me, for such aberrations as the New Thought, Coughlinism, Osteopathy, and the New Deal.

Sincerely yours,
H. L. Mencken

To Ezra Pound
[PT-CC]

November 28, 1936

My dear Pound: [7]

You are something behind-hand with that tirade, but if you want to print it I surely have no objection. Everything you say has been said before, first by the war patriots, then by the Ku Kluxers, then by the Anti-Saloon League brethren, then by the Harding visionaries, then by the Coolidge ditto, then by the apostles of Hoover's New Economy, and now by the New Dealers and Union Square Communists, with

---

[6] Earl Browder (born in 1891) was general secretary of the Communist Party in the United States from 1930 until 1944. He was expelled from the party in 1946.

[7] About this letter, Mencken writes: (Ezra Pound) is now doing radio crooning for the Italians. I have known him for many years. In the 1930's he became converted to the Douglas scheme of Social Credit, and began bombarding me with long letters on the subject. When I refused to be converted he took to abusing me. The first of these letters is my response to a long tirade. He must have answered politely, for my second letter seems less violent. I saw him in New York in 1939, but since then have had only one or two brief notes from him. (H. L. Mencken to Julian P. Boyd, December 1, 1942.) In fact there seems to have been a voluminous exchange of letters between them after 1936.

applause all along the line by the Single Taxers, chiropractors, anti-vivisectionists, sur-realists, anti-Darwinians, Rotarians, Kiwanians, thought-transferers, Fundamentalists, Douglasites, pacifists, New Thoughters, one-crop farmers, American Legionaires, osteopaths, Christian scientists, labor skates, and kept idealists of the *New Republic.*

In brief, you come to the defense of quackery too late. All you say or can say has been said 10,000 times before, and by better men. I say better men because there is plainly a quantitative if not a qualitative difference between quackeries, and hence between the gullibility of their customers. Thus, the imbecility of the New Thought is obviously a shade less painful than that of Fundamentalism, and the imbecility of the Townsend Plan is appreciably less obvious than that of the Douglas Plan. Indeed, it must appear to every man not afflicted by the believing neurosis that there is more sense in even T. S. Eliot's surrender to High Church Episcopalianism than there is in your succumbing to the Douglas rumble-bumble.

You made your great mistake when you abandoned the poetry business, and set up shop as a wizard in general practise. You wrote, in your day, some very good verse, and I had the pleasure, along with other literary buzzards, of calling attention to it at the time. But when you fell into the hands of those London logrollers, and began to wander through pink fogs with them, all your native common sense oozed out of you, and you set up a caterwauling for all sorts of brummagem Utopias, at first in the aesthetic region only but later in the regions of political and aesthetic baloney. Thus a competent poet was spoiled to make a tin-horn politician.

Your acquaintance with actual politics, and especially with American politics, seems to be pathetically meagre. You write as if you read nothing save the *New Masses.* Very little real news seems to penetrate to Rapallo. Why not remove those obscene and archaic whiskers, shake off all the other stigmata of the Left Bank, come home to the Republic, and let me show you the greatest show on earth? If, after six months of it, you continue to believe in sorcery, whether poetical, political or economic, I promise to have you put to death in some painless manner, and to erect a bronze equestrian statue to your memory, alongside the one I am setting up in honor of Upton Sinclair.

Meanwhile, please don't try to alarm a poor old man by yelling at him and making faces. It has been tried before.

[*Unsigned*]

1937

To Ezra Pound
[PT-CC]

January 12, 1937

Dear Pound:

Whether you read the *New Masses* or don't read it, you at least argue precisely like the comrades. The world is out of kink; *ergo,* let us sample every new peruna that comes along. I can see no difference between the Douglas scheme and any other of the current quackeries. They all hold out vain hopes to poor and miserable people, and can only make them more unhappy. Some tin-horn messiah is now trying out Douglasism in one of the Western provinces of Canada. It is doing about as well as the Single Tax did in New Zealand. That is to say, it is driving all civilized people out of the place, and giving the *Chandala* nothing but a headache.

It seems to me that one of the prime jobs of every educated man on this earth is to denounce charlatans. New ones are always popping up, and the common run of idiots are always succumbing to them. There is little if any difference between one and another. The Hoover New Economy was no better and no worse than the New Deal. Communism in all its essentials is on all fours with primitive Christianity. And all the jackasses who now try to embellish literature by writing gibberish are only bastard sons of Euphuism.

I invite you again to come home, shave off your medieval disguise, and see the show. If you don't revolt against it in ten days, then

I'll have you put to death as hopeless. The country reeks with frauds, and the only thing to be said in favor of them is that many of them are very amusing. It is a gorgeous spectacle, but it has no more significance than a duel between Tom cats. When it is over the poor fish who now sweat with hope will still be slaves, doomed to dull and ignominious toil for scoundrels, world without end.

I have just got out of hospital and am shoving off to Florida for a week of sunshine. I haven't had a holiday for nearly two years. What floored me was a throat infection—not dangerous, but a great nuisance.

I am sending you a dozen Gideon Bibles.

[*Unsigned*]

To THEODORE DREISER
[UP]

[*On January 12th, Dreiser asked Mencken what he thought of the current literary trends, particularly in the field of fiction, and requested a list of the most notable works written during the past ten years.*]

H. L. Mencken
1524 Hollins St.
Baltimore
January 22, 1937

DEAR DREISER:

I'll probably be back in New York before you leave finally. The week in Florida gave me a big lift, and I begin to feel like work again. My desk, of course, is piled mountain high, and it will take me a little while to dig through the accumulation. I suggest that we have dinner alone and go through the matters you discuss. It seems to me that there is a great deal of quackery in literature, as there is in politics. Most of the geniuses discovered by the Communists are simply imbeciles. But I have considerable confidence in young Farrell, despite his political hallucinations. His new book, just out, contains some really excellent stuff.[1]

I saw Gloom several times during the Autumn. She came to Baltimore to visit her brother, who was laid up here in hospital. She

[1] James T. Farrell's new book: *A World I Never Made* (New York: The Vanguard Press; 1936).

looked to be in excellent health, and was in her usual depressed but amiable spirits.

I surely hope that you find a buyer for your house. The real estate market seems to be improving rapidly. Down in Florida the realtors are prancing around in their old form. Every one I saw had on a new suit of clothes and a new hat.

Yours,
M.

◇◇◇◇◇◇◇◇◇◇◇◇◇

To EDWARD STONE[2]
[UV]

H. L. Mencken
1524 Hollins St.
Baltimore
March 1, 1937

DEAR MR. STONE:

In my own mind my debt to Nietzsche seems very slight, though I confess that other people seem to have put a larger value on it. I read him at the suggestion of Harrison Hale Schaff, head of the firm of J. W. Luce and Company of Boston, which had published my little book on George Bernard Shaw in [1905]. My knowledge of Nietzsche at that time was very superficial. Most of his books had not been translated. I tackled the original German and found it dreadful going. However, after a winter of hard work, I managed to formulate a more or less coherent idea of his system, and upon that basis I wrote my book. It made an unexpected success, and is still in print. It should have been revised long ago, but Schaff for some reason or other refuses to let me touch it.

There has been no biography of me since Goldberg's. The gaps it leaves could be very easily filled. I am naturally interested in your project, and if I can give you any help, I'll certainly be delighted to do so.

Sincerely yours,
H. L. Mencken

---

[2] Edward Stone wrote *H. L. Mencken's Debt to F. W. Nietzsche,* M.A. thesis (University of Texas, June 1937).

◇◇◇◇◇◇◇◇◇◇◇◇◇◇

To Edgar Lee Masters
[OFP]

H. L. Mencken
1524 Hollins St.
Baltimore
March 12, 1937

Dear Masters:

I hear from a clerical friend at Princeton that More's end was very beautiful.[3] He died with the Holy Scriptures in his hand and in the hope of a glorious resurrection. He was buried by the Free Masons, with the assistance of the Elks, and no less than three clergymen took part in the services. They closed with a mass singing of the old hymn, "Whiter Than Snow".

I am sorry that I never met More. We had some pleasant enough exchanges ten or twelve years ago. He really knew a great deal, but all his thinking was corrupted by piety. He could never see the thumping contradictions in his books. In one of them, after proving the complete imbecility of all the cardinal Christian doctrines, he embraced them with a whoop at the end. Such men, it seems to me, are not hard to understand. The poisons of piety still run in their veins, and they are never able to think quite clearly.

I am hoping to get to New York very soon, and to have the honor of beholding you.

Yours,
M.

To Edward Stone
[UV]

H. L. Mencken
1524 Hollins St.
Baltimore
March 31, 1937

Dear Mr. Stone:

My book on Nietzsche was written many years ago, and it was not until afterward that I met Dr. Oscar Levy, the owner of the English

[3] More: Paul Elmer More (1864–1937), the critic and writer.

rights to his works. Dr. Levy is a physician, and was well acquainted with both Nietzsche and his sister. He tells me that there is no reason whatever to believe that Nietzsche was a syphilitic. His illness, in fact, suggested strongly that he was not. As I recall it, Dr. Levy is in some doubt about Nietzsche's virginity, but on that point my recollection is not quite clear. I have not met Dr. Levy for three years, though I am in frequent communication with him. If you want to write to him, tell him that I suggested it. His address is Hotel Masséna, Monte Carlo, Monaco.

[. . .] I must confess that I didn't read his [O'Brien's] book very attentively. I am thus unable to express any opinion about it.[4]

Sincerely yours,
H. L. Mencken

To Edgar Lee Masters
[ofp]

H. L. Mencken
1524 Hollins St.
Baltimore
April 17, 1937

Dear Masters:

When you set John Dewey to thinking you really put him in peril of his life. He is a teacher, not a thinker. Go read any of his books save his Ethics, which apparently was written by his collaborator Tufts. Old John himself is the dullest writer heard of on earth since Apostolic times. I defy any man to read ten pages of him without scratching.

The current pinks amuse me greatly. They are in for a dreadful disappointment—indeed, I am half convinced that their uproars will eventually bring in some sort of Fascism. As for me, I don't care. Long before the concentration camps open I'll be an angel.

Yours,
M.

---

[4] The book was *Forward with Roosevelt,* written in 1936 by Patrick Joseph O'Brien and published by the John C. Winston Co., Philadelphia.

To Edward Stone
[UV]

H. L. Mencken
1524 Hollins St.
Baltimore
May 3, 1937

Dear Mr. Stone:

I refuse absolutely to let you pay postage on the return of your manuscript. I have had great pleasure reading it, and only hope that it gets into print, so that I may have a permanent copy.

As you know, I was under the impression that my debt to Nietzsche was very slight. I must say now that your argument rather shakes me. Such influences are exerted, it appears, very insidiously. I was picking up Nietzscheisms without being aware of them, and they undoubtedly got into my own stuff. Certainly you maintain your thesis with immense plausibility, and, as I say, I am half inclined to confess conversion to it.

My best thanks for your friendly interest. I shiver when I think of the immense work that you put into the thesis. I only hope that you didn't carry away the determination to read me no more.

Sincerely yours,
H. L. Mencken

To Roscoe Peacock
[OFP]

H. L. Mencken
1524 Hollins St.
Baltimore
May 12, 1937

Dear Peacock:

It is not the lack of better men that causes Luce to employ pinks; it is simply the fact that they are cheaper. At least four-fifths of the really competent authors of the country are against the present reign of hooey. I marvel that some one doesn't set up a conservative weekly and turn them loose. Such a weekly, if it were carried on with wit, would be an immediate and permanent success. As things stand, the pinks have all the sounding boards.

The editors accumulated by Luce are mainly incompetent. Both *Fortune* and *Time* are inaccurate and silly. The style of writing that they have popularized is palpably fifth rate.

Yours,
Mencken

To WHEELER SAMMONS, JR.[5]
[YU]

H. L. Mencken
1524 Hollins St.
Baltimore
May 14, 1937

DEAR MR. SAMMONS:

Thanks very much for the chance to read your thesis, and especially for your extreme generosity. You treat me humanely indeed, and I assure you that I am grateful. The copy that you so kindly sent me will go into my archives, and when I am converted into an angel it will pass to the public library here in Baltimore. Thus it is assured of being cherished throughout the remaining history of the unfortunate human race.

My publisher wants me to do my reminiscences, but I find myself little inclined to write about my professional career. What interests me most, looking backward through the years, is my childhood here in Baltimore. The town was extraordinarily backward and barbaric in those days, but also extraordinarily pleasant. I have thought of doing a small volume on it, to be called "Happy Days", or something of the sort. It would deal with my first twelve years. The years following can wait—if indeed I ever write about them at all. My somewhat wide acquaintance among authors has convinced me that most of them are dull fellows. All literary reminiscences, it seems to me, read pretty much alike.

My best thanks again for your friendly interest.

Sincerely yours,
H. L. Mencken

---

[5] Wheeler Sammons, Jr., had written a B.A. dissertation at Harvard on "H. L. Mencken, Humorist and Reformer". He was the son of Wheeler Sammons, well-known publisher and world-wide specialist in economics and political science.

(1937)

To Blanche Knopf
[AAK]

H. L. Mencken
1524 Hollins St.
Baltimore
July 7, 1937

Dear Blanche:

God knows I wish I could drop in on you at Pocasset, but I fear it will be impossible before August 6th. Some time ago I rashly undertook to do a series of articles on the Johns Hopkins Hospital for the *Sun.* The job looked easy, but now that I am in it I find that it is full of grief. The amount of stuff I am writing is not large, but getting the material for it involves making a great many visits to the hospital to consult the various chiropractors. When I finish the job I'll know more about the place than anybody in it.

There is an excellent book in George S. Schuyler, the colored author who used to write in the *American Mercury.* Schuyler is the best writer the Negroes have ever produced, and moreover, he is a highly intelligent man. If you could induce him to do a frank book on the present situation of his people in this country it would probably make a sensation. He loves to tell the truth, and the truth in this case is full of surprises. He is the bitter enemy of all the uplifters who presume to uplift the darker races. Some time when I am in New York we must get hold of him and talk the thing out with him. I really believe that he could give you something extraordinary.

Yours,
H. L. M.

To Oswald Garrison Villard
[PT]

Baltimore, August 16, 1937

Dear Mr. Villard:

I find your letter on my return to Baltimore. It rather surprises me, for it is news to me that your article has been dropped—if, indeed, it be a fact. I am going to the office and I'll inquire about it and write to you again. John Owens told me some time ago that he was extremely hard pressed for space, but he said nothing about stopping any feature then running.

It is excellent news that you are doing your memoirs. Certainly I hope you write them at length, and tell the whole truth. You have seen a lot of interesting things, and you know how to describe them.

I am toying with the idea of doing a brief volume of my first twelve years. It would be a sort of picture of Baltimore during the 80's, with incidental discussions of the origin and growth of my own theological system. Certainly writing such a book would be a lot of fun.

Broun, it seems to me, has become the perfect jackass. I can imagine nothing more idiotic than his proceedings at St. Louis. He has wrecked the Newspaper Guild. For one, I am convinced that it was needed, and that if it had been properly managed it might have done a lot of good, not only to newspaper men, but also to decent newspapers. There was no opposition to it in the *Sun* office here. But it is impossible, of course, to ask newspaper executives to swallow the St. Louis programme, and to accept such an ass as Broun as the dictator of American journalism.

Sincerely yours,
H. L. Mencken

To ALFRED A. KNOPF
[PT]

Baltimore, September 15, 1937

DEAR ALFRED:

I hear from Leary, Stuart that your office reports "In Defense of Women" out of print, and that it is also out of print in the dollar Doubleday edition. Do you think it would be worth while to revise and reissue it? As it stands, the text is somewhat archaic, and I'd hesitate to see any more copies come off the same plates. But I believe I could revise it in a month of work, and make it more or less salable again.

My present plan is to tackle "Advice to Young Men" almost at once. I have put it off during the Summer in order to clear off various minor jobs, but now I begin to feel like writing again. It promises to be a short book—probably not much larger than "In Defense of Women".

I could tackle "In Defense of Women" immediately after finishing "Advice to Young Men".[6]

Yours,
M.

To WILLIAM LYON PHELPS
[PT]

Baltimore, October 4, 1937

DEAR BILLY:

A note from Governor Cross indicates that I am expected to deliver a formal lecture to your customers on the Bergen Foundation. This news really appalls me. I am very little interested, in fact, in current American literature, and concocting a plausible lecture on the subject would stagger me. Wasn't it our understanding that all I'd have to do would be to appear before your students and answer questions? If that can be arranged I'd certainly much prefer it. Let me hear about this.[7]

Yours,
H. L. M.

To WILLIAM LYON PHELPS
[PT]

Baltimore, October 9, 1937

DEAR BILLY:

Thanks very much. You relieve me immensely. It would help me further if you would ask some of your bright young men to form a *few questions in advance.* That would give me a good start. Once I am wound up, I go ahead at full speed. Better still, send me a few questions of your own. I hate to put this burden on you, but I think the show will be better if it is free and easy than if I attempt a formal lecture.

---

[6] The new edition of *In Defense of Women* was never done; *Advice to Young Men* was planned for years by Mencken, but was never written.

[7] Mencken was scheduled to speak before the students at Yale; he actually refused to deliver a formal lecture, but simply answered questions.

My book shows that the date is November 15th and the time 5 P.M. If that is incorrect let me know.

Yours,
M.

To JAMES M. CAIN[8]
[OFP]

H. L. Mencken
1524 Hollins St.
Baltimore
October 18, 1937

DEAR JIM:

Digging up the notes for "The Charlatanry of the Learned" was really much simpler than it looks. I discovered some excellent old German encyclopedias at the Peabody Library, and they contained everything that I wanted. My brother was working on a book at the same time, and spending nearly every evening at the Peabody. I would join him there, and after a couple of hours of easy prospecting, we'd proceed to Schellhase's kaif and there get down a few beers. It was a pleasant life, and my trachitis gradually disappeared.

The meaning of *cluck* I don't know. It seems to suggest Ku Klux, but that resemblance may be deceptive. I wish we had some decent etymologists in this great Republic. The professionals are all dubs. They regard it as *infra dig.* to put in any time on the words used every day by 125 million of the plain people.

Lippmann's book, like all of his books, leaves me flat.[9] It seems to me that he is best in short articles. Whenever he launches upon a long argument it begins to sag, and in the end the effect is feeble. I have never been able to understand the great popular success of some of his earlier books. He writes beautifully, but I always get the feeling that he is afraid to offend.

---

[8] James M. Cain (born in 1892): ex-Baltimore *Sun* reporter, and novelist. He wrote *The Postman Always Rings Twice* (New York: Alfred A. Knopf; 1934) and many other novels.

[9] The Walter Lippmann book was *An Inquiry into the Good Society* (Boston: Little, Brown and Co.; 1937).

When are you returning to the Orient? I surely hope it will be soon.

Yours,
M.

◇◇◇◇◇◇◇◇◇◇◇◇◇◇

To ALBERT G. KELLER
[OFP]

H. L. Mencken
1524 Hollins St.
Baltimore
December 31, 1937

DEAR KELLER:

Baker I never knew—somewhat strangely. I came close to him several times, but never actually met him.

Tell your daughter that I have been trying to get a Bible suitably elegant. The modern editions all seem to me to be too scientific. The Book I remember as a boy was full of gaudy and horrible illustrations, some of which impressed me with a sense of sin that I have never quite got rid of.

I envy you that daily slug of whiskey. I enjoy Scotch more or less, but it doesn't agree with me. My system, I suppose, was built for malt liquor. Even wine, though I love it, has a tendency to upset me. Everything in this world is managed badly. The human body is the greatest botch ever seen in the universe.

I surely hope that you are feeling better, and that you'll be lucky in 1938. My brother and I are planning to take a brief trip to the West Indies in a few weeks. We haven't had a holiday for a long while. We'll probably put in ten days sleeping on the ship.

Sincerely yours,
M.

1938

◇◇◇◇◇◇◇◇◇◇◇◇◇◇◇◇◇◇◇◇

To Sinclair Lewis
[yu]

H. L. Mencken
1524 Hollins St.
Baltimore
January 7, 1938

Dear Red:

It was my duty as a Christian to defend you. Once the book is out the Communist brethren will probably lay on with great ferocity.[1] My guess is that they are feeling rather sick. The news from Russia certainly can't be very comforting.

I haven't had a holiday for more than two years, so I am thinking of taking a couple of weeks in the West Indies. I'll probably sail week after next. Unfortunately, my brother, who is going with me, must return early in February, so the trip will have to be short. When I get back I'll give myself the honor of waiting on you.

Don't you ever come down this way any more? Certainly it is your duty as a patriot to visit Washington now and then. Please bear in mind that Baltimore is only forty miles away, and that the trains now make it in forty-one minutes.

Yours,
M.

---

[1] Sinclair Lewis's book: *The Prodigal Parents* (New York: Doubleday, Doran and Co.; 1938).

(1938)

To [X]
[OFP]

H. L. Mencken
1524 Hollins St.
Baltimore
January 18, 1938

DEAR [X]:

It is a grand pleasure to encounter an agnostic who is not a convert from Methodism. My own free-thinking ancestry is much like yours. My father and grandfather before me were scoffers at the holy Christian religion, though both of them seem to have got along pretty well with clergymen, as, indeed, I do myself. I suspect that you and I keep rather quiet about our lack of belief simply because it is not a novelty to us. The loud atheists are always former Presbyterians or Baptists. Some time ago an organization calling itself "The American Association for the Advancement of Atheism" invited me to join it. On investigating its literature I found that its president was a former evangelical clergyman. His bellowings simply disgusted me, and so I refused to have anything to do with him.

I incline to believe that your chances of placing the book with Macmillan are excellent. If he fails, don't hesitate to try the Yale University Press. The faculty running it are by no means bigoted Yankees. On the contrary, they seem to have open minds, and to be ready to print anything that really interests them. That is true to some extent of the Oxford Press also. It has shown a considerable enterprise and, indeed, in many fields has far outreached the commercial publishers.

I am going to the West Indies on Friday—my first holiday for two and a half years. Unfortunately, my brother, who is traveling with me, will have to be back here early in February, so our trip will be very short. I propose to go to sleep as soon as I hit the ship, and to remain snoring until we reach Jamaica.

Sincerely yours,
H. L. Mencken

(1938)

To James H. Gipson[2]
[OFP]

[J. H. Gipson had asked Mencken what sort of book he would like to receive for a gift.]

The Evening Sun
Sun Square
Baltimore, Md.
April 15, 1938

Dear Mr. Gipson:

All I can say is that as I grow older I read fiction with decreasing interest. For verse I never had much taste, and I am now somewhat too old, of course, to take any great interest in juveniles. In general I prefer books dealing with the exact sciences but after that comes biography, with travel third.

My very best thanks.
Sincerely yours,
H. L. Mencken

To Albert G. Keller
[OFP]

The Evening Sun
Sun Square
Baltimore, Md.
April 23, 1938

Dear Keller:

My term of servitude here will end on May 7th. I agreed to sweat and suffer for three months only. After I clear out I'll probably put in a month getting my private business in order and then go to Germany. I haven't been there for ten years and I am eager to find out what is

---

[2] James H. Gipson (born in 1885): president and co-founder of *The Caxton Printer's, Ltd.;* he specialized in publishing books by authors from the western United States.

going on. Whether I'll write anything for publication remains to be seen.

My guess is that the new spending program will go through with a whoop. It will take a hero to stand up against it and there are very few heroes in either House. The reorganization racket was much easier. But with millions of money on the counter most of the brethren will go along.

The Thomas Mann stuff simply eludes me. I certainly do not share Knopf's idea that it is magnificent. I have tried to read it at various times, but always fail to get any distance.

I am in a low state of health, chiefly because of lack of air and lack of exercise, but once I am liberated I shall recover quickly.

Sincerely yours,
Mencken

To Edward Stone
[uv]

H. L. Mencken
1524 Hollins St.
Baltimore
September 26, 1938

Dear Mr. Stone:

I deplore your dedication to pedagogy, and only hope that the coming war will release you. You may go into it an Assistant Professor of English, and come out a Major General. If you so desire, my chaplain will be instructed to offer prayers to that end.

Thanks for the chance to see your very eloquent tribute to Wolfe. He died here so quickly after his arrival that I didn't get the chance to see him. He was, in fact, virtually unconscious when he got here. My late wife was a great admirer of his books, and constantly urge[d] me to read them, but I must confess that they seemed to me to be rather hard going. If he had lived five years longer he'd have got rid of many of his defects. I met him only a few times, but had a great liking for him. There was something charmingly boyish about him. Next to Sinclair Lewis, he was the most modest author I ever encountered.

Sincerely yours,
H. L. Mencken

To Roscoe Peacock
[OFP]

H. L. Mencken
1524 Hollins St.
Baltimore
November 21, 1938

Dear Peacock:

La Brokaw is a clever woman, and I'll look up her piece in *Stage*. I have known her for some years. Unfortunately, I have yet to see her two plays.[3]

I needn't tell you that I agree with you thoroughly. Unluckily, satire is something that most American editors seem to be afraid of. I think the reason is that very few people penetrate it. Nine times out of ten it is taken quite seriously. I often had that experience with it in my *American Mercury* days. You may recall, also, an ambitious satire that I launched in 1915 or thereabout—a burlesque history of the bathtub. It is still taken quite seriously by many persons who should know better, and has even got into the encyclopedias.[4]

I pray for you regularly, and hope that the effects are not deleterious.

Yours,
M.

To Vincent Starrett
[OFP]

H. L. Mencken
1524 Hollins St.
Baltimore
December 5, 1938

Dear Mr. Starrett:

It goes without saying that I'll be delighted to autograph those two volumes of Selected Prejudices. Let them come to me as above, and I'll return them promptly.

[3] La Brokaw: Mrs. Claire Boothe Luce, then a playwright.

[4] There is at the Enoch Pratt Free Library in Baltimore a fat collection of clippings and documents concerning the famous "Bathtub Hoax", which was actually perpetrated on December 28, 1917, in the columns of the New York *Evening Mail*.

As you have probably noticed, they are *English* translations of selections from my American volumes. I deliberately sat down to claw my native American into orthodox English. When the first volume came out it was an unexpected success, and so Cape insisted on another. I never proceeded to a third, simply because I had exhausted the available material. Many of the essays in the six volumes printed here were basically unintelligible to Englishmen, and could not be translated into their language.

It was pleasant to hear from you.

Sincerely yours,
H. L. Mencken

1939

To Joseph Hergesheimer
[OFP]

[*Joseph Hergesheimer, who had published practically nothing since 1934, had expressed misgivings as to his talent for writing; he was contemplating a new novel, which he actually never wrote.*]

H. L. Mencken
1524 Hollins St.
Baltimore
April 6, 1939

Dear Joe:

Somehow or other, I am delighted to hear that you are reducing your staff. After all, every extra servant is an extra problem. August and I have tried down here to live as simply as possible, and it seems to work. Why not drop down some day and put in the evening with us?

I am still convinced firmly that you and I are very far from antiques. You have more than one first-rate book in you, and I predict formally that you'll prove it within a year. As for me, I have actually begun a new manuscript. It is that volume of reminiscences of my early youth, and three chapters are already on paper. They are trivial stuff, but I am in hopes that they won't be unamusing.

The curse of this literary trade is that it often throws us into moods of depression. I gather that you are in one now. I floundered around in the same way for a year after Sara's death, and pulled myself together only by hard work on "The American Language", fourth edition. Last Spring I got into the dumps again, and couldn't do any decent work until after Christmas, despite two trips abroad. Now, by some miracle, I begin to feel alive again, and if the Holy Ghost doesn't floor me once more I'll probably finish the book by the end of the Summer. The Knopfs, as usual, are pressing me, but I am not going to be hurried.

I surely hope that Dorothy's illness has passed off. She wrote to me once while you were away, but that was some time ago.

Baker's finish was quick and painless. He had some sort of bone disease that hardly incommoded him until ten days before his death. After he got to [the] hospital his kidneys gave out, and then he developed pneumonia. It would be hard to imagine a more placid death. The class that he ran for so many years has been abolished, and I am rather glad of it. As you know, he introduced me to Sara, and I had been haranguing his girls for nearly sixteen years.

Yours,
[*H. L. Mencken*]

To THEODORE DREISER
[UP]

[*Dreiser had recently edited* The Living Thoughts of Thoreau.]

H. L. Mencken
1524 Hollins St.
Baltimore
April 8, 1939

DEAR DREISER:

Thanks very much for the copy of the Thoreau book. Rather curiously, I know relatively little about Thoreau, and so it will be an especial pleasure to read your selections. For some reason or other, I have always felt a sort of antipathy toward him—probably because he was a New Englander and something of a transcendentalist. Looking through your collection, I am surprised by the range of his ideas. I had always thought of him as a sort of nature lover.

The ignorance of the so-called intelligentsia is really appalling. I encountered a college professor some time ago who had never heard of Sam Blythe. I am told, by the way, that Blythe is living in California. If you ever encounter him please give him my best regards.

I am plugging away at my book, with various longish interruptions. Doing it is a lot of fun, but whether anybody will want to read it remains to be seen.

The idealists at Washington are determined to get us into a war, and I begin to suspect that they may have their wish. The next one will be very much worse than the last one. I am planning to become a spy hunter. If you don't want me to denounce you the first week you had better send me a good box of five-cent cigars.

Yours,
M.

◇◇◇◇◇◇◇◇◇◇◇◇◇

To THEODORE DREISER
[UP]

[*On March 11th, Mencken had sent Dreiser a few clippings from the* Congressional Record, *his favorite reading, containing a radio address by Alexander Woollcott on the admission of German refugee children to the United States.*]

H. L. Mencken
1524 Hollins St.
Baltimore
April 17, 1939

DEAR DREISER:

Off hand I can't think of any good digest of Kant's philosophy. Those that I am acquainted with are even more difficult than the original. However, I am making inquiries, and if I find out anything I'll pass it on. Kant was probably the worst writer ever heard of on earth before Karl Marx. Some of his ideas were really quite simple, but he always managed to make them seem unintelligible. I hope he is in Hell.

I sent you a few more clippings from the *Congressional Record* the other day. Please don't indulge yourself in any sneers. The men who contribute to the *Record* are genuine patriots, and deserve the veneration of all Christian citizens.

Yours,
M.

To THEODORE DREISER
[UP]

H. L. Mencken
1524 Hollins St.
Baltimore
April 19, 1939

DEAR DREISER:

Masters, who knows a great deal about philosophy, tells me that George Henry Lewis's history of it remains one of the best books ever done on the subject. I read it many years ago, but recall it only vaguely. Masters also thinks well of Durant's "Story of Philosophy", but here I dissent. It seems to me that Durant is a very superficial fellow. In general, metaphysics seems to me to be very hollow. Half of it is a tremendous laboring of the obvious, and the other half is speculation that has very little relation to the known facts. Altogether, I think I'd support a law drafting all philosophers into the army.

I am going to Washington tomorrow to harangue a meeting of newspaper editors. It is always a depressing job. They are, taking one with another, a very innocent class of men. They always believe, deep down in their hearts, whatever they hear from official bigwigs.

Yours,
M.

To THEODORE DREISER
[UP]

H. L. Mencken
1524 Hollins St.
Baltimore
April 24, 1939

DEAR DREISER:

If any one ever started a decent paper in Southern California the natives would lynch him. Now that you are on the scene, I advise you to read the Los Angeles *Times* carefully. It is really almost incredible.

Thanks for the clipping about the death of Wright. He was a great liar, but nevertheless an amusing fellow. He gave Rascoe a great deal of the blather that Rascoe printed in his introduction to the Smart Set Anthology. Later on he tried to blame it on Nathan, but I know where the stuff came from. I saw Wright only a few times in recent years. Two or three years ago he brought his wife down to Baltimore for surgical treatment.

Yours,
M.

◇◇◇◇◇◇◇◇◇◇◇◇◇

To GEORGE S. SCHUYLER
[OFP]

H. L. Mencken
1524 Hollins St.
Baltimore
May 10, 1939

DEAR MR. SCHUYLER:

The Pulitzer prize editorials are always preposterous—in fact, I am toying with a scheme to print a collection of them as a comic book. You will recall the one called "Who is Coolidge?" I am still half convinced that the author wrote it with his tongue in his cheek. I hope you lay on with proper ferocity. I am convinced, as you are, that we are headed for a dictatorship in this great Republic. Roosevelt is hot to horn into the European mess, and his wizards believe that if he can scare the country sufficiently, it will be possible to reëlect him next year. I am inclined to agree that this is sound political dope.

I have just read your violent assault on Comrade Bilbo.[1] Admittedly, he is a master ass; nevertheless, I suspect that there may be some sense in his scheme. After all, the future of the Negro in this country doesn't look any too hopeful. It might not be a bad idea to try a return to Africa. It could not be attempted, of course, on the heroic scale imagined by Comrade Bilbo, but nevertheless it might be at-

[1] About this letter, Mr. Schuyler writes: Bilbo was (Theodore) Bilbo, a rabid racist hailing from Poplarsville, Miss., who had been Governor . . . and was later Senator. A professional bigot, he was not without that pawky sense of humor which distinguishes the backwoods cracker.

tempted. Once 10,000 smart American gentlemen of color had got to Africa, the Liberian oligarchy would begin to wither and fade away. I may do a piece on this subject a bit later on. Let us not understimate Comrade Bilbo because he is a notorious jackass. So was Martin Luther.

Another matter: has anyone tried to interest Aframericans in dyes and bleaches to change the color of their hair? They seem to spend an enormous amount of money on hair-straighteners, but all such great inventions leave their locks coal-black, with a patent leather finish. The other day, I saw a colored girl in Baltimore whose hair was definitely brown. Her complexion was much darker, and the combination was really very striking. I suspect that if some smart fellow began vending a dye to produce yellow, red, and even green and purple, hair, he would earn an honest fortune.

My brother and I are still hoping to see you in Baltimore.

Sincerely yours,
H. L. Mencken

To Alfred A. Knopf
[AAK]

H. L. Mencken
1524 Hollins St.
Baltimore
May 15, 1939

Dear Alfred:

Have you ever thought of doing a book of the dissenting opinions of Hugo Black? They are sometimes almost insane, but they are often written with considerable skill. I believe that a volume of them, brought out, say, next January, with a competent introduction by some intelligent lawyer, would have a chance. A companion volume might be made of the dissenting opinions of Justices Butler and McReynolds. They set forth the old interpretation of the Constitution with great clarity and skill, and often penetrate the sophistries of the majority in a very amusing manner. It was when Holmes was in a minority that he did his best work, and the same thing is true of Butler and McReynolds.

I believe that there is an interest in minority opinions, and that both of these volumes might be profitable. However, I suggest finding out first whether the volume of Holmes's dissents made any money. If it didn't, there is no chance for Black, Butler and McReynolds.

Yours,
M.

◇◇◇◇◇◇◇◇◇◇◇◇◇◇

To H. L. DAVIS
[OFP]

H. L. Mencken
1524 Hollins St.
Baltimore
May 17, 1939

DEAR MR. DAVIS:

How are you? And what are you up to? I had hoped to hear from you long ago. Is the new novel making good progress? As for me, I have begun work on a small and inconsequential volume of reminiscences. Writing it is a lot of fun.

I have been reading Steinbeck's "Grapes of Wrath". It seems to me to be a very poor job. It is full of pink hooey, and contains some very stilted and ineffective writing. When I put it beside "Honey in the Horn" I really laugh. Steinbeck, of course, is getting encomiastic notices in the pink weeklies, but that is of no significance. They always praise any book that blames every bellyache on Wall Street.

Sincerely yours,
H. L. Mencken

◇◇◇◇◇◇◇◇◇◇◇◇◇◇

To H. L. DAVIS
[OFP]

H. L. Mencken
1524 Hollins St.
Baltimore
July 24, 1939

DEAR MR. DAVIS:

I advise you to avoid those *New Yorker* pieces.[2] They are mere fragments of the book, and some of them are rather scanty. At the

---

[2] Selections from *Happy Days* ran in *The New Yorker.*

moment I am laid up, but I am hoping to get back to the job very shortly, and to finish the book by the end of the Summer. I'll be delighted to send you a copy of it when it comes out.

Wolfe's stuff I never could read.[3] My late wife was a great admirer of it and often urged me to tackle it, but every time I did so I was driven away. I knew Wolfe slightly. He was a very amiable fellow, but he always seemed to me to be almost as confused as Sherwood Anderson.

I hope the book is going on prosperously. Those first chapters were really superb.

Sincerely yours,
H. L. Mencken

To JOSEPH HERGESHEIMER
[OFP]

H. L. Mencken
1524 Hollins St.
Baltimore
September 16th [1939]

DEAR JOE:

Your difficulties with these pieces really puzzle me: they seem to be quite without sense. If I were editor of the *New Yorker* I'd certainly nail "The Alabaster Locket" instantly, and if I were editor of the *Saturday Evening Post* I'd do the same to "Garibaldi Was a Bum". Did Chambrun ever send "Garibaldi" to *Esquire?* If not, I suggest that there is probably a ready market there. To be sure, *Esquire* is a lousy magazine, but nevertheless it is a market. As for "The Thistle of Ayr" I think it would fit admirably into *Harper's.*

A few minor suggestions:

1. The Era of God Will (p. 7 and 9 of "The Thistle of Ayr") should be The Era of Good Feeling.

2. The first two sentences of "The Alabaster Locket" are redundant, and a shade confusing. The whole story belongs to Florence.

3. In places, the punctuation seems to me to be a trifle confusing. For example, in the sentence beginning "At last" in the last paragraph of p. 4 of "The Alabaster Locket". Again, in the first paragraph of p. 1

[3] Wolfe: Thomas Wolfe, the novelist.

of the same: "He was a serious painter", etc. There are a good many other examples. I have some doubt that omitting commas is a good idea. It is apt to haul up the reader, and it smells too much of the current quacks.

I like all three pieces, and as I say, I marvel that you have had any difficulties about them. They are good stuff, and they are genuine Hergesheimer. I hope you keep on blazing away on the same path. Soon or late it will pay.

Our session was exactly right. The right people and the right talk. Hay fever let me go all the while I was in West Chester. It came back here, but not severely. I begin to feel more or less normal.

The penultimate chapter of my little book got itself written today, despite the infernal heat. I hope to finish the job by the end of next week. Unhappily, I seem doomed to be interrupted by an extraordinary burst of visiting firemen, some of them female.

Yours,
M.

◇◇◇◇◇◇◇◇◇◇◇◇◇◇

To EZRA POUND

H. L. Mencken
1524 Hollins St.
Baltimore
October 4, 1939

DEAR POUND:

The *Sun* is supporting Roosevelt in a large way, and so I assume that there is no chance of your joining its foreign staff. I am sorry indeed. I nominated you in due form, and believe that you'd have been a valuable acquisition. My own liberty is still unmolested, and I enclose two proofs of it. How long this will last God only knows.

My belief is that Roosevelt will horn into the war at the first chance. He is, to be sure, still bellowing about keeping the United States out of it, but no rational man takes such talk seriously. All of his principal advisers are violent Anglomaniacs, and I think he is also one himself. If the United States horns in it will be impossible for me to write anything, or more accurately, to print anything. I'll probably do what I did the last time; that is, devote myself to a job that has nothing to do with the current carnage. I have several such projects in view. It is always possible, of course, that England and France may decide to come to terms, but at this writing it seems rather improbable.

Let me hear what you are up to, and how things look from the Italian side.

Yours,
Mencken

To Blanche Knopf (Mrs. Alfred A. Knopf)
[PT]

Baltimore, October 27, 1939

Dear Blanche:

My regular price for going to the theatre is, as you know, $1,000 cash in advance. I'll reduce it to $500 for the Day play, but I don't think that I can go below that.[4]

When I'll get to New York I don't know, but it will probably be soon. More of this anon.

Yours
H. L. M.

To Jim Tully
[OFP]

H. L. Mencken
1524 Hollins St.
Baltimore
November 3, 1939

Dear Jim:

Whoever argues against first person stories is simply foolish. Some of the greatest fiction in the world has been written in that form; for example, Joseph Conrad's "Youth".

I'll get hold of *Esquire* and the *Forum* tomorrow and read both your article and McClure's. I hope you are making good progress with "Out of My Heart". The title is excellent.

I hear from Dreiser now and then, but not often. You speak of him as *prematurely* old. The plain truth is that he is *actually* old. In a year or two he'll be 70, and ready for the body-snatchers. What he is up to at the moment I don't know. If he never writes another line in this life he will be remembered for the magnificent work he did in his forties.

I have got rid of my little book of reminiscences, and am now

---

[4] The Day play was, of course, *Life with Father.*

toying with a Dictionary of Quotations that has been on the stocks for many years. I have accumulated almost 30,000 cards, and they contain a great many salty quotations that are not in any other book. Whether I'll ever be able to finish the job remains to be seen. I begin to smell the breath of angels.[5]

M.

To JOSEPH HERGESHEIMER
[OFP]

H. L. Mencken
1524 Hollins St.
Baltimore
December 5, 1939

DEAR JOE:

Your wire must have reached here just after I left for New York. When I got there Alfred Knopf told me that he had stopped off to see you and that you were in excellent health and full of sin.

Within a day or two you will receive a copy of my new book. Please note that it is not to be published until January 22, and that until then it is for your private eye alone. It is trivial stuff, but there are parts of it that may conceivably amuse you. I should say that it is about eighty per cent. truth. The rest consists of icing on the cake.

Why don't you and Dorothy run down to Baltimore sometime and have lunch with me? I can imagine nothing pleasanter.

Yours,
[*H. L. Mencken*]

To ALBERT G. KELLER
[OFP]

H. L. Mencken
1524 Hollins St.
Baltimore
December 15, 1939

DEAR KELLER:

For some reason or other, Goethe has always failed to lift me. I read him first in an English translation. It was a bad one, and it seems

---

[5] The *Dictionary of Quotations* was published in 1942 by Alfred A. Knopf.

to have poisoned me against him. My old friend Henry Wood, who was professor of German at the Johns Hopkins for years, was a violent Goethe fan and used to quote him constantly. He labored with me violently, but never made any impression on me. To this day Goethe seems to me to be somehow inferior. I grant you that this is nonsense, but there is the fact.

The theological pressure that you speak of never bothered me in my nonage. My mother went to church now and then, but her doctrinal ideas seem to have been very vague, for I never heard her mention them. I think she went simply as a sort of social gesture. My father accompanied her no more than two or three times in my recollection, and even then he went under protest. Religion was simply not a living subject in the house. It was discussed now and then, but only as astrophysics might have been discussed. I grew up believing firmly that it was unimportant, and I am still of that opinion. In consequence, my toleration runs beyond the common. It never occurs to me to dislike a man because of his faith.

Whether my book will pay for itself remains to be seen. So far there have been no reports from Knopf's drummers. They will not tackle their customers until after Christmas. My own guess is that the book will not do very well. But I have been fooled in the past, and in both directions.

I seize the opportunity to hope that you are lucky in 1940. Christmas in this house is always a dismal festival, and I may try to evade it by leaving the city. Unfortunately, I have not been able to find any suitable retreat. Two years ago I was laid up in the hospital over Christmas, and enjoyed it immensely. Everywhere else there is some evocation of the ghastly Christmas spirit.

My best thanks for those corrections. *Jimson* is obviously right. I'll have it inserted in the next edition, if there ever is one.

Sincerely yours,
Mencken

(1939)

◇◇◇◇◇◇◇◇◇◇◇◇◇◇

To William Lyon Phelps
[ofp]

H. L. Mencken
1524 Hollins St.
Baltimore
December 15, 1939

Dear Billy:

Your letter really delighted me. My very best thanks. I started that book in a trivial mood, but as it grew under my hand it gradually occurred to me that there was really a story in it. It interested me especially to hear that your own youth was substantially like mine. Certainly our lives since have run along parallel tracks. I only hope that when the time comes to depart this world you will not accompany me to that inferno which all the theologians tell me is bound to be my eternal habitation. Certainly you deserve better than that.

Let me hear of it whenever you head this way and we'll have a session, and a long one. I can imagine nothing pleasanter. Meanwhile, I hope you are lucky in 1940. The year just closing has been a dreadful one.

Yours,
M.

To Theodore Dreiser
[up]

[*On December 17, 1939, Dreiser had written to Mencken:*

Thanks for Happy Days—which came three or four days ago. I've been squinting into it here & there and have read, so far, the preface, the Universe, the training of a gangster and some odd paragraphs including the last in the book. I keep it beside my bed to read mornings & midnight—mostly—entirely in fact—to cheer myself up a bit. Your angle is certainly your angle and there is no other to compare therewith. It's read and chuckle and that's why it will be passed along and read. I see myself reading it all just as I see myself taking another highball—to lift me up a bit. I hope sincerely you'll go on with other periods—being your critical self all the way. This country needs just such an autobiography.

And you're almost 60! Kind heaven! You sound like a racketeering youngster of 27 or 8. Luck. Regards

—Dreiser

Already I've been asked the loan of it!

To hell with Xmas.

All the way through this book I am compelled to note how unlike Henry W. Longfellow you are.]

H. L. Mencken
1524 Hollins St.
Baltimore
December 22, 1939

DEAR DREISER:

When you mention Longfellow you touch a tender chord. All of my early poetical work was written in imitation of him, and at one time my admiration for him actually went to the length of growing whiskers. In my later years I have somehow slipped out of his orbit, unquestionably to my damage as patriot and Christian.

Knopf wants me to do a series of reminiscences, each covering a decade, but I shy from the idea. "Happy Days" sets a mood that it would be impossible to keep up in the later years. My teens, for example, were full of loud alarms, and it would sound idiotic to treat them as I deal with my first ten years. In my twenties I was gay again, and also in my thirties, but since the age of forty I have been full of a sense of human sorrow. This sense has frequently taken the virulence of an actual bellyache.

I hope that you are in the best of health, and that you see nothing but good luck in 1940.

Yours,
M.

1940

To JIM TULLY
[OFP]

H. L. Mencken
1524 Hollins St.
Baltimore
January 22, 1940

DEAR JIM:

I never listen to debates. They are dreadful things indeed. The plain truth is that I am not a fair man, and don't want to hear both sides. On all known subjects, ranging from aviation to xylophone-playing, I have fixed and invariable ideas. They have not changed since I was four or five years [old].

The Chaplin book sounds interesting indeed. You may well throw overboard anything that Frank Harris wrote on the subject. He was the most unreliable man ever heard of. He not only had a very faulty memory, he was also a magnificent liar.

If you are managing the Rev. Billy Knight, I suggest bringing him to Baltimore. Sin is rampant in this part of the world, and a good revival would be of benefit to the inhabitants. The blowing up of Prohibition ruined all the evangelical clergy, and since that time the Devil has been running wild.

Yours,
M.

(1940)

To THEODORE DREISER
[UP]

H. L. Mencken
1524 Hollins St.
Baltimore
April 19, 1940

DEAR DREISER:

I hear vaguely that you have been ill, and I only hope that you have made a complete recovery. Let me hear about it when you feel like it. I am somewhat wobbly myself, but still manage to get through a reasonable day's work.

Among other things, I am putting in some finishing licks on a book of quotations that has entertained me off and on for thirty years. I started it for my own use, and it has now grown to 30,000 cards. I am thinking of bringing it out early next year. Have I your permission to print a few brief quotations from your own works? They come chiefly from "Art in America" and "Hey Rub-a-Dub-Dub", and are never more than two sentences long. I assume that all of the copyrights of your books are now in your hands. I'll write to Max Schuster also, but understand that he has only a license to print.

The *New Masses* brethren sent me a circular in which you are made to speak of the *New Masses* as "our magazine". Is this authorized? If so, have you turned Communist? I certainly hope you haven't. It must be manifest to any one that Communism stands in contempt of the imperishable truths of our holy Christian religion.[1]

Yours,
H. L. M.

[1] Theodore Dreiser officially joined the Communist Party on July 20, 1945.

To Samuel A. Nock[2]
[OFP]

H. L. Mencken
1524 Hollins St.
Baltimore
May 16, 1940

Dear Dr. Nock:

Rather curiously, I have never read "Life With Father", though I lately saw the play. It covers the same general ground as "Happy Days", but obviously enough the two books differ enormously. They are both as far from "Tom Sawyer" as the police regulations of Abilene, Texas, are from the Ten Commandments.

It is conceivable that I may get into your general region during the Summer. If so, we must certainly sit down for a session. I am afflicted at the moment by lumbago, but in all probability it will pass off quickly. I have a busy Summer ahead.

Sincerely yours,
H. L. Mencken

To Herbert F. West
[OFP]

H. L. Mencken
1524 Hollins St.
Baltimore
August 9, 1940

Dear Mr. West:

If you want to file my Baltimore *Sun* pieces, I'll be glad to send you clippings. Unhappily, the series will probably have to end very soon. It will be impossible to discuss the war frankly once Roosevelt horns into it. I hear from Washington that he is determined to do so at the very earliest chance.

The most interesting book that I have read of late is "Peaks and Lamas", by Marco Pallis, published by Knopf. Pallis is a Greek denizen of England, who went to the Himalayas to climb peaks and lingered to study Buddhism. Buddhism seems to me to be complete hooey; nevertheless, Pallis manages to make his investigation of it interesting.

[2] Dr. Samuel A. Nock (born in 1901): author, vice-president of the Kansas State College.

He writes extremely well, and has produced a thoroughly unusual and interesting book.

I lately plowed through the four volumes of Sandburg's "Lincoln". They are full of immensely interesting stuff, but it seems to me that Sandburg has made a mess of the writing—indeed, there are plenty of places in which it must strike any reader that he is puzzled by his own material and can't figure out its significance. Nevertheless, it must be said for him that he is honest. Despite his theory that old Abe was a noble character, he doesn't hesitate to present the massive evidence to the contrary.

I have been reading of late a number of old books, for example, "The City of God", by St. Augustine, and "Leviathan", by Thomas Hobbes. "The City of God" struck me, once more, as a farrago of nonsense. It is really amazing that any one should ever have taken it seriously as a work of either theology or philosophy. "Leviathan", on the contrary, delighted me all over again. It is certainly one of the most interesting books ever written.

Sincerely yours,
H. L. Mencken

◇◇◇◇◇◇◇◇◇◇◇◇◇◇

To ALFRED A. KNOPF
[AAK]

H. L. Mencken
1524 Hollins St.
Baltimore
September 25, 1940

DEAR ALFRED:

I'll certainly be delighted to come to Purchase on Sunday. Hay fever is still more or less annoying, but the overt symptoms have disappeared, and what mainly bothers me is a persistent malaise. No doubt an hour in the fresh air will help it.

The Pratt Library not only spelt *Prejudices* wrong; it also adorned its window with a placard crediting me with discovering a whole list of authors who were known almost before I was born. Under the circumstances, I was estopped from protesting.

I hear from Blanche that she'll be here on Thursday night. We'll meet then, and probably again on Friday at lunch.

Yours,
M.

◇◇◇◇◇◇◇◇◇◇◇◇◇◇

To Huntington Cairns
[OFP]

H. L. Mencken
1524 Hollins St.
Baltimore
October 4, 1940

Dear Cairns:

I hate the radio so violently that I hesitate to say yes, but I should add that you really tempt me. Unhappily, the most powerful temptation is radiated by Aristotle's "Nichomachean Ethics", always a great favorite of mine. You have set it down for discussion on October 27th. God knows where I'll be on that day. I am joining the Willkie funeral train in New York on Tuesday, and shall stick to it during its New England tour. After that I'll be at the disposal of the *Sun,* so I can't make any engagement until after election. I'd much prefer, if it is all the same to you, to postpone the whole matter until after January 1st. I can then discuss it with better comfort. In any case, I warn you that it will take an engine of at least 300,000 horse power to induce me to croon.

I hope you are in Baltimore soon. We meet far too seldom.

Yours,
H. L. Mencken

To Blanche Knopf
[AAK]

H. L. Mencken
1524 Hollins St.
Baltimore
October 23, 1940

Dear Blanche:

Unhappily, a Willkie meeting is promised to Baltimore for October 30th, and so I'll be unable to come to the party to Lesser. Please give him my very best. The firm is immensely lucky to have him, and I hope you restrain him by force if he begins talking of enlisting in the navy and going out to fight the Japs. Tell him that it is a bad idea, for the Pacific ocean is the deepest on earth.

I suggest sticking to Grove until he definitely withdraws. I believe he'd make a better book than Polvogt.[3]

Various manuscripts of some promise have passed through my hands during the last week or two. One is a book called "The Foreign Language Press in New York", prepared by the Federal Works Agency. So far as I know, no publisher has it. It is in charge of Frederick Clayton, director of the New York City WPA Writers' Project, 110 King Street, New York.

The second is a novel dealing with red caps, written by Reginald Clyne, 463 Manhattan Avenue, New York City. This Clyne is himself a red cap. I encountered him in the Pennsylvania station a couple of weeks ago. He introduced himself and asked me to read his book. It is no masterpiece, but nevertheless it may be worth putting through your mill. I hesitate to recommend it, but I think someone in the office should read it.

The third manuscript is a large dictionary of slang by two criminals locked up in the Virginia penitentiary at Richmond. The one in charge of the piece is Clinton A. Sanders, and his official address is 500 Spring Street, Richmond, Va. The thing is large, but it consists of straight matter. I am not sure whether such a thing will sell, but it occurs to me that you may want to look at it yourself. If so, a line to Mr. Sanders will bring it.

My head infection has passed off, but I still feel a bit rocky. God willing, I'll certainly see you in New York on November 6th.

Yours
H. L. M.

To JAMES T. FARRELL
[OFP]

H. L. Mencken
1524 Hollins St.
Baltimore
November 20, 1940

DEAR MR. FARRELL:

Those swine will run on for a little while longer, and then the inevitable reckoning will come. It is appalling to think of the damage

[3] Probably Russell Clark Grove, a New York nose and throat specialist who wrote *Sinus* for Alfred A. Knopf. The other books mentioned in this letter were not published.

they have done during the last five or six years. I am tempted constantly to tear up my oath and resume book reviewing, if only for the purpose of putting down a series of gross and blatant quacks. Unhappily, I have other irons in the fire, and moreover, I believe that twenty-five years of book reviewing was enough. It is a dreadful chore, and I am sorry for even the pinks who have to practise it.

The news that Dreiser has succumbed to the Stalinists is not surprising. The old boy is the most innocent idiot ever heard of. His political ideas are those of a child of seven, and he always succumbs to plausible quacks. I have never known a man whose general ideas were less reasonable and accurate.

Willkie wrote very few of his own speeches. They were mainly done by a small brain trust, headed by Russell Davenport. Willkie, of course, revised them, but apparently his revisions were not very extensive. He was always at his best when he got to the end of his manuscript and began to extemporize.

Yours,
H. L. Mencken

◇◇◇◇◇◇◇◇◇◇◇◇◇◇

To JOSEPH HERGESHEIMER
[OFP]

H. L. Mencken
1524 Hollins St.
Baltimore
December 9, 1940

DEAR JOE:

I suggest Thursday, January 23rd. If that is all right, let me know and I'll see you at Wilmington at 3:44. I assume that we'll be able to escape early the next day. I'll probably have to be back in Baltimore by the afternoon.

I have nearly finished White's "Shelley". Shelley seems to me to have been, not only an idiot, but also a scoundrel. Nevertheless, White somehow makes him interesting. The book is a ghastly chore, but I have got through it without any actual pain. Such things really must be done. I wish there were an equally good biography of Mark Twain.

I seize the opportunity to hope that you are lucky in 1941. My love to Dorothy.

Yours,
[*H. L. M.*]

(1940)

To JAMES T. FARRELL
[OFP]

H. L. Mencken
1524 Hollins St.
Baltimore
December 11, 1940

DEAR MR. FARRELL:

Thanks very much for the chance to see your blast against Mortimer J. Adler. You describe him precisely. I hear confidentially that Holy Church is full of hopes that he will submit to baptism anon. If the ceremony is public I'll certainly attend. I invite you herewith to come along in my private plane. I assure you that there will be plenty of stimulants aboard.

I am distressed to hear about the carbuncle, and only hope that all of the accompanying discomforts have passed off. It is a dreadful thing to try to work when ill. I have been at it for the last three or four months, and making heavy weather of it. Superficially, I seem to be all right, but there are various discomforts that keep me unhappy.

If I were twenty years younger I'd tackle Mumford, Brooks and company and give them something to think of. Dreiser, it seems to me, differs considerably from Darrow. For one thing, as you say, he is much less intelligent, and for another thing, he is rather more honest. His belief in spooks and banshees is quite real, and I have always predicted that he'd end a confessing Christian. I hear from the old boy very seldom. He sends me an article now and then, but I suppose he assumes that my politics are wicked.

I never see Mike Gold's idiocies. The fact that he is denouncing me violently, however, doesn't surprise me. I gave him a hand in his early days. Such [. . .] always prove their independence of spirit by libeling those who have tried to help them. Mike had a certain mild talent, but politics, of course, ruined it. When the pogroms start in this great Republic he will probably be one of the first victims.[4]

I hear from Washington that war is now inevitable. The only

---

[4] Michael Gold was then writing a series of articles for the *Daily Worker* later to be collected into a book: *The Hollow Men* (New York: International Publishers; 1941); in one of them, he attacked Mencken as a reactionary.

question at issue is whether Roosevelt will horn in with or without a formal declaration.

Don't forget to let me know where you print your blast against Mumford. I am very eager to read it.

Sincerely yours,
H. L. Mencken

1941

To Harry Elmer Barnes[1]

[PT]

[*Mencken wanted to retire from the Baltimore* Evening Sun, *but Paul Patterson, the owner, prevailed on him to remain at least as news consultant at half his previous salary. In 1948 Mencken completed his last assignment for the paper: the coverage of the conventions at Philadelphia.*]

Baltimore, January 20, 1941

Dear Barnes:

My very best to Parshley the next time you see him.

I am pulling out of the *Sun* in a couple of weeks. It seems silly to go on trying to tell the truth in a paper that has swung so far toward Roosevelt. My relations with the brethren are excellent, but it seems to me that my continuance is bound to embarrass both of us. I have, as you know, no great yen to instruct and edify the plain people. So far as I am concerned, they can believe anything they damn please. I am continuing my connections with the *Sunpapers* in other capacities, and I hope that my increased leisure will give me the chance to finish a couple of books that have been under way for some time.

All this is for your private eye. No announcement will be made.

Yours,

M.

[1] Harry Elmer Barnes (born in 1889): educator, historian, and sociologist.

To L. M. Birkhead[2]
[OFP]

H. L. Mencken
1524 Hollins St.
Baltimore
January 22, 1941

My Dear Pastor:

I read your two reprints on Freedom of Assembly with great interest. Some really difficult problems are involved in the matter, and I hope to discuss them in an article a bit later on. My series on the war in the Baltimore *Sun* will end in a week or two. It seems to me an affectation to be printing such things in a paper which is supporting the war violently, and swallowing the usual English nonsense.

I believe there is another difficulty in the anti-Semitic question. After all, a man who believes sincerely that the Jews are a menace to the United States ought to be allowed to say so. The fact that he is wrong has got nothing whatsoever to do with it. The right to free speech involves inevitably the right to talk nonsense. I am much disturbed by the effort of the New York Jews to put down criticism. It seems to me that they are only driving it underground, and so making it more violent.

I had not heard the charge that Steinbeck is a Jew. It seems to me that "Grapes of Wrath" is an excellent piece of work, but that he spoiled it by inserting those *New Republic* editorials between the chapters. They were extraordinarily banal, and they lowered the tone of the whole book.

Sincerely yours,
H. L. Mencken

[2] Leon Milton Birkhead (born in 1885) was a Unitarian clergyman and writer; he had served Sinclair Lewis as technical adviser in the writing of *Elmer Gantry*.

To L. M. Birkhead
[OFP]

H. L. Mencken
1524 Hollins St.
Baltimore
January 31, 1941

Dear Pastor:

I have put in many a long hour sweating over the problem you raise. My guess is that in the last analysis it is insoluble. However, I am always inclined to give free speech the right of way, and so I believe that anti-democratic propaganda should be permitted—that is, so long as it does not advocate actual violence. As soon as the law attempts to distinguish between sound and unsound opinions, free speech goes out of the window. There is simply no way to get rid of that difficulty.

I am much disturbed by the efforts of the Jews in New York to put down criticism of themselves. I don't share the common prejudice against them, but nevertheless I can't imagine any reason why a man who entertains it shouldn't be free to say so. Every time the Jews procure the jailing of some poor idiot who denounces them from a soapbox they provide the way for dreadful retribution hereafter. My fear is that they will get a large part of the blame for the present war, here as elsewhere. Too many of them have been whooping it up. I assume, of course, that its issue will be uncomfortable for the United States. On that point I have no doubt whatsoever. Scotching Hitler will turn out to be an enormously heavier job than scotching the Kaiser.

I trust that you are leading a sober, Christian life, and reading only good books. As for me, I am in the midst of writing another bad one.

Sincerely yours,
H. L. Mencken

(1941)

To JIM TULLY
[OFP]

H. L. Mencken
1524 Hollins St.
Baltimore
April 7, 1941

DEAR JIM:

I hear from New York agents that Dreiser has returned to the Coast. He spent his whole time in New York in communion with the pinks. The old boy is really an idiot politically speaking. He protests constantly that the Jews exploit him and misrepresent him, but nevertheless he always falls for it when they tackle him with fresh blandishments.

I had a dream last night in which I saw an army of 100,000,000 angels descending upon England to save it. Inasmuch as you had a decent Christian education, you know more about such things than I do, and so I pass on the news to you. Some of the angels were colored, but the majority were white.

Yours
H. L. M.

To JULIAN P. BOYD
[PU]

[*Mencken had just returned from a trip to Havana.*]

H. L. Mencken
1524 Hollins St.
Baltimore
May 13, 1941

DEAR DR. BOYD:

I dropped in on President Dodds again yesterday, but found that he was still forbidden visitors. However, I heard from the hospital that he is making excellent progress, and I am hoping to see him before the end of the week. I shall then inquire if his doctor permits him the use of alcoholic refreshments.

Ford Madox Ford's letters are probably far more valuable than his manuscripts. He always seemed to me to be a grossly overestimated writer, but he had close relations with many first-rate men and his files are probably full of good stuff. Personally, I regarded him as a jackass.

My Cuban trip seems to have given me a lift, and I am once more at work on my book.

Sincerely yours,
H. L. Mencken

◇◇◇◇◇◇◇◇◇◇◇◇◇

To CHANNING POLLOCK
[PT]

Baltimore, May 23, 1941

DEAR CHANNING:

Some of these days we must certainly sit down and talk it over. It begins to seem like long, long years since I last had the honor of witnessing you.

I share your resentment of the imbecile way in which the world is managed. I was never more alive mentally than I am at this minute, but my old carcass is beginning to crack, and so my hours of work have to be shortened constantly. However, I am still hoping to last long enough to produce two or three more books.

Yours,
M.

◇◇◇◇◇◇◇◇◇◇◇◇◇

To JAMES T. FARRELL
[OFP]

H. L. Mencken
1524 Hollins St.
Baltimore
May 30, 1941

DEAR MR. FARRELL:

The best of luck with "Ellen Rogers". It sounds immensely interesting. I needn't tell you that I am delighted to hear that you are extending the plan of the O'Neill–O'Flaherty saga. I am convinced that it is really first-rate stuff, and that the world will discover that fact soon or late. The idiots who denounce it will be remembered only as idiots.

I agree with you thoroughly about Woodrow Wilson's style. It was really terrible. Have you ever seen the book called "The Story of a Style" by William Bayard Hale? It deals with Wilson's writing in a thoroughly realistic and merciless manner. No man knew Wilson better than Hale. At the time the United States broke into the last war the book was suppressed, and copies of it are now rare, but I think that there is one in the New York Public Library.

I am hard at work on my early newspaper reminiscences. It is mainly bawdy stuff, but here and there I indulge myself in a few philosophical flip-flops. My illness during the Winter lost me eight weeks, and as a result I am behindhand with the manuscript. However, it is now going pretty well, and I hope to finish it by the end of June.

Brooks seems to me to be an extraordinarily hollow and silly fellow.[3] I have known him for years and used to have some respect for him, but no more. It doesn't surprise me to hear the story that you tell. It is an axiom for which I have never encountered an exception that a man full of moral indignation is always dishonorable. MacLeish I have never met. He is only too obviously a hollow ass.

Sincerely yours,
H. L. Mencken

To Alfred A. Knopf
[PT]

Baltimore, July 22, 1941

Dear Alfred:

I note what you say about the Beer matter. There must be plenty of good material in my book reviews. I assume that they are in your office files.

Why doesn't some one print a really decent looking King James Bible? All those issued by the regular publishers have a funereal air, and most of them are bound idiotically. There are some better Bibles in modern translation, but no sensible man wants to read a modern translation. What is needed is a simple Bible without notes, giving the

[3] Brooks: Van Wyck Brooks.

King James text precisely, and bound so that it looks like a good book, not like a scarecrow to alarm sinners. If you ever think of doing such an edition, I'll be glad to write an introduction for it. The King James is a really magnificent work, and deserves to be read as literature. It is stupendously superior to all the other texts, and it should be read in the orthodox form, not rearranged à la Sutherland Bates.

Yours,
M.

◇◇◇◇◇◇◇◇◇◇◇◇◇

To LOU WYLIE (MRS. L. W. VAN SICKLEN)
[OFP]

H. L. Mencken
1524 Hollins St.
Baltimore
August 18, 1941

DEAR MISS WYLIE:

I trust that your adventure with Putnam doesn't discourage you. Sometimes it takes a long while to place a book, but if you have patience it can be done. I can't, of course, judge the wisdom of the suggested rewriting. You must decide that matter for yourself. I haven't the slightest doubt that whatever you do will improve the book, and that you'll place it with a good publisher soon or late.

Please give my best to John McClure. I moan and beat my breast every time I think of his abandonment of writing. I hear through various returning explorers that he devotes his whole time to newspaper work. Newspaper work is good so far as it goes, but it doesn't go far enough.

I predict formally that the old Huey Long crowd will once more reach its former political heights. It has the tremendous power of the New Deal behind it. I am thoroughly pessimistic about the future of American politics. There was a time when it seemed likely that its worse corruptions would be abated, but of late they have been increasing, and my guess is that before the war ends they will reach hitherto unattained heights. After all, very few Americans are in favor of honest government. The overwhelming majority is not for anything that promises loot.

Sincerely yours,
H. L. Mencken

To Ben Abramson[4]
[YU]

H. L. Mencken
1524 Hollins St.
Baltimore
October 2, 1941

Dear Mr. Abramson:

Thanks very much for your note. I only hope you like "Newspaper Days" just as well after the humanizing effects of that gin have worn off. By a strange coincidence, I was full of the same beautiful drug at the time you were reading the book.

If I went on with those reminiscences they would probably make, not five volumes, but twenty-five. In all probability, "Newspaper Days" will be the last. The teens lying between it and "Happy Days" were so like any other teens that I hesitate to write about them, and the years following "Newspaper Days" bring up too many still living men.

I wore not one mezuzah, but no less than ten during the hay-fever season. They failed completely. If you have one with a real punch in it I'll be delighted to have it but if it is simply the usual fraud I refuse to take it.

God help us all! I hope to see you in Chicago very soon.

Sincerely yours,
H. L. Mencken

To Ellery Sedgwick
[PU-CC]

H. L. Mencken
1524 Hollins St.
Baltimore
November 1, 1941

Dear Sedgwick:

I find your letter of October 28th on my return to Baltimore. I needn't tell you that I was delighted to hear that you really liked "Newspaper Days". You can imagine that I had a swell time writing it.

---

[4] A Chicago bookseller.

It is, of course, mainly directed at old newspaper men. Maybe I'll do a companion volume on my magazine adventures at some future time. Unhappily, that future time begins to draw rather short. Day by day I note the accumulating signs of senility. Only too soon I'll be an angel in Heaven, prancing and cavorting around the throne.

I often wonder what would have been the consequence if I had accepted your offer so long ago. I was tempted sorely, and it was mainly my desire to remain by my mother here in Baltimore that made me say no. On the whole, it was probably a wise decision, for I have been more comfortable here than I'd ever have been in New York. Nevertheless, I suspect now and then that staying here cut off some good opportunities.

Don't you ever rove the country any more? I'd certainly like to see you in Baltimore. The victuals here remain eatable, and the bartenders are really magnificent.

Sincerely yours,
H. L. Mencken

1942

To HENRY M. HYDE[1]

[PU]

[*Baltimore?*]
March 5, 1942

DEAR HENRY:

I enclose a clipping of a piece that was printed under your name in the *Evening Sun* of March 3rd. I observe that the copy readers struck out the article from in front of the first word of the second paragraph, and so made you write like a contributor to *Time*. I offer you my condolences on this outrage. All the young reporters are imitating *Time*, but we old-timers must stand for the English language.

I pray for you incessantly.

Yours,
[*H. L. Mencken*]

[1] Henry M. Hyde (1860–1951): author and journalist; he was Washington correspondent for the Baltimore *Evening Sun*.

◇◇◇◇◇◇◇◇◇◇◇◇◇

To H. L. DAVIS
[OFP]

H. L. Mencken
1524 Hollins St.
Baltimore
April 17, 1942

DEAR MR. DAVIS:

I have driven a nail into my radio, and so I get a reasonable amount of peace. Also, I have poured a quart of molten sealing wax over my phonograph. God knows I wish I could do something comparable to the telephone. Having suffered under it for forty years I should be more or less used to it by now, but the plain fact is that I jump every time it rings.

I hope that work is going well with you again, and that your book will soon be finished. As for me, I have wasted nearly a year on a long record that can't be published. When I began it I was convinced that it was worth reducing to paper, but now I develop some doubts. However, the job is done, and so I suppose I should rejoice.

The coming Summer promises to provide Christian men with the best show seen on earth since the Crusades. I am looking forward to it with the most eager anticipations. I only hope that if the Japs actually take California they are polite to you.

Sincerely yours,
H. L. Mencken

◇◇◇◇◇◇◇◇◇◇◇◇◇

To JAMES T. FARRELL
[OFP]

H. L. Mencken
1524 Hollins St.
Baltimore
April 17, 1942

DEAR MR. FARRELL:

Your plan to do a novel on American politics is interesting indeed. Needless to say, I'll be delighted to give it any help that is possible. Let us sit down together some day and discuss it. Once I hear about it in more detail I'll be able to offer you more rational advice about the materials. They are enormous in quantity. My own files, in fact, are heavy with them. I have followed the politicoes for more than forty years, and know a great many. Rather curiously, political novels have been rare in this great Republic. Many years ago I induced Harvey Fergusson to do one, with Washington as the scene. The result was a book called "Capitol Hill". It was not bad, but it never made much of an impression. Fergusson was familiar with the materials at first hand, for his father had been a Congressman, and he had been brought up in Washington and afterward became a newspaper man there.

I agree with you thoroughly about Anderson. It should be said in defense of his autobiography, of course, that it was put together by others after his death. It contains some fairly good stuff, but in the main it seems to me to be rubbish. His self-consciousness increased as he grew older. In the days when I first knew him he was writing simply and directly, and some of the things he did were unquestionably first-rate. But as he began to receive attention he became a sort of actor, and in his last days I found it impossible to get any pleasure out of him. He resented that fact more or less, and so I fare rather badly in his book.[2]

I don't blame you for tiring of fiction. Every man is wearied now and then by his main job. Sometimes I am almost tempted to spit on my hands and do a book of verse. It would be dreadful, true enough, but it might conceivably do me some good.

Sincerely yours,
H. L. Mencken

◇◇◇◇◇◇◇◇◇◇◇◇◇◇

To Albert G. Keller
[OFP]

H. L. Mencken
1524 Hollins St.
Baltimore
June 5, 1942

Dear Keller:

Unhappily, my ignorance of Goethe is so dense that I fear I can't help you. It occurs to me that what may be troubling you is simply

---

[2] In his *Memoirs,* Sherwood Anderson accuses Mencken of having remained blind to the merits of *Winesburg, Ohio,* then boasting that he had recognized its value from the first. The truth is that Mencken had written a very favorable review of the book in the August 1919 *Smart Set.*

an aberration of memory. Certainly the quotation from "Torquato Tasso" is substantially identical to the one you have in mind. It has been my experience that the memory often effects such similar changes. More than once in compiling my Dictionary of Quotations I was astonished to discover that a quotation that I remembered clearly was also remembered inaccurately. I wish I could help you, but I am simply not competent.

Here in Maryland the same horrible weather that you mention has been going on. At the end of April the cold winds set up an inflammation in my naso-pharynx, and in a little while it got so violent that I had to go to the Johns Hopkins Hospital. I was laid up there for two weeks. The new sulfanol drugs cured the infection, but I came out of the place greatly depleted, and I am still somewhat shaky. Several jobs that I am hoping to tackle must be deferred until I am restored to complete normalcy.

There is only one way to buck the magazines, and that is to keep hard at it. It is, of course, a great advantage to know what is already in them, but I should add that most editors like to print, now and then, something that is in sharp contrast to their usual stuff. I am convinced that if you bang away you'll find a ready and profitable market. God knows the American magazines need the sort of stuff that you have to offer. Nine-tenths of their contents are written by literati who know precisely nothing. I'll look up the *Fortune* series at once, though I should add that *Fortune* seems to me to be a wretchedly bad magazine.

I agree with you thoroughly about Billy Phelps.[3] I have been in contact with him for many years, and have a high opinion of him. As you say, he is completely free from the idiotic pretentiousness that marks so many of his colleagues of the English faculty.

It is not true that I hate poetry. That report flows out of the fact that I once attempted, perhaps unwisely, to investigate its nature. I was convinced then, and I am still convinced, that it is a sort of escape mechanism—in brief, it is made up mainly of sonorous and impressive statements of the obviously not true. People always assume that any theory of that sort involves a moral judgment. Certainly it does not in my case. I can see no objection whatsoever to stating the obviously not true, provided the result is beautiful. In scientific writing, of course, it would be absurd, but we are talking of poetry, not science.

---

[3] Billy: William Lyon Phelps.

I hope that you are comfortable in Maine. In all probability, I'll stick to Baltimore during the Summer. I really feel comfortable in hot weather. What fetches me is cold, especially when it is accompanied by wind.

Yours
H. L. M.

◇◇◇◇◇◇◇◇◇◇◇◇◇◇

To CHANNING POLLOCK
[PT]

Baltimore, July 13, 1942

DEAR CHANNING:

I not only authorize you to print that passage; I insist upon it. I am only sorry that you did not mention the fact that I was one of the most eminent piano players of that era—in fact, I had only one real rival in the whole United States, and that was Nick Longworth. He was the doyen of all the Cincinnati professors. We used to compare notes in his later years.[4]

I am delighted to hear that you are doing your autobiography. It has long been my contention that every literate man is under a sort of obligation to humanity to set down what he has seen and heard. Incidentally, Dr. Julian P. Boyd, librarian of Princeton, is toying with a scheme to do a volume of my letters while I am still alive. If you have any in your files, and he applies to you for the loan of them, this is simply to say that I approve his enterprise. He is walking into a really formidable job but seems to be determined to go through with it.

I have just got out of hospital, after some minor surgery, but seem to be recovering fast and hope to be fully restored to normalcy in a few days.

Yours,
H. L. M.

---

[4] In his autobiography, *Harvest of My Years* (Indianapolis, New York: The Bobbs-Merrill Co.; 1943), Channing Pollock made short references to H. L. Mencken, one of them being to the effect that once they both toured the red-light districts of Baltimore.

To Van Wyck Brooks
[OFP]

H. L. Mencken
1524 Hollins St.
Baltimore
July 14, 1942

Dear Brooks:

Thanks very much for your letter. I am passing on the news to Boyd, and you'll probably hear from him in the near future.

It is pleasant indeed to know that you and Carl Sandburg were thinking of me. I have not had any direct communication with him for some years, but there was a time when we saw each other more or less, and exchanged a frequent correspondence.

I surely hope that you'll be heading this way at some time in the near future, and that you'll let me see you in Baltimore. I have just got out of hospital, where I enjoyed some minor surgery, but my recovery seems to be swift and I am already feeling almost normal.

Yours,
H. L. Mencken

1943

To Huntington Cairns
[PT]

1524 Hollins Street
Baltimore, Maryland
January 15, 1943

Dear Huntington:

Thanks very much for the reprint of your treatise on Plato's Theory of Law. I have read it with the utmost pleasure, but I should add at once that it has not disposed of my apparent congenital dislike of Plato. I was simply born an Aristotelian, and nothing that you or I can do will ever change that fact. When I put my nose into "Nicomachean Ethics" I begin to feel at home at once, but the Platonic Dialogues irritate me constantly, and apparently incurably. I give you Plato's discussion of lawyers on your page 385 as a specimen of his almost invariable loose thinking. There is, to be sure, a case against lawyers, as there is a case against the holy saints, but I am sure that he doesn't state it.

God help us one and all! I hope you'll be coming this way soon again. We meet much too seldom for my comfort.

Yours,
M.

(1943)

To JAMES T. FARRELL

UP]

H. L. Mencken
704 Cathedral St.
Baltimore
February 18, 1943

DEAR MR. FARRELL:

Please don't make excuses for holding that list. You are free to keep it as long as you please. Whenever you are actually done with it, let me have it here.

It seems to me that your criticism of "Sister Carrie" is extraordinarily penetrating and convincing. It suggests a sort of recreation for you: why don't you do a series of critical ideas on your principal contemporaries, and then bring them out as a book? I believe that it would have an excellent chance. Nine-tenths of the current criticism is done by imbeciles who measure everything with the Marxian yardstick. Dreiser, without doubt, is one of the worst writers ever seen on earth. Nevertheless, he has something that is hard to match. I well recall the enormous impression that "Sister Carrie" made on me when I read it back in 1902. I was also knocked off my feet by "Jennie Gerhardt". The later books seem to me to be less impressive, and I have never been able to convince myself that "An American Tragedy" is really first-rate work.

I hear that Dreiser is now laboring away at a book to be called "The Bulwark". He started it to my knowledge in 1912 or thereabout, but then laid it away.

Yours,
M.

(1943)

To DUDLEY NICHOLS[1]
[YU]

H. L. Mencken
1524 Hollins St.
Baltimore
March 9, 1943

DEAR MR. NICHOLS:

Thanks very much for your letter, and my most abject apologies for putting you to so much trouble. I happened upon the address of Ernest Booth a little while after I wrote to you, and was soon in communication with him. What he is doing, I don't know precisely, but I got out of him the information that I was seeking.

It seems to me that your suggestions about the psychology of the criminal are excellent. The artist, obviously, is a closely allied species, and not infrequently the two coalesce.

I know Henry Miller quite well, and have a high opinion of some of his work. To be sure, he now and then gets drunk on words, but it is not often. His style is really marvelously effective, and it seems to me that he has something to say. I was unaware of the fact that he is in California and, in truth, haven't heard from him for a couple of years.

Incidentally, if you have any of my letters in your file, and a request reaches you from Dr. Julian P. Boyd for the loan of them, this is simply to say that I agree. Boyd is the librarian at Princeton, and he is planning to bring out a book of my letters while I am still alive. He is a charming fellow, and may be trusted to return anything that he borrows.

Sincerely yours,
H. L. Mencken

[1] Dudley Nichols (1895–1960): a movie director. He produced several films after plays by Eugene O'Neill.

(1943)

To THEODORE DREISER
[UP]

H. L. Mencken
1524 Hollins St.
Baltimore
March 19, 1943

DEAR DREISER:

I note what you say in your letter of March 13th. I surely hope that if you ever finish that autobiographical trilogy you push on to four volumes, and devote the fourth to the period since 1911. It has been full of rich experience.

What, precisely, are your ideas about the current crusade to save humanity? I have seen many statements of them, chiefly in the Communist papers, but most of those statements seemed to me to be incredible. Are you supporting the war, and if so, to what extent? I recall that during the last great struggle for democracy our ideas were virtually identical, but I somehow gather the impression that you have changed your mind this time. Have you ever printed anything on the subject? I observe that the Communists have ceased of late to list you as one of them, and I assume that this has been done in response to your protests. I continue of the opinion, as always, that they are a gang of frauds.

Some time ago E. H. O'Neill, of the University of Pennsylvania library, came down to Baltimore to see me. He told me that the Dreiser bibliography that he has under way has now reached really formidable proportions. I hope and assume that it will be printed soon or late. O'Neill says that he hopes to make it really exhaustive. It will include not only everything that you have published yourself, but also everything that has been written about you, not omitting book reviews.

Yours,
M.

[*Dreiser answered this letter in the following terms on March 27, 1943:*

You ask: "What, precisely, are your ideas about the current crusade to save humanity". Personally, I do not know what can save humanity unless it is the amazing Creative force which has brought "humanity", along with its entire environment into being. I, myself, in my day have cursed Life and gone down to the East River from a

$1.50 a week room in Brooklyn to a canal dock to quit. My pride and my anger would not let me continue, as I thought. And yet a lunatic canal boatman ferrying potatoes from Tonawanda to the Wallabout Market in Brooklyn did. Wanting me as a companion to accompany him on his return trip to Tonawanda, he stated as his excuse for his liberality or charity that he "thought maybe I was trying to run away from my wife". And my wife was in the west living on her parents while I struggled and starved on alone. To a guy with a total of 15 cents left and a $1.50 week room to return to, this brought an ironic laugh and, in consequence, a change of mood that saved me from going to Tonawanda and instead—the next day—moved me to cross over to Manhattan Island with a new idea. But I will have to write A Literary Apprenticeship before you can learn all about that. Incidentally, that is why I said to you that A Literary Apprenticeship would be a scream.

For not more than five years from that date I was Editor-in-Chief of all the Butterick Publications at a fat salary. My predecessor as editor had—on being discharged—committed suicide. And you ask me about the "Current crusade to save humanity". My answer is that I do not know positively—nor do I think that anyone else does so know,—that is, that it will be saved. It may go under.

And certainly many phases of it—the lunatic rich with their asinine control of billions—should go under, just as did the French Monarchists—Louis XIV, XV, XVI and Charles I in England. And as the Russian Czarist system up to 1917 should have and did go under. For if there is any reason for saving humanity surely it should not be that of starving and murdering it. No life of any kind, in my humble opinion, is better than that. For I do not believe in slavery or starvation. For if, with all that we know through modern science,—agronomy, medicine, economy and education—we cannot do better by the average man than I saw in Russia in 1927—(the left-over miseries of the Czarist Regime) also in England in 1911, '12, '26, '28, '38—and Spain, France and Belgium, then I think humanity had better be allowed to pass. For I have pity. And pity suggests that no humanity at all is better than what I have seen here and there,—many fractions of the United States included.

I know you have no use for the common man since he cannot distinguish himself. But I have—just as I have for a dog, a worm, a bird, a louse or any living or creeping thing. The use that I see is contrast and so interest for you and for me. For without these where would either you or myself or humanity, as a whole, be? Where? The interest and charm of life—where would it be? And for whom? Your unsaved humanity? I do not follow that course of reasoning. For without natural universal interest in all phases of created life this night I would take a sleeping potion that would end the argument for me. As for you—you might live on without mental interest of any kind, assuming that you could and also chose to do so. But I cannot even see it as possible.

You see, Mencken, unlike yourself, I am biased. I was born poor. For a time, in November and December, once, I went without shoes. I saw my beloved mother suffer from want—even worry and wring her hands in misery. And for that reason, perhaps—let it be what it will—I, regardless of whom or what, am for a social system that can and will do better than that for its members—those who try, however humbly,—and more, wish to learn how to help themselves, but are none-the-less defeated by the trickeries of a set of vainglorious dunces, who actually believe that money—however come by—the privilege of buying this and that—distinguishes them above all others of the very social system which has permitted them to be and to trick these others out of the money that makes them so great. Upon my word! To be more specific—for Christ's sake!

As for the Communist System—as I saw it in Russia in 1927 and '28—I am for it—hide and hoof. For like Hewlett of Canterbury, who wrote that fascinating book on England and Russia, I saw its factories, its mines, its stores, its Komissars, with at least ten of whom I discussed the entire problem.

On their hands, at that time, they had the recuperation and future welfare of some 180,000,000 people that included millions of Mohammedans, Buddhists, Nomads and God knows what else. And better educated, and higher thinking, and more kindly and courageous men and women, I have never met in my life. In my humble estimation their equals in this country are few indeed. In sum, I conceived a passionate respect for that great people and still retain it,—a people who, in so far as I could see, wished humanity to survive on a better plane than ever it had known before,—not die or starve or be made slaves of. And the love I conceived for them then, and that passionate admiration I also developed there, I still retain, as also, I have for their writers, artists and musicians since ever I became aware of their enormous gifts. If you question my judgment here, show me a Chekhov, a

Dostoyevsky, a Tolstoy, a Gogol, a Moussorgsky in all the history of American art and American reaction to American life and I will sit up in silent reverence, for their equals I do not know.

As for Doctor, Professor Mencken—to me, of course, he is sui generis. Never has there been in this or any other country before, in so far as I know, one like him! And, sadly, I fear, there will not soon be another. He seems to me to lack faith in anything and everything save the futility of everything—which is a Voltairean approach to all that is, and that amuses me. But for all the bull-headed faults and ironic conclusions of said Heinrich—I love and always will love him—be the final estimate of said Dreiser or said Mencken what it may.

Darling—don't forget that I remember how, almost fatalistically, you arrived in my life when, from a literary point of view, I was down and out, and you proceeded to fight for me. Night and day apparently. Swack! Smack! Crack! Until finally you succeeded in chasing an entire nation of literary flies to cover. It was lovely! It was classic. And whether you choose to slam me right or left, as is your wont, in the future, Darling Professor, Doctor, I will love you until the hour of my death. And don't pull any Edgar Allan Poe stuff in connection with my forgotten grave either. Do you hear me? Or, I'll come back and fix you. And how!

Love and kisses from
[*Dreiser*]

P.S. *As for the American Communists—well there are—or were and still are, I assume,—many fakirs and flies and camp followers who hope to pick up a living out of the cause. They have never interested me and I have never been interested by their gyrations and genuflections. I am—and have been—content to deal with the Russian Government direct—its foreign office, its American Ambassador, its consuls, etc. I have written for Pravda often and have answered many cables that have come to me direct.*

P.P.S. *If your really want to bother with my social viewpoint why not read America Is Worth Saving? It is there in full.*

I have now nine extra letters from you. When they reach 15 I'll send you the dates and send them on together with my answers, if you say so, to the U.P. in Philadelphia.]

(1943)

◇◇◇◇◇◇◇◇◇◇◇◇◇◇

To Arthur Davidson Ficke[2]
[YU]

H. L. Mencken
1524 Hollins St.
Baltimore
April 21, 1943

Dear Mr. Ficke:

I am distressed indeed to hear that you are ill, and only hope that this spell passes off with dispatch.

What you say about those old days of the *Smart Set* naturally touches me. We had a lot of fun in that era, and though our purposes were certainly not lofty, it is pleasant to hear that they left some traces. I have, of late, been amusing myself by digging through my letter-files of the *Smart Set* period. They are very bulky, and I am trying to get some order into them so that the PH.D.'s of the future may be able to mine them with some success. They are full of letters from authors, and many of these letters are extremely interesting, for they discuss the work of the writers.

I hope you let me see you sometime in New York. I expect to be there toward the end of this week but, unhappily, I'll be pretty well on the jump. A trip planned for a month ago had to be abandoned on account of illness, and I am now beset by delayed engagements. However, I'll certainly be back during the Spring, and I trust that a chance will offer for a session then.

Sincerely yours,
H. L. Mencken

To Harry Elmer Barnes
[PT]

August 27, 1943

Dear Barnes:

The *Progressive* brethren sent me a dozen copies of the magazine, and I have been going through them with great pleasure.[3] Without question, they are coming nearer to telling the truth than any other

[2] Arthur Davidson Ficke (1883–1945): the American poet.
[3] The *Progressive,* a weekly magazine founded in 1929.

group of American editors. The newspapers have simply abrogated their proper function. They are all hewing close to the party line.

God knows I'd like to see you, but I hesitate to make a train trip in these days. Hay fever seems to be pretty severe this year, and I am intensely uncomfortable. Happily, I have several routine jobs in hand that keep me pleasantly occupied, and so I do not repine.

If you see my Uncle Julius, please tell him that I pray for him regularly.

Yours,
[*Unsigned*]

◇◇◇◇◇◇◇◇◇◇◇◇◇◇

To HARRY ELMER BARNES
[PT]

September 2, 1943

DEAR BARNES:

I'd certainly like to do something for Rubin, but I simply can't concoct anything within his pattern. I am so constituted that I have to either Tell It All or stay silent altogether. In this war, as in the last, it seems to me to be most rational to save up what I have to say until it can be said freely. You, yourself, manage the thing very adroitly, but I am not so skillful.

Hay fever is middling bad this year, but I still manage to get some work done. I am up to my ears in the supplement to "The American Language". It will take me a year at least.

Yours,
[*Unsigned*]

◇◇◇◇◇◇◇◇◇◇◇◇◇◇

To GEORGE JEAN NATHAN
[CU]

H. L. Mencken
1524 Hollins St.
Baltimore
November 4, 1943

DEAR GEORGE:

My very best thanks. You relieve my mind considerably. I was in great fear that I had got a lot of baloney into that list. You will be rewarded post-mortem, and in a rich and even lavish manner.

Bromley and I had a really swell time. He is an excellent lawyer, and he fed me beautifully. The government's attorney, Hassell, turned out to be an almost fabulous jackass. He gave me such leads that I was genuinely amazed. God knows I wish you had been present to take a hand.

I see nothing in Rascoe's raving. If he ever writes anything that is really dreadful, let me have a clipping of it. Soon or late, of course, some one will throw him for a dreadful fall. I am strongly against quarreling publicly with such lice. That is one thing he hopes we'll do. In six months Roy Howard will fire him and he'll be on the beach again.[4]

Yours,
M.

◇◇◇◇◇◇◇◇◇◇◇◇◇◇

To JAMES T. FARRELL
[UP]

H. L. Mencken
704 Cathedral St.
Baltimore
November 15, 1943

DEAR MR. FARRELL:

I see no reason why you should bother about those reviews. They are so obviously prejudiced that no sensible man credits them. You are probably never going to accumulate a large public, but nevertheless, you'll make steady progress, I am sure, and in the end you'll find yourself in a really solid position. The fact that a great many imbeciles have yipped at you will only help you.

I agree with you thoroughly about most of the so-called slang now prevailing. It is invented, of course, by smarties who really understand nothing whatsoever about the processes of folk psychology. Fortunately, their inventions seldom if ever get into the actual speech of the people. All slang, of course, is invented by individuals, not by groups, but nevertheless it must accord with the speechways of the group or it is bound to fail. I have myself suggested at least a hundred words in my time, but only two or three of them have ever got anywhere. Some of the rest still have some currency among the so-called intelligentsia,

[4] Roy W. Howard was editor and president of the New York *World-Telegram*.

but the intelligentsia have nothing whatsoever to do with the common speech. Their influence upon it, indeed, is almost as slight as that of the grammarians.

I have begun to read "My Days of Anger", and like it immensely. It seems to me that your writing shows a constant improvement. It was good to start with, but now you are perfecting your technic. When you attempt anything it always comes off.

It has been calculated by a talented theologian of my acquaintance that every one of us will have to sweat in Purgatory for ten million years for every second of sin on this earth. It is thus obvious that an old man will have a worse time of it than boys hanged at the age of 16 or 17. My own accumulation, I greatly fear, is now almost infinite—in fact, I definitely despair of salvation. If there is any truth whatsoever in either the text of Holy Scriptures or the teachings of Holy Church, I am very likely to go straight to Hell, without any preliminary pause in Purgatory.

It is good news that you are doing a book of short stories. I have read several notices in the papers about your New York novel. I surely hope you spit on your hands and let go. The best of luck!

Sincerely yours,
H. L. Mencken

◇◇◇◇◇◇◇◇◇◇◇◇◇◇

To Walter F. White
[YU]

H. L. Mencken
1524 Hollins St.
Baltimore
December 6, 1943

Dear Walter:

I have read the manifesto of your committee in an humble and prayerful spirit, but can only report that it seems to me to be buncombe. If you wrote it, then you will have a bad quarter of an hour when you face the post-mortem F.B.I. I can see no evidence whatever that the English, if victorious in the present war at American expense, will make any effort to carry out the programme outlined in your Item 7, nor do I believe that the pledges you ask for from candidates for office, if you get them, will be worth anything. You already have virtually all of them from Roosevelt, but how many are being carried out?

All the frauds will promise you everything you ask for, and all the honest men, if any, will be daunted by the visible impossibility of doing anything effectual. Race relations never improve in war time; they always worsen. And it is when the boys come home that Ku Klux Klans are organized. I believe with George Schuyler that the only really feasible way to improve the general situation of the American Negro is to convince more and more whites that he is, as men go in this world, a decent fellow, and that amicable living with him is not only possible but desirable. Every threat of mass political pressure, every appeal to political mountebanks, only alarms the white brother, and so postpones the day of reasonable justice. The immediate problem is not to get more and more gaudy jobs for professional Negroes—including, for example, that of admiral in the Navy—, nor is it to force the doors of hotels, clubs and stores that only the rich could patronize; it is not even to get useless (and probably venal) votes for a horde of poor black ignoramuses in the South. It is to protect the Negro, if it can be done, against the inevitable attempt of white competitors on the lower levels to dispose of him by outrage and murder. Here in my own town of Baltimore, where race relations have been peaceful for generations and no Negro has been denied his vote in my time, every thoughtful person, black or white, is made uneasy by the possibilities ahead. The war industries have brought in huge gangs of barbaric white crackers from the South and on their heels have come other gangs of black refugees from Southern White Christianity. It is not hard to figure out what will happen when the flood of government money runs out, and these two gangs begin fighting for the marginal jobs. . . .

[Incomplete]

1944

◇◇◇◇◇◇◇◇◇◇◇◇◇◇◇◇◇◇◇◇

To GEORGE JEAN NATHAN
[CU]

H. L. Mencken
1524 Hollins St.
Baltimore
February 24, 1944

DEAR GEORGE:

I hope the new book is making good progress. My own seems to be moving very well. It is, of course, a dreadfully tedious job, but I somehow enjoy it. It doesn't need a psychoanalyst to discover that there is a pedant hidden in Henry.

Masters seems to be virtually blotto. I had a note from him the other day, but it was brief and it said nothing. In it, however, he hinted that when he escapes at last, if he ever does, he'll probably begin suit against the authors of that libel. It will be interesting to find out how it was launched.

Edgar Selwyn's death was a real blow to me, and when it was followed almost immediately by Art Kudner's I began to rock.[1] Worse, three other old friends passed out within the same week. It is later than we think.

Yours,
M.

---

[1] Edgar Selwyn (1875–1944): ex-actor and dramatist. Art(hur) Kudner (1890–1944): advertising man, contributor to *The Atlantic Monthly.*

(1944)

To James T. Farrell
[UP]

H. L. Mencken
1524 Hollins St.
Baltimore 23
June 5, 1944

Dear Mr. Farrell:

The quick surrender of the Canadians does not surprise me in the slightest. They are a highly dubious lot and their attempts on American magazines are even more idiotic than their attempts on American books. You will observe that the name of the offending functionary is not revealed, and that you thus have no remedy against him at law.

I certainly hope you do that article on George Ade. He is one of the underestimated men. I am convinced that his short stories are much better than his fables. Some of them are really superb pieces of buffoonery.

Dreiser came to New York to accept a prize from the American Academy of Arts and Letters. I didn't come to see him, for I simply couldn't endure any such transaction. For more than thirty years on end the members of the Academy devoted themselves very largely to trying to cry him down. For him to now take a cash prize from them seem to me to be intolerable. I think I'd rather starve first.

I surely hope that you settle down at Pleasantville and find it agreeable. I am more and more convinced that New York is a bad place for a working author. I keep out of it as much as possible.

"To Whom It May Concern" has not yet reached me, but I assume that it is on its way.

Sincerely yours,
H. L. Mencken

To JAMES T. FARRELL
[UP]

H. L. Mencken
1524 Hollins St.
Baltimore
July 4, 1944

DEAR MR. FARRELL:

Thanks very much for the chance to read your excellent article on Lardner. I think your analysis of him is completely accurate. The essential thing about him was his utter disbelief in human pretension. He saw the fraud in what are commonly regarded as the higher motives.

I marvel that some one doesn't sit down quietly and do a serious philosophy (or maybe I should rather say psychology) on some such assumption. If I had two lives to live I'd tackle it myself. Unhappily, I am so hard beset by work long-promised, and even contracted for, that I'll be an angel in Heaven long before the time offers to tackle any such enterprise.

Lardner was an extremely interesting man. One of his remarkable peculiarities was the extraordinary slowness of his speech. He talked at the rate of no more than thirty words a minute. He was, in the days when I knew him best a considerable boozer, but he was extremely interesting even in his cups. I have put in many a pleasant evening with him at Rogers' old saloon in Sixth avenue.

Sincerely yours,
H. L. Mencken

To HARRY ELMER BARNES
[OFP]

H. L. Mencken
1524 Hollins St.
Baltimore
July 18, 1944

DEAR BARNES:

God knows I'd like to take your advice, but it seems to me to be completely impossible. If I resumed writing about the current scene I'd collide with the censorship before I had got beyond the second paragraph of the first article. It is simply impossible for me to deal with such quacks without using them roughly. The official censorship is only the half of it, and not the worse half. Every newspaper and magazine in America is also operating a volunteer censorship that goes much further. Thus I am convinced that it would be an impossible thing for me to discuss the current news, and so I have shut down my plant sine die. The new book, meanwhile, keeps me jumping. It is a really dreadful job, but I somehow enjoy it.

I am enclosing a formula for a new cocktail that I have lately invented. I can recommend it heartily. Unfortunately, it lacks a name. If you have any suggestions to offer, I'll be glad to submit them to my pastor.

Yours,
M.

To VICTOR T. RENO[2]
[OFP]

H. L. Mencken
1524 Hollins St.
Baltimore
July 18, 1944

DEAR MR. RENO:

Thanks very much for those copies of the San Quentin *News.* If you encounter any other such glossaries I certainly hope you let me see them.

It goes without saying that I'll be delighted to embellish the Hirshberg book.[3] Let it come to me as above. I am glad to hear that you found "Living Philosophies" so quickly.[4] My own copy has somehow disappeared, but I think I can pick up another in New York. My contribution to the book was really based on an article that I had contributed to the *Nation* some time before. But I put in a lot of hard work

---

[2] A collector of Menckenians. He lived on the Pacific coast.

[3] The Hirshberg book: *What You Ought to Know about Your Baby* (New York: Butterick Publishing Co.; 1910), a hack job that Mencken had performed for a Baltimore physician.

[4] *Living Philosophies* (New York: Simon and Schuster; 1931), edited by Will Durant, contained an essay by Mencken: "What I Believe". It had previously appeared not in the *Nation,* but in the *Forum* for September 1930.

improving it, and I agree with you that it is one of the most effective things I have ever written.

Sincerely yours,
H. L. Mencken

To Bernard Smith[5]
[AAK]

H. L. Mencken
1524 Hollins St.
Baltimore–23
October 5, 1944

Dear Smith:

I can think of no answer to your argument. You are, in fact, completely right. I approved the Follett scheme mainly because two assumptions were in my mind. One was that it would probably not go any further. The other was that the best of Bierce is in the epigrams, not in the stories. I see no objection to including a few of the stories in the volume you have in mind but I am convinced that only a few are likely to interest the readers of today. Bierce's best stuff is not in his fiction but in his witticisms. Some of the epigrams are magnificent and so are some of the fables. If the book turns out to be a success it will always be possible to bring out a second volume based on a closer gleaning. There is an enormous mass of matter in the Neale edition. Nine-tenths of it, of course, is simply newspaper stuff and of no possible interest to the present generation.

Sincerely yours,
H. L. Mencken

[5] One of the editors of Alfred A. Knopf.

1945

To GEORGE JEAN NATHAN
[CU]

H. L. Mencken
1524 Hollins St.
Baltimore–23
February 8, 1945

DEAR GEORGE:

That Winchell story is made out of the whole cloth. Certainly I'd have heard of it if there had ever been a divorce. I marvel that New York endures its gossip mongers so docilely. Whenever they deal with anything of which I have personal knowledge they are 100 per cent wrong.

I have finished my book, and also a chapter for a cooperative history of American literature, projected by a posse of super-pedagogues. This last almost broke my back. It was difficult indeed to get a coherent account of the subject into small space.[1]

I am not sure as yet about the precise date of my arrival in Gomorrah. I'll write to you again.

Yours,
M.

[1] The history of American literature here mentioned is the *Literary History of the United States,* edited by R. Spiller and others (New York: The Macmillan Co., 1946). H. L. Mencken contributed the chapter on the American language.

To GEORGE JEAN NATHAN
[CU]

H. L. Mencken
1524 Hollins St.
Baltimore–23
February 22, 1945

DEAR GEORGE:

Hearst is a man of impeccable taste in literature; hence his veneration for my compositions. Unhappily, I simply can't do anything for his great family papers. In these days of saving the world my whole vocabulary is forbidden. I couldn't write a column on politics without bringing down the professional patriots. It is much easier to turn to other subjects and let the country be damned.

I hope we'll be seeing each other the week of March 12th.

Yours,
M.

To BRADFORD F. SWAN[2]
[YU]

H. L. Mencken
1524 Hollins St.
Baltimore–23
March 1, 1945

DEAR MR. SWAN:

The true first edition of "The Artist" is accurately described in the Frey bibliography. My inscription in the Hogan copy must have been in error. Unhappily, I can't tell you how many copies of the so-called acting edition of "Heliogabalus" were published. It might be a good idea to write to Alfred Knopf. Perhaps his records will show.

I had some very pleasant interchanges with Henry B. Fuller in his last days. He was a charming man. Unhappily, I never met him face to face. I tried hard to induce him to contribute to the *Smart Set,* but by that time he had pretty well abandoned writing.

Let that list come along at your convenience. Perhaps I'll be able to suggest some way to fill the gaps in it.

[2] Bradford F. Swan (born in 1907) is theatre and art critic of the *Providence Journal;* he began collecting H. L. Mencken when he was in high school, and amassed a considerable collection that he later gave to the Yale Sterling Library.

Needless to say, I'll be delighted to have that article on fruit-growing by Dreiser. My souvenirs of him are to go to the New York Public Library on my departure for bliss eternal. They include a great many curious odds and ends. Along with them will go a set of photostats of my letters to him. I got them from the University of Pennsylvania Library a couple of years ago.

I know nothing about Groff Conklin save that he wrote to me about that Smart Set Anthology. His partner in the enterprise was a lowly swine named Burton Rascoe. When I refused to let Rascoe mine my files he retorted by printing a vituperative preface to the book, full of libel on both me and Alfred Knopf. I made no protest, for I never object to such things. Knopf, however, was advised that some of Rascoe's statements were damaging to his business, so he forced the publishers to change the text. In all this transaction Conklin conducted himself decently. All the swinery was ascribable to Rascoe.

I am glad that the Newberry Library has acquired the Fuller papers. The old boy is seldom mentioned today, but soon or late he will be resurrected.

Sincerely yours,
H. L. Mencken

To BRADFORD F. SWAN
[YU]

H. L. Mencken
1524 Hollins Street
Baltimore 23, Md.
April 3, 1945

DEAR MR. SWAN:–

Rather curiously, I have been toying myself, for many years, with the idea of a funeral service for the admittedly damned. Ten or twelve years ago I began to draw it up with the help of my late wife, but her death threw me off it, and I have never resumed. She was herself a complete agnostic and much more anti-clerical than I am, but I had to call in a High Church Episcopal rector for her funeral, to avoid scandalizing her Alabama relatives beyond endurance, just as I had had to call in another to marry us. In the latter case, there was the further consideration that civil marriage is unknown in Maryland. One must either submit to a pastor or go outside the State.

The funeral of my own father, a really violent agnostic, was carried on by the Freemasons, but there was also a clergyman. The Masons shoved him into the background, but vitiated their Boy Scout deed by bringing along a trumpeter who shook the neighborhood with blue notes. My grandfather was also laid away to Christian moans—at the command of my step-grandmother, the legal owner of his carcass.

To avoid any such mishaps in my own case I have left strict orders that my clay is to be taken immediately after death to an undertaker's studio, that no one is to see it, that no flowers are to be spread upon it, and that it is to be cremated absolutely without ceremony. My sister will probably object on the ground that all Baltimore will be aghast, but I have pledged my brother (and executor) to see that the programme is carried out. I have announced to the public more than once that I am to be stuffed post mortem, and offered to the National Museum at Washington, but I hear confidentially that taxidermy is still too backward to achieve the job; moreover, the Maryland laws, which date from the Thirteenth Century, probably prohibit it.

I am too old to give you much help, but I am certainly greatly interested. Let me hear of it when you have the service sketched out. My plan included using some of the more antinomian passages in the Bible—say from the Book of Job. There is an immense mass of material. I believe it should be arranged somewhat like the Episcopal Prayer-Book, with plenty of alternate passages in prose and verse. It should be printed in the same way, with headings in Old Black.

Sincerely yours,
H. L. Mencken

To JAMES T. FARRELL
[UP]

H. L. Mencken
1524 Hollins St.
Baltimore 23
May 5, 1945

DEAR MR. FARRELL:

Needless to say, I'll be delighted to see you whenever you get into these wilds. Let me know of it as far in advance as possible, so that I may clear off the time. I'll probably be here all Spring, and nearly all Summer.

I have read your article on Dreiser with great interest. It is, indeed, excellent stuff. Unhappily, I find myself in some doubt that he is really the sociologist that you make him out. My belief is that his economic, psychological and political reflections are really afterthoughts, and that in most cases they are very far from profound, and even far from intelligent. His moving force in his earlier books was simply to depict the life of struggling people. He had been one himself, and he had a great pity for the whole class. His rationalization of their difficulties came considerably later. I am convinced that "An American Tragedy" was not only not the best of his books, but one of the worst. Certainly "Jennie Gerhardt" was a much more moving piece of writing.

I am told that Hickey, the London columnist, is a Jew like Winchell. What his original name was I don't know. He has invented a number of excellent phrases, including *Lord Haw Haw.* Winchell's emergence as a great Jewish statesman is really preposterous. He should stick to his last.

Yours,
H. L. Mencken

◇◇◇◇◇◇◇◇◇◇◇◇◇

To JAMES T. FARRELL
[UP]

H. L. Mencken
1524 Hollins St.
Baltimore 23
August 17, 1945

DEAR FARRELL:

I am playing with an idea of doing a sort of chronicle of my adventures as editor—in fact, I have already got a substantial part of it on paper. Have I ever asked you to send me a little better account of yourself than is to be found in the press-sheets and reference books? If not, I do so now. Please don't let any such enterprise interfere with your regular work. But if a dull afternoon ever comes along, and you feel like recreating yourself by writing about your adventures in this vale, I'll be delighted to have a copy of the product.

I want to make my narrative as interesting as possible, and I am introducing into it some rather intimate accounts of people I have known. I needn't add that nothing will be printed in my lifetime that would embarrass anyone. All the essential documents, however, will be preserved, and posterity will be free to consult them after, say, 1975 in the library where I propose to deposit them.

Hay fever so far has bothered me very little. I am full of vaccines, and it is possible that they may give me a measurable amount of relief.

Yours,
H. L. Mencken

To James T. Farrell
[UP]

H. L. Mencken
1524 Hollins St.
Baltimore 23
August 31, 1945

Dear Farrell:

What I had in mind was simply a brief memorandum on your beginning. What suggested to you the idea of writing, and how did you make your start? I'd like, if possible, to have the name of the first thing of yours that got into print. I assume that it was a magazine or newspaper piece.

Please don't go to any trouble in the matter. I found myself needing the information for my own narrative, and it occurred to me that it might entertain you to write it down. A man's memory fades as he grows older, and it is thus of some value to get the record straight while it is still clear in mind.

If you ever have an idle afternoon, and feel like making a memorandum, I'll certainly be delighted to have it. I speak of an idle afternoon lightly, but I am well aware that you probably never have any. Neither do I.

Yours,
H. L. Mencken

To Sinclair Lewis
[YU]

H. L. Mencken
1524 Hollins St.
Baltimore–23
October 15, 1945

Dear Red:–

I am not going to tell you that "Cass Timberlane" is comparable to "Babbitt" or "Elmer Gantry" (all except the last 30,000 words, which you wrote in a state of liquor), but it seems to me to be the best thing you have done, and by long odds, since "Dodsworth". It has the same defects that "Dodsworth" had: the woman is such a bitch that it is hard to imagine a sensible man falling for her. But you have a right to set your own story, and in "Cass Timberlane" you have managed it admirably. There is not a trace of the banality that I howled against in "Ann Vickers". There is none of the patriotic fustian that made me sick in "It Can't Happen Here". There is no going to pieces toward the end, as in "Gideon Planish". In brief, a well-planned and well-executed book, with a fine surface. I liked the Assemblages of Husbands and Wives especially. The authentic Red, foul and full of sin, shows up in them. They are searching and swell stuff, though I protest that frigging is much less important in marriage than you seem to make it out. The main thing is simply talk. It is boredom that makes the lawyers fat.

The country swarms with subjects for your future researches. You did the vermin of the Coolidge era, but those of the Roosevelt and post-Roosevelt eras are still open—the rich radical, the bogus expert, the numskull newspaper proprietor (or editor), the career jobholder, the lady publicist, the crooked (or, more usually, idiotic) labor leader, the press-agent, and so on. This, I believe, is your job, and you have been neglecting it long enough. There are plenty of writers of love stories and Freudian documents, though not many as good at it as you are, but there is only one real anatomist of the American Kultur. I think it stinks, but whether it stinks or not is immaterial. It deserves to be done as *you* alone can do it.

Please don't let the fact that you are approaching bliss eternal stay you. You have done a better book at 60 than you were doing at 50. I myself have printed five since 60, and all of them have sold better than those done 20 years ago. Moreover, I have yielded nothing in them to the current hooey: in all of them I stick to my guns. You are, of course, further gone in sin than I am, but you have just proved that you are still very much alive, so I renew my old urgings and solicitations, and curst be him who first cries "Hold! Enough!" You have no duty to humanity, to be sure: to hell with humanity. But you owe something to Red Lewis, the poor immigrant boy from Poland.

Seeing you on the water-wagon affects me like seeing you on your knees. It is intolerably obscene. But if it is necessary, then let us forget it. At any moment the quacks may order me to join you. If so, I shall thank them for their advice—and retire to a brewery.

This letter is too long, but it is now too late for you to do anything about it. I hope your next book, whatever its theme, shows the hero kicking some pestiferous woman in the ass and throwing her out to the Italians. I am, God knows, no gynephobe, but I like women who appreciate their men. We bucks do a great deal for them. We defend them, support them, soothe their frenzies, and even admire them. I think they deserve that admiration—but not when they try to make slaves of men who are their betters. In any combat between superior and inferior I am for No. I. So is our Heavenly Father.

I hope that "Cass" is selling well, and that you are not laying out all your lucre on ice-cream sodas. If you had any fixed place of abode, like a decent Christian, and it were near to Baltimore we might meet now and then and think up nasty names for our enemies. But God seems determined to keep us apart. Maybe we will meet in Heaven. I surely hope not.

Yours,
H. L. M.

1946

To Helen Dreiser (Mrs. Theodore Dreiser)
[UP]

H. L. Mencken
1524 Hollins St.
Baltimore–23
January 18, 1946

Dear Mrs. Dreiser:

Thanks very much for your two letters. You tell me precisely what I wanted to know, and I am certainly delighted to have it. I am only sorry that I couldn't get to Los Angeles for the funeral. If I get to the Coast during the year, I'll certainly come to see you. Meanwhile, you must let me hear of it whenever you head eastward yourself. Maybe I can give you some aid with the business of getting all the books brought out in an uniform edition. There are some, of course, that are apparently hopeless. That happens to the works of every author. But there are others that will deserve new editions, and I incline to believe that Doubleday will undertake them. He is certain to do so if "The Bulwark" has a good sale.

I hope you give serious consideration to a book of memoirs. I don't think you should undertake a formal life of Dreiser, but simply an account of him as you saw him. The woman who did a book on him ten or twelve years ago has broken into the papers in New York with what purports to be an authoritative statement of his ideas, and I gather that she is planning to revise her former work.[1] Inasmuch as she

[1] The woman, etc.: Dorothy Dudley, who wrote *Forgotten Frontiers; Dreiser or the Land of the Free* (New York: H. Smith and R. Haas; 1932).

seems to be pinkish in politics, she will probably devote herself mainly to Dreiser's relations with the Communists. This was an unimportant detail of his life. He will be remembered, not as a politician, but as a novelist, and I think he'll be remembered for a long, long while. I'll get hold of *Life* magazine and take a look at that funeral story.

Once my current book is off my hands, I'll probably begin work on a memoir of my own, describing my relations with Dreiser from 1906 onward. It is, however, not certain that I'll be able to tackle this job, and in any case I'll probably not print the result. It will be less a book than a detailed record for the use of scholars of the future.

I surely hope that you are in good health and reasonably good spirits. I have been disabled for a week past by an injury to my foot. It is not very painful, but it makes it impossible for me to wear a shoe, so I am somewhat handicapped.

Sincerely yours,
H. L. Mencken

◇◇◇◇◇◇◇◇◇◇◇◇◇◇

To HELEN DREISER (MRS. THEODORE DREISER)
[UP]

H. L. Mencken
1524 Hollins St.
Baltimore–23
January 30, 1946

DEAR HELEN:–

That letter was Dreiser at his best, and his best was incomparable. I remember seeing you in Baltimore at the time the two of you started South together. It was, to be precise, on December 12, 1925, for my mother was desperately ill in hospital and died the next day. I remember how I resented his leaving you to sit in a cold car up the street, and how I resented likewise his aloof indifference to my mother's illness. It was a long while afterward before I ever felt close to him again. But I should have known him better. There was a curiously inarticulate side to him, and it often showed up when he was most moved. If I had another life to live I think I'd attempt a long study of him, trying to account for him. But it is now too late.

I have done a preface for "An American Tragedy". It is poor enough stuff and I had some difficulty with it, for I put the book much below some of his others, especially the first half. It must have been back in 1908 or 1910 when he showed me the first sketch of the early chapters—those describing the street preacher. But I hope the preface [serves] its purpose. So far I have not heard from Zevin. My own copy of "An American Tragedy" is buried deep in the Mencken papers at the library here, and Zevin had to dig up one for me in New York.

I hope you bear in mind your own book. Write it exactly as it comes to you. If I can give it any help let me know.[2] My best thanks for the copy of the letter.

Yours,
H. L. M.

◇◇◇◇◇◇◇◇◇◇◇◇◇◇

To HELEN DREISER (MRS. THEODORE DREISER) [UP]

H. L. Mencken
1524 Hollins St.
Baltimore–23
February 4, 1946

DEAR HELEN:

The introduction that I wrote for Zevin does not attempt anything beyond the most superficial criticism. It is mainly devoted to reminiscences of Dreiser, with special attention to his method of work. I sent it to Zevin last week, but so far have not heard from him. Whether or not he likes it, I don't know.

It is too late for me to do a book on Dreiser, simply because I have grown old and have too many other irons in the fire. My present schedule will keep me jumping for three or four years at least, and I begin to doubt that I'll be fit for work by the time it is completed—indeed, it will rather surprise me if I don't find myself an angel in Heaven.

I remember that December day very clearly. Dreiser parked your car on a hill about a block from my house, and we had been sitting at the fire for some time before I learned that you were in it. I thereupon rushed out to the place, dragged you out of it and brought you in to warm up. We had a drink or two, and then you and he started off for the South. My mother died the next day. I naturally expected some communication from him, but none came in. This irked me consider-

[2] Helen Patges Dreiser eventually published *My Life with Dreiser* (Cleveland: World Publishing Co.; 1951).

ably, and we were on cool terms for some years afterward. Eventually, however, we came together again, and in his later years we were very friendly. I could never, of course, follow him into his enthusiasms for such things as spiritualism, Communism and the balderdash of Charles Fort, but that never made any difference between us, for some of my ideas were just as obnoxious to him.

I didn't understand from Zevin that his edition of "An American Tragedy" was to be a part of a Memorial Edition—in fact, I gathered that he was bringing out only the one book. If he offers to do the others, it seems to me that it will be a good idea to let him go ahead. He is a very enterprising fellow, and should be able to sell a good many copies.

I am delighted to hear that you are going on with your book. If I can give you any help with it, you know that I'll be more than glad to do so. I have a great many records that may be of use to you. All of them will go to the New York Public Library at my death.

Yours,
H. L. Mencken

To George Jean Nathan
[CU]

[*Mencken was suing a neighbor whose dog prevented him from working by its continual barking.*]

H. L. Mencken
1524 Hollins St.
Baltimore–23
February 25, 1946

Dear George:

That barking dog disappeared within twenty-four hours after I entered my suit, but I am pressing the business, and demanding damages. What the result will be remains to be seen. The dog's bark did not sound like Dreiser; it rather suggested Paul Armstrong.

That Ass Smith is still at it. This month he describes me as an imitator of Brann, the iconoclast, and says that I have never approached him. Is the fellow insane, or is he simply malicious? See *Encore*, page 318.

I'll be back in Gomorrah on Tuesday, March 12th. If you are free for that evening, please don't forget that I owe you a dinner. Let me know about this.

The best of luck with the book. My own is making pretty fair progress.[3]

Yours,
M.

◇◇◇◇◇◇◇◇◇◇◇◇◇◇

To Julian P. Boyd
[PU]

H. L. Mencken
1524 Hollins St.
Baltimore–23
April 1, 1946

Dear Julian:

I suggest the first week in June. Will that be convenient? If not, then let us make it the second week. In May I'll probably be pretty well occupied. I am very eager to hear about your plans for a revived *North American Review*. Obviously, there is a magnificent chance for a really independent and intelligent magazine. All of those now existing, including especially the *Virginia Quarterly Review,* have got down to the level of small town editorial writing.

Let us have a session with the brethren when we meet. Tell George Brakeley that I am looking forward with the pleasantest anticipations to another visit to his bar.

I am just recovering from my usual Spring bout with a head infection. It was middling severe this year and I am still somewhat dilapidated, but I am able to work.

Sincerely yours,
M.

---

[3] The book: G. J. Nathan's *Theatre Book of the Year* (New York: Alfred A. Knopf; 1946). My own: *Supplement II, The American Language* (New York: Alfred A. Knopf; 1948).

(1946)

◇◇◇◇◇◇◇◇◇◇◇◇◇◇

To Julian P. Boyd
[pu]

H. L. Mencken
1524 Hollins St.
Baltimore–23
June 6, 1946

Dear Julian:

It was a pleasant visit indeed, thanks to you and Grace. Please give her my devotion. My brother was naturally enormously delighted with those fish fossils. I was rained out twice in New York, but nevertheless managed to survive.

I am writing to George Brakeley suggesting that you and he come down to Baltimore on either July 11th or July 18th for a quiet session at the Maryland Club. That will be the very heart and center of the mint julep season, and it will also be a swell time for eating crabs. Let me know about this at your convenience.

The more I think of it the more I am convinced that the brethren at the country club had better decide on a programme before they go any further. I don't mean that they should take a rigid party line, but simply that they should determine their general position, and choose their associates accordingly. Nothing is feebler than a magazine of opinion which admits all shades thereof. People who buy such things want to be supported in their own opinions without being addled by controversies. All attempts to set up magazines devoted to free discussion have failed. Such is the advice and so are the conclusions of the oldest and wisest man now extant on earth.

Yours,
H. L. M.

◇◇◇◇◇◇◇◇◇◇◇◇◇◇

To James T. Farrell
[up]

H. L. Mencken
704 Cathedral St.
Baltimore
June 12, 1946

Dear Mr. Farrell:

I long ago suspected that Dreiser was led into the Marxist corral by his present widow. She avoids the subject very carefully in writing to me. If I ever do my reminiscences of Dreiser I'll produce plenty of proof that in all such matters he was a poor jackass. For many years he believed firmly in spiritualism. I always predicted that if he lived long enough he'd leap back upon the bosom of holy church.

I hope you blister those Canadian blackmailers in your open letter. They are a pestiferous lot and devote themselves busily to annoying American magazines.

If you actually get down into these wilds in July let me have news of it as far ahead as possible, so that I can arrange to be here.

Yours,
H. L. Mencken

To Bradford F. Swan
[YU]

H. L. Mencken
1524 Hollins St.
Baltimore–23
October 24, 1946

Dear Swan:

Inasmuch as the New York Public Library will get all of my letters and perhaps also a number of other things, I incline to believe that it is a good idea to give your own collection to Yale. That will provide at least one more anchor against oblivion. Why I should care about oblivion I simply can't tell you. My earnest belief is that when I die at last I'll be dead forever and all over. The larval PH.D.'s, of course, will probably be snuffling my bones for a few years afterward.

That dog's-eared copy of "The American Language" was not the first edition, as I recall it, but the fourth. It is my work copy and I am still using it for Supplement II. When the job is done at last, I'll be delighted to give it to you.

Yours,
H. L. M.

1947

◇◇◇◇◇◇◇◇◇◇◇◇◇◇◇◇◇◇◇◇

To JAMES T. FARRELL
[UP]

H. L. Mencken
1524 Hollins St.
Baltimore 23
July 17, 1947

DEAR FARRELL:

It doesn't surprise me in the slightest to hear that the military big-wigs in Berlin have refused to permit the German translation of Studs Lonigan. They are, to the best of my belief, complete jackasses. I have been carrying on a correspondence for weeks past regarding their ruling that I can't send copies of the *Congressional Record* to a professor in the University of Berlin. They try to put the blame on the Russians, but they are themselves responsible.

It is good news that you are at work on the second volume of Bernard Clare. The first volume sticks in my mind. Some time ago a Canadian newspaper man asked me to nominate the best living American novelist. I sent in the name of a Chicago Irishman named Farrell.

Why in hell don't you hire a cheap printer to make some letterheads showing your address? Every time I enjoy the honor of receiving a communication from you it takes my secretary ten or fifteen minutes to find out where my reply is to be sent. If there are no printers in

New York, let me know and I'll have some letterheads printed here.

I hope to see you soon.

Yours,
H. L. Mencken

◇◇◇◇◇◇◇◇◇◇◇◇◇◇

To JULIAN P. BOYD
[PU]

H. L. Mencken
1524 Hollins St.
Baltimore–23
October 20, 1947

DEAR JULIAN:

I hope you went to hear that lecture on the God of the Atom. The atom bomb, I have long preached, is the greatest invention that Yahweh has made since leprosy. Certainly it has given great glory to the Christian physicists of this country. Try to imagine a decent cannibal throwing it on a town full of women and children.

My book is riding me hard. The two indexes are really infernal. However, I am taking a couple of days out to visit Joe Hergesheimer, and I hope to finish the whole bloody business by the middle of November.

Yours,
H. L. M.

◇◇◇◇◇◇◇◇◇◇◇◇◇◇

To BRADFORD F. SWAN
[YU]

H. L. Mencken
1524 Hollins St.
Baltimore–23
October 30, 1947

DEAR SWAN:

I offer you my condolences, though with a reservation. The best years in my experience are the forties. After fifty a man begins to deteriorate, but in the forties he is at the maximum of his villainy.

"Chapters of History" is the tentative title for a possible section of my omnibus volume.[1] I am not sure that I'll be able to include it—indeed, I am beginning to doubt that it will be possible to print the book at all. Knopf reports that the collapse of book sales is really appalling.

I am sorry that I didn't meet Mr. Brown in Washington. Some of the talk that I heard at the conference irritated me, and I made an unexpected but somewhat violent speech. I surely trust that our Heavenly Father has forgiven me.[2]

Sincerely yours,
M.

To James T. Farrell
[UP]

H. L. Mencken
1524 Hollins St.
Baltimore 23
November 29, 1947

Dear Farrell:

Thanks very much. I'll send a book to Souvarine at once.

I hope you devote yourself assiduously to that Clare volume, and that you finish it long before the end of 1949.

Ibsen used to fascinate me, but in recent years I find him rather a bore.

Yours,
M.

---

[1] My omnibus volume: *The Days of H. L. Mencken* (New York: Alfred A. Knopf; 1947).

[2] The conference: possibly a Gridiron Club dinner in Washington. Mr. Brown: Sevellon Brown III, the editor of the *Providence Journal.*

1948

To F. Gary Bivings
[PT]

[F. Gary Bivings, then a student at Princeton University, had just written his B.A. *thesis: "Militant Individualism: An Analysis of the Social Attitudes of H. L. Mencken".]*

H. L. Mencken
1524 Hollins St.
Baltimore–23
May 3, 1948

Dear Mr. Bivings:

I have now read your thesis, and with great pleasure. It seems to me that you have done a really first-rate job. Some of your conclusions, to be sure, rather surprise me, but I certainly do not object to them. You state your case very clearly and effectively, and there is evidence of hard and intelligent work on every page. You probably overestimate my belief in laissez-faire. As a matter of fact, I have denounced it off and on for years, and embrace it in the end because any alternative seems to me ten times worse. This is especially true of the socialist alternative. It would wreck civilization without doing any decent man any good whatsoever.

I'd like to have a copy of the thesis. If you say so, I'll have it copied here. I'll then turn over your own manuscript to Hamilton Owens.

My congratulations on an excellent job.

Sincerely yours,
H. L. Mencken

To BRADFORD F. SWAN
[YU]

H. L. Mencken
1524 Hollins St.
Baltimore–23
October 28, 1948

DEAR SWAN:

I am dreadfully sorry to hear of your mother's serious illness. I surely hope that she is comfortable, and that she will show a quick recovery. Such things are always alarming, but nine times out of ten they pass off without leaving much damage.

Julian Boyd has been cherishing his fantastic scheme for four or five years past. I predict formally that he will never execute it. If he undertook to print my letters he'd have to leave out all the really good ones or risk seeing his book burnt by the common hangman.

I have long had a rule against accepting honors of any sort, and I am perhaps the only American author of my years who is not an LL.D. I long ago let it be known that I'd make an exception in favor of a D.D., but so far no one has taken me up.

I had to decline that invitation from the Elizabethan Club at Yale. I found that I was accumulating too many speaking engagements. I like to holler, but it takes an enormous amount of time.

Sincerely yours,
H. L. M.

1950

To FANIA MARINOFF (MRS. CARL VAN VECHTEN) [YU]

[*On November 24th, 1948, H. L. Mencken was stricken by cerebral thrombosis and could never again resume an active literary life. However, he was still able to dictate his correspondence to his secretary, Mrs. John Lohrfinck, and lost none of his previous good spirits, as the following letter will show:*]

H. L. Mencken
1524 Hollins St.
Baltimore–23
April 7, 1950

DEAR MRS. VAN VECHTEN:

Mr. Mencken sends his best thanks for your Easter card. He asks me to tell you that during the present week, of course, he has devoted his whole time to the church. He went to services this morning at 4 A.M. and he tells me that he will remain until 11.35 this evening. He sends you his best.

Sincerely yours,
[*Mrs. John W. Lohrfinck*]
Secretary to Mr. Mencken

1956

To JUDY BRILHART

[*Copy sent by Mrs. Lohrfinck to the Editor*]

Baltimore, Md.
January 25, 1956

DEAR JUDY:

That elegant stuff has arrived and my brother and I are really delighted to have it. We enjoy such things immensely.

I am sorry that we have not seen you of late, but I hope that you'll be coming in sometime before long. My illness is still very bad and it is not likely that I'll be able to get around much longer.

Yours,
[*Dictated by H. L. Mencken*]

[*H. L. Mencken died on January 29, 1956. This is his last letter. It was addressed to a little girl, aged 12, the daughter of Mrs. Walter Brilhart, after she had sent Mencken a box of caramels as a token of friendship.*]

INDEX

A Note About the Author

H. L. MENCKEN was born in Baltimore in 1880 and died there in 1956. Educated privately and at Baltimore Polytechnic, he began his long career as journalist, critic, and philologist on the Baltimore *Morning Herald* in 1899. In 1906 he joined the staff of the Baltimore *Sun,* thus initiating an association with the *Sun* papers which lasted until a few years before his death. He was co-editor of the *Smart Set* with George Jean Nathan from 1914 to 1923, and with Nathan he founded in 1924 *The American Mercury,* of which he was editor until 1933. His numerous books include *A Book of Burlesques* (1916); *A Book of Prefaces* (1917); *In Defense of Women* (1917); *The American Language* (1918—4th revision, 1936); *Supplement I* (1945); *Supplement II* (1948); six volumes of *Prejudices* (1919, 1920, 1922, 1924, 1926, 1927); *Notes on Democracy* (1926); *Treatise on the Gods* (1930); *Treatise on Right and Wrong* (1934); *Happy Days* (1940); *Newspaper Days* (1941); *Heathen Days* (1943); *A Mencken Chrestomathy* (1949); *Minority Report* (1956); and *The Bathtub Hoax* (1958). Mencken also edited several books; he selected and edited *A New Dictionary of Quotations* (1942). He was co-author of a number of books, including *Europe after 8:15* (1914); *The American Credo* (1920); *Heliogabalus* (a play, 1920); and *The Sunpapers of Baltimore* (1930).

A Note on the Type

THE TEXT of this book is set in CALEDONIA, a Linotype face designed by the late *W. A. Dwiggins* (1880–1956), the man responsible for so much that is good in contemporary book design and typography. Caledonia belongs to the family of printing types called "modern face" by printers —a term used to mark the change in style of type-letters that occurred about 1800. Caledonia borders on the general design of Scotch Modern but is more freely drawn than that letter.

Composed, printed, and bound by
KINGSPORT PRESS, INC., Kingsport, Tennessee.
Paper manufactured by
S. D. WARREN COMPANY, Boston.
Typography and binding based on designs by
W. A. DWIGGINS